HOUGHTON MIFFLIN

Ma**t**h

MATHEMATICS

Cover Activity: *Students gather and analyze data for Numbers as News, Module Opener, pages 290–291. Students (shown here clockwise from left): Carmina Ramirez, Kevin Russell, Tracy Zindell, Scott Kawamoto, Jamileh McKnight.*

HOUGHTON MIFFLIN

Math

MATHEMATICS

Program Authors
Harry Bohan
Gerlena Clark
Heather J. Kelleher
Charles S. Thompson

Contributing Authors
Nadine S. Bezuk
Frank A. Holmes
Jean M. Shaw
Lucia Vega-Garcia

Houghton Mifflin Company·Boston

Atlanta • Dallas • Geneva, Illinois • Princeton, New Jersey • Palo Alto

Authors and Contributors

Nadine S. Bezuk
Associate Professor of Mathematics
  Education
San Diego State University
San Diego, CA

*Contributing Author,
Developer of Concept and
Materials for* Math to Go

Harry Bohan
Professor of Mathematics Education
Sam Houston State University
Huntsville, TX

*Program Author,
Developer of Philosophy
and Grades 3-6*

Gerlena Clark
Los Angeles County Mathematics
  Consultant
Los Angeles, CA

*Program Author,
Developer of Philosophy
and Teacher Training Materials*

Heather J. Kelleher
Former Classroom Teacher
  and Doctoral Student
University of British Columbia
Vancouver, BC, Canada

*Program Author,
Developer of Philosophy
and Grades 1–2*

Jean M. Shaw
Professor of Elementary Education
University of Mississippi
University, MS

*Contributing Author,
Developer of
Kindergarten Level*

Charles S. Thompson
Professor of Education
University of Louisville
Louisville, KY

*Program Author,
Developer of Philosophy
and Grades 3–6*

Lucia Vega-Garcia
Bilingual Education Director
Santa Clara County Office of Education
San Jose, CA

*Contributing Author,
Developer of Teacher
Support for Students
Acquiring English*

Acknowledgments

Grateful acknowledgment is made for the use of the following material: **42** From "E.T.—The Extra-Terrestrial" in *Roger Ebert's Movie Home Companion 1993 Edition,*copyright © by Roger Ebert. —Continued on page 527

Developed and produced by Ligature

Printed in the U.S.A. ISBN: 0-395-67913-3
23456789-D-98 97 96 95 94

Specialists

Brenda Gentry-Norton
Research Associate
Program for Complex
 Instruction
Stanford University
Palo Alto, CA

*Consultant for Assessment
Philosophy and Materials*

Brenda Glen
Classroom Teacher
Balderas Elementary School
Fresno, CA

*Field Test Coordinator and
Developer of Teacher's Edition
Notes, Grades 5–6*

Joan L. Hopkins
Classroom Teacher
Escondido Elementary School
Palo Alto, CA

*Field Test Coordinator and
Developer of Teacher's Edition
Notes, Grades K–2*

Betty Iehl
Educational Consultant
San Gabriel, CA

*Developer of Teacher's Edition
Notes, Grades 4 and 6*

**National Center to Improve
the Tools of Educators**
Douglas Carnine, Director
Edward Kameenui, Associate
 Director
University of Oregon
Eugene, OR

*Developer of Alternate Strategies
Materials, Grades 2–6*

Mary Anne O'Neal
Educational Consultant
Carson, CA

*Developer of Teacher's Edition
Notes, Grades 3 and 5*

Annie Podesto
Staff Development Specialist
Stockton Unified School
 District
Stockton, CA

*Consultant for Assessment
Philosophy and Materials*

Sally Y. Wong
Title VII Adviser
Los Angeles Unified School
 District
Los Angeles, CA

*Developer of Teacher's Edition
Notes, Grades 3–6*

Field Test Teachers

Kindergarten Modules
Traci Assad, Fall River Summer School Program, Fall River, MA •
Susanne Burke, Holmes School, Dorchester, MA • **Leland Clarke,**
Holmes School, Dorchester, MA • **Beverly Letendre,** Fall River
Summer School Program, Fall River, MA • **Sarah Outten,** Slade
Regional Catholic School, Glen Burnie, MD • **Debbie L. Rea,**
Escondido School, Stanford, CA • **Pat Robinson,** Escondido School,
Stanford, CA

Grade 1 Modules
Robin Crawley, Holmes School, Dorchester, MA • **Suraya Driscoll,**
River Heights School, East Grand Forks, MN • **Nancy Matthews,**
Douglas School, Douglas, MA • **Mary Miller,** Holmes School,
Dorchester, MA • **Johanna Roses,** Baker School, Chestnut Hill, MA •
Elaine Kuritani Tsumura, Marrama School, Denver, CO

Grade 2 Modules
Najwa Abdul-Tawwab, Holmes School, Dorchester, MA • **Mary Jane
Brown,** Forwood School, Wilmington, DE • **Joan L. Hopkins,**
Escondido School, Stanford, CA • **Dorene Odom,** Holmes School,
Dorchester, MA • **Ida R. Wellington,** Washington School, Oakland, CA

Grade 3 Modules
Robin Burstein, Greenwood School, Des Moines, IA • **Joanne
Castelano,** Slade Regional Catholic School, Glen Burnie, MD • **Diane
Rezek Fator,** Emerson School, Berwyn, IL • **Linda Griffiths,** Kennedy
School, San Diego, CA • **Michele Hilbing,** Slade Regional Catholic
School, Glen Burnie, MD • **Sharnell Jackson,** Decatur School,
Chicago, IL • **Janet M. Laws,** Lombardy School, Wilmington, DE •
Patricia Y. Lynch, Lombardy School, Wilmington, DE • **Efraín
Meléndez,** Dacotah Street School, Los Angeles, CA • **Doris Miles,**
Sandburg School, Wheaton, IL • **Ricki Raymond,** Piper School,

Berwyn, IL • **Deb Schantzen,** River Heights School, East Grand Forks,
MN • **Bonnie Schindler,** Kennedy School, San Diego, CA • **Theresa
Sievers,** Komensky School, Berwyn, IL • **Kimberly Bassett
Whitehead,** Lombardy School, Wilmington, DE

Grade 4 Modules
Lynda Alexander, St. Elizabeth School, Chicago, IL • **Betty
Coleman,** Parkman School, Chicago, IL • **Karen DeRon-Head,**
Armour School, Chicago, IL • **Keith Libert,** Escondido School,
Stanford, CA • **Joe Montoya,** Horace Mann School, Rapid City, SD •
Robert Poncé, Niños Heroes School, Chicago, IL

Grade 5 Modules
Lynnise H. Akinkunle-Gool, Niños Heroes School, Chicago, IL •
Doris Buffo, Balderas School, Fresno, CA • **Ronni K. Cohen,** Burnett
School, Wilmington, DE • **Valerie De George,** Greeley School,
Chicago, IL • **Brenda Glen,** Balderas School, Fresno, CA • **Brenda
Leigh,** River Heights School, East Grand Forks, MN • **Cynthia L. Lew,**
Madison School, Pomona, CA • **Lisa Palacios,** Pleasant Hill School,
Carol Stream, IL • **Kathryn Peecher,** Revere School, Chicago, IL •
Cindy Sardo, Burnett School, Wilmington, DE • **Henry A. Simmons,**
Balderas School, Fresno, CA • **Delorise Singley,** Oakwood Windsor
School, Aiken, SC • **Cecilia Maria Vasquez,** Balderas School, Fresno,
CA • **Michelle Wilson,** Jefferson School, Fresno, CA

Grade 6 Modules
Dorothy Cooper Jones, Banneker Achievement Center, Gary, IN •
Albert Martinez, Marianna Avenue School, Los Angeles, CA •
Sharon Oechsel, Hiawatha School, Berwyn, IL • **Christopher G.
Reising,** Kennedy School, San Diego, CA • **Lee Wirth,** Pershing
School, Berwyn, IL

Reviewers

Kathryn A. Alexander, Macon Middle School, Brunswick, GA
(Grade 6 modules) • **Sherry Bailey,** Richland School District #2,
Columbia, SC (Grade 5 modules) • **Elsbeth G. Bellemere,**
Scarborough School District, Scarborough, ME (Grade 5 modules) •
Sharon L. Cannon, Myrtle Beach Middle School, Myrtle Beach, SC
(Grade 6 modules) • **Cleo Charging,** White Shield School,
Roseglen, ND (Grade K modules) • **Judy C. Curtis,** Colfax School,
Denver, CO (Grade 3 modules) • **Myra S. Dietz,** Carroll School #46,
Rochester, NY (Grade 6 modules) • **W. L. Duncker,** Midland School
District, Midland, TX (Grade 5 modules) • **Donna Marie Falat,**
Longfellow School, Bridgeport, CT (Grade 2 modules) • **Linda
Gojak,** Hawken School, Lyndhurst, OH (Grade 6 modules) •

Annette D. Ham, Waltersville School, Bridgeport, CT (Grade 5
modules • **Feliciano Mendoza,** Miles Avenue School, Huntington
Park, CA (Grades 5 and 6 modules) • **Kenneth Millett,** Department
of Mathematics, University of California, Santa Barbara, CA (Grade
6 modules) • **Rita Nappi,** Read School, Bridgeport, CT (Grade 4
modules) • **Mahesh Sharma,** Cambridge College, Cambridge, MA
(Grades K and 6 modules) • **Patricia E. Smith,** Crosswell School,
Easley, SC (Grades 3 and 4 modules) • **Bonnie Townzen,** Lubin
School, Sacramento, CA (Grade 1 modules) • **Angelia W. Whiting,**
Beardsley School, Bridgeport, CT (Grade 1 modules) • **Pamela
Yoka,** Covedale School, Cincinnati, OH (Grade K modules)

Contents

MODULE 3

Nature and Numbers

113

Contents

MODULE 4

177 **Let's Get Growing!**

Contents

MODULE 7
Shaping Your World
337

MODULE 8

401 # No Purchase Necessary

Math Power

The goal of this book is to help you build your **math power.** Math power means being able to understand and use math.

REASONING AND PROBLEM SOLVING

Learning to think mathematically and developing your skills as a problem solver are important parts of building math power.

CONNECT AND COMMUNICATE

By communicating about math, you can make your thinking clearer and find connections between new math ideas and the math you already know.

As your math power grows, you'll use math more and more in your daily life. Math power can help you in shopping, planning activities, or working on your favorite hobby.

Math power can also help people in their jobs. Whatever job you may have one day, you can be pretty sure that it will involve math. Discuss with your class some ways that restaurant managers, artists, plumbers, and dentists use math in their work.

These students are showing some keys to math power. When you see one of these keys in your book, you will know that the question or activity below it can help you build math power.

TOOLS AND TECHNIQUES

Math power is knowing how and when to use tools such as calculators and computers and when it's faster to use mental math.

DRAWING TO LEARN

Building math power also involves drawing to help you understand and solve problems and to share your thinking with others.

Ongoing Investigation

Which Shapes Tessellate?

First of all, what is an investigation? It is an open-ended problem. In other words, you will not reach a single right answer. In fact, your investigation can lead to many answers and even to other questions. You will find many investigations in this book. The one described on these pages is called an ongoing investigation because you will work on it all year.

1 Goal

This year, investigate tessellations with your classmates. Find out which shapes tessellate and which ones don't. Start today by experimenting with regular polygons.

2 Tessellation Information

You are probably asking, "What does *tessellate* mean?" Here is a description that you can use throughout your investigation. *A shape tessellates if copies of it can be fitted together to cover a surface with no spaces between and no overlaps.*

You'll see examples of tessellations on these pages. As you begin working with tessellations, you will notice them all around you—in ceramic tiling, flooring, and stained-glass windows.

3 Making the Shapes

Work with a group to make several copies of all the regular polygons. Remember that, by definition, a regular polygon has sides of equal length. You can use any of these methods:

- Trace the shapes on this page.
- Use the Geometry Tool or pattern blocks to trace shapes.

equilateral triangle

square

hexagon

pentagon

octagon

4 Hands-On Experimentation

Experiment to find out which regular polygons tessellate. Remember that the shapes can be positioned in any way, just as long as they touch at one point. When you're done, you might want to glue or paste your tessellations onto sheets of construction paper to save in your portfolio.

HOUGHTON MIFFLIN MATHEMATICS
Drawing to Learn   Geometry Tool

Keep in Mind

Remember to do these things as you experiment:

☐ Test all the regular polygons.

☐ Write a statement about your observations, including which regular polygons tessellate and which do not.

5 Conclusions

Can you think of a reason why some shapes tessellate and others don't? Did this experiment bring up questions that you want to investigate further? Were you able to make more than one pattern from the tessellating figures? Write a statement of your observations. Then meet with your class to share your team's findings.

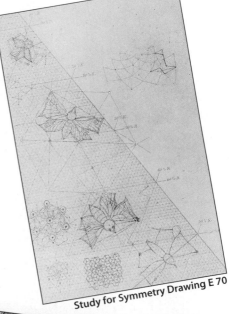

Study for Symmetry Drawing E 70

6 Look Ahead

During the year, you will have more opportunities to experiment with tessellations. Youwill add colors and shapes to make unique designs. Along the way you may come up with fascinating tessellations—as well as mathematical discoveries. Join the surprising world of the artist Escher!

The Dutch artist M. C. Escher (1898–1972) often used tessellations in his work. His astounding visual effects are due in large part to Escher's knowledge of mathematics.

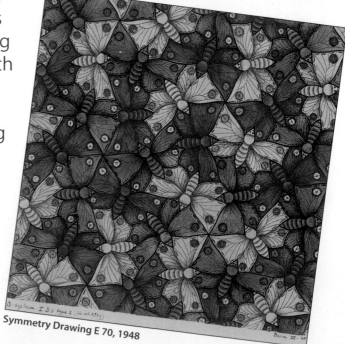

Symmetry Drawing E 70, 1948

Say It with Numbers

SECTION A

Making Sense of Your Data

SECTION B

Looking at Parts of a Set

SECTION C

Analyzing the Middle

How would you tell people of the future about your life today? Some people build time capsules to pass on knowledge about themselves. What do you want people to know about you one thousand years from now?

SECTION D

Exploring the Other Side of Zero

Creating the Past

What ideas and items would you include in a time capsule? Before deciding, investigate what is important to you and your class.

Word Bank

- mean
- median
- mode
- negative integers
- pictograph
- range
- stem-and-leaf plot

1 Make a Collage

Cut out or copy photos, graphs, and other items from newspapers and magazines that describe you and your class. Use the items to create a collage on your own or with your group.

② Describe Current Trends

What do your classmates like? List what you think are your classmates' favorite foods, games, and classes. Explain how you made your choices.

③ Build and Store

Brainstorm what type of material you will use to build your time capsule. Where will you store it? How can you help people in the future find it?

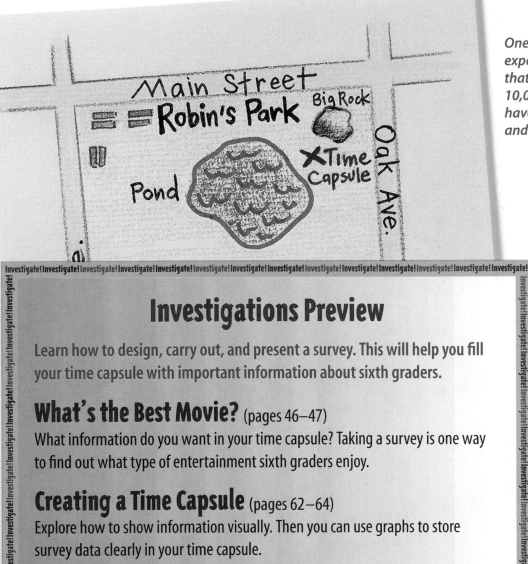

One time capsule expert estimates that more than 10,000 capsules have been buried and lost.

Investigate! Investigate! Investigate! Investigate! Investigate! Investigate! Investigate! Investigate! Investigate! Investigate! Investigate! Investigate!

Investigations Preview

Learn how to design, carry out, and present a survey. This will help you fill your time capsule with important information about sixth graders.

What's the Best Movie? (pages 46–47)
What information do you want in your time capsule? Taking a survey is one way to find out what type of entertainment sixth graders enjoy.

Creating a Time Capsule (pages 62–64)
Explore how to show information visually. Then you can use graphs to store survey data clearly in your time capsule.

LESSON 1

What Do You Think?

Look at one another's collages. Does anyone show what he or she does for fun? How can you discover what your classmates like to do? What would free-time activities tell people of the future about today's culture?

ACTIVITY 1 Create a Survey

With Your Group Brainstorm a list of free-time activities. Choose one of the activities and write five survey questions about it.

What other survey topics do you want to add to the list?

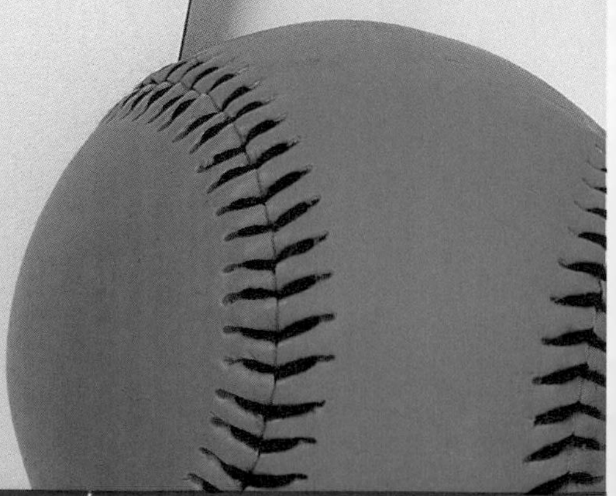

Free-Time Activities

Reading
Playing soccer
Dancing
Listening to music

1 Has your group developed good survey questions? Before deciding, discuss how you could improve the questions below.

In Your Journal What makes a survey question good? List three things to look for.

a. How would you change this question to get more specific information?

b. Why might this question be interpreted in various ways?

1. Do you like music?

2. Do you go to the movies often?

3. What is your favorite type of music?
   a. country
   b. classical
   c. jazz

c. Why might you want other responses to this question?

4. Do you think that the NBA should expand?

d. Do you think everyone would understand this question? Explain.

5. Do you go sledding or ice skating more often?

e. Why would some people not be able to answer this question?

2 Revise your group's questions as needed. Now predict the results you will get from surveying your entire class. Share your predictions with your class.

5

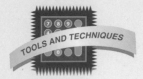
Answers to survey questions are often numbers, categories, comments, or either yes or no. Which answers work best for graphing the responses? Why?

3 One representative from each group will survey the rest of the class. After surveying everyone, representatives should return to their original group and share the collected data.

ACTIVITY 2 Analyze Your Data

With Your Group What does your data tell you? Use the sample below to help you analyze the responses to your group's survey.

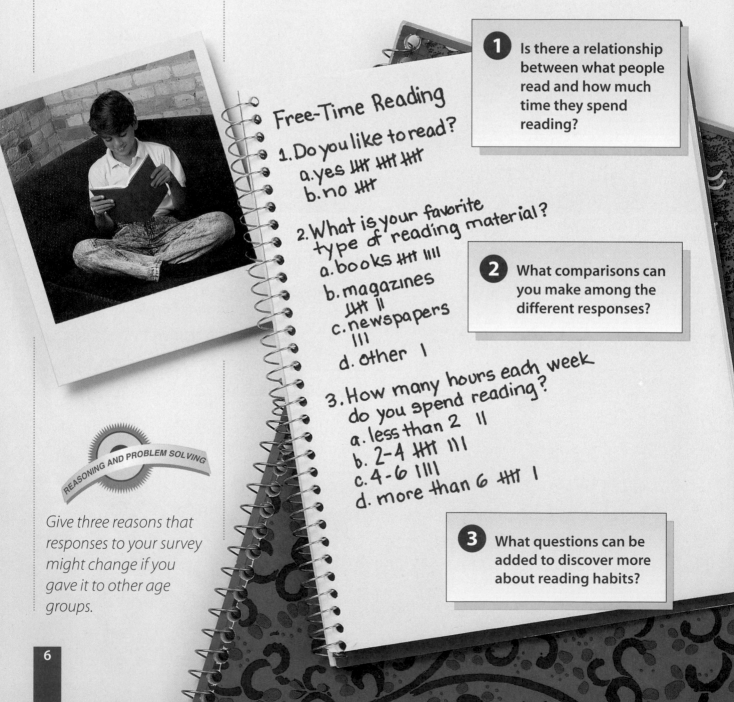

Free-Time Reading

1. Do you like to read?
   a. yes ⫻⫻⫻ ⫻⫻⫻ ⫻⫻⫻
   b. no ⫻⫻⫻

2. What is your favorite type of reading material?
   a. books ⫻⫻⫻ IIII
   b. magazines ⫻⫻⫻ II
   c. newspapers III
   d. other I

3. How many hours each week do you spend reading?
   a. less than 2 II
   b. 2-4 ⫻⫻⫻ III
   c. 4-6 IIII
   d. more than 6 ⫻⫻⫻ I

1 Is there a relationship between what people read and how much time they spend reading?

2 What comparisons can you make among the different responses?

3 What questions can be added to discover more about reading habits?

REASONING AND PROBLEM SOLVING

Give three reasons that responses to your survey might change if you gave it to other age groups.

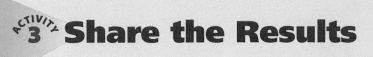

³ Share the Results

With Your Partner How will you communicate your survey results to the class? Look at the responses that are completely different. What do they tell you?

Create a chart to show the data.

How can you use your data to describe a typical student in your class? Write a short description.

Try It!

Rewrite the survey questions so they are good questions.

1. Do you do homework?
2. Do you like food?
3. Do you swim?
4. Do you sleep often?

Write out in words two numerals between the following.

5. 23,545 and 23,550
6. 11,010 and 11,020
7. 110,540 and 120,540
8. 120,650 and 120,660
9. 179,432 and 180,432
10. 111,111 and 111,121

Think About It

11. Explain how a survey may be accurate or misleading.

Show Your Data

You can choose many different kinds of graphs to represent your data. How do you know which graphs to use?

What You'll Need
- grid paper
- ruler

ACTIVITY 1 What Works Best

With Your Class Discuss which type of graph will work best with your group's data.

1 From this **pictograph**, how do you know the number of students who were surveyed?

2 Why is it easy to see what response is given most often or least often by looking at a pictograph?

3 Do any of the numbers on the pictograph surprise you? If so, why?

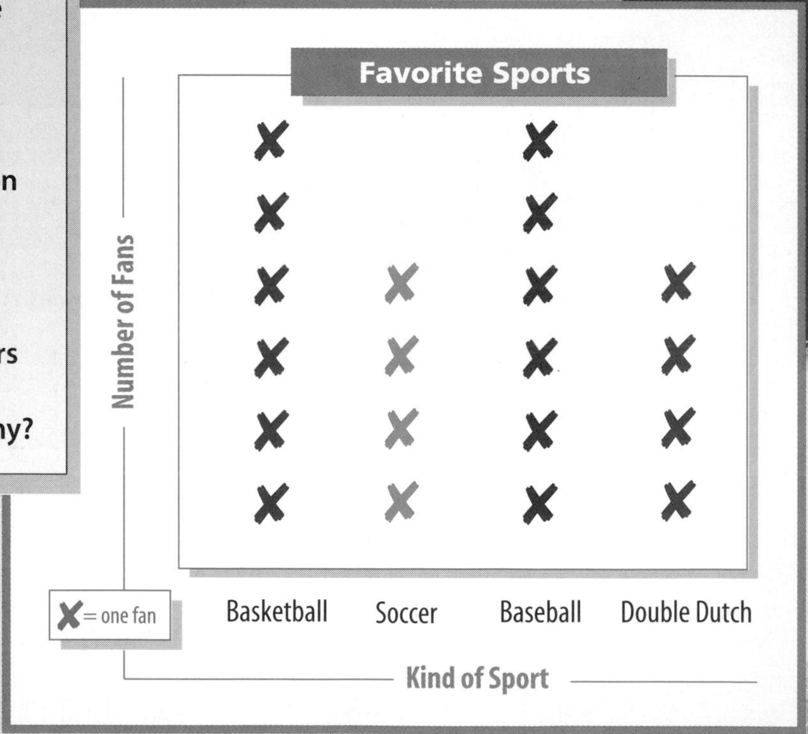

Favorite Sports

✗ = one fan

Basketball Soccer Baseball Double Dutch

Number of Fans

Kind of Sport

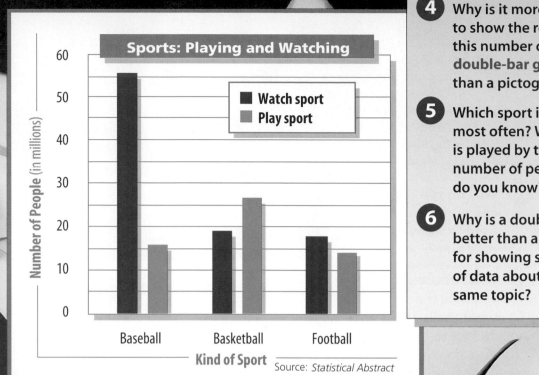

Sports: Playing and Watching

Number of People (in millions)

- ■ Watch sport
- ■ Play sport

Kind of Sport: Baseball, Basketball, Football

Source: *Statistical Abstract of the United States 1992*

4 Why is it more appropriate to show the results from this number of people in a **double-bar graph** rather than a pictograph?

5 Which sport is watched most often? Which sport is played by the least number of people? How do you know?

6 Why is a double-bar graph better than a pictograph for showing several sets of data about the same topic?

This **stem-and-leaf plot** at right shows winning scores for college football teams on October 9 and 16, 1993. The plot shows scores with tens as stems and ones as leaves.

7 The score 30 is in red. Where is the score 27? How often did 27 occur?

8 What other numbers occur more than once?

9 On the stem-and-leaf plot, what is the greatest value? least value?

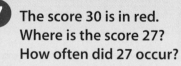
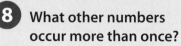

Winning Football Scores

Stem	Leaf
0	
1	
2	0, 1, 4, 4, 7, 7, 7, 8, 8, 8
3	**0**, 1, 4, 4, 5, 6, 8, 8, 9
4	0, 1, 2, 4, 5, 5, 5
5	8, 3
6	8

Source: *Chicago Tribune*

10 Why do you think line graphs are often used to show change over time?

11 What would you estimate the sales of basketballs and tennis rackets to be in 1983? How do you know?

12 When were sales of the two items about the same?

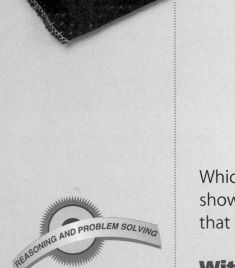

Sales of Sports Equipment

■ Basketballs
■ Tennis rackets

Total Sales (in millions)

Year

Source: *The Sporting Goods Market,* 1991

Which data from your survey, if any, would best be shown as a line graph? What questions could you ask that would be shown on a line graph?

With Your Group Discuss which graphs will best represent your data. Now try plotting your data on graphs. With each graph, write an explanation of why you chose the particular graph to show the data.

REASONING AND PROBLEM SOLVING

How is a double-line graph like a double-bar graph? How are they different?

ACTIVITY 2 Graphs Around Us

On Your Own Complete Graph It. Then choose and complete one of the three options that follow it. Share your results with your class.

What You'll Need
• *grid paper*
• *ruler*

Graph It Make a graph showing the amount of time you spend on various free-time activities during a typical week. Describe the graph and how it represents your data.

Do you like to spend time with your friends? Do you play a musical instrument?

1 **Graph Maker** Choose a graph from your collage on page 2. How could you show the same data for another purpose? Make another graph.

2 **Sales Representative** Use the line graph on page 10 to write a persuasive paragraph. Convince someone they should buy more of your basketballs to sell at their sports store.

TOOLS AND TECHNIQUES

Graph makers frequently round the numbers they use. Explain why they would do so.

3 **Data Collector** Survey your class and a group of adults about the amount of time they spend watching and playing various sports. Make a double-bar graph to compare the data. Write a summary of your conclusions.

Do You Remember?

Try It!

Explain why Exercises 1–4 would or would not be a good way to represent the data. Then complete Exercise 5.

TEST SCORES		
Week	English	Science
1	81	71
2	70	75
3	75	75
4	83	78
5	80	80
6	85	85
7	76	90
8	98	94

1. pictograph

2. line graph

3. stem-and-leaf plot

4. double-bar graph

5. Graph the test score data.

Write the numbers below from least to greatest.

6. 966; 1,112; 955; 1,192

7. 408,078; 48,087; 487; 487,000

8. 6,238; 16,900; 60,000

9. 2,324; 2,432; 2,342; 2,234

10. 10,101; 110,101; 11,011; 100,001

Think About It

11. Use the chart above. Predict the test scores in week 9.

Size Up Your Sample

Do you ever sing along with the radio? Take a survey and predict how many people in the United States sing with the radio too.

ACTIVITY 1 Radio Sing-Along

With Your Group Discover if your group is typical of all students in your class, all sixth graders, and all people in the country.

1 **Survey Your Group** Who sings along with the radio in your group? To find out, take a survey. Based on your data, estimate how many people in your class sing along with the radio. Explain how you made your estimate.

ACTIVITY OPTION

Surveys usually use a random sample. Make a plan to show how you could randomly choose students in your school to survey.

13

2 **From Group to Class** Combine data from all groups. Was your prediction for the class accurate? Explain. You can use your class data to make predictions about larger groups of people. Think about the number of people from your class that sing with the radio. How many people in your school or in your state would you expect to sing along with the radio?

3 **From Class to Country** Maybe your class is representative of the whole country. Based on your class results, about how many of the 260 million people in the United States would you predict sing along with the radio? Explain how you made your prediction.

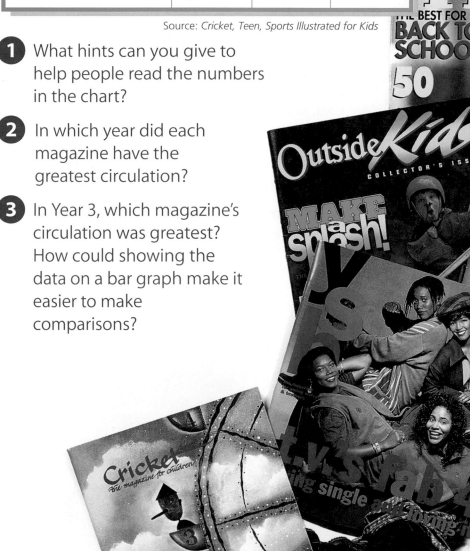

ACTIVITY 2 Magazine Numbers

With Your Group What magazines do you like reading? How many students do you think read *Teen*? Estimate how many different magazines are published in a year. Can you believe it is more than 11,000,000?

What You'll Need
- *grid paper*
- *ruler*

Magazine Circulation			
	Year 1	**Year 2**	**Year 3**
Sports Illustrated for Kids	856,366	880,597	930,890
Teen	1,169,279	1,152,865	1,163,724
Cricket	105,000	110,000	100,000

Source: *Cricket, Teen, Sports Illustrated for Kids*

1 What hints can you give to help people read the numbers in the chart?

2 In which year did each magazine have the greatest circulation?

3 In Year 3, which magazine's circulation was greatest? How could showing the data on a bar graph make it easier to make comparisons?

4 Make a multiple bar graph to represent the data on the chart. Why would rounding the data to the nearest ten thousand help you make your bar graph?

5 Identify trends you see in the circulation data. Predict each magazine's circulation for Year 4.

Circulation Game

With Your Partner In the following game, imagine you are a circulation manager for a magazine. Write a one-digit number on each of ten slips of paper. On the back of each, write a reason why circulation might go up or down. Put the slips in a box.

What You'll Need
- *10 slips of paper*
- *box*

Free poster in this issue.

Circulation goes up.

1 Pull five number slips. Make the least possible number. This is your starting circulation. Rearrange them to make the greatest possible number. This is your circulation goal. Record your numbers and return your slips to the box.

Price increases.
Circulation goes down.

2 Pull four number slips. Use the numbers on the slips to create the amount to add to or subtract from your starting circulation.

3 Put the slips back in the box. Pull one to find the action to take. Take turns until one player reaches his or her circulation goal.

DRAWING TO LEARN

Make a pictograph. Show the circulation for the newspapers in the Try It! What will each symbol represent? How many symbols will you draw for each newspaper?

Starting Circulation: 13,458
Circulation Goal: 85,431

Do You Remember?

Try It!

Use the chart. Write a question and answer that requires the following:

1. rounding to the nearest million

2. rounding to the nearest thousand

3. identifying the greatest number

4. identifying the smallest number

5. ordering numbers

Top-Selling U.S. Newspapers
Wall Street Journal 1,852,863
USA Today 1,540,698
New York Times 1,201,970
Los Angeles Times 1,164,388

Source: *Information Please Almanac 1993*

When divided by 6, which numbers have a remainder of 2?

6. 20   7. 63   8. 74

9. 96   10. 248   11. 320

Think About It

12. When might you round the numbers in the chart?

LESSON 4 Part of It All

TOOLS AND TECHNIQUES

The fraction $\frac{3}{4}$ could represent parts of a set, such as 3 of 4 students. Or, $\frac{3}{4}$ could represent parts of a whole, such as 3 of 4 pieces of pizza.

The time capsule about your class wouldn't be complete without information on favorite foods! What are some of your favorite foods? Many sixth graders rank pizza as the food they like best. Do you?

ACTIVITY 1 Taste Tally

With Your Class Find out your classmates' favorite kinds of pizza. What different pizza toppings do students like?

 Write five survey questions about pizza toppings.

 Survey your classmates to find the number of students who prefer each type of topping.

3 Write as fractions the part of your class that prefers each type of pizza. To find the most popular, order the fractions from greatest to least.

a. How would you write as a fraction the part of your class that prefers cheese pizza?

b. How did you choose the numerator and the denominator?

c. Are the denominators for each of the fractions you wrote the same or different? Explain why this happened.

In Your Journal Do any students in your class dislike pizza? Explain how you would include their responses when ordering the fractions.

On Your Own Draw a graph, a picture, or a diagram. Show how the fractions compare the choices of your class. Share with your class how you compared fractions and ordered them from greatest to least.

$$\frac{8}{25} > \frac{3}{25}$$

Favorite Pizza Toppings

Topping	Number Preferring Topping / Total Number of Students
Cheese	$\frac{8}{25}$
Mushroom	$\frac{3}{25}$
Pepperoni	$\frac{6}{25}$
Sausage	$\frac{5}{25}$
Spinach	
None	

REASONING AND PROBLEM SOLVING

Suppose after eating the pizza you find that you have $2\frac{3}{4}$ pizzas left over. How could you find the number of $\frac{1}{4}$-pizza servings that are left?

ACTIVITY 2 Placing the Order

With Your Partner You know what kinds of pizza your classmates prefer. Now find the number of each kind of pizza to order for a class party.

1 Estimate how many whole pizzas you need to buy. Plan on each person eating $\frac{1}{4}$ pizza.

Whole Pizzas
1 cheese
1 mushroom
1 pepperoni

Half and Half Pizzas
1 half cheese,
half mushroom

$$\frac{6}{4} = 1\frac{2}{4}$$

2 Draw a model to show each student's order. Then write how many of each kind of pizza to order. If it is less than 1, write the fraction. If it is more than 1, use a **mixed number**—a whole number and a fraction.

$$\frac{9}{4} = 2\frac{1}{4}$$

3 Explain in writing how you decided the number of each kind of pizza to order.

Pizza Preferences

On Your Own Compare what other groups prefer on their pizza to your class. Do item a or b. Write a summary of what you find.

a. Survey ten people your age outside of class.
b. Survey ten people of various ages.

In Your Journal Explain how you would tell a friend to rewrite $\frac{7}{4}$ as $1\frac{3}{4}$ or $1\frac{1}{4}$ as $\frac{5}{4}$.

Do You Remember?

Try It!

Write the greatest number. If it is a fraction greater than 1, write it as a mixed number. Otherwise, write it as a fraction greater than 1.

1. $1\frac{2}{3}, \frac{1}{3}, \frac{4}{3}$

2. $1\frac{1}{4}, \frac{6}{4}, \frac{9}{4}$

3. $1\frac{2}{5}, \frac{8}{5}, 1\frac{4}{5}$

4. $\frac{6}{4}, \frac{1}{4}, \frac{7}{4}$

5. $2\frac{2}{3}, 1\frac{1}{3}, \frac{7}{3}$

6. $2\frac{1}{3}, \frac{5}{3}, 2\frac{2}{3}$

Write $>$, $<$, or $=$.

7. $\frac{1}{4} \bullet \frac{5}{4}$

8. $\frac{5}{4} \bullet 1\frac{1}{4}$

9. $2\frac{1}{3} \bullet \frac{8}{3}$

Decide if the answer is even or odd. Write *E* or *O*. Find only the answers that are even.

10. $463 + 35$

11. $447 + 393$

12. $4,659 + 112$

13. $3,455 + 156$

14. $6,738 + 234$

15. $2,374 + 435$

Think About It

16. Explain how you rewrite a mixed number as a fraction.

More or Less?

DRAWING TO LEARN

Try drawing a diagram to help you compare these fractions.

You probably found that the toppings preferred by your survey groups varied. How can you compare fractions with different denominators?

ACTIVITY 1 Comparing Groups

With Your Partner Assume that in one group $\frac{4}{5}$ preferred cheese and in another $\frac{7}{10}$ preferred cheese. Which group had a greater part that liked cheese pizza? Finding **equivalent fractions** with the same, or common, denominator is a way to compare.

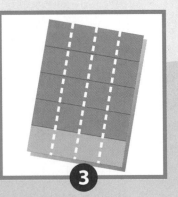

1 Shade a sheet of paper to show $\frac{4}{5}$. Then fold it in half across the shaded part of the paper.

2 Open the paper. Record the equivalent fraction you made. How could you use the common denominator you made to help compare $\frac{4}{5}$ and $\frac{7}{10}$?

3 Try to make more equivalent fractions for $\frac{4}{5}$ by folding your paper into halves again. Explain what happens.

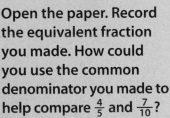

What happens to the numerator when you fold the paper in half? What happens to the denominator?

ACTIVITY 2 Greater or Less?

TOOLS AND TECHNIQUES

With Your Partner Look at the survey results below. Compare the part of the students in each group who preferred cheese pizza. Why might paper folding be a difficult way to compare these fractions? Describe the method you use.

To make more equivalent fractions, you can repeat folding the paper. What are four equivalent fractions for $\frac{7}{10}$?

D'Juana's Class
Pizza Preferences

cheese	$\frac{12}{30}$
pepperoni	$\frac{5}{30}$
onion	

Rob's Combined Group's
Pizza Preferences

cheese	$\frac{24}{60}$
pepperoni	$\frac{8}{60}$
onion	

Think back. What happened to the numerator and denominator each time you folded the paper to make equivalent fractions? How can you write equivalent fractions without drawing a picture or folding paper?

TOOLS AND TECHNIQUES

Recognizing common multiples can help you compare fractions. Some multiples of 4 are 4, 8, 12, 16, 20, 24, and multiples of 6 are 6, 12, 18, 24, 30, 36. One common multiple of 4 and 6 is 12. Name another.

ACTIVITY 3 Why Does It Work?

With Your Class Complete the comparisons.

$$\frac{12}{30} = \frac{12 \times 60}{30 \times 60}$$

$$\frac{24}{60} = \frac{24 \times 30}{60 \times 30}$$

- How does each method work?
- Why does it work?
- How do these methods compare with yours?
- Which way do you prefer?

$$\frac{12}{30} = \frac{12 \div 6}{30 \div 6}$$

$$\frac{24}{60} = \frac{24 \div 6}{60 \div 6}$$

$$\frac{12}{30} = \frac{12 \times 2}{30 \times 2}$$

Do You Remember?

Try It!

Identify the equivalent fraction pairs.

1. $\frac{1}{4}, \frac{10}{40}$
2. $\frac{3}{12}, \frac{12}{36}$
3. $\frac{5}{8}, \frac{12}{32}$

Arrange the fractions from least to greatest.

4. $\frac{2}{3}, \frac{1}{4}, \frac{2}{5}$
5. $\frac{5}{6}, \frac{2}{3}, \frac{3}{6}$
6. $\frac{3}{5}, \frac{10}{15}, \frac{5}{15}$

Think about place value. Find the number you must subtract to change the digit 6 to 0.

7. 463
8. 4,659
9. 83,647
10. 56,394
11. 23,639
12. 162,437

Think About It

13. Tell how you found equivalent fractions in Exercises 1–3.

Deciding by Decimals

Do you ever see or read reviews? A review, like the one below, may be one person's opinion or the combined opinions of several people.

ACTIVITY 1 Order Another Way

With Your Class How do you like your school cafeteria lunches? Design a survey that asks about five lunch menu items. Use a scale like the one shown to rate the lunches. Have each person in your group take the survey.

How does assigning a number value to each choice help you analyze your data?

Yuck	So-so	Okay	Good	Yum!
1	2	3	4	5

14   Section 2 • USA Tribune • January 3, 1994

○|○ Restaurant Reviews

Falafel With Flair!

25

Look at how these numbers are rounded.

4.08 → 4.1

4.75 → 5

4.25 → 4

4.825 → 4.83

Explain how rounding with decimals is like rounding with whole numbers.

What You'll Need
- *Tracing Tool or grid paper*

0.5
0.05
0.005
0.0005

ACTIVITY 2 ▷ Comparing Ratings

With Your Group Use a calculator to find the average rating your group gave to each menu item. Your calculator display probably shows some **decimals.** How do you know what the decimals you found mean?

1 Use what you already know to help you.
- You can write a fraction or a mixed number to show part of something.
- You know that each place in our number system is ten times greater than the place to its right.

a. If 0.5 is 5 tenths, why is 0.05 called 5 hundredths?
b. How will you read the 5 in 0.005?
c. How do you know that the 5 in 0.0005 is in the ten-thousandths' place?

Average Rating for Egg Rolls

4 + 3 + 5 + 3 = 15

4)‾15‾

4

3

5

3

2 Use the chart. How can you decide which lunch got the highest rating? the lowest rating?
- Draw decimal squares or use your Tracing Tool to show what each rating means and how it compares.
- Use what you know to list your group's ratings from highest to lowest.

ACTIVITY OPTION

Find ten different examples of decimals used in newspapers. Write a description of how each of the decimals was used.

Group A	Average Rating
Tuna sandwich	1.5
Hamburger	3
Pizza	4.25
Tacos	4.5
Egg rolls	3.75

3 Expand your survey to students outside your class.
- Find average ratings and write a review for your school newspaper. Your review should explain how you got your information and any recommendations you want to make.

Many reviewers award stars for their ratings. You can, too!

ACTIVITY 3 Decimal Fractions

With Your Partner How can you compare decimals? Roll five number cubes. Make the greatest possible decimal that is less than 1 from these numbers. Then make the least decimal that is less than 1 from these numbers. Your partner then rolls the cubes and tries to make a decimal greater than your greatest number and less than your least number.

Do You Remember?

Try It!

Arrange the decimals in order from least to greatest.

1. 0.33, 0.303, 0.3033   **2.** 2.303, 2.3313, 2.33

3. 0.522, 0.5, 0.534   **4.** 5.501, 5.51, 5.0551

Some of the exercises have errors. Fix any errors. Write *C* if the exercise is correct.

5. 1.51 > 1.4   **6.** 3.453 < 3.42   **7.** 0.73 > 0.733

Find the answers that end in 0. Explain how you know.

8. 7,536 + 274   **9.** 4,383 + 1,462   **10.** 122 + 3,408

11. 4,974 − 3,500   **12.** 1,904 − 1,904   **13.** 6,384 − 4,096

Think About It

14. Describe errors found in Exercises 5–7. How would you help someone who made mistakes like these?

Possible Percents

Percents compare amounts per hundred. In fraction form, percents use 100 as a denominator. How is a percent like a decimal?

ACTIVITY 1 Presenting Percents

With Your Partner The circle graph shows one group's favorite Chinese and Chinese American foods.

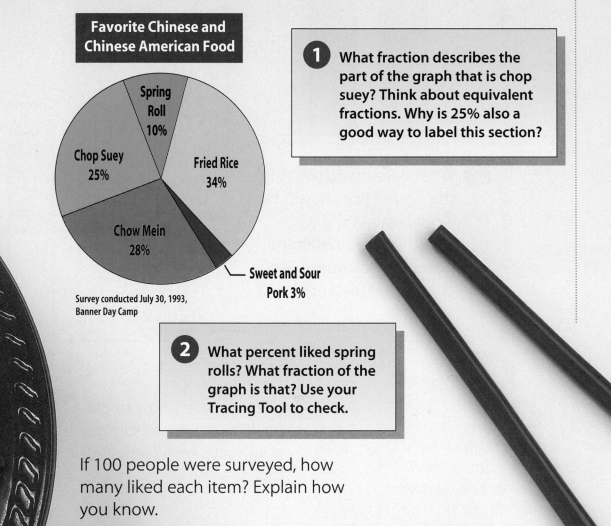

Favorite Chinese and Chinese American Food

Spring Roll 10%

Chop Suey 25%

Fried Rice 34%

Chow Mein 28%

Sweet and Sour Pork 3%

Survey conducted July 30, 1993, Banner Day Camp

1 What fraction describes the part of the graph that is chop suey? Think about equivalent fractions. Why is 25% also a good way to label this section?

2 What percent liked spring rolls? What fraction of the graph is that? Use your Tracing Tool to check.

If 100 people were surveyed, how many liked each item? Explain how you know.

What You'll Need
• *Fraction Tool or grid
paper and ruler*

ACTIVITY
2 Picturing Percents

With Your Class It's easy to find percents when there are 100 in the group. The food survey, however, was given to 71 campers. You can estimate the number of campers who chose each item by drawing a percent-bar model. Use your Fraction Tool to sketch a percent-bar model like the one shown. Then discuss the questions.

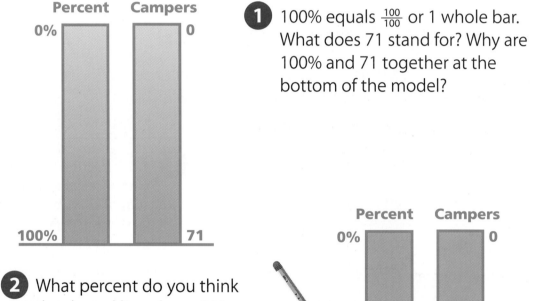

1 100% equals $\frac{100}{100}$ or 1 whole bar. What does 71 stand for? Why are 100% and 71 together at the bottom of the model?

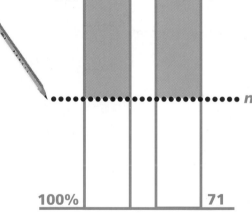

2 What percent do you think the dotted line shows? How would estimating where 50% is help you estimate how many campers liked chop suey? fried rice?

REASONING AND PROBLEM SOLVING

Why might thinking of a rounded number like 70 or a compatible number like 72 help you estimate?

3 Use what you know to draw dotted lines for 25% and 75%. Estimate the number of campers who named each food as their favorite.

With Your Group Use what you know about estimating 25%, 50%, and 75% to estimate the number of campers who chose each kind of juice.

Which of these fruit juices do you like the best?	
Apple	34%
Cranberry	8%
Grape	27%
Orange	31%

Data collected Banner Day Camp
July 30, 1993

✓ **Self-Check**

Think about fraction equivalents for percents to help you estimate.

- *50% = $\frac{1}{2}$*
- *25% = $\frac{1}{4}$*
- *75% = $\frac{3}{4}$*

How would you find half of a number? How would you find one fourth or three fourths?

4 Think about 25%. How can you estimate 27%, 31%, and 34% of the campers? Show your work. Where should the line be for 8%? How do you know? How many campers is that?

5 How can you tell if you made good estimates? Use the percents and make a model of your class. How many students does 27% represent? Show all juices.

What's for Dinner?

What do people in the United States like to eat?
To find out, answer eight of the following ten items.

Use the chart to help you answer Exercises 1, 2, and 3.

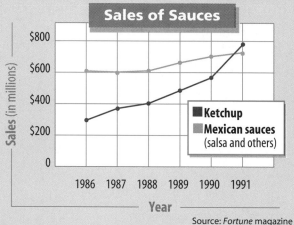

Sales of Sauces

Sales (in millions)

$800
$600
$400
$200
0

■ Ketchup
■ Mexican sauces
(salsa and others)

1986 1987 1988 1989 1990 1991

Year

Source: *Fortune* magazine

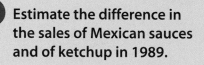

1 Estimate the difference in the sales of Mexican sauces and of ketchup in 1989.

2 In 1986 what fraction of the total sales of Mexican sauces and ketchup were Mexican sauces?

3 In 1986 sales of Mexican sauces were 50% of ketchup sales. What fraction of ketchup sales is that?

4 In a 1986 survey, restaurants called about 240 of 900 menu items ethnic foods. In 1991 about 360 out of 1,000 were labeled ethnic. In which year were ethnic foods more common? Explain.

5 In 1989 consumers ate an average of 2.6 pounds of spinach each. Express this amount as a fraction.

6 In 1989 consumers ate 15.7 pounds of rice per person. Write this amount as a mixed number.

7 Each year, a typical consumer eats $5\frac{4}{5}$ pounds of broccoli and $5\frac{7}{10}$ pounds of green beans. Which food do people eat more of? Explain how you know.

Use percent bars to help you answer Exercises 8, 9, and 10.

8 At 6 pounds per person in 1988, broccoli eaters ate 66% more broccoli than they did in 1977. About how many pounds per person were eaten in 1977?

9 A survey found that 75% of people in the United States have eaten Chinese food. If the U.S. population is 260 million, about how many have eaten Chinese food?

10 About 25% of the U.S. population has eaten Japanese food. With 260 million people, about how many people is that?

Chocolate

The word *chocolate* comes from the Aztecs, the Native Americans who lived in what is now Mexico. They had a drink like cocoa that they called *xocatyl*. Would you put anything into your time capsule about chocolate? Answer the following questions to find out more about chocolate production and consumption.

1 People make chocolate from cocoa beans. Write in words the amount of cocoa produced in Ghana in 1992.

2 What was the total production of cocoa from the top three cocoa-producing countries in 1992?

Cocoa Production		
(in thousands of metric tons)		
Country	**1901**	**1992**
Ghana	1	280
Ivory Coast	little	760
Nigeria	little	130
Brazil	18	368
Malaysia	little	170
World Total	115	2,358

Source: *FAO Quarterly Bulletin of Statistics 1992*

3 Why would showing the data in this table on a double-bar graph be difficult?

4 People planted the first cocoa trees in West Africa in 1879. Estimate the percent of world production that came from Ghana, West Africa, in 1901.

5 The 124 million people in Japan eat about 384 million pounds of chocolate each year. How much is this per person?

6 In A.D. 600, the Maya began growing cocoa beans in what is now southern Mexico. They used the beans as money. One rabbit cost 8 beans. How many rabbits could you buy for 100 beans?

Aztec stone figure of a man holding a cocoa pod, from between 1440 and 1521.
The Brooklyn Museum: Museum Collection Fund

7 *Mole* is a Mexican sauce. It includes about 1 ounce of chocolate for each 2 cups of tomatoes. How much chocolate would go with 1 quart of tomatoes?

8 Cocoa trees first grew in what is now Brazil. What fraction of world production came from Brazil in 1901?

9 In Switzerland, a country of about 7 million people, chocolate sales are 19.4 pounds per person per year. How much chocolate is sold in Switzerland?

Check Your Math Power

10 In 1992, which country produced about 30% of the world's cocoa? Explain how you know.

LESSON 8 Movie Favorites

DRAWING TO LEARN

Show in a sketch your prediction of how many students in your class like horror, comedy, action, or fantasy movies.

What kind of movies do you enjoy? Do most sixth graders enjoy the same kinds of movies? Explain why you might want to include movie data in your time capsule.

ACTIVITY 1 Movie Reviews

With Your Class   Survey sixth graders to find how their movie preferences compare with yours.

1 Use the three questions below. Add at least three of your own. Take the survey within your class and record the results.

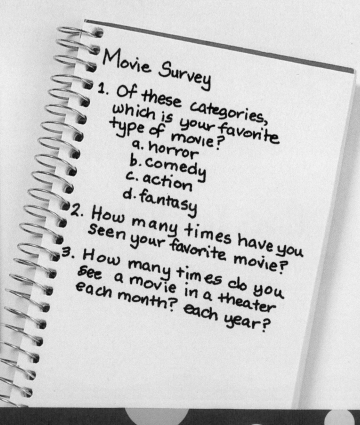

Movie Survey

1. Of these categories, which is your favorite type of movie?
   a. horror
   b. comedy
   c. action
   d. fantasy

2. How many times have you seen your favorite movie?

3. How many times do you see a movie in a theater each month? each year?

2 How would you describe the movie preferences of a typical member of your class?

Movie Survey

1. Of these categories, which is your favorite type of movie?

Comedy	Horror	Action	Fantasy
11	6	9	4

How might responses of sixth grade classes vary?

Some movies could be part of more than one category. Explain how that might affect your data.

THE STORY THAT TOUCHED THE WORLD.

A STEVEN SPIELBERG FILM

E.T.
THE EXTRA-TERRESTRIAL

2 A Closer Look

With Your Group How did you and your class decide on what was typical? Take a look at some ways you can analyze your data.

How many times have you seen your favorite movie?

I I I I I I I I I 2 2 2 2 2 2 2 2 3 3 3 4

The range is 3.

> The difference between the greatest and the least is the **range**. How would you find the range?

> The **median** is the middle number when the responses are ordered from least to greatest. Explain how you would find the median. If three more people gave 1 as a response, why would the median be 1.5?

1 1 1 1 1 1 1 1 1 2 ②2 2 2 2 2 2 2 3 3 3 4

The median is 2.

1 1 1 1 1 1 1 1 1 2 2 2 2 2 2 2 2 3 3 3 4
⎵ 9 ⎵ 8 ⎵3 ⎵1

The mode is 1.

> The **mode** names the response that occurs most often.
> • How is finding the mode like finding what's most popular?
> • What kind of business would be interested in this response?

CONNECT AND COMMUNICATE

How can you remember that the median is the middle number?

1 1 1 1 1 1 1 1 1 2 2 2 2 2 2 2 2 3 3 3 4

$1 \times 9 = 9$
$2 \times 8 = 16$
$3 \times 3 = 9$
$4 \times 1 = 4$
_____
38

$38 \div 21 = 1.8095238$

The mean is 1.8.

The **mean** is one kind of average. How was the mean calculated?

- What does 1.8 tell you and why was it rounded?
- How can clustering, or seeing where numbers group, help you estimate the mean?

ACTIVITY 3 · Going to Extremes

With Your Group According to *The Guinness Book of World Records,* Gwilym Hughes saw 20,064 movies between 1953 and 1991. That's a mean of 528 per year! If you include Hughes in the group below, what happens to the range, median, mode, and mean?

Movies Seen in a Theater During the Past Year

2 4 5 5 10 10 12 13 14 16 20 27

On Your Own Find the mean, median, mode, or range as appropriate for each question in your movie survey.

REASONING AND PROBLEM SOLVING

What numbers could you have added to the data that would not have changed the mean and range as much as Hughes's numbers did?

ACTIVITY 4 Boxes with Whiskers

With Your Partner You've found the range, median, mode, and mean. A good way to show a lot of data in one place is to use a box-and-whisker plot.

Movies Seen in a Theater During the Past Year

2 4 5 5 10 10 12 13 14 16 20 27

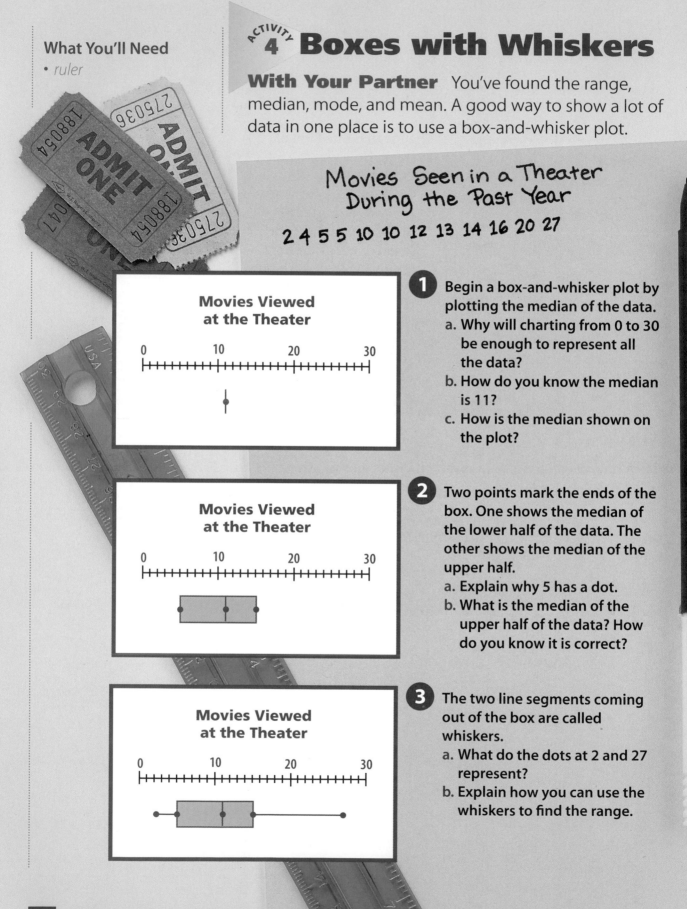

1 Begin a box-and-whisker plot by plotting the median of the data.
  a. Why will charting from 0 to 30 be enough to represent all the data?
  b. How do you know the median is 11?
  c. How is the median shown on the plot?

2 Two points mark the ends of the box. One shows the median of the lower half of the data. The other shows the median of the upper half.
  a. Explain why 5 has a dot.
  b. What is the median of the upper half of the data? How do you know it is correct?

3 The two line segments coming out of the box are called whiskers.
  a. What do the dots at 2 and 27 represent?
  b. Explain how you can use the whiskers to find the range.

4 Look at the box-and-whisker plot.
   a. Explain what each dot shows.
   b. What numbers are inside the box? How do you know?
   c. Would a bar graph be suitable for this data? Explain.

Movies Viewed at Home Last Year

0   10   20   30   40   50   60

On Your Own Select data on one of the questions in your survey. Explain how a box-and-whisker plot would show your data and why it would be useful.

Do You Remember?

Try It!

Find the mean, median, and range for each set of numbers.

1. 2, 4, 6, 8, 10, 1

2. 88, 72, 94, 85, 91, 90

3. 42, 8, 72, 68, 6

4. 2.5, 6.8, 8.05, 12.2, 9.3

5. 17, 12, 19, 15, 10

6. 25, 55, 34, 50, 11, 35, 36

Choose the best method for you to find each product. Write *P* (pencil-and-paper), *M* (mental math), or *C* (calculator). Find the product.

7. 9×35

8. 90×235

9. 23×652

10. $60 \times 4{,}000$

11. 25×75

12. 30×80

Think About It

13. What does a box-and-whisker plot show you that a table does not? Explain your answer.

LESSON 9 Alike and Different

CONNECT AND COMMUNICATE

In Your Journal *How are students in your class like adults? How are they different? Discuss how you could show these similarities and differences in a diagram.*

Every time you use an equals sign, you are comparing one number with another. Now compare things that are not numbers.

ACTIVITY 1 All, Some, or None?

With Your Group The movie *E.T.—The Extra-Terrestrial* is one of the most popular movies ever made. How can you use your comparison skills to help you analyze the movie?

LITERATURE

In this review of E.T. *by Roger Ebert, notice the contrast between the two leading characters.*

The movie's hero is one particular little boy named Elliott. He is played by Henry Thomas in what has to be the best little boy performance I've ever seen in an American film. He doesn't come across as an overcoached professional kid; he's natural, defiant, easily touched, conniving, brave, and childlike. He just *knows* there's something living out there in the backyard, and he sits up all night with his flashlight, trying to coax the creature [E.T.] out of hiding with a nearly irresistible bait: Reese's Pieces. The creature, which looks a little like Snoopy but is very, very wise, approaches the boy. They become friends.

Roger Ebert's Movie Home Companion

With Your Class One way to compare data is by drawing a Venn diagram. Use the review and picture to make a Venn diagram that compares Elliott and E.T.

Comparing Elliott and E.T.

Elliott
E.T.

- brave
- childlike

- has two eyes

- looks like Snoopy
- very wise

Self-Check *Check your Venn diagram by filling in sentences like these:*
- *Only Elliott is ___?___.*
- *Only E.T. is ___?___.*
- *Both Elliott and E.T. are ___?___.*

1 What characteristic do both Elliott and E.T. share? How is it shown on the diagram?

2 What words describe Elliott but not E.T.? What words describe only E.T.? Where does each go in your diagram?

With Your Partner You can also use Venn diagrams to compare numbers. Choose a, b, or c. Share your results with your class.

3 Use at least ten numbers for each Venn diagram.
a. multiples of 4 and 6
b. numbers divisible by 2, 3, and 4
c. Make your own rule.

Numbers Divisible by 2, 3, and 4

2

3

2

4 12 3

4

'60s Fun

Suppose you found a suitcase that a group of sixth graders in 1968 had filled as a time capsule. How old would these former sixth graders be today? What can you learn about what sixth graders were like in 1968?

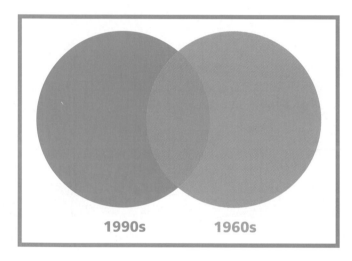

1990s   1960s

1 In which section on the Venn diagram would you put a picture of basketball star Michael Jordan? Explain.

2 On the Venn diagram, which section would you put movies in? Why?

3 On the Venn diagram, hip hop music would go in the blue section. What does this placement tell you about the history of music?

4 In 1968 about 23% of all households had color television sets. If the total number of households was 61 million, about how many had color televisions?

5 Skateboards cost between $1.98 and $50.00 in the mid-1960s. What was the range of prices?

6 Look at the chart. What is the mean ticket price for the years 1959–1968?

7 Explain whether you think the ticket prices in this chart are means, modes, or medians.

 8 What is the range of ticket prices shown on the chart below?

Typical Movie Ticket Prices	
Year	Price
1959	$0.51
1960	$0.69
1961	$0.69
1962	$0.70
1963	$0.85
1964	$0.93
1965	$1.01
1966	$1.10
1967	$1.20
1968	$1.31

Source: *Reel Facts,* by Cobbett S. Steinberg

9 In 1964 baseball star Roberto Clemente hit 12 home runs. In the following four seasons, he hit 10, 29, 23, and 18 home runs. Does the mean show his typical season? Explain.

10 You didn't live in the '60s but you were 6 once. Make a Venn diagram that compares you at 6 years old and now.

Investigation

What's the Best Movie?

Imagine that your class is making a time capsule. Since movies are popular entertainment, you decide to include one movie. Which movie would you choose? Do some research to help you make your decision.

1 Decide whether your movie will represent how sixth graders live today or what kinds of movies they like to watch.

2 Develop and conduct a survey of at least ten sixth graders about five selected movies. What survey questions will give you information that can help you choose a movie?

3 Analyze and present your data. Determine the mean, mode, median, and range as appropriate. Draw a graph for each survey question.

4 Based on your survey choose one movie to include in your time capsule. Use your survey data and write a one-page summary to convince your classmates to support your choice. You may also want to use sketches, quotations, or other research.

Option What other types of entertainment do you want to represent in your time capsule? Collect and analyze data on them. Then write a report explaining why some other item should be included in your time capsule.

Need quotations from:

actors
songs
interviews
reviews

Ask Yourself

☐ What should the movie represent?
☐ How many people should you survey?
☐ Will mean, mode, or median be most helpful?
☐ How does the survey suggest which movie to choose?
☐ What graphs best represent the data?

Covering New Ground

C an you have less than nothing? How would you describe it? Think about what you might put into a time capsule about something less than nothing.

What You'll Need
• *grid paper*

ACTIVITY 1 **What's the Story?**

With Your Partner Take a look at a non-numerical graph—a graph without numbers.

1 Use your imagination to write a story about the graph below. Share your story with the class. Use the Tools and Techniques to help you.

When reading a non-numerical graph, describe each major point on the graph. Also, explain why the graph line rises and falls.

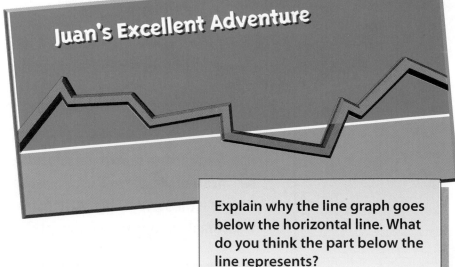

Juan's Excellent Adventure

Explain why the line graph goes below the horizontal line. What do you think the part below the line represents?

2 Present your story to the class. After everyone is finished, compare stories.
  - Did any groups have similar explanations for the same points?
  - Were any explanations completely different?
  - Which story best described the graph?

3 Design another bar graph to show something specific about Juan's adventure that does not appear on the first graph.

How could you make sure that everyone who looks at your non-numerical graph reads it the same way?

What You'll Need

- *6 strips of red paper*
- *6 strips of black paper*
- *spinner or compass, ruler, and paper clip*
- *1 cube labeled 1–6*

ACTIVITY 2 Below Zero

Have you ever owed anyone money? Have you heard of below-zero temperatures? How could you communicate this information? Over the centuries people have developed different ways for representing these numbers.

With Your Partner Discuss how the following systems work.

1 **Red or Black** In ancient China, people used red bamboo sticks to show numbers greater than zero. Black sticks showed numbers less than zero. Try this system with your partner.

a. Make a spinner that is half red and half black.

b. Roll a number cube and spin the spinner to discover the number you will represent. Record the color and number.

c. Use red or black strips of paper to show your number. Explain whether the number is greater than or less than zero. Show at least ten numbers.

2 **Around the Number** The
Hindus once used a circle around a
number to show a number less
than zero.

a. Rewrite your Chinese numbers
using the Hindu system.

b. Decide how you can order
numbers less than zero and
numbers greater than zero.

c. Write an explanation of how
your order works.

Chinese System	Hindu System
				4	4
|||||| 6 owed	6̥
||| 3 owed	3̥

3 **On the Line** Today many people use positive (+)
and negative (−) symbols to communicate about
different types of numbers. **Positive integers** are
the counting numbers but not 0 (1, 2, 3, 4, 5 . . .).
Negative integers are the opposite of positive
integers. They show numbers less than zero.

a. Read this number
as "negative six."

b. How can you use the number
line to tell if you ordered the
numbers you wrote in the
Hindu system correctly?

```
◄──┬─┬─┬─┬─┬─┬─┬─┬─┬─┬─┬─┬─┬─┬──►
      −6       −3 −2   0 1   3 4      7
```

c. The numbers −1 and 1
are opposites, and −2
and 2 are opposites.
What is the opposite of
3? 4? −3? −4? 5? 6?

d. Opposites are the same
distance from zero but in
the opposite direction.
Copy the number line
and show all the
opposites.

DRAWING TO LEARN

*Try developing your own
system for showing
negative numbers.*

Section D: Exploring the Other Side of Zero 51

DOWN THE LINE

What You'll Need
- *gameboard*
- *spinner or compass, ruler, and paper clip*
- *1 cube labeled 1–6*

ACTIVITY 3 Game Time!

With Your Group You will use a number cube and spinner to play Down the Line. The goal is to land on 10 or −10 and then work toward 0. The winner is the first person to land on 0. If you roll a number that takes you beyond 10 or −10, you lose your next turn.

1 Start at Zero
To find out who goes first, everyone should roll the cube. The person with the highest roll should start the game. All players will start on 0.

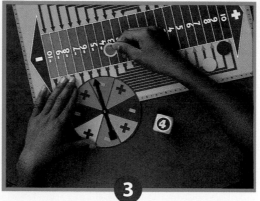

Roll the Cube
Each person rolls the cube. The number rolled is the number of spaces you move.

Spin for + or −
Spin a spinner like the one above. If the spinner lands on −, move toward the negative-sign end on the number line. If it lands on +, move toward the positive sign on the number line.

4 The Opposite
If one player lands on an integer that is the opposite of an integer someone else is on, both players go back to zero.

Do You Remember?

Try It!

Write the opposites for the following numbers.

1. 14   **2.** −8   **3.** −3   **4.** 9   **5.** −12   **6.** 20

Order the numbers from least to greatest.

7. 4,000; 440; 4,040; 4,400   **8.** 81,021; 81,201; 82,001

9. 5,996; 6,000; 5,868; 6,086   **10.** 37,240; 37,420; 37,042

Think About It

11. Write an explanation for how you know what the opposites are for Exercises 1–6.

LESSON 11 Plotting Your Point

The grid system allows archeologists to keep track of where they find "accidental time capsules."

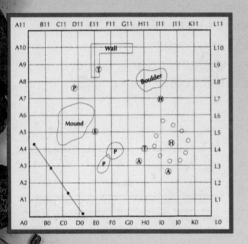

Archeologists use a grid system to record the exact location of an artifact. To discover more about coordinate grids, do Activity 1. Then try Activities 2, 3, and 4 in any order.

How do archeologists label their grid systems? Can you think of any other grids that are labeled the same way?

ACTIVITY 1 Finding Your Way

With Your Class The coordinate grid system works differently from the archeologist's grid. You can see one difference by looking at a number line.

1 Look at the number line below. Why are both positive and negative numbers used?

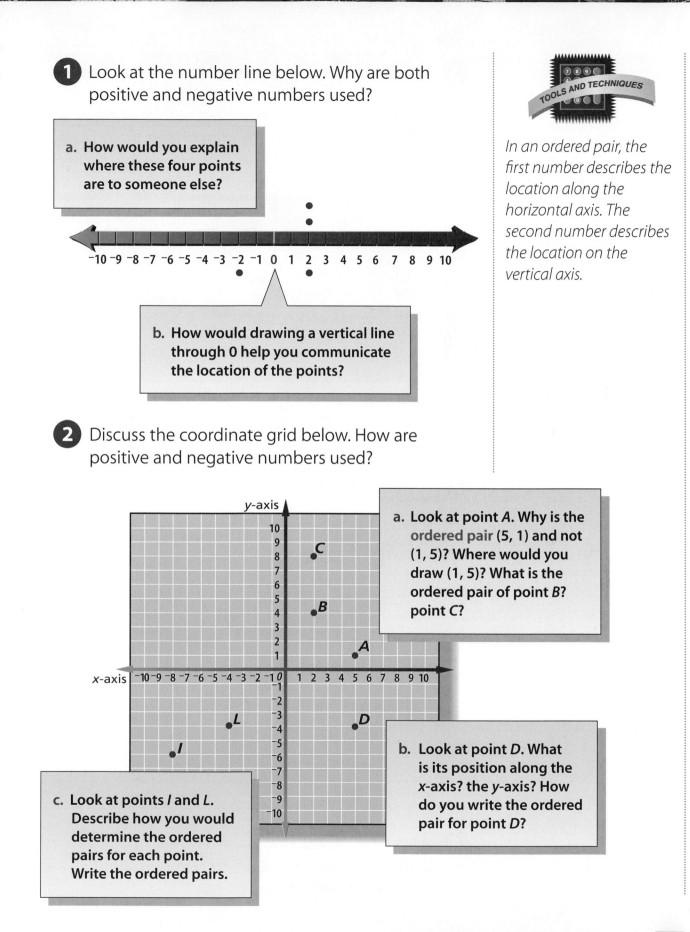

a. How would you explain where these four points are to someone else?

In an ordered pair, the first number describes the location along the horizontal axis. The second number describes the location on the vertical axis.

TOOLS AND TECHNIQUES

b. How would drawing a vertical line through 0 help you communicate the location of the points?

2 Discuss the coordinate grid below. How are positive and negative numbers used?

a. Look at point _A._ Why is the ordered pair (5, 1) and not (1, 5)? Where would you draw (1, 5)? What is the ordered pair of point _B?_ point _C?_

b. Look at point _D._ What is its position along the _x_-axis? the _y_-axis? How do you write the ordered pair for point _D?_

c. Look at points _I_ and _L._ Describe how you would determine the ordered pairs for each point. Write the ordered pairs.

3 The coordinate grid is divided by the *x*-axis and *y*-axis into four **quadrants.** In your journal make a chart like the one below. Fill in your chart with all the points you plot, the sign for each coordinate, and the quadrant in which the point is located. Plot at least five points in each quadrant.

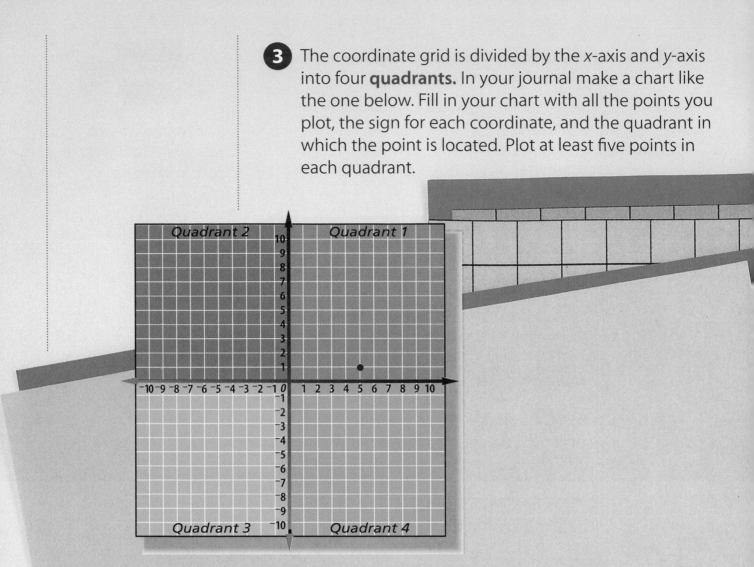

Point	Sign	Quadrant
(5,1)	(+, +)	1

4 Write a rule about how to determine a point's quadrant by looking at which numbers are positive and which are negative.

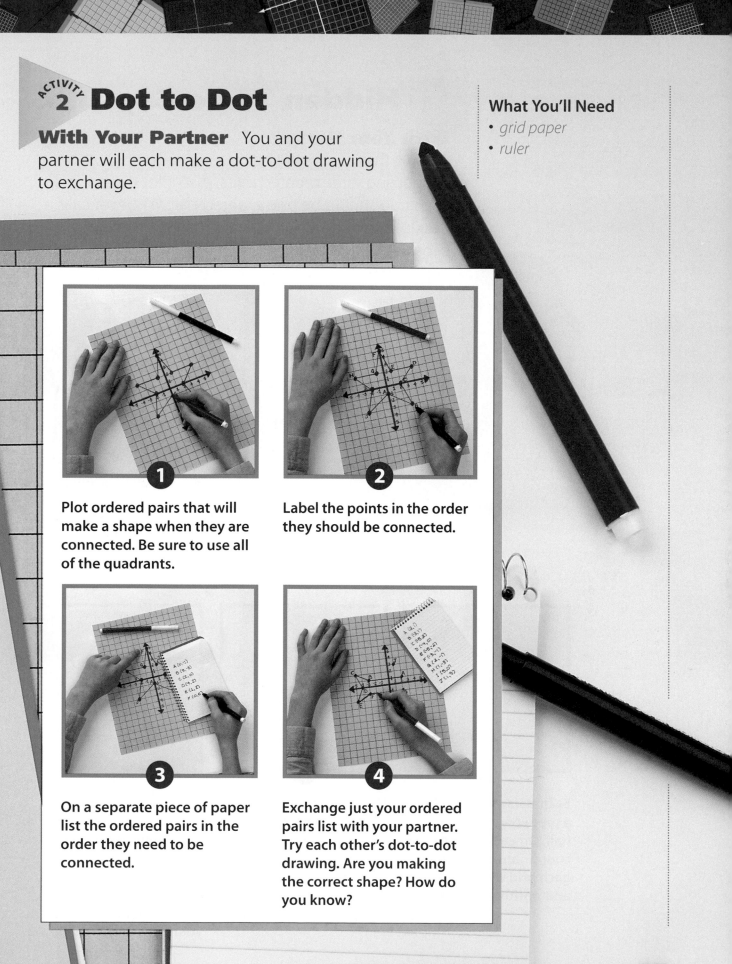

ACTIVITY 2 Dot to Dot

With Your Partner You and your partner will each make a dot-to-dot drawing to exchange.

What You'll Need
- *grid paper*
- *ruler*

1 Plot ordered pairs that will make a shape when they are connected. Be sure to use all of the quadrants.

2 Label the points in the order they should be connected.

3 On a separate piece of paper list the ordered pairs in the order they need to be connected.

4 Exchange just your ordered pairs list with your partner. Try each other's dot-to-dot drawing. Are you making the correct shape? How do you know?

ACTIVITY 3 Hidden Time Capsule

With Your Partner Each person plots a time capsule that is represented by a line segment connecting three ordered pairs. Also, plot three traps. Each trap should be one ordered pair. Whoever calls a trap loses one turn. To finish the game, both time capsules should be found.

1 Each person should fold a piece of grid paper in half. On each half draw a coordinate grid. Label each grid with negative and positive numbers.

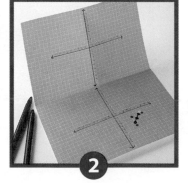

2 Use the bottom grid to plot your time capsule and three traps.

3 Take turns naming ordered pairs where you think your partner's time capsule is hidden. On the top grid use a check to mark off ordered pairs called that miss. Mark your finds with a circle.

ACTIVITY 4 Secret Message

With Your Partner Each letter of the alphabet is shown on the grid below. What word is spelled by the letters at these points: (9, 2), (−7, 8), (−6, 7)? Did you and your partner get the same word? Write a message to exchange with your partner using at least ten letters.

✔ **Self-Check**

In the grid below, which points are in the same quadrant as (−, +)?

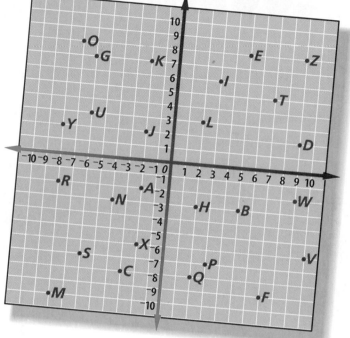

Try It!

Use the grid above. Write the ordered pair for the following points.

1. *A*   **2.** *Z*   **3.** *F*   **4.** *M*   **5.** *N*

Order the following exercises from least remainder to greatest.

6. 469 ÷ 8   **7.** 641 ÷ 7   **8.** 908 ÷ 9

9. 2,341 ÷ 6   **10.** 3,000 ÷ 7   **11.** 433 ÷ 5

Think About It

12. What do the points (5, 2), (−5, 2), (−5, −2), and (5, −2) have in common?

Looking Back

Choose the right answer. Write *a, b, c,* or *d* for each question.

1. Which pair would round to the same whole number?

   a. 3.4, 3.6   **b.** 3.0, 3.5
   c. 2.9, 3.3   **d.** 2.4, 3.2

2. Which set of numbers is in order from least to greatest?

   a. 4, ⁻5, 11, ⁻13 **b.** ⁻13, ⁻5, 4, 11
   c. ⁻5, ⁻13, 4, 11 **d.** 11, 4, ⁻5, ⁻13

3. Use a percent-bar model to find 25% of $300.

   a. $25   **b.** $75
   c. $150   **d.** $300

4. Which numbers are *not* equivalent?

   a. $\frac{4}{9}, \frac{24}{54}$ **b.** $\frac{5}{11}, \frac{50}{110}$

   c. $\frac{6}{20}, \frac{12}{40}$ **d.** $\frac{7}{20}, \frac{1}{4}$

5. How many zeros are in the number six million one thousand fourteen?

   a. 1   **b.** 2
   c. 3   **d.** 4

6. Use the bars below to estimate 75% of 120. What two numbers is it between?

   a. 61–80   **b.** 81–100
   c. 101–120   **d.** 121–140

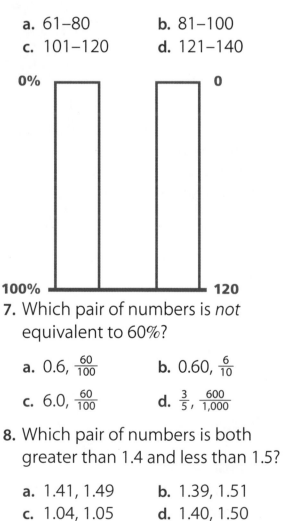

7. Which pair of numbers is *not* equivalent to 60%?

   a. 0.6, $\frac{60}{100}$ **b.** 0.60, $\frac{6}{10}$

   c. 6.0, $\frac{60}{100}$ **d.** $\frac{3}{5}, \frac{600}{1,000}$

8. Which pair of numbers is both greater than 1.4 and less than 1.5?

   a. 1.41, 1.49   **b.** 1.39, 1.51
   c. 1.04, 1.05   **d.** 1.40, 1.50

9. Which number divided by 9 leaves a remainder of 6?

    a. 255   **b.** 627

    c. 940   **d.** 1,006

10. Which set of numbers is in order from greatest to least?

    a. $4\frac{3}{8}, 3, 2\frac{3}{4}, \frac{9}{10}, \frac{1}{2}$

    b. $\frac{1}{2}, \frac{9}{10}, 2\frac{3}{4}, 3, 4\frac{3}{8}$

    c. $3, 4\frac{3}{8}, \frac{9}{10}, \frac{1}{2}, 2\frac{3}{4}$

    d. $4\frac{3}{8}, 3, 2\frac{3}{4}, \frac{1}{2}, \frac{9}{10}$

11. Which pair of numbers is *not* equivalent?

    a. $\frac{37}{7}, 5\frac{2}{7}$ **b.** $9\frac{1}{9}, \frac{28}{3}$

    c. $12\frac{2}{3}, \frac{114}{9}$ **d.** $\frac{84}{8}, 10\frac{1}{2}$

12. Which set of ordered pairs is correctly matched with the points shown on the grid?

    a. A is $(^-1, 2)$, B is $(^-2, 2)$, C is $(4, 5)$
    b. A is $(1, ^-2)$, B is $(2, ^-2)$, C is $(4, 5)$
    c. A is $(1, 2)$, B is $(2, 2)$, C is $(4, ^-5)$
    d. A is $(1, 2)$, B is $(2, ^-2)$, C is $(4, ^-5)$

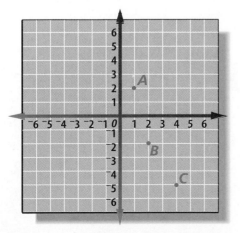

13. Which would be best described by a negative number?

    a. height of a building
    b. chairs in a library
    c. average of test scores
    d. money you owe

Check Your Math Power

14. Explain how you would describe the typical height of players on the basketball team shown below.

15. On four tests a student scored 86, 94, 83, and 89. Add two more test scores that would result in a mean of 90 for the six tests.

16. On a coordinate grid, plot four points that describe a parallelogram with no right angles.

MODULE 1

Investigations

Creating a Time Capsule

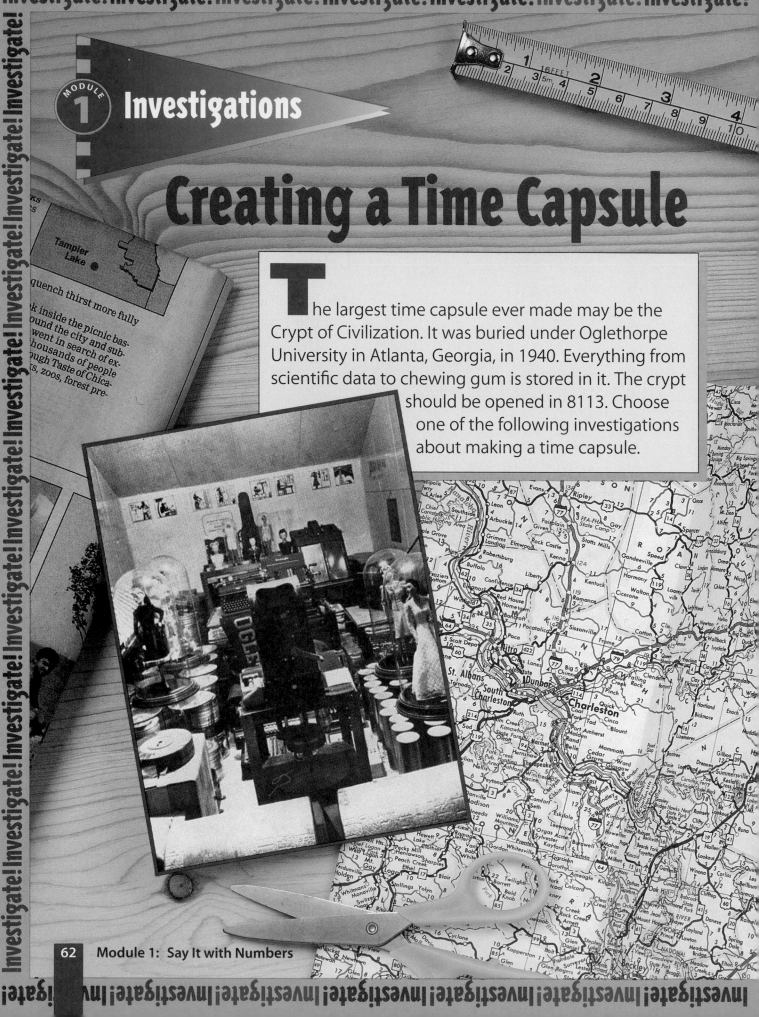

The largest time capsule ever made may be the Crypt of Civilization. It was buried under Oglethorpe University in Atlanta, Georgia, in 1940. Everything from scientific data to chewing gum is stored in it. The crypt should be opened in 8113. Choose one of the following investigations about making a time capsule.

Investigation A

Your Class Time Capsule

Create a class time capsule. Each student must provide something for it. How will you persuade your classmates that what you provided is appropriate to include in the capsule?

1. Create and conduct a survey on a topic that has not been surveyed in this module. Analyze your data, using appropriate statistics and graphs. Explain to your class why you think people in the future should see your display.

2. Choose what your class wants to store in the class time capsule.

3. Discuss how to build a container, where to store it, and how to communicate with people who might not speak your language. Draw a map to show the location of the time capsule.

Keep in Mind

Your report for your time capsule will be judged on the following points:

☐ Did you use means, modes, medians, and ranges appropriately to summarize your information?

☐ Did you use appropriate graphs to show your data?

☐ Were your directions for finding the time capsule clear?

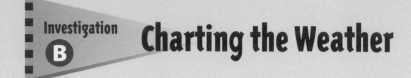

Investigation B

Charting the Weather

For one week, keep track of the high and low temperatures, the amount of rain or snow, and the wind speed. Write a report for a time capsule comparing your data with the average data for the week.

Computer Option

If you are on a computer network, send a weather survey out over it. Collect and analyze your data. Write a report explaining which places have weather similar to yours.

Investigation C

A Video Time Capsule

As a class, make a one-hour video to include in your time capsule. Your video should include examples of the use of graphs, statistics such as mean or mode, and negative numbers. Take a survey to find out what topics to show. Decide how much time to spend and which groups will show each topic. Divide into groups, plan your segments, and begin taping.

Getting Around

Whether you're going around the block or around the world, getting there takes planning and skill. In this module you'll use a scale ruler to estimate distance. You'll also learn about mixed numbers, integers, factors, and functions. At the end of the module, you'll use what you know to plan a journey to Antarctica.

SECTION
A

Time and Distance

SECTION
B

Factors and Multiples

SECTION
C

Working with Fractions

SECTION
D

Integers and Functions

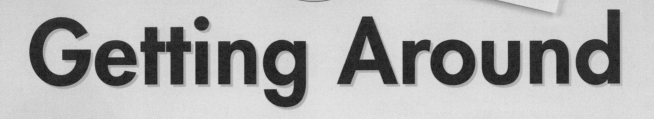

From Here to There

Every time you leave one place and head for another you answer a series of questions. Where am I going? How can I get there from here? What's the best way to travel? How long will it take? Use the answers to these questions to help you plan a trip.

❶ Plan

With a group, pick three places to visit. Think about where these places are and what the weather is like there. How would the location and weather affect your answers to the questions above?

❷ Consider

Make a list of your reasons for choosing each place. Is the place near or far? How long will it take to get there—hours? days? Will you use more than one kind of transportation?

Sea-The-World
CRUISES

Thunder
Bay

S U P E R I O

Entries/Entrées   Visas

Departures/Sorties

3 Investigate

Choose one of your three destinations. Create a travel plan to present to the class. On a poster, include the following:

- an outline map showing where you are and where you're going
- transportation you will use
- an estimate of how far and how long you will travel

Word Bank

- **composite number**
- **function**
- **greatest common factor (GCF)**
- **inverse operation**
- **least common multiple (LCM)**
- **prime factorization**
- **prime number**
- **variable**

TOPEKA & TALLAHASSEE RAILROAD
Train Schedule

Chicago...St. Paul...Portland/Seattle

7
Daily

◄ Train Number ►

Investigate! Investigate! Investigate! Investigate! Investigate! Investigate! Investigate! Investigate! Investigate! Investigate! Investigate! Investigate! Investigate! Investigate! Investigate!

Investigations Preview

Learn how to read maps and schedules and to add and subtract integers and mixed numbers. Using these skills can help you get from here to there.

Circles and Paths (pages 86–87)

How can you find and figure out mathematical patterns in circles?
Use what you learn to help you look for math patterns elsewhere.

Getting Around Antarctica (pages 110–112)

How can you use what you know to plan a journey to Antarctica?
Use what you learn about addition, subtraction, and map reading to help you make a detailed travel plan.

Spokane, WA (Coeur d'Alene, ID)	(MT)			20A
	(PT)			6 45A
Thru Cars Chicago–Portland				4 48A
Spokane, WA				1 55A
Pasco, WA (Kennewick, Richland)			Dp	12 40A
Wishram, WA (The Dalles)				28
Bingen-White Salmon, WA			Ar	11 30P
Vancouver, WA				8 38P
...rtland, OR				6 42P
...kane, WA		(PT)		6 05P

LESSON 1 It's About Time

When you travel a long distance, you may be going to a new time zone. When it's noon where you live, it's midnight on the other side of the globe.

What You'll Need
- *world globe*
- *strip of adding machine tape*
- *string or measuring tape*

ACTIVITY 1 **24 Time Zones**

With Your Group Use a globe to identify the different time zones of the world.

1 Measure the globe's circumference at the equator. Cut your paper to the same length as the circumference. Divide it into 24 equal sections.

2 Wrap the paper strip around the globe. Why don't the time zones match the meridians exactly?

3 Write your time on 1 section of your paper strip. Figure out the times in the other zones and write them in.

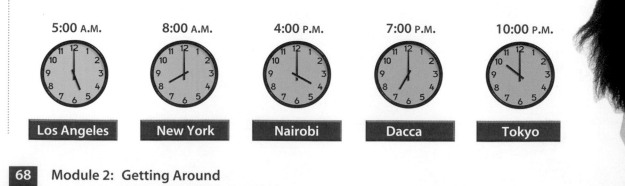

5:00 A.M. — Los Angeles 8:00 A.M. — New York 4:00 P.M. — Nairobi 7:00 P.M. — Dacca 10:00 P.M. — Tokyo

ACTIVITY 2 ▸ Time and Place

With Your Group   Use your time zone strip and the time zone map below to find these answers.

1 What time zone do you live in? What are the time zones immediately east and west of you?

2 Locate a city in each of the four time zones shown. Write the name on your strip. What time is it in each of these cities?

3 Write three questions about time differences between places in different parts of the United States. Share your questions with the class.

✔ **Self-Check** *If you're having trouble figuring out time differences, draw or think about a clock. Remember to add or subtract hours from time zone to time zone.*

ACTIVITY 3 — Travel Times

On Your Own Use the charts and your time zone strip to answer five of these questions.

Time Zones

Hawaii–Aleutian	Alaska Standard	Pacific	Mountain	Central	Eastern
Honolulu	Anchorage	Los Angeles	Denver	Chicago	New York
Kailua	Nome	Seattle	Santa Fe	Milwaukee	Cleveland
Hilo	Juneau	Portland	Cheyenne	Houston	Columbia
Kaneohe	Fairbanks	Vancouver	Edmonton	New Orleans	Montreal

1 When it is midnight in New York, what time is it in Montreal? in Seattle?

2 When it's 9:00 P.M. in Columbia, what time is it in Juneau? in Honolulu? What is the time difference between Columbia and the other two cities?

Flight Schedule

From	To	Depart	Arrive
New York	Los Angeles	8:00 A.M.	10:28 A.M.
Cleveland	Chicago	7:24 A.M.	7:42 A.M.
Milwaukee	Chicago	7:58 A.M.	8:40 A.M.
Portland	New York	6:51 A.M.	1:54 P.M.
Montreal	Houston	10:55 A.M.	2:40 P.M.
Chicago	New Orleans	11:50 A.M.	1:49 P.M.

3 Suppose you fly from Cleveland to New Orleans through Chicago.
a. What is the total flight time?
b. How much time is there between flights in Chicago?

4 Choose two flights you would like to take. What is the total flight time for each? Did you account for the time zone changes? Explain.

5 Which of the two flights you chose will take the longest time? How much more time will it take than your other flight?

6 When flying west, will you gain or lose time? Explain.

ACTIVITY 4 Using a Scale Ruler

On Your Own Kilometers (km) or miles (mi) can be used to measure long distances. A scale ruler will help you estimate distances on a map.

What You'll Need

- *2-by-10-cm strip of cardboard*

CONNECT AND COMMUNICATE

In Your Journal Do you think it is possible to tell from a map the actual distance from place to place? Why or why not?

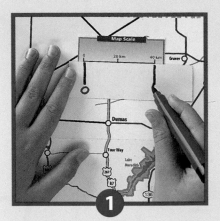

1

Put a strip of cardboard along the scale line on the map key. Mark off the beginning and ending points and label them. How many kilometers does this section represent?

2

Mark 1$\frac{1}{2}$ centimeters (cm) on your scale. What distance does this represent? Mark three other points on your scale. Write the distance for each.

3

Use your scale ruler to draw segments that represent these distances:
a. 80 km b. 50 km c. 25 km

Map Scale

0   20 km   40 km

3 cm = 20 km

Buenavista

385   87   136

Panhand

Amarillo

Vega

27

Marion

Exercises and Problems

On the Road

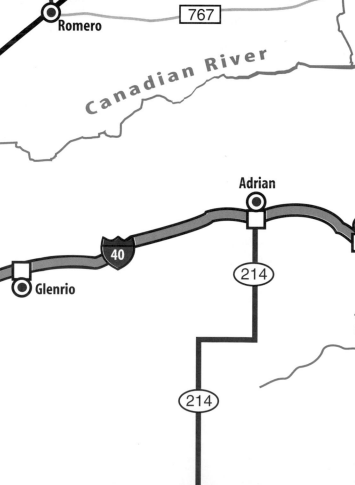

Use this map and the scale ruler you made in Activity 4 to answer these questions. Remember that you can't find the actual distance but you can make a reasonable estimate.

Parallel lines never intersect. Perpendicular lines meet at right angles. On a map, roads may seem to be parallel or perpendicular to one another.

1 Name two routes that seem parallel to Route 385.

2 Which two routes seem perpendicular to Route 40?

3 About how many kilometers is it from Channing to Vega?

4 About how far is it from Vega to Dalhart?

5 Which is the longer trip, from Romero to Dalhart or from Panhandle to Gruver? About how much longer?

6 The Commutative Property of Addition states

$$a + b = b + a.$$

Use measurements to illustrate this property for any trip on the map.

Map Scale

0   20 km   40 km

3 cm = 20 km

Dalhart

54

87

Hartley

Channing

767

Romero

385

Canadian River

Adrian

Vega

40

214

Glenrio

385

214

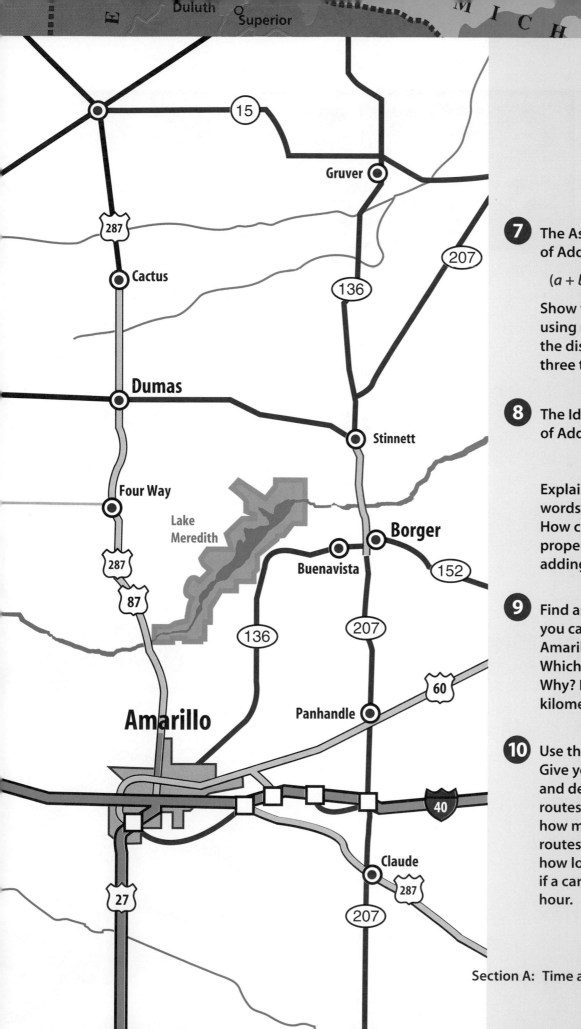

7 The Associative Property of Addition states

$$(a + b) + c = a + (b + c).$$

Show this property using measurements for the distances between three towns.

8 The Identity Property of Addition states

$$n + 0 = n.$$

Explain in your own words what that means. How could the identity property be applied to adding distances?

9 Find as many ways as you can to get from Amarillo to Borger. Which way is shortest? Why? How many kilometers is it?

10 Use the map to plan a trip. Give your starting point and destination, the routes you will take, and how many kilometers the routes cover. Estimate how long the trip will take if a car travels 60 km an hour.

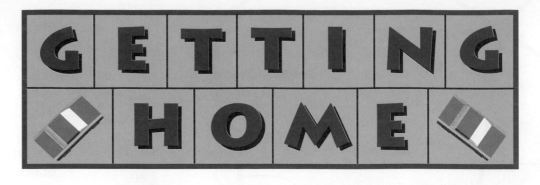

GETTING HOME

You will use many decimal numbers as you play the Getting Home game. What do you think you will learn about decimals during the game?

ACTIVITY 1 ▶ How Far? How Much?

With Your Group Read the game rules and discuss them. The object of the game is to get home by the shortest route for the least money. Be sure everyone understands how to play. As you play, you can keep track of your totals on a sheet of paper.

What You'll Need
- *gameboard*
- *game pieces*
- *cube labeled 1–6*
- *play money*

ACTIVITY OPTION

See whether you can improve the game by writing new rules or revising those given here. When you have finished, trade rules with another group and try out each other's version of the game.

Getting Home Rules

1. Each player gets $20 travel money.

2. Roll a number cube. Move that number of spaces.

3. Keep a running total of the kilometers you travel.

4. Pay any toll you pass over. Buy gas before reaching 300 km or pay a $20 towing fee and move to the nearest gas station.

5. Subtract what you spend from your $20. If you run out of money, jump directly to the cash station, collect $20, and lose one turn.

6. When you get home, add your total distance to the total money you spent. The player with the lowest score wins.

What You'll Need
- *gameboard*

ACTIVITY 2 Planning Ahead

With Your Partner Discuss the game you played in Activity 1. How did you figure out your route?

1 You could have planned ahead by figuring out the total tolls on different routes. Did you notice that the toll stops had different prices? One route on the gameboard has the following tolls.

A letter used to represent a value is a **variable**. Suppose $2.80 is **a,** $3.50 is **b,** and $4.25 is **c.**

  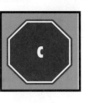  

1a + 1b + 1c + 1b + 1a means total tolls

You can use a computer spreadsheet to evaluate an algebraic expression. Put the value for each variable in a cell. Then put the expression in a cell. The computer will calculate the value.

2 You can combine like terms to get new **expressions.**

Keep in mind that in mathematics $2a = 2 \times a$.

2a + 2b + 1c   1c + 2a + 2b

a. How do these expressions differ from the one in Step 1?
b. Why can't you add $2a + 2b$?
c. Substitute the values for *a, b,* and *c,* and compare the values of the three expressions.

3 A variable can be given any value. Suppose the values of the variables were changed as follows.

_a_ = $3.07   _b_ = $1.04   _c_ = $2.15

4 Using these values, find the value for the expressions in Step 2. How do your answers compare?

5 Choose a route on the gameboard. Write an expression using variables to represent some of the distances or tolls. How do the variables help you find the total distance or cost?

Try It!

Do You Remember?

Add and subtract like terms. Match the expressions that are alike. Use $a = 2$, $b = 3.5$, and $c = 2.5$ to find the value of each equation.

1. $2a - 1b + 2a$ **2.** $1a + 3b + 1c$

3. $5a + 4b - 3a$ **4.** $3b + 2a + 1b$

5. $1a + 3a - 1b$ **6.** $4b + 1c + 1a - 1b$

Estimate the quotients.

7. $38 \div 3$ **8.** $75 \div 5$ **9.** $120 \div 8$

10. $720 \div 8$ **11.** $85 \div 6$ **12.** $1{,}260 \div 4$

Think About It

13. Where in Exercises 1–6 did you use the Commutative Property? Write your answer.

REASONING AND PROBLEM SOLVING

Why are the Associative and Commutative Properties important? Give an example of a situation in which you might use these properties.

LESSON
3

Just the Factors

Many mathematicians spend time studying number patterns. Try the following activities to discover some tricks that will help you with these patterns.

What divisibility rules can you use to find the factors of a number?

REASONING AND PROBLEM SOLVING

ACTIVITY 1 **How Many Factors?**

With Your Partner You can divide on your calculator to find factors. If the quotient is a whole number, you have found two factors.

1 Pick any three-digit number. Divide and list the factors. See who can find the most factors.

357 | 1 × 357 | 3 × 119
         | 7 × 51 | 17 × 21

2 Compare your lists. Did you and your partner find all the factors? How can you tell?

3 Find the factors for at least four more numbers. How can looking at the last digit help?

ACTIVITY 2 Prime or Composite?

With Your Partner About 230 B.C., Eratosthenes, a Greek mathematician, found a way to identify **prime numbers.** A prime number has exactly two factors, 1 and the number itself. Use a hundred chart to find the primes between 1 and 100.

1

2

3

Cross out 1. Why isn't 1 a prime number? Draw a circle around 2. Multiples of 2 are products of 2 and other numbers. Cross out the multiples of 2.

Draw a circle around 3 and cross out its multiples. Why are some multiples of 3 already crossed out?

Find the next unmarked number. Is it prime? Continue until all the numbers are circled or crossed out. What is the last number to be crossed out?

4 List all the circled numbers. These are all the primes less than 100.

5 Except for 1, all the crossed-out numbers are called composite numbers. Write a definition for composite numbers.

DRAWING TO LEARN

Try making a chart with the first 100 numbers written in rows of 6. How does this chart differ from the first? Now arrange the numbers in rows of 12. How does this chart differ from the other two?

Write an explanation telling why 1 is neither a prime number nor a composite number.

ACTIVITY 3 Using Primes

With Your Class Writing a composite number as the product of its factors is called factoring. Expressing a composite number as the product of prime factors is called **prime factorization**.

1 Making a factor tree is one way to help you with prime factorization.

Start with any factorization of the number that does not use 1.

$$24$$
$$6 \times 4$$
$$2 \times 3 \times 2 \times 2$$

If one or both of the factors are not prime, add another branch to the tree.

Continue until all the numbers on the bottom branches are prime.

2 Make another factor tree for 24. Start with 8 and 3. What is the result? What is the result if you use 2 and 12?

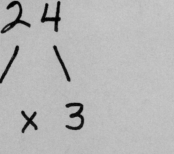

$$24$$
$$8 \times 3$$

$$24$$
$$2 \times 12$$

With Your Partner Make some factor trees of your own.

3 Make as many factor trees as you can for 36.
   a. Write the prime factorization.
   b. How many prime factorizations are there for 36?

4 Find the prime factorizations for 60 and 42. Share your answers with the class. How many prime factorizations does each number have?

CONNECT AND COMMUNICATE

In Your Journal What properties tell us that all of these factorizations are the same?

   $2 \times 3 \times 5$ $3 \times 2 \times 5$
   $5 \times 3 \times 2$ $5 \times 2 \times 3$

Do You Remember?

Try It!

If the number is composite find the prime factorization.

  1. 41   **2.** 12   **3.** 42   **4.** 27

Find the number. Use the prime factorization to list at least three composite factors.

  5. $2 \times 3 \times 2 \times 3$ **6.** $5 \times 5 \times 5 \times 3$
  7. $5 \times 3 \times 3 \times 7$ **8.** $2 \times 5 \times 2 \times 3 \times 2$

Write true addition and subtraction statements.

  9. 2.02; 31.5; 33.52   **10.** 6,875; 387; 6,488

 11. 8.76; 9; 0.24   **12.** 9.87; 12.316; 2.446

 13. 1,254; 2,443; 3,697 **14.** 16.5; 5.88; 10.62

Think About It

15. In Exercises 5–8, how did having the prime factorization help you find the composite factors?

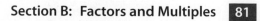

In Common

ACTIVITY
1 **Diagramming Factors**

On Your Own Making a Venn diagram is one way of finding common factors.

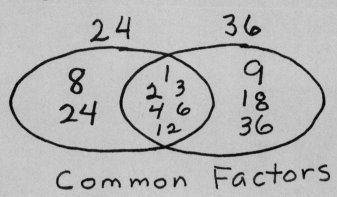

24   36

Common Factors

1 What are the common factors of 24 and 36? Which factor is the greatest? This factor is called the **greatest common factor (GCF)**.

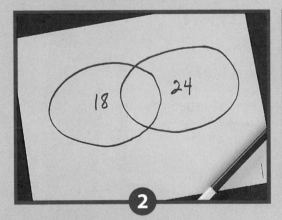

2

To find common factors of 18 and 24 start with drawings of the two sets.

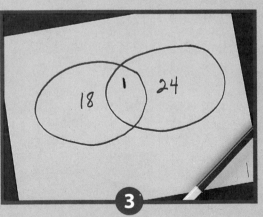

3

We can start with a 1 in the overlap. Why? Continue. Find the GCF.

4 Find the GCF in these number pairs.

a. 18, 27   b. 15, 55   c. 18, 23

Common Primes

With Your Partner Another way to find the GCF is to use the prime factorizations of two numbers.

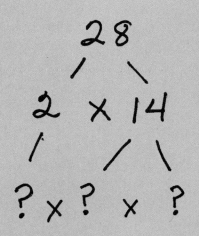

28
/ \
2 × 14
/ / \
? × ? × ?

40
/ \
4 × 10
/ \ / \
? × ? × ? × ?

1 Find the prime factorization of each number.

$28 = \boxed{2} \times \boxed{2} \times 7$

$40 = \boxed{2} \times \boxed{2} \times 2 \times 5$

2 Compare the prime factorizations. Circle the prime factors that are the same.
  a. What is the product of the circled factors of 28? Is it a factor of 28?
  b. What is the product of the circled factors of 40? Is it a factor of 40?
  c. What is the GCF of 28 and 40? Explain why you cannot find a greater common factor.

3 Find the GCF of each number pair.

a. 16, 20 b. 18, 45 c. 28, 42

✔ Self-Check *When finding the LCM of two numbers, how do you know how many multiples to list? Explain.*

ACTIVITY 3 Search for Multiples

With Your Class You can use Venn diagrams or prime factorizations to find the common multiples of two numbers.

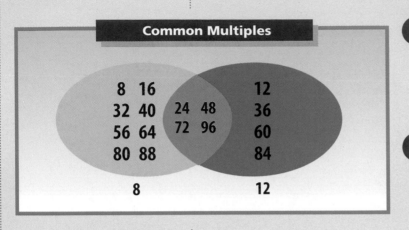

Common Multiples

8 16		12
32 40	24 48	36
56 64	72 96	60
80 88		84
8		12

1 Look at the Venn diagram on the left. Are all of the multiples of 8 and 12 shown?

2 What are the common multiples? What is the **least common multiple (LCM)** of 8 and 12?

3 Use the prime factorizations on the tablet to build the least common multiple of 8 and 12.

 a. Start by listing the prime factorization of 12, $2 \times 2 \times 3$. Why must all of these factors be included in the LCM?

 b. What factors must the LCM have to be a multiple of 8?

 c. Why do you need to add only one more 2?

 d. Multiply to find the LCM.

$8 = 2 \times 2 \times 2$
$12 = 2 \times 2 \times 3$

LCM
↓
$2 \times 2 \times 3$
↓
$2 \times 2 \times 2 \times 3$

4 Use a Venn diagram or prime factorization to find the LCM of 6 and 9.

$$6 = 2 \times 3$$

$$9 = 3 \times 3$$

$$\text{LCM} = ?$$

5 Find the LCM for each number pair.

a. **4, 8**　　b. **5, 9**　　c. **6, 10**

6 Which method works best for finding the least common multiple? Why?

The product of two numbers is equal to the product of their GCF and LCM. Write an explanation of how this works, and show at least three examples.

Try It!

Write the common factors. Circle the GCF.

1. 20, 35　**2.** 16, 20　**3.** 24, 36　**4.** 22, 33

Find the LCM and the GCF.

5. 3, 5　　**6.** 8, 15　　**7.** 15, 75　　**8.** 36, 60

Order the integers from least to greatest. Add one smaller and one larger integer to each list.

9. ⁻7, ⁻4, 6　　**10.** 3, ⁻3, 2　　**11.** 6, 15, 12

12. 6, ⁻1, ⁻8, 5　　**13.** ⁻6, ⁻8, ⁻1, ⁻10

Think About It

14. Can two numbers have a greatest common multiple? Explain your answer in writing.

Try to think of another way to find the LCM of two numbers. Share your method with the class.

Investigation

Circles and Paths

There's more than one path you can take to get around a circle. Make some circular designs and see if you notice any interesting mathematical patterns.

1 Choose a number—for example, 8. Use your Fraction Tool or compass to mark eight points at equal distances around the circumference of the circle.

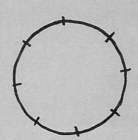

2 Pick a second number that is less than the first, such as 2. Choose a place to start. Use a straightedge to connect every second point.

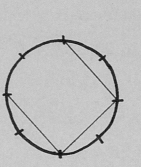

3 Keep going until you return to the starting point. This is a path. If all points are not connected, move over one point and begin a new path. You might want to do this next path in a different color.

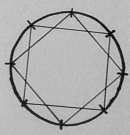

4 How many paths are in your circle? Make a chart like the one on this page to show your results. Describe your design. What do you notice about the paths and the number of points you used to create the design? Explain.

5 Now try using other numbers to create different designs. Review your explanation. Does it apply to your new designs?

number of Points	Connect every...	number of paths
8	2	
8	3	2
12		
12		
24		

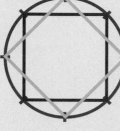

Ask Yourself

- ☐ What mathematical relationship do you see between the number of paths and the numbers you used?
- ☐ How did you find the relationship between the paths and the number of points?
- ☐ What math did you use—addition, multiplication, division?
- ☐ How did the circles you created affect your explanation of the patterns?
- ☐ How could you explain these circle patterns to a friend?

Math by Mail

Suppose that you are employed by the Mercury Express Mail Company in Topeka, Kansas. Each day it is your job to solve problems like the following.

1 Ms. Rivera is mailing 16 dictionaries to Beaumont, Texas. Each dictionary weighs 1.5 pounds (lb). How much will it cost to send the package by air?

2 Mr. Johnson is sending an 8-lb box of marbles to his nephew in Juneau, Alaska. How much will it cost to send by ground?

3 Ms. Kaba's package contains three pairs of gloves for her nieces in Fargo, North Dakota. Each pair of gloves weighs about 6 ounces (oz). What is the cost to ship by air?

4 How much would Ms. Kaba save by using ground delivery?

5 One package contains six 12-oz jars of cocoa and five 1-lb bags of pretzels. How much will ground delivery to Long Beach, California, cost?

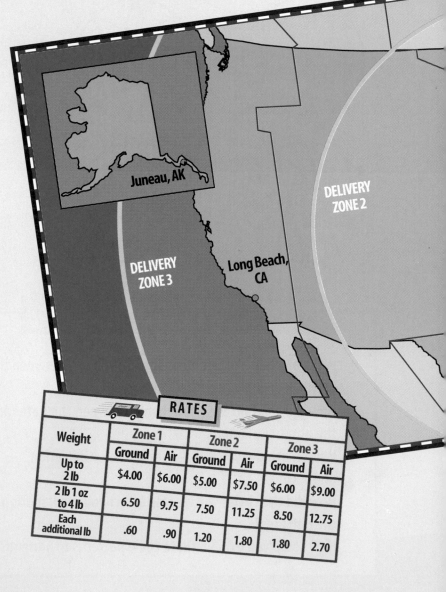

Weight	Zone 1		Zone 2		Zone 3	
	Ground	Air	Ground	Air	Ground	Air
Up to 2 lb	$4.00	$6.00	$5.00	$7.50	$6.00	$9.00
2 lb 1 oz to 4 lb	6.50	9.75	7.50	11.25	8.50	12.75
Each additional lb	.60	.90	1.20	1.80	1.80	2.70

6 Packages are separated by weight for shipping. Put these packages in order from least to greatest by weight: 12.25 lb, 16.87 lb, 12.04 lb, 16.75 lb, 12 lb, 11.95 lb.

7 Mr. Mahdi has two 3-lb items and four 5-lb items to ship. How can he divide them into 2 packages of equal weight?

8 What if Mr. Mahdi had four 3-lb items and six 5-lb items? How could these be divided into 2 packages of equal weight?

9 Each week, the Ticky Tack Company ships twelve 75-lb cartons of tacks to Springfield, Massachusetts. What is the least it would cost to ship them? What would be the total cost for 1 year?

DELIVERY ZONE 3

DELIVERY ZONE 2

DELIVERY ZONE 1

Springfield, MA

Fargo, ND

Omaha, NE

★ Topeka, KS

Springfield, MO

Tulsa, OK

Beaumont, TX

Check Your Math Power

10 For any size package, what is the cost difference between ground delivery and air delivery? Create a chart or rule to answer this question quickly.

LESSON 5 Plus and Minus

Horses, once a very important means of travel, create a problem in this Jewish folktale.

Three men pooled their money and for 2,700 rubles bought 17 horses in partnership. One had paid half of the money, another a third, and the third man a ninth. But, when the time came to divide the horses, they did not know how to do it. So they went to the rabbi for advice.

"Let me sleep on the matter overnight," he told them. "Come back tomorrow morning and bring your horses with you."

At the appointed hour the following morning the three partners brought their horses to the rabbi. The rabbi went into his stable and led out his own horse. Mounting it, he drew up alongside the 17 horses.

"My good friends," he said, "there are now 18 horses here. You who paid one-half, take 9 horses. You, who paid a third, take 6 horses. You, who paid one-ninth, take 2 horses. Altogether you, therefore, have the 17 horses disposed of."

Then the rabbi led his own horse back to the stable and returned to his Talmud.

From *A Treasury of Jewish Folklore*
edited by Nathan Ausubel

Were you able to figure out how the rabbi used his math power to divide the horses? The secret lies in being able to add the fractions $\frac{1}{2}$, $\frac{1}{3}$, and $\frac{1}{9}$.

ACTIVITY 1 Parts of a Whole

On Your Own You need to be able to add like fractions and know some things about equivalent fractions. If you do, you can use *your* math power to add fractions such as $\frac{1}{2}$ and $\frac{1}{3}$.

Why is it harder to add $\frac{1}{2}$, $\frac{1}{3}$, and $\frac{1}{9}$ than it is to add $\frac{1}{9}$, $\frac{2}{9}$, and $\frac{3}{9}$?

What You'll Need
- *Fraction Tool or ruler*

1

Use your Fraction Tool to draw and shade a bar representing $\frac{1}{2}$.

2

Now draw and shade a bar that represents $\frac{1}{3}$.

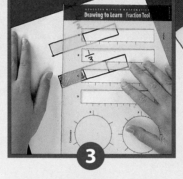

3

Lay your Fraction Tool over the shaded portions. What other fractions would fit the shaded area?

Draw bars of fractions equivalent to $\frac{1}{2}$. Draw bars of fractions equivalent to $\frac{1}{3}$.

$\frac{1}{2}$

$\frac{1}{3}$

How does what you know about multiples help you find common denominators?

4 Do any of the bars you drew have the same denominator in both the $\frac{1}{2}$ set and the $\frac{1}{3}$ set? How might these bars help you find the sum?

5 Kim used 6ths and Ty used 12ths to find the sum. Will they get the same sum? Explain.

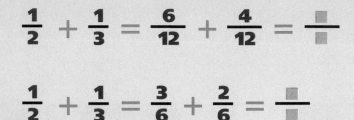

$$\frac{1}{2} + \frac{1}{3} = \frac{6}{12} + \frac{4}{12} = \frac{\blacksquare}{\blacksquare}$$

$$\frac{1}{2} + \frac{1}{3} = \frac{3}{6} + \frac{2}{6} = \frac{\blacksquare}{\blacksquare}$$

6 Sometimes sums or differences should be in simplest terms. Use the Fraction Tool to solve these equations.

   a. $\frac{1}{6} + \frac{1}{2} = n$ **b.** $\frac{1}{4} + \frac{2}{3} = n$ **c.** $\frac{2}{3} - \frac{1}{6} = n$

ACTIVITY 2 **Fractions: + and –**

With Your Partner Your Fraction Tool helped you take the first step in solving the rabbi's riddle. You added $\frac{1}{2}$ and $\frac{1}{3}$ to get $\frac{5}{6}$.

1 To finish you must add $\frac{5}{6}$ and $\frac{1}{9}$. How can you find equivalent fractions without using the Fraction Tool?

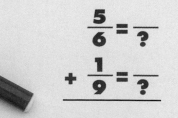

$$\frac{5}{6} = \frac{}{?}$$

$$+ \frac{1}{9} = \frac{}{?}$$

2 Does your sum help you see how the rabbi solved the problem? How did using his own horse help?

3 Find equivalent fractions for each pair. Then find the sums or differences.

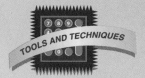

Use your calculator to find the common denominator. Multiply the denominators. Then divide the result by the greatest common factor.

a. $\dfrac{1}{4}$
   $+\dfrac{1}{3}$

b. $\dfrac{5}{6}$
   $-\dfrac{3}{5}$

c. $\dfrac{4}{7}$
   $-\dfrac{1}{3}$

d. $\dfrac{3}{8}$
   $+\dfrac{5}{6}$

Do You Remember?

Try It!

Add or subtract. Then write the answers in order from least to greatest.

1. $\dfrac{5}{6} - \dfrac{5}{12} = n$ **2.** $\dfrac{7}{10} + \dfrac{1}{5} = n$ **3.** $\dfrac{2}{3} - \dfrac{1}{4} = n$

4. $\dfrac{3}{5} + \dfrac{1}{8} = n$ **5.** $\dfrac{5}{6} - \dfrac{3}{4} = n$ **6.** $\dfrac{1}{2} + \dfrac{9}{14} = n$

Estimate answers to the nearest whole number.

7. $2.09 + 6.872$ **8.** $10.509 + 0.795$ **9.** $0.446 + 0.549$

10. $4.04 - 0.582$ **11.** $5.2 - 3.8$ **12.** $1.79 - 0.988$

Think About It

13. When is the least common denominator the same as the product of the denominators? Explain in writing.

LESSON 6 Mixed Numbers

✔ **Self-Check** *Use what you know about factors to find equivalent fractions. If a numerator and a denominator have a common factor, you can simplify the fraction.*

ACTIVITY 1 Wholes and Parts

With Your Partner Bicycles are another way of traveling. Two bikers started out on a $3\frac{3}{10}$-mi. bike race. After the first 5 minutes, Tanya had completed $1\frac{7}{10}$ mi and Lila had completed $1\frac{2}{10}$ mi. How much farther did each racer have to go to finish?

1 How would you solve the problem? Talk it over with your partner.

    a. Why is it easier to figure out Lila's remaining distance than Tanya's?

    b. How did you find Tanya's remaining distance?

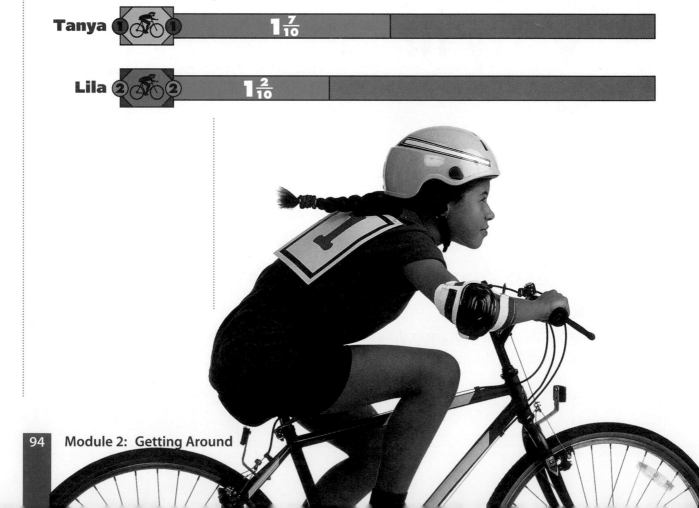

Tanya ① 🚲 ① $1\frac{7}{10}$

Lila ② 🚲 ② $1\frac{2}{10}$

2 Ben counted by tenths from $1\frac{7}{10}$ to $3\frac{3}{10}$ to find out how much farther Tanya had to go. Try Ben's method.

3 Hakeem changed both numbers to fractions greater than 1. Try Hakeem's method.

4 Rosa said she made a trade, just as she did when subtracting whole numbers. Rosa said that $3\frac{3}{10} = 2\frac{13}{10}$.

5 Why wouldn't Rosa's method work for a problem like the one below? To what could you change $6\frac{3}{8}$ so Rosa's method would work for a subtraction like the following?

Draw to show how the Associative, Commutative, and Identity Properties of Addition apply to fractions.

$$6\frac{3}{8} \rightarrow 5\,\cancel{\frac{13}{8}}$$

$$-2\frac{5}{8} \qquad -2\frac{5}{8}$$

Think about the number that's crossed out. What part of the number is wrong?

6 Which method do you like better? Why?

If you have a calculator that calculates fractions, you can simplify the sum or difference by using the **Simp** *key.*

What You'll Need
- *2 bags or boxes to hold slips of paper*

Add It Up

On Your Own   Adding mixed numbers, like subtracting them, sometimes requires regrouping.

1   Try working these exercises by yourself. Compare your answers with those of a partner. Which need regrouping?

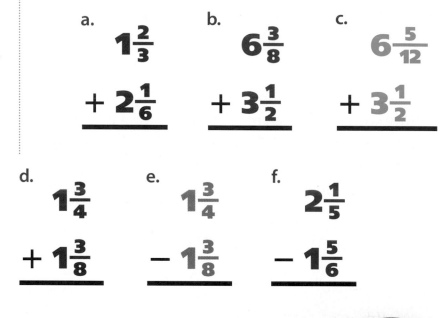

a.
$$1\frac{2}{3}$$
$$+\,2\frac{1}{6}$$

b.
$$6\frac{3}{8}$$
$$+\,3\frac{1}{2}$$

c.
$$6\frac{5}{12}$$
$$+\,3\frac{1}{2}$$

d.
$$1\frac{3}{4}$$
$$+\,1\frac{3}{8}$$

e.
$$1\frac{3}{4}$$
$$-\,1\frac{3}{8}$$

f.
$$2\frac{1}{5}$$
$$-\,1\frac{5}{6}$$

With Your Group Practice
adding and subtracting mixed numbers.

2 Work together to make up many
different fractions less than 1. Write
each one on a small card or slip of
paper and drop it into a box or bag.
Then write the numbers 1–9 and drop
them into a second box or bag.

3 Take turns picking out two whole numbers and
two fractions. Use them to make up two mixed
numbers. Estimate the sum of the two numbers.
Estimate the difference between the numbers.
Then calculate the actual sum and difference.

ACTIVITY OPTION

*Make up 12 addition and
subtraction exercises with
mixed numbers. Hold a
contest with another
group in which you solve
each other's exercises.
The first group to correctly
finish all 12 wins.*

Exploring Atlanta

Atlanta, the capital of Georgia, is the birthplace of Martin Luther King, Jr. Use the map of Atlanta to practice measuring distances and working with mixed numbers. Use the edge of a sheet of paper to make yourself a map scale you can use to measure map distances. Estimate all distances to the nearest $\frac{1}{4}$ inch (in.).

Birthplace of Martin Luther King, Jr.

1 The house where King was born is now a national historic site. What is the site's distance from the State Capitol?

2 King attended Morehouse College. How far is that school from his birthplace?

3 You can explore Atlanta's past at the Atlanta Historical Society. How far is that place from the King birthplace?

 4 The Cyclorama has a huge circular painting of the Civil War Battle of Atlanta. How far is the Cyclorama from the Historical Society?

 5 Add all the distances you got in Exercises 1–4. What's the sum?

 6 Find the two sites on the map that are about $\frac{1}{2}$ mi apart.

7 Which two schools on the map are about $1\frac{2}{10}$ mi apart?

A helicopter flies from the Governor's Mansion to the Arts Center, then to the Centers for Disease Control, then to the State Capitol.

 8 What is the distance of each flight as a mixed number in simplest terms?

 9 What is the total distance?

 10 How much farther is it from the Governor's Mansion to the Arts Center than from the Centers for Disease Control to the Capitol?

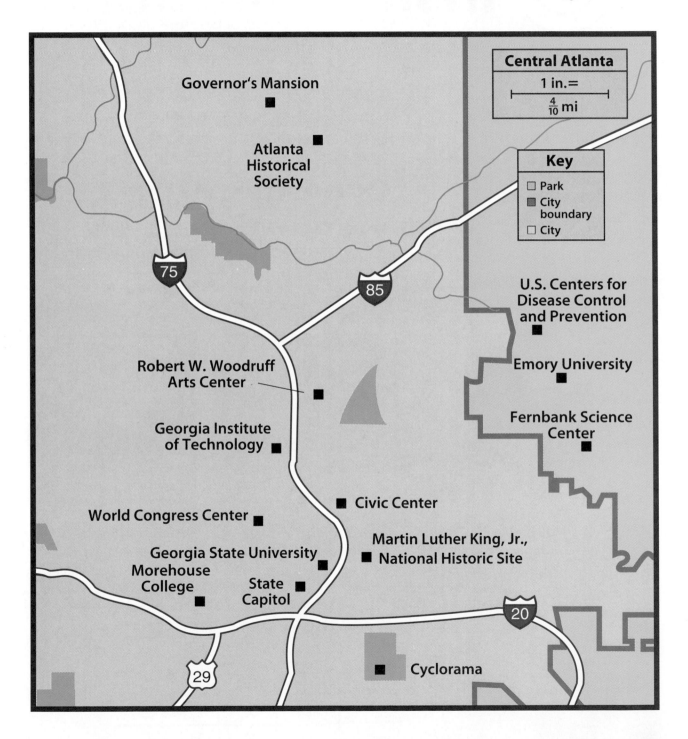

LESSON 7 Inside Integers

Tminus 5 minutes and holding." For space flights, NASA uses negative integers to count mission time *before* takeoff and positive integers for time *after* takeoff.

ACTIVITY 1 Opposites Attract

With Your Group In this game the blue number cube and counters represent positive numbers and the red cube and counters represent negative numbers.

What You'll Need
- *20 blue and 20 red counters*
- *1 blue cube labeled 1–6*
- *1 red cube labeled 1–6*

1

Roll both cubes. Take the number of red and blue counters shown. Match each blue counter with a red. Return the matched counters.

2

Record your turn on a chart like the one below. On your next turn, throw either a red or a blue cube. Get the number of counters shown.

3

Return any matches. Record your turn. Play five rounds. The player with the fewest counters is the winner.

roll	blue	red	results
1	4	3	1 blue
2	1	3	2 red

ᴬᶜᵀᴵᵛᴵᵀʸ 2 Positive and Negative

With a Partner Matching red and blue counters is one model for adding integers. For example, matching 4 blue counters and 3 red counters is like adding 4 and ⁻3. The number line can also be used as a model for adding integers.

1 What does the first move on this number line show? What does the second move show? How does the number line fit the equation?

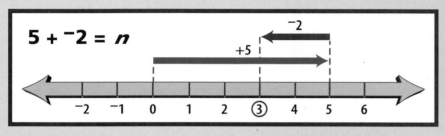

$$5 + {}^-2 = n$$

2 Explain how this number line fits the equation. What would the number line for $6 + {}^-6$ look like? Write a statement about the sum of any integer and its opposite.

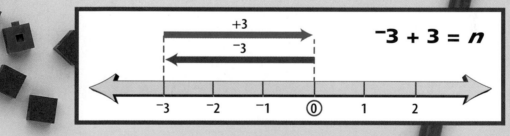

$${}^-3 + 3 = n$$

3 Draw number lines to show these equations.
a. $^-4 + 2 = n$ b. $n = 9 + {}^-9$
c. $n = 7 + 2$ d. $^-7 + {}^-2 = n$

4 Write a paragraph explaining what happens when you add these integers: positive + positive, negative + negative, positive + negative.

What You'll Need

- *20 blue and 20 red counters*
- *1 blue cube labeled 1–6*
- *1 red cube labeled 1–6*

ACTIVITY 3 # Turning It All Around

With Your Group Addition and subtraction are **inverse operations.** Thinking about the related addition can help make sense of the subtraction.

1 Write the equations shown below.

$$\square - \triangle = n$$

$$\triangle + n = \square$$

a. Roll the red cube. Write that number in the triangle.
b. Show the number of red counters.
c. Roll the blue cube. Write that number in the square.
d. What is *n*?

What color counters must you add to the 5 reds to end up with 3 blues? How many must you add?

2 This time roll the red cube twice. Record the first roll in the square. Use counters. Solve for *n*.

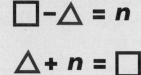

What color counters must you add to the 6 reds to end up with 4 reds? How many must you add?

$$\boxed{^-4} - \triangle{^-6} = n$$

$$\triangle{^-6} + 2 = \boxed{^-4}$$

REASONING AND PROBLEM SOLVING

In Activity 1 you rolled both number cubes at the same time. Why do you roll one at a time when subtracting?

102 Module 2: Getting Around

3 Try these subtractions. Use your counters and cubes. Record the first throw in the square each time. Throw:
  • a red cube then a red cube
  • a red cube then a blue cube
  • a blue cube then a red cube
  • a blue cube then a blue cube.

$$\square - \triangle = n$$

✔ **Self-Check** *Write an addition equation to fit each of your solutions.*

 ACTIVITY 4 Lay It on the Line

With Your Partner Think about using the number line to model subtraction of integers.

1 Would you move forward or backward to get from 4 to ‾2? How many steps?

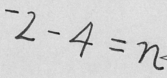

$$‾2 - 4 = n$$

Think: $4 + n = ‾2$

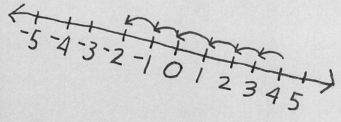

2 Make up three more subtraction equations with negative numbers. Show them on the number line. Then look for patterns and share your findings with the class.

Section D: Integers and Functions   103

3 Use any method to work these pairs.

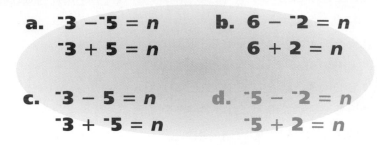

a. $^-3 - ^-5 = n$ b. $6 - ^-2 = n$

    $^-3 + 5 = n$ $6 + 2 = n$

c. $^-3 - 5 = n$ d. $^-5 - ^-2 = n$

    $^-3 + ^-5 = n$ $^-5 + 2 = n$

How do the answers in each pair compare? How are
the paired equations the same? How are they
different? Write a rule that allows you to change
subtraction equations to addition equations.

Do You Remember?

Try It!

Write an inverse equation. Find the value of n.

1. $12 - 20 = n$ **2.** $n = ^-12 - ^-8$ **3.** $^-2 - ^-3 = n$

4. $n = 0 - ^-20$ **5.** $^-10 - 8 = n$ **6.** $n = ^-12 - ^-12$

Tell whether the sum will be greater than or less than zero.
If greater than zero, find the answer.

7. $^-24 + 25$ **8.** $^-212 + ^-212$ **9.** $15 + ^-15 + 36$

Order from greatest to least.

10. $3\frac{1}{3}, \frac{2}{3}, 2\frac{2}{3}$ **11.** $\frac{4}{5}, 2\frac{1}{5}, \frac{1}{5}$ **12.** $1\frac{4}{9}, 1\frac{1}{3}, \frac{2}{3}$

13. $7\frac{1}{10}, \frac{7}{10}, 8\frac{7}{10}, \frac{5}{10}$ **14.** $\frac{4}{8}, \frac{3}{8}, 5\frac{1}{8}, \frac{8}{8}$ **15.** $1\frac{3}{4}, 1\frac{5}{6}, 5\frac{10}{6}, 1\frac{1}{2}$

Think About It

16. Explain in writing why $^-10 - 10 = ^-20$.

Function Time

ᴬᶜᵀᴵⱽᴵᵀʸ 1 Number Decoder

With Your Partner Here's a trick you can use to amaze your friends. You need to remember only a few simple steps.

What You'll Need
- *1 blue cube labeled 1–6*
- *1 red cube labeled 1–6*

1 Have your partner roll two number cubes, one red and one blue. Say that without seeing the cubes you will tell which number was rolled on each cube. Have your partner do the following. Remember: the red cube stands for a negative number.

Number Decoder

1. **Multiply the number on the blue cube by 5.**
2. **Add 3.**
3. **Multiply by 2.**
4. **Subtract the number rolled on the red cube and tell the result.**

You figure out the answer:
Mentally subtract 6 from the result. The tens' digit will be the number on the blue cube. The ones' digit will be the number on the red cube.

2 Practice the trick on your partner a few times. Then switch roles.

3 Try to explain how the trick works. You can use a paragraph, a chart, a drawing, or even an equation.

CONNECT AND COMMUNICATE

Why is a table the most effective way to set up function inputs and outputs?

ACTIVITY
2 **Commuter Computer**

On Your Own The Japanese bullet train can travel at a peak speed of 130 mi per hour. See if you can discover a rule for showing how far it can travel in various amounts of time.

1 Make a table showing how far the train would travel at peak speed in the following times: 1 hour, 2 hours, 6 hours.

Input (hours)	1	2	3	6	12	24
Output (distance)	130	?				

2 Explain the relationship between the input and output numbers in your table. One way to show this relationship is to use a variable for the input, such as 130*n*.

3 A relationship in which a given input always has the same output is called a **function**. Write a function rule for each table below.

Input	12	6	7	9
Output	6	0	1	3

Input	1.5	3	6
Output	3	4.5	7.5

4 Look at the first input and output in each table above. For each input find a new rule that will give the same output as before.

ACTIVITY 3 Guess the Function

With Your Class Use what you know about functions to play this game.

1. Write a function on a slip of paper. Your function can include more than one step and can include fractions, decimals, or mixed numbers.

2. Draw an input/output table to show your group. Ask them to figure out the function rule. The first person to correctly answer presents the next function rule.

3. Select one of your group's input/output tables for the class to solve.

ACTIVITY OPTION

Guess the Function can be played by two teams. One team writes the function rule while the other tries to guess what the rule is.

$$n \div 2$$

$$(n + 1) \times 2$$

Do You Remember? Try It!

Make an input/output table. Use the numbers 1–10.

1. Add your age. 2. Multiply by 2. 3. Subtract 10. 4. Add $\frac{1}{2}$.

Make a table using the given values.

5. $12 - r$; $r = -2, -1, 0, 1, 2$

6. $s - 10$; $s = 0, 1, 2, 3$

7. $4t + 1.5$; $t = 1, 2, 3$

8. $\frac{1}{v}$; $v = 1, 2, 3, 4, 5$

Write the greatest number. Write fractions greater than 1 as mixed numbers, mixed numbers as fractions.

9. $\frac{5}{6}, \frac{11}{12}, \frac{13}{12}$

10. $\frac{6}{5}, \frac{3}{10}, \frac{10}{10}, 1\frac{1}{10}$

11. $\frac{3}{9}, \frac{1}{3}, \frac{7}{6}$

12. $\frac{5}{8}, \frac{3}{4}, \frac{9}{8}, \frac{13}{16}$

Think About It

13. What do you notice about the output values in Exercises 5–8? Explain your observation in writing.

Looking Back

Choose the right answer. Write *a*, *b*, *c*, or *d* for each question.

1. Which statement shows the Associative Property of Addition?
   a. $4 + 1.002 = 5.002 + 0$
   b. $9.2 + {}^-6.85 = 2.35$
   c. $2.8 + (4.9 + 1) = (2.8 + 4.9) + 1$
   d. $23 + (8 - 10) = 10 + (10 + 1)$

2. For which equation does $n = 3$?
   a. $10 + (7 - 14) = n$
   b. $n \times 3 = 12$
   c. $3 + 3 = n + 4$
   d. $n = 0 + {}^-3$

3. Which has the correct solution?
   a. $2.25 + 1.004 + 0.563 = 3.927$
   b. $7.54 - 4.351 = 3.191$
   c. $1.119 + 3.8 + 9.024 = 13.943$
   d. $23.73 + 2.8606 - 10.5 = 16.0904$

4. Which equation will have the same solution as $3x + (2y - 1x) = 2z$?
   a. $2z = 3x + 2y - 1x$
   b. $(3x + 2y) - 1x = 2z$
   c. $2x + 2y = 2z$
   d. all of the above

5. Which is the prime factorization of 36?
   a. 6×6
   b. $2 \times 2 \times 9$
   c. 2×3
   d. $2 \times 2 \times 3 \times 3$

6. Which is the prime factorization of 48?
   a. $2 \times 2 \times 2 \times 2 \times 3$
   b. 2×3
   c. 4×12
   d. $2 \times 2 \times 2 \times 3$

7. What is the greatest common factor of 36 and 48?
   a. $2 \times 2 \times 2 \times 2$
   b. $2 \times 2 \times 2 \times 2 \times 3$
   c. $2 \times 2 \times 3$
   d. 2×3

8. What is the least common multiple of 42 and 56?
   a. $2 \times 3 \times 7$
   b. 7×7
   c. $2 \times 2 \times 2 \times 3 \times 7$
   d. 2×7

Use the grid for Exercises 9–12. Write a, b, c, or d.

9. Which line segments are parallel?
   a. *AE, FI*
   b. *CN, NO*
   c. *IJ, KN*
   d. *JK, LO*

10. Which line segments are perpendicular?
    a. *EH, MN*
    b. *CB, GH*
    c. *CD, KL*
    d. *AG, AB*

11. Which line segment is neither parallel nor perpendicular to any other one shown?
    a. *FI*
    b. *LO*
    c. *JK*
    d. *EM*

12. What is the total distance along the route *BI, IJ, JK, KL*?
    a. $2\frac{3}{4}$ mi
    b. $3\frac{1}{2}$ mi
    c. $3\frac{7}{8}$ mi
    d. $2\frac{2}{3}$ mi

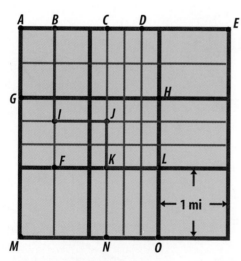

13. Which of the following is ordered from least to greatest?
    a. $\frac{3}{27}, \frac{2}{9}, \frac{1}{4}$
    b. $\frac{1}{2}, \frac{2}{3}, \frac{1}{4}$
    c. $\frac{5}{9}, \frac{10}{18}, \frac{15}{27}$
    d. $\frac{8}{16}, \frac{5}{10}, \frac{1}{2}$

Use the number line to answer the following questions.

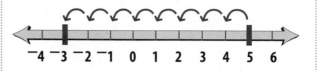

14. What equation does the number line show?
    a. $5 - 8 = n$
    b. $n = 8 + 5$
    c. $n + 5 = 8$
    d. $8 - n = 5$

15. What does *n* equal in the correct answer to question 14?
    a. $n = {}^-3$
    b. $n = 13$
    c. $n = {}^-13$
    d. $n = {}^-8$

16. Which is the related addition equation for ${}^-a - b = {}^-c$?
    a. $a + b = c$
    b. $a + b = {}^-c$
    c. ${}^-c + b = {}^-a$
    d. ${}^-b + {}^-a = {}^-c$

Check Your Math Power

17. A bluefin tuna can swim about 45 miles per hour. About how far can it go in 15 minutes?

18. Create a function table to show how far the tuna would travel in 4–12 hours.

19. Write a function rule for this table.

Input	2	3	7	9
Output	5	7.5	17.5	22.5

MODULE 2 Investigations

Getting Around Antarctica

Every school day you take a trip. You go from home to school. You plan the best route and choose your transportation according to the distance you have to travel. You decide when to leave home so that you reach school on time. Now use this experience to help you plan a journey to the Byrd Science Station in Antarctica.

Investigation A   Heading South

1 From the moment you step out your door until you reach Byrd Station, you need to follow a well-planned route. Use maps to help you decide how to get there. Write a detailed description of the land, sea, and air routes you will follow. List the kinds of transportation you will use.

2 Once you know your route, find out about how far you will be traveling. What is the distance on each "leg," or part, of your trip? You may need to create a scale ruler to help you estimate distances.

3 Estimate how long it will take you to get to Byrd Station. What is the average speed of the transportation you will use? How can you use information about speed and distance to figure out how long the trip will take?

4 Create a detailed map showing your route and the distance. Also create a travel plan telling what kinds of transportation you will use and how long the trip will take. Present your map and plan to the class.

Keep in Mind

Your presentation will be judged by how well you do the following things.

☐ How well do you show what you know about addition to help you figure distances?

☐ How well do you describe why you chose a particular kind of transportation?

☐ How clearly does your travel plan show and explain your route and the time your trip will take?

Investigation B — Around the World

Use your math skills to plan a trip around the world. Decide what kinds of transportation you will use and where you will use them. Create a map that shows your route and the distance you will travel between stops. Use all of this information to create an itinerary that shows how long your journey will take.

Ongoing Investigation — Tessellating Quadrilaterals

Extend your investigation of tessellations to a variety of quadrilaterals.

1 Try creating tessellations with some or all of the kinds of quadrilaterals shown on this page. To make your patterns, you can trace the shapes or use your Geometry Tool to draw them. You can draw your own quadrilaterals—just make sure none of the sides or angles are congruent.

2 Add your tessellations to your portfolio. Also include a note describing what you've discovered. How are your tessellations similar? How are they different? Do all quadrilaterals tessellate?

Rectangle

Trapezoid

Parallelogram

Rhombus

Quadrilateral

Nature and Numbers

How far is the sun? How many ladybugs would you find in an acre of prairie? The math in this module helps you count, measure, and work with nature. You will use some enormous numbers. You will also use numbers that can help measure the tiniest things you can imagine.

SECTION

A

Powers of Ten

SECTION

B

Rectangles and Prisms

SECTION

C

Circles and Cylinders

SECTION

D

Decimal Division

113

How Big?

Objects in nature come in all sizes. A giant sequoia tree might be 10 times taller than trees in your neighborhood. A moss plant might be 10,000 times smaller than the tree it lives on. What does 10 times mean? 10,000 times? Size up the world of nature.

Anole
length: 12 centimeters
mass: 8 grams

Philodendron Leaf
length: 6 centimeters
mass: 0.02 grams

1  **Size It!**

About how many times longer than the leaf is this anole? As much as 10? About how many times heavier is the lizard?

② Compare!

How would you compare the length of a pine cone with the height of the entire tree? How would you compare your own height with that of the tree?

Word Bank
- area (*A*)
- circumference (*C*)
- cylinder
- diameter (*d*)
- exponent
- order of operations
- power of ten
- radius (*r*)
- volume (*V*)

③ Chart!

What is 10 times as big as an anole? What is 10,000 times as big? Make a chart that increases by tens: 1 ×, 10 ×, 100 ×, 1,000 ×, 10,000 ×. Fill it in with your estimates of sizes of things in nature. Check your estimates in an encyclopedia.

Pine Cone
length: 8 centimeter
height of pine tree: 30 meters
mass of one seed: 10 milligrams

Investigations Preview

Find formulas that will help you work with 2- and 3-dimensional shapes. Expand your multiplication and division skills to big and small numbers.

Room to Grow (pages 144–145)
How would you design a garden where space and soil are scarce? Knowing the formulas for area and volume will help.

Waste Watch (pages 174–175)
Do you know how much space garbage takes up in the natural landscape? Use your new design and math skills to figure it out. Use this information to help increase awareness about waste disposal in your community.

LESSON
1

Looking at Powers

The photos on these pages are from the book *Powers of Ten* by Philip and Phylis Morrison. What do you think the title means?

In Your Journal Write a brief description of each photo. Make sure it is clear which picture you are talking about.

A man picnics in a Chicago park. In the second picture, you move high above him and see a wider area.

ACTIVITY 1 Using the Power

With Your Class The first photo shows a space 1 meter by 1 meter. Notice how the scene changes from picture to picture. Look at the measure by each photo.

1 meter

1 How does the width of the space shown change? Describe the pattern, using words or a drawing.

10 meters

2 How many times greater is the width shown in the second picture than the width in the first? the width in the third than the width in the second?

3 Now examine this place-value chart. How is it like the pattern in the pictures?

Ten thousands	Thousands	Hundreds	Tens	Ones
1	0,	0	0	0

4 Think about the next picture in this series. What width or distance will it show? Turn the page to find out.

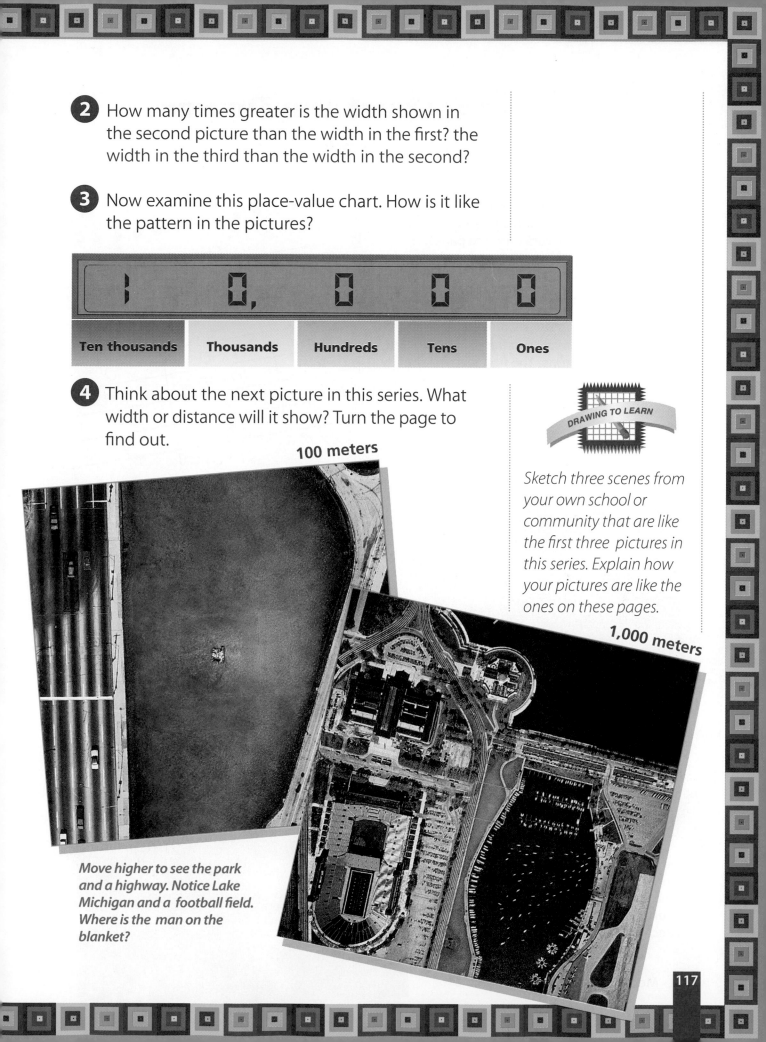

100 meters

1,000 meters

Move higher to see the park and a highway. Notice Lake Michigan and a football field. Where is the man on the blanket?

DRAWING TO LEARN

Sketch three scenes from your own school or community that are like the first three pictures in this series. Explain how your pictures are like the ones on these pages.

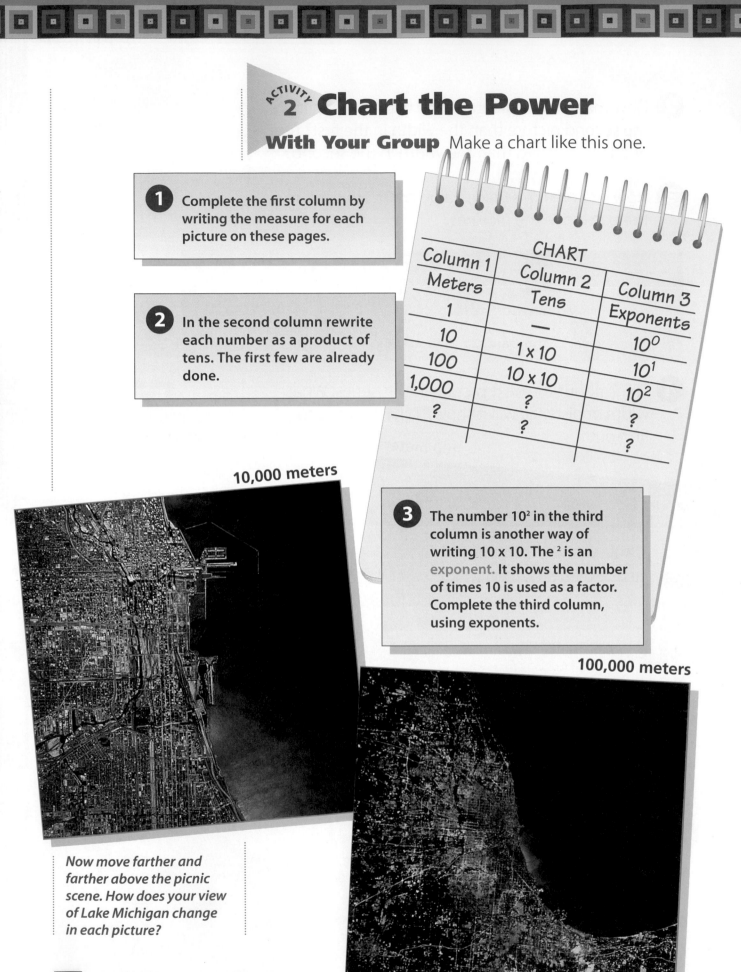

ACTIVITY 2 Chart the Power

With Your Group Make a chart like this one.

1 Complete the first column by writing the measure for each picture on these pages.

2 In the second column rewrite each number as a product of tens. The first few are already done.

CHART

Column 1 Meters	Column 2 Tens	Column 3 Exponents
1	—	10^0
10	1 x 10	10^1
100	10 x 10	10^2
1,000	?	?
?	?	?
		?

3 The number 10^2 in the third column is another way of writing 10 x 10. The ^{2} is an **exponent**. It shows the number of times 10 is used as a factor. Complete the third column, using exponents.

10,000 meters

100,000 meters

Now move farther and farther above the picnic scene. How does your view of Lake Michigan change in each picture?

1,000,000 meters

What do you notice about the exponent and the number of zeros in the original number?

4 Any number that can be written as all tens is called a power of ten. Now try to explain why the authors called their book *Powers of Ten*.

10,000,000 meters

Now you move from a cloud pattern to a view of Earth. How many steps did it take to get there from the picnic blanket?

100,000,000 meters

What You'll Need
- *grid paper*
- *scissors*
- *tape*

ACTIVITY 3 **Seeing Powers**

With Your Class Make models to show how the length of something changes when you increase it by powers of ten.

1 Cut out 1 square from a sheet of grid paper. This shows 10^0, or 1.

2 Now cut out a strip that is 10 times as long or 10^1. Make another strip that shows 10^2. Use tape as you need to.

TOOLS AND TECHNIQUES

Calculator On your calculator multiply any number by 10. When you get your answer, press the equal sign once more. What happens?

3 Keep making strips that increase in length by the next power of ten. What power of ten makes a strip as long as your classroom?

ACTIVITY 4 **Calculate the Power**

On Your Own Use a calculator to help discover a rule for multiplying and dividing by powers of ten.

1 In any whole number there is a decimal point that you don't see. For example, 7 = 7.0. What happens to the decimal point when you multiply by 10? by 100? by 1,000?

2 Choose any whole number from 1 to 9. Multiply it by consecutive powers of ten. Record.

$$7 \times 1 = 7$$
$$7 \times 10 = 70$$
$$7 \times 100 = 700$$
$$7 \times 1,000 =$$

3 Now think of a number like 2.75. What is the product if you multiply by 10? by 100? Explain. Use your calculator to check. Predict what will happen if you multiply by 1,000. Check.

4 Now divide. Predict the answer when you divide 2.75 by 10. Check with your calculator.

$$10\overline{)2.75} = ?$$

5 What will happen when you divide 2.75 by 100? by 1,000?

6 Write a generalization for multiplying and dividing by powers of ten.

✓ **Self-Check** *Test your generalization by working these problems.*

$14 \div 10,000$ $1,500 \times 100$
14.3×10 $3 \div 1,000$
23.3×100 $23.3 \div 100$

Do You Remember?

Try It!

Write in standard form. Then arrange the answers from least to greatest.

1. 7×10^3 **2.** $17 \div 10^3$ **3.** 7×10^2
4. 7×10^6 **5.** $7 \div 10^9$ **6.** $7 \div 10^5$

Complete.

7. 300 in. = _____ ft **8.** 15 mi = _____ ft **9.** 1.5 mi = _____ yd
10. 9 ft = _____ in.   **11.** 423 yd = _____ ft **12.** 33 mi = _____ ft

Think About It

13. Which is greater, $5 \div 10^7$ or $5 \div 10^5$? Explain.

LESSON 2 To the Stars

Our galaxy has stars that are 6 billion years old. You can write 6 billion as 6,000,000,000. Scientists have a more convenient way to write large numbers, though.

10²¹ meters

Now move farther into space to see the entire Milky Way Galaxy. Can you see our sun? It is one of the galaxy's 200 billion stars!

ACTIVITY 1 Starry Numbers

With Your Class In **scientific notation** a number can be written as the product of a number between 0 and 10 and a power of ten.

1 Here's a way to write 6 billion in scientific notation.
   a. Rewrite 6,000,000,000 like this.
   b. Next rewrite using tens.
   c. Then use an exponent to show the number of times multiplied by 10.

$6 \times 1,000,000,000$

$6 \times (10 \times 10 \times 10 \times 10 \times 10 \times 10 \times 10 \times 10 \times 10)$

6×10^9

2 Write these numbers in scientific notation. How did you decide on the exponent for each number?
   a. 500,000
   b. 5,000,000
   c. 5,000,000,000

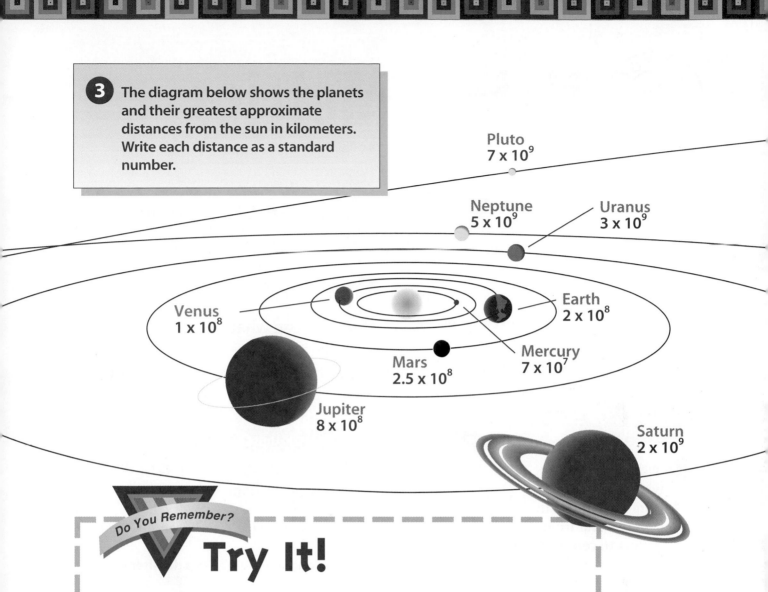

3 The diagram below shows the planets and their greatest approximate distances from the sun in kilometers. Write each distance as a standard number.

Pluto
7×10^9

Neptune
5×10^9

Uranus
3×10^9

Venus
1×10^8

Earth
2×10^8

Mars
2.5×10^8

Mercury
7×10^7

Jupiter
8×10^8

Saturn
2×10^9

Do You Remember?

Try It!

Use scientific notation to rewrite these numbers. Then arrange the numbers from least to greatest.

1. 5,000,000,000 **2.** 400,000,000
3. 20,000,000 **4.** 6,000,000
5. 1,000,000,000 **6.** 60,000,000

Find each answer to the nearest tenth.

7. $3.34 + 91.2 = n$ **8.** $243.9 + 119.33 = n$ **9.** $332.96 - 9.47 = n$
10. $1433 - 287.83 = n$ **11.** $33.48 + 88.9 + 136.23 = n$

Think About It

12. Explain what happens to the decimal point when you change scientific notation to standard form.

Nature Metrics

Use the metric system to follow the nature trail. The chart will help.

ACTIVITY 1 On the Trail of Tens

With Your Group Use what you know about multiplying and dividing by powers of ten to answer the questions about the chart. Show how you got your answers.

1 What happens when you change from millimeters to centimeters? from meters to centimeters?

Metric Units		
Length	**Mass**	**Capacity**
millimeter (mm) 0.001 m	**milligram (mg)** 0.001 g	**milliliter (mL)** 0.001 L
centimeter (cm) 0.01 m	**centigram (cg)** 0.01 g	**centiliter (cL)** 0.01 L
decimeter (dm) 0.1 m	**decigram (dg)** 0.1 g	**deciliter (dL)** 0.1 L
meter (m)	**gram (g)**	**liter (L)**
kilometer (km) 1,000 m	**kilogram (kg)** 1,000 g	**kiloliter (kL)** 1,000 L

2 What happens when you go from grams to milligrams? from grams to kilograms? Write a generalization for changing from one metric unit to another.

NATURE TRAIL

3 Choose a unit and start your nature hike. Choose the most appropriate unit on each of the three signs below. Explain your choice.

DEER LAKE AND RESERVE

Total paved roads:

200,000 m

200 km

2,000,000 dm

DEER LAKE

Depth:

50 m

0.05 km

500 dm

DEER LAKE DAM

Water through dam per hour:

1,000,000 L

1,000 kL

10,000,000 dL

4 Change the unit by rewriting the measurements shown on the next two signs. Use a more appropriate unit. Explain how you did it.

NATURE CENTER

See our

Smallest Beetle:	0.005 cm
Longest Snake:	150 cm
Tallest Tree:	0.042 km

ECOLOGY POND

Capacity:

6,000 L

What You'll Need

- *balance or coat hanger, paper cups, paper clips*
- *1-L measure*
- *seeds, beans, or small items as centimeter cubes*
- *centimeter ruler*

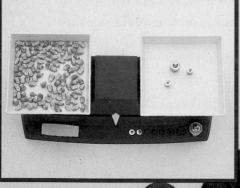

Esti-Metric

With Your Group How good a judge are you when it comes to estimating metric mass, capacity, and length? Choose two activities and see.

Beans by the Bag Use any objects about the size of beans.

a. Place a handful of the objects in a bag. Take turns holding the bag in one hand and estimating the mass.

b. Use a balance scale to find the mass. How close are your estimates?

c. How many handfuls of beans would make a mass of 1 kg? Estimate. Then check your estimate.

How Many Are in There?

Use a 1-L container and any small objects.

d. How many of the objects would fill the 1-L container? Write your estimate. Fill the container and check your estimate.

e. If you filled a 1-L jar with sand and another one with beans, would the number of grains of sand be the same as the number of beans? Why or why not?

250ml

VIT LAB

PP 135 MA

Meter Readers Now try length.

f. Estimate the lengths of the flower and the leaf. Give your estimate in centimeters and meters.

g. How can you find the actual length? Why might a ruler not give you the exact answer?

h. Estimate the length of other items both large and small. Are your estimates close to the actual measurements?

ACTIVITY OPTION

Which has a greater mass, an unpopped kernel of corn or a popped one? a brick or a chalkboard eraser? Write five questions like these. Exchange with a partner and experiment to find the answers.

Do You Remember?

Try It!

Estimate the length of each object in metric units. Then put the objects in order of length from shortest to longest.

   1. a ball-point pen   **2.** your foot   **3.** a skateboard
   4. your school flagpole   **5.** a telephone receiver

Use mental math to get your answer.

   6. 429×10 **7.** 402×10 **8.** $1{,}420 \times 10^2$
   9. 14.23×10 **10.** 423.0×10 **11.** 1.42×10^3

Think About It

12. Explain your method of estimating the lengths for Exercises 1–5.

LESSON
4

Saving a Prairie

10⁵ meters

Nearly all the land you see in the photograph on the left was once a large, grassy prairie. Today it is cities and farms. In 1990, volunteers in Illinois helped in an experiment. In one weekend they moved a remaining piece of prairie that had been sold for its gravel.

Photos by Rob Panzer

Recently acquired for preservation, prairie near south suburban Markham displays huckleberry and heath asters.

Prairie companions

The Conservancy's business is to save nature's Rembrandts

By Stevenson Swanson
Environment writer

The story of the legal headaches, the paperwork, the serpentine turns of a creeping bureaucracy can wait. They are not the point. An open field, its knee-high grass dotted with pale gold, purple and sunset red, and animated by the season's grasshoppers and the last of the birds—that is the point.

These 100 acres of the Prairie State are the core of the Indian Boundary Prairies, in south suburban Markham, a scattering of four large undeveloped tracts that will amount to more than 400 acres if all are preserved. It is hard to overstate the importance of this acreage. Prairie remnants are typically only a people dozen acres, and prairie restoration projects are usually smaller than that.

"This is the largest, best-quality prairie left in Illinois," said Steve Packard, science and stewardship director of the Illinois chapter of the Nature Conservancy. "And as messy as the legal cobwebs look, it's worth putting in the time to get this."

Packard and others have only recently swept away the cobwebs that had entangled 761 parcels of land at Indian Boundary, bringing the portion that has been preserved to more than 200 acres. The work that went into the project has been called the most complex land acquisition in the history of conservation in Illinois.

It is another in a string of notable accomplishments for the little-known estate arm of the Nature Conservancy, the environments conservation movement. What makes a first-class

lady's tresses, prairie gentian.
"D.H. Lawrence described the color of the prairie gentian as 'a deep and hurtful blue,'" Packard said. "They the very last flowers of fall."

Site manager Ron Panzer, a naturalist at Northeastern Illinois University, values the Indian Boundary lands for their abundant animal life. At the first 100-acre alone, he estimates there are 3,000 species, including a few gray fox and several rare Fra ground squirrels.

The difference between railroad rights-of-way and cemeteries (the most ant remnants) and this prair animals don't survive on cities," he said "This is contemporary stand probably have 90 or 9 species that were once is large enough than species of papaipema in the Midwest

These large sites sur Century because they agricultural land. The 20th Ce for o

An Aphrodite butterfly.

The gray fox, a prairie denizen.

These lilies are rarely found outside the prairie.

Around the Edge

ACTIVITY 1

With Your Group Volunteers divided the prairie into rectangles. They did this so certain plants and animals would be kept together. They measured the **perimeter,** the distance around each rectangle.

✓ **Self-Check** *After you use a formula to find the perimeter of the rectangle on this page, add up the sides to check your answer.*

1 How many different ways can you think of to find the perimeter of this rectangle?

5 m

3 m

> **How do you know what the missing measures for this rectangle are?**

2 Did you use a formula to find the distance around the rectangle? One formula you might have used is $P = 2 \times (l + w)$.

3 These examples show how two different students used the formula above. Why did they get different answers?

4 Which answer is correct? How do you know?

5 Can you see why you need to have special rules when you are working with more than one operation? How do the parentheses in the formula $P = 2 \times (l + w)$ help tell what to do?

5

3

Ⓐ $P = 2 \times l + w$
$P = 2 \times 5 + 3$
$P = 13$

Ⓑ $P = 2 \times l + w$
$P = 2 \times 5 + 3$
$P = 16$

[Order of Ops]

What You'll Need
- *gameboard*
- *cube labeled 1–6*
- *counters*

ACTIVITY 2 Order of Play

With Your Partner There are rules for the order in which you add, subtract, multiply, and divide. These are called the **order of operations**.

> As you calculate, follow these rules:
> - First do the operations in parentheses.
> - Then multiply and divide from left to right.
> - Finally, add and subtract from left to right.

The Order of Ops games will help you use these rules.

Ops 500 Begin by placing your counters on Start. Then take turns. After each turn, find the total of all your answers. The first player to reach 500 wins.

1 Roll the number cube and move the number of squares shown on the cube.

2 On a sheet of paper, write the expression that is on your square.

3 Roll the cube four times. Then write those numbers in the blanks on your paper. You choose the order.

4 Place parentheses in the expression where they will help you get the greatest possible value. Record.

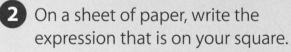

$$\underline{3} + \underline{6} + \underline{4} \times \underline{2}$$

$$3 + 6 + 4 \times 2 = 17$$
$$(3 + 6 + 4) \times 2 = 26$$
$$3 + (6 + 4) \times 2 = 23$$

Ops Match You need one counter. The object is to use parentheses to make the value of the expression as close as possible to the number the counter is on. The first player to get 10 points wins.

Calculator *When you use your calculator to find the perimeter of a rectangle or to play Order of Ops, use the parentheses keys.*

① To begin, move to the first square. Copy that square's operations on a sheet of paper.

② Take turns rolling the number cube four times. Write your numbers in the blanks in any order.

③ Write parentheses in the expression. Don't forget—you want to have the value of the expression be as close as possible to the number the counter is on. The closest value gets a point.

④ Move the counter to the next square and repeat Steps 1–3.

What You'll Need
- *centimeter ruler*
- *centimeter grid paper*

ACTIVITY OPTION

Use grid paper. Cut out rectangles and make your own irregular field. Rearrange parts to form fields of different shapes. Does the perimeter change? Explain.

ACTIVITY 3 Crooked Edges

With Your Group Find the perimeter of this irregular figure.

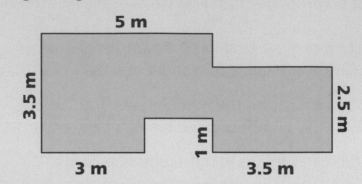

5 m

3.5 m

2.5 m

1 m

3 m

3.5 m

1 Try these two methods on grid paper.
  a. Divide the figure into smaller rectangles.
  b. Fill in the sides of the figure so it forms one big rectangle.

2 Did either way help you find the perimeter? If so, was one a better method? Explain.

Do You Remember?

Try It!

Will the expression give the perimeter? Explain.

1. $2 \times l + 2 \times w$ **2.** $2 \times l + w$ **3.** $2 \times (l + w)$ **4.** $4 \times l$ **5.** $l + l$

Use the letters to name the following on the large rectangle.

6. the height   **7.** a line segment
8. the width   **9.** a set of parallel lines
10. intersecting line segments

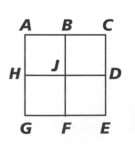

A   B   C

H   J   D

G   F   E

Think About It
11. Write an explanation telling how to find the perimeter of a rectangle without using a formula.

Cover the Prairie

How much space will a rectangle of prairie need when it is moved? The volunteers had to know the rectangle's **area,** or the surface covered.

ACTIVITY 1 Transplanting a Page

With Your Group Look at the squares that line the side and the bottom of this page. They are from a photograph of a prairie.

1 How could you find the number of squares you need to cover this entire page? Try more than one way.

2 Write a formula for finding the area of a rectangle.

3 Try your formula on these rectangles.

a.

6 m

3 m

b.

3 m

5 m

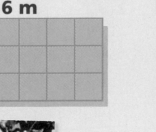
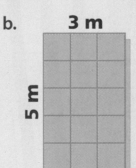

4 A square is a special kind of rectangle. Write a formula for finding the area of a square.

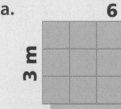

133

What You'll Need

- *centimeter ruler*
- *centimeter grid paper*

DRAWING TO LEARN

Draw all the rectangles you can with a 30-m perimeter. Try the method you used in Activity 2. Explain how you did it.

ACTIVITY 2 Movable Fences

With Your Group   You have a 20-m length of fence to enclose a rectangular section of prairie.

1 Draw all the different rectangles you can with a perimeter of 20 m.

2 Do the areas stay the same? Explain.

3 Repeat Steps 1 and 2 for a perimeter of 36 m.

4 Which rectangles have the greatest area in both cases? Why?

5 Write a generalization telling which rectangle of a given perimeter gives you the greatest area.

9

1

$1 \times 9 = 9$

8

2

$2 \times 8 = 16$

7

3

$3 \times 7 = 21$

3 Square a Rectangle

On Your Own Find a way to multiply square units when you don't know the length of their sides.

1 What is the length of this rectangle in terms of *r*? the width?

What does r^2 mean? How does it help you understand area?

2 Copy the rectangle. Why is the small square labeled r^2?

3 Draw lines to connect all the opposite points. Then describe the area of the rectangle in terms of r^2.

4 Draw a model and solve:

  a. $7r \times 8r = $ ▧   **b.** $12t \times 8t = $ ▧

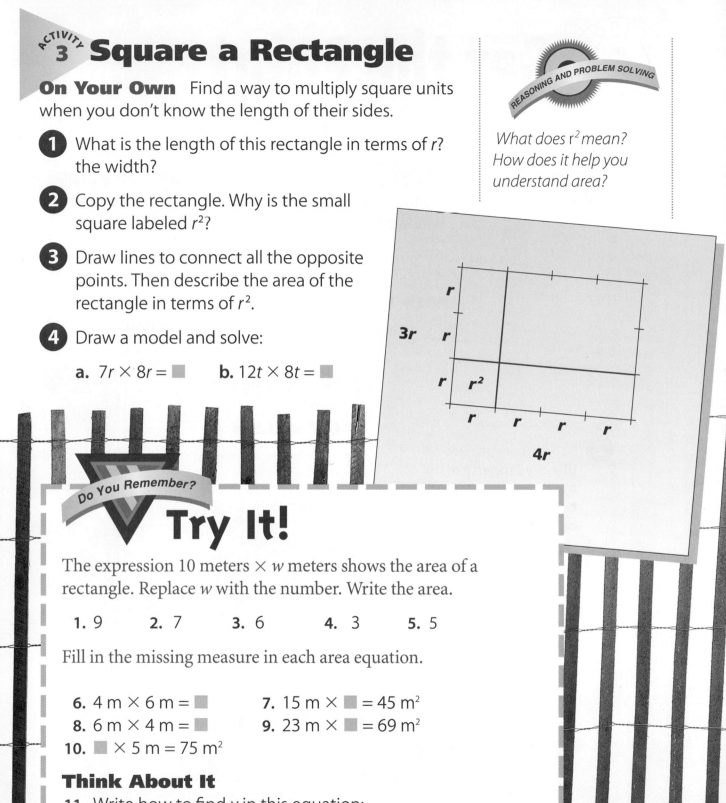

Do You Remember?

Try It!

The expression 10 meters × *w* meters shows the area of a rectangle. Replace *w* with the number. Write the area.

  1. 9   **2.** 7   **3.** 6   **4.** 3   **5.** 5

Fill in the missing measure in each area equation.

  6. $4 \text{ m} \times 6 \text{ m} = $ ▧   **7.** $15 \text{ m} \times $ ▧ $ = 45 \text{ m}^2$
  8. $6 \text{ m} \times 4 \text{ m} = $ ▧   **9.** $23 \text{ m} \times $ ▧ $ = 69 \text{ m}^2$
  10. ▧ $ \times 5 \text{ m} = 75 \text{ m}^2$

Think About It

11. Write how to find *y* in this equation:
  y meters × 12 meters = 36 square meters

LESSON (6) Get the Point

CONNECT AND COMMUNICATE

Any number between 0 and 1 is less than 1 and can be written in decimal form.

To find the area of rectangular plots of the prairie, you multiplied the length by the width. Sometimes the length and width are stated as decimals.

ACTIVITY 1 Point by Point

With Your Group Use number sense to help you estimate the area of this prairie section.

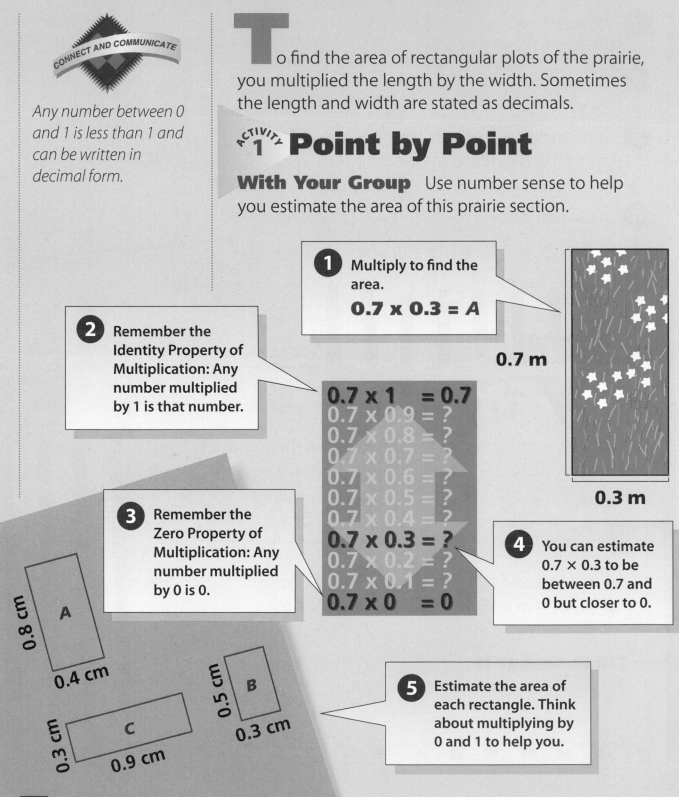

1 Multiply to find the area.

0.7 x 0.3 = A

0.7 m

0.3 m

2 Remember the Identity Property of Multiplication: Any number multiplied by 1 is that number.

$$0.7 \times 1 = 0.7$$
$$0.7 \times 0.9 = ?$$
$$0.7 \times 0.8 = ?$$
$$0.7 \times 0.7 = ?$$
$$0.7 \times 0.6 = ?$$
$$0.7 \times 0.5 = ?$$
$$0.7 \times 0.4 = ?$$
$$0.7 \times 0.3 = ?$$
$$0.7 \times 0.2 = ?$$
$$0.7 \times 0.1 = ?$$
$$0.7 \times 0 = 0$$

3 Remember the Zero Property of Multiplication: Any number multiplied by 0 is 0.

4 You can estimate 0.7×0.3 to be between 0.7 and 0 but closer to 0.

5 Estimate the area of each rectangle. Think about multiplying by 0 and 1 to help you.

A — 0.8 cm, 0.4 cm

B — 0.5 cm, 0.3 cm

C — 0.3 cm, 0.9 cm

ACTIVITY 2 — What's the Rule?

With Your Class How can you find the exact product of 0.7 × 0.3? One way to multiply decimals is to think about the array that is formed on a hundredths' square.

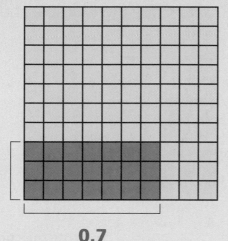

0.3

0.7

0.7 x 0.3 = 0.21

Make a sketch on a hundredths' square to show 0.6 × 0.6.

On Your Own Must you always use a hundredths' square to multiply decimals?

1 Study the examples on the right. Describe the pattern you see in the three products.

2 Write a rule for placing a decimal point when you multiply decimals.

3 Try out your rule with items a, b, and c below. Use your calculator to see if your rule works.

```
  0.3
x 0.2
-----
 0.06
```

```
  0.03
x 0.2
------
 0.006
```

```
  0.06
x 0.02
------
0.0006
```

a. 0.5
  x 0.9

b. 0.08
  x 0.4

c. 0.06
  x 0.02

ACTIVITY 3 ▷ The Point of Decimals

With Your Partner You can also use estimation to know where to place the decimal point in the product.

1 The digits in the product are correct. Only the decimal point is missing. Copy the example and write the decimal point.

> **a. Multiply the whole number parts, 5 and 14.**

14.12
x   5.13
_____
724356

> **b. Which whole number is closest to the correct answer— 7, 72, or 724?**

> **c. Write the correct answer by placing the decimal point.**

2 Copy these examples. Estimate to place the decimal point.

2.13
x 10.94
_____
233022

8.025
x 6.2
_____
497550

7.31
x 4.7
_____
34357

3 Try using the rule you wrote in Activity 2. Do you get the same product?

4 Explain how you would find the product for the following.

a.   3.26
x 0.05
_____

b. 16.3
x 2.4
_____

c.   3.7
x 1.033
_____

ACTIVITY 4 Garden²

What You'll Need
- *centimeter ruler*
- *centimeter grid paper*

With Your Partner   Plan a neighborhood garden. You have a 1-km² plot.

1 Divide the plot into three unequal rectangles. Each rectangle must have a different area.

2 Draw your plans.

3 Find and label the perimeter and area of each rectangle. Use kilometers and square kilometers.

4 Provide at least two designs.

1 km

1 km

Do You Remember?

Try It!

Find the area of a rectangle 3.5 m long if the width is:

1. 1.3 m   **2.** 0.9 m   **3.** 0.3 m   **4.** 7.7 m   **5.** 0.5 m

Explain in writing why each answer is reasonable or unreasonable.

6. 57.63 + 20.18 = 77.81   **7.** 34.21 + 44.09 = 7,830

8. 1,247 + 2,604 = 385.1   **9.** 33,632 + 25,799 = 79,431

10. 64,187 + 28,273 = 9,246.0

Think About It
11. How are the decimals in question 6 alike?

Digging In!

The prairie movers dug up chunks of dirt around plant roots. They transplanted three-dimensional pieces of prairie like these.

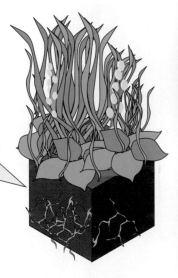

> A **rectangular prism** has three dimensions: length, width, and height.

> A **cube** is one kind of rectangular prism. How is it different from the prism on the left?

What You'll Need
- *grid paper*
- *centimeter cubes*
- *scissors*
- *tape*

ACTIVITY 1 Fill It Up!

With Your Group Measure the **volume**—the number of cubes that fit inside—of some rectangular prisms. Make three different-sized boxes like the one in the picture. Find the volume of each.

1 Make a three-sided guide box from grid paper.

2 Fill the bottom with an array of centimeter cubes. How many cubes cover the base?

3 Then add layers to fill the box. The total number of cubes is the volume.

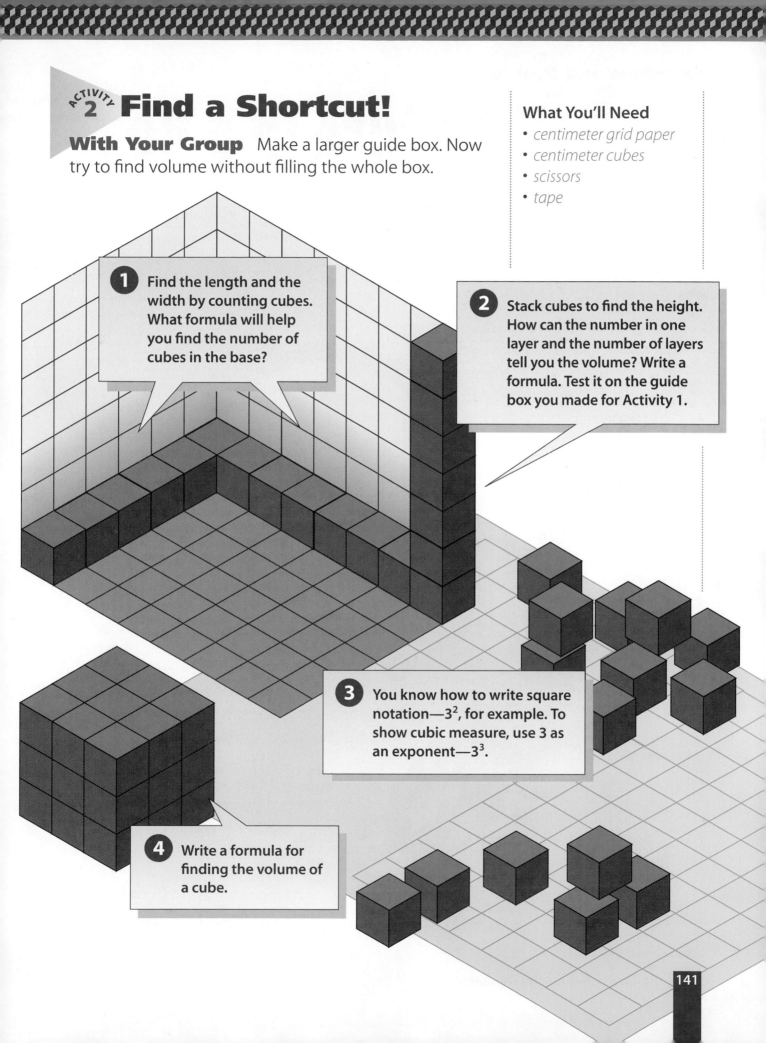

Find a Shortcut!

ACTIVITY 2

With Your Group Make a larger guide box. Now try to find volume without filling the whole box.

What You'll Need
- *centimeter grid paper*
- *centimeter cubes*
- *scissors*
- *tape*

1 Find the length and the width by counting cubes. What formula will help you find the number of cubes in the base?

2 Stack cubes to find the height. How can the number in one layer and the number of layers tell you the volume? Write a formula. Test it on the guide box you made for Activity 1.

3 You know how to write square notation—3^2, for example. To show cubic measure, use 3 as an exponent—3^3.

4 Write a formula for finding the volume of a cube.

Nature in a Box

Imagine you're working on a project with a variety of seeds. Use what you know about volume, area, and perimeter to solve the problems.

Coconuts

1 A coconut is a very large seed. One coconut takes up a space about 12 cm × 12 cm × 14 cm. What is the volume of a box large enough to store 6 coconuts? 20 coconuts?

2 In square meters, what is the area covered by 10 coconut boxes with bases 12 cm × 12 cm?

Sunflower Seeds

3 About 115 wild sunflower seeds fill a box 5 cm × 4 cm × 1 cm. Give the dimensions of another box that could hold the same number of seeds.

4 What would be the volume of a box needed for 800 seeds? How do you know?

5 How many boxes with a base 7 cm wide and 10 cm long fit on a shelf 1 m × 4 m?

6 Estimate the volume of a tiny box about the size of a sunflower seed. Explain how you found the answer.

Scarlet Runners

7 A scarlet runner is a bean. It's a seed much bigger than a sunflower seed. Eleven beans fit in a box 5 cm × 4 cm × 1 cm. What is the volume of a box for 1,000 scarlet runners ?

8 You should plant scarlet runners about 7.6 cm apart. How much area does this give each plant to grow?

7.6

7.6

7.6

7.6

9 How many scarlet runners could you plant in a garden area 5 m × 6 m? Draw a diagram to help you.

10 Think again about the box that is 5 cm × 4 cm × 1 cm. If there are 5 scarlet runner beans in the box, about how many sunflower seeds will fit in the rest of the box?

Investigation

Room to Grow

Use all the information on these pages to plan two different gardens that are about 80 m². Your plans should include diagrams with all dimensions labeled. Also include the types of plants and numbers of plants that fit into each garden.

1 Different kinds of plants need different amounts of growing space. Use information from the chart or from a gardening book to determine how much space your plants need.

Planting Chart	
Plant Name	**Distance Between Plants**
impatiens	8 cm
sweet peas	15 cm
lettuce	25 cm
carrots	9 cm
sweet potatoes	30 cm
radishes	8 cm

2 What shape will each garden be? Make one of your gardens an interesting, irregular shape. Be sure you know how to find the area.

3 If your plants are going to grow well, you should probably add a layer of topsoil that is about 15 cm deep. Topsoil is measured in cubic centimeters.

4 Is one of your plans better than the other? Give a reason for your answer.

Ask Yourself

☐ What are the things you need to consider when making your plans?

☐ Does each plan have all the information you were asked to include?

☐ How can you tell whether your design allows enough space for your plants to grow properly?

☐ How can you make sure that the area of each garden is about 80 m²?

☐ How could you explain your garden plans to a friend so that he or she could make the gardens?

Bug Out!

Plants and insects live in delicate relationship. Insects help spread seeds, and plants provide food for insects. You cannot move a prairie without moving the bugs!

1. Biologists put insects in an ice chest to move them. The cold slows them down. If an insect flies best at a body temperature of 38°– 40°C, and the insect's temperature is 20°C, how many degrees must its temperature rise before it can fly away?

2 One student converted 38°C to Fahrenheit using this formula: $F = 1.8 \times C + 32$. The student's answer was 126°F. Is the answer correct? Explain how you know.

3 Each insect is stored in a tiny plastic case in the ice chest. If each case has a volume of 233.54 cm³, and there are 66 insects, what does the volume of the ice chest have to be?

4 Would the boxes above fit inside a chest 30 cm × 22.5 cm × 23.6 cm? Explain your answer.

5 A biologist estimates that there are 1.2 million ants, 0.054 million wasps, and 6,200 dogfaced butterflies in 1 km² of prairie. What is the estimated total of these three populations?

6 Some ants can carry 50 times their own weight. To equal this feat, how much would you have to lift in kilograms? in pounds?

7 Bees make honey from different kinds of plants. If clover honey costs $.99 per jar, and alfalfa honey costs $1.29 per jar, how much would you save by buying 10 jars of clover honey instead of the same amount of alfalfa honey?

Check Your Math Power

8 For every person on earth, there are 200 million insects. Explain how you think someone might have figured this out.

9 Some people say that when the weather is mild you can estimate the temperature in Fahrenheit. Just count the times a cricket chirps in 15 seconds and add 40. Work out a formula to estimate the temperature in Celsius using cricket chirps. To convert Fahrenheit to Celsius, subtract 32 and multiply by $\frac{5}{9}$.

Baltimore Checkerspot and Eyed Brown Butterfly Populations

1987: 25 BC, 5 EB
1988: 18 BC, 23 EB
1989: 15 BC, 15 EB
1990: 9 BC, 42 EB
1991: 26 BC, 52 EB
1992: 10 BC, 46 EB
1993: 43 BC, 40 EB

10 Use the data in the field notebook. Make a graph comparing the populations of two kinds of butterflies on 10 m² of prairie over 7 years. Describe what the graph does and doesn't tell you.

LESSON **8**

Round in Circles

1,000 meters

Flying in an airplane over Chicago, you might see the scene on the left. Flying over some parts of the western United States, you might see circular fields like the one below. Crops that grow in this field are irrigated by a rotating pipe.

The distance around a circle is called the **circumference** (*C*).

The pipe forms the circle's **radius** (*r*)—a line segment from the circle's center to its edge. Sprinklers spray water as the pipe goes around.

If the pipe extended in both directions, it would form a **diameter** (*d*)—a line that passes through the circle's center, connecting two points on the edge.

ACTIVITY 1 Drawing in Circles

On Your Own How can you find the circumference of a circular field? Draw five different circles with your compass.

What You'll Need
• compass
• string

1 Choose a radius. If the radius is 10 cm, what is the diameter? How do you know?

2 Position your compass where you want the center point of your circle to be.

3 Revolve the pencil around the center point. Why is the center point important?

4 For each circle, draw a diameter. Use string to compare the length of the diameter with the length of the circumference.

5 How can you use what you discovered to make an estimate of the circumference of any circle? Write a formula to show this.

ACTIVITY 2 Circle the Field

With Your Group Revise your formula to get a more accurate measurement of the circumference.

1 The Greek letter π, or pi, stands for the relationship between the diameter and the circumference. Usually you can round the value of π to 3.14.

2 Rewrite the formula you wrote in Activity 1 to use π. Do you think this will give an exact answer or an estimate? Explain.

TOOLS AND TECHNIQUES

You can use the π key on your calculator when working with circle formulas. What does your calculator display when you press π?

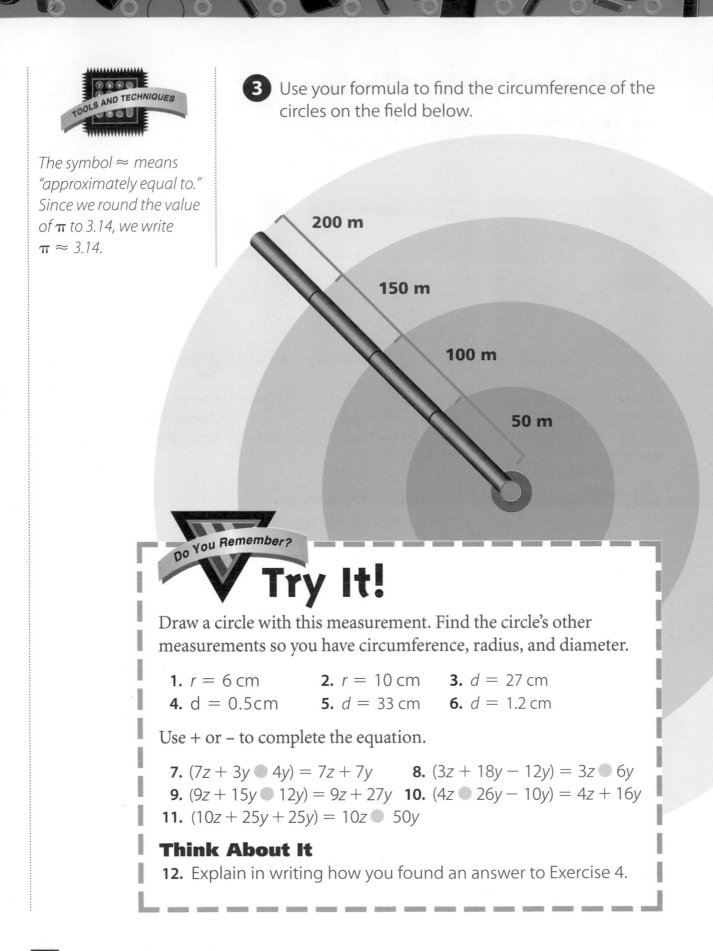

3 Use your formula to find the circumference of the circles on the field below.

TOOLS AND TECHNIQUES

The symbol ≈ means "approximately equal to." Since we round the value of π to 3.14, we write π ≈ 3.14.

200 m

150 m

100 m

50 m

Do You Remember?

Try It!

Draw a circle with this measurement. Find the circle's other measurements so you have circumference, radius, and diameter.

1. $r = 6$ cm   **2.** $r = 10$ cm   **3.** $d = 27$ cm
4. d = 0.5 cm   **5.** $d = 33$ cm   **6.** $d = 1.2$ cm

Use + or – to complete the equation.

7. $(7z + 3y \bullet 4y) = 7z + 7y$ **8.** $(3z + 18y - 12y) = 3z \bullet 6y$
9. $(9z + 15y \bullet 12y) = 9z + 27y$ **10.** $(4z \bullet 26y - 10y) = 4z + 16y$
11. $(10z + 25y + 25y) = 10z \bullet 50y$

Think About It

12. Explain in writing how you found an answer to Exercise 4.

Inside the Circle

How much space do you have for crops on a circular field? Knowing the area will help.

ACTIVITY 1 Square a Circle

With Your Partner With a compass draw a circle with a radius of 4 cm. Draw a diameter. Draw a second diameter to form a right angle with the first.

1 **How Many *r*'s?** Use *r* to label each line segment that goes from the center to the circumference. What does *r* stand for?

What You'll Need
- *centimeter ruler*
- *compass*

REASONING AND PROBLEM SOLVING

Is it possible to draw a circle that has a diameter of 8 cm and a radius of 6 cm? Why or why not?

Section C: Circles and Cylinders 151

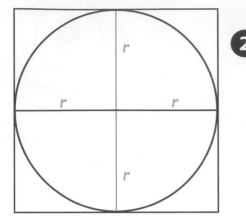

2 The Outside Square
Use a ruler to draw a square outside the circle. Describe the area of the large square, using *r*.

3 The Inside Square Now draw a square like this inside the circle. How can you use *r* to describe the area of the inner square?

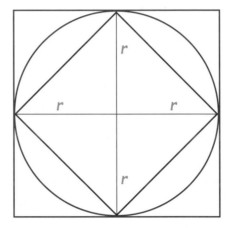

4 Between the Squares You know the area of the outer square and of the inner square. How would you estimate the area of the circle? Write a formula for the area of a circle.

5 Plug-in π A common formula for area of a circle is $A = \pi r^2$. Did your estimate come close to that? Explain.

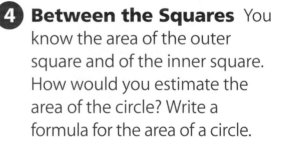

2 Circles to Draw

With Your Group Use your compass to plan your own patterns of circular fields. Label the diameter, circumference, and area of each circle you draw.

1 Plan a pattern of circular fields. You want to use the fewest pumps to water the largest space. Draw and explain your plan.

2 Fields aren't always rectangles. Plan two patterns of circle irrigation on an irregular field. Draw and explain your plan for each.

What You'll Need
- *compass*
- *ruler*

DRAWING TO LEARN

Use your compass to draw plans for something besides irrigation fields. Plan a playground or maybe a roller-skating course.

Nature's Circles

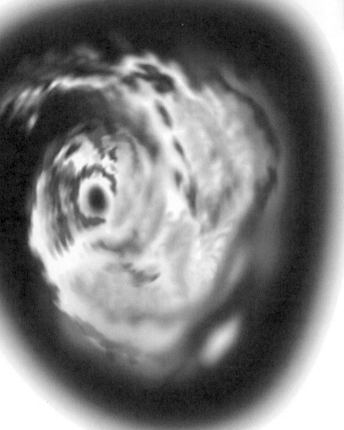

Use what you have learned about circles to measure these circles in nature.

Hurricane!

1 A typical hurricane might be about 400 km in diameter. What would be the circumference of a hurricane that size?

2 What would the area be?

Around a Pond

3 You want to jog 1,000 m. How many times will you have to run around this pond? How do you know?

4 How much area does the pond cover? How do you know?

5 How did knowing about circumference and area help you get your answers?

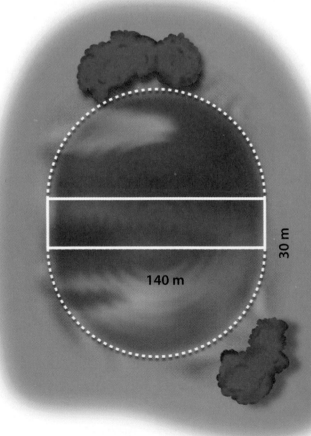

140 m

30 m

Volcano!

6 The enormous crater of La Garita volcano in Mexico is about 45 km across its center. Use what you know about circles to tell more about the crater.

To Earth's Center

7 This cross-section diagram shows a "slice" of Earth at its center. What is the circumference of Earth's inner core at the point shown in this diagram?

8 About how much area does the inner core cover at this point?

9 What is the diameter of the entire planet at this point? the circumference?

10 How much total area does the diagram show? How do you know?

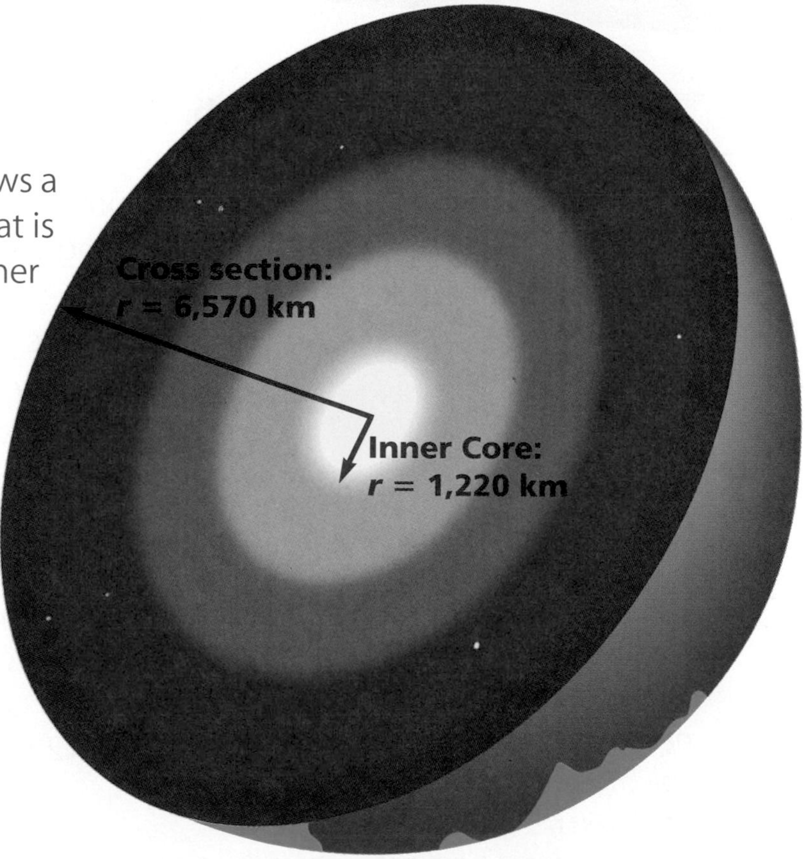

Cross section:
r = 6,570 km

Inner Core:
r = 1,220 km

LESSON 10

Silo Shapes

What else has the shape of a silo? The shape is called a **cylinder.** How would you describe it?

ACTIVITY 1 Circle Boxes

With Your Group How many cubic meters (m³) of grain can a silo hold? You need to find the volume.

Farmers store grain in cylinder-shaped silos. What other cylinders can you think of?

1 Think about how you found the volume of a rectangular prism.

   a. How did you find the area of the base?

   b. How did knowing that help you find the volume of the rectangular prism?

2 Now use the rectangular prism to help you discover how to find the volume of a cylinder. Use the diagram below.

   a. Create a method for finding the volume of a cylinder. How is this method like that for finding the volume of a rectangular prism? How is it different?

   b. Find the volume of these cylinders:
   - $d = 10$ cm; $h = 30$ cm
   - $r = 12$ m; $h = 25$ m

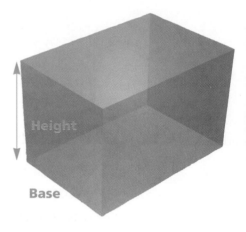

✓ **Self-Check**

A cylinder with a base radius of 5 cm and a height of 25 cm has a volume of 1,962.5 cm³. See if you get that answer with your formula. If not, revise your formula.

ACTIVITY 2 Expanding Cylinders

With Your Group Build an expanding cylinder. It will show how volume changes as a cylinder's base area or height changes.

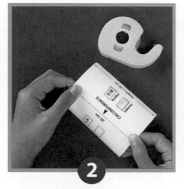

What You'll Need
- *scissors*
- *tape*

1 Cut out the cylinder strips and tape together. Cut out the boxes labeled *radius* and *volume*.

2 Form a cylinder with a circumference of 10 cm. Notice that the cylinder's height and radius are labeled.

3 Find the volume. Write it in the *volume* box. Do the same for the 15- and 20- cm marks on the strip.

4 **Exploring Cylinders** Work with some expanding cylinders. Make a presentation for other groups. Explore questions like these. Explain each answer.

a. How does volume change when circumference doubles?

b. How does it change when height doubles?

c. How might you triple volume?

d. How does volume change when radius doubles?

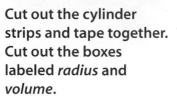

Cylinder Puzzlers

With Your Group Choose two of these cylinder puzzles.

1 **Cylinder Wrap!** Take a look at the dimensions of this cylinder. How much paper would you need to "gift-wrap" it? Leave the top and bottom open. Explain how you got your answer.

Height = 27 cm

Radius of base = 12 cm

2 **Plan a Silo** Imagine you are building silos. Find the diameter and height of a silo with approximately these capacities. Make a diagram to show your plan. Use a calculator and what you have learned about volume of a cylinder.

a. 3,000 m³   **b.** 2,600 m³   **c.** 1,800 m³

ACTIVITY OPTION

Bring in labels from cans. Peel off the labels carefully. Use the length and width of each to find the volume of the can. Tell how you did it.

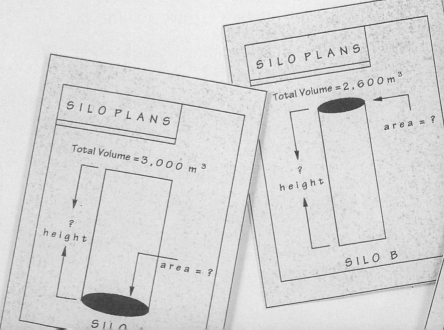

SILO PLANS

Total Volume = 3,000 m³

? height

area = ?

SILO

SILO PLANS

Total Volume = 2,600 m³

area = ?

? height

SILO B

3 **Tennis, Anyone?** The circumference of the opening of this tennis ball can is about 22.75 cm. About how tall is the can? How do you know?

a. What is the diameter of the can?

b. How does that compare to the height of one ball?

Do You Remember?

Try It!

Estimate which cylinders have a volume greater than 500 cm³.

1. $r = 10$ cm; $h = 10$ cm   **2.** $r = 5$ cm; $h = 20$ cm
3. $r = 3$ cm; $h = 5$ cm   **4.** $r = 10$ cm; $h = 5$ cm
5. $r = 20$ cm; $h = 22$ cm   **6.** $r = 5$ cm; $h = 10$ cm

Multiply each diameter by 100. Tell which circles will be the same.

7. $d = 0.03$ m   **8.** $d = 0.030$ m   **9.** $d = 0.003$ m
10. $d = 0.0300$ m   **11.** $d = 0.00300$ m   **12.** $d = 0.3$ m

Think About It

13. Explain in writing how you made your estimates for Exercises 1–6.

LESSON 11 Decimals in Nature

The trees growing together have a message for the poet. What does the poem tell you about nature?

We have grown together you and I
Like two trees I saw once
Sharing a common root.
One tree gave shade,
The other light.
The trees grew strong and tall together.
They protected one another.
One tree was home to the other.
One tree was always looking out.
They endured the cold together.
They lived when there was no rain.
The trees shared sunlight and sky.
They shared earth and water.
The trees that I saw once
Grew together until at last
When winter came they died
And went back to the earth as one.

From War Cry on a Prayer Feather:
Prose and Poetry of the Ute Indians
by Nancy Wood

Charting the Parks

With Your Partner The United States National Parks System protects some of the country's natural areas. Use the information in the chart.

1 How many times greater than Acadia is Sequoia National Park?

$$
\begin{array}{r}
1 \\
39\overline{)402} \\
\underline{39} \\
12
\end{array}
$$

In the division above, 39 is the **divisor** and 402 is the **dividend.**

    a. Complete the division to find the **quotient.**

    b. What is the remainder? Do you need to use it? Explain.

2 How many times smaller than Glacier National Park is Acadia? How do you know?

3 What is the average number of acres in the six parks on the graph? How would the average change if you did not include Glacier?

4 Try these divisions. Show your work.

    a. $45\overline{)3,076}$ **b.** $19\overline{)47,890}$

Sizes of National Parks
(in thousands of acres)

1,000
900
800
700
600
500
400
300
200
100

1,014
920
572
520
402
39

Acadia Sequoia Great Smoky Isle Royale Olympic Glacier

DRAWING TO LEARN

Find information about visitors to the national parks. Design and draw a graph that shows the most popular parks and the number of visitors per acre.

ACTIVITY 2 Treasured Giant

With Your Group One of the world's tallest known trees stands in Redwood National Park in California. This tree is 367.8 ft tall. How many times taller is it than a person who is 5 ft tall?

1 You already know how to find the answer if both the divisor and the dividend are whole numbers.

$$
\begin{array}{r}
735 \text{ R3} \\
5{\overline{\smash{\big)}\,3{,}678}} \\
\underline{-3\ 5} \\
17 \\
\underline{-15} \\
28 \\
\underline{-25} \\
3
\end{array}
$$

$5{\overline{\smash{\big)}\,367.8}}$

2 How do you think you divide when the dividend is a decimal?

3 Make a plan to divide $5{\overline{\smash{\big)}\,367.8}}$ Try out your plan.

4 Does your plan work? Use multiplication to check. Describe how you would do that. Adjust your plan if you need to.

5 The height of how many 5-ft people would equal the height of the tree?

6 Try solving these.

a. $7{\overline{\smash{\big)}\,46.83}}$ b. $18{\overline{\smash{\big)}\,586.8}}$

c. $32{\overline{\smash{\big)}\,1{,}996.8}}$ d. $41{\overline{\smash{\big)}\,2{,}095.1}}$

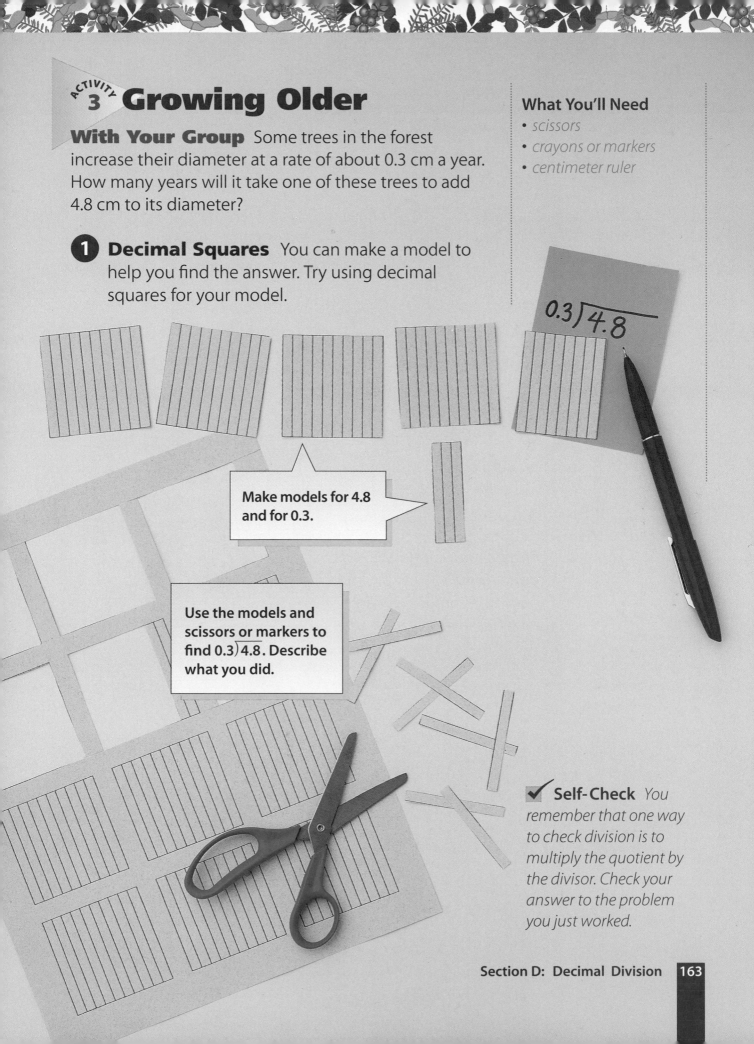

ACTIVITY 3 ▸ Growing Older

With Your Group Some trees in the forest increase their diameter at a rate of about 0.3 cm a year. How many years will it take one of these trees to add 4.8 cm to its diameter?

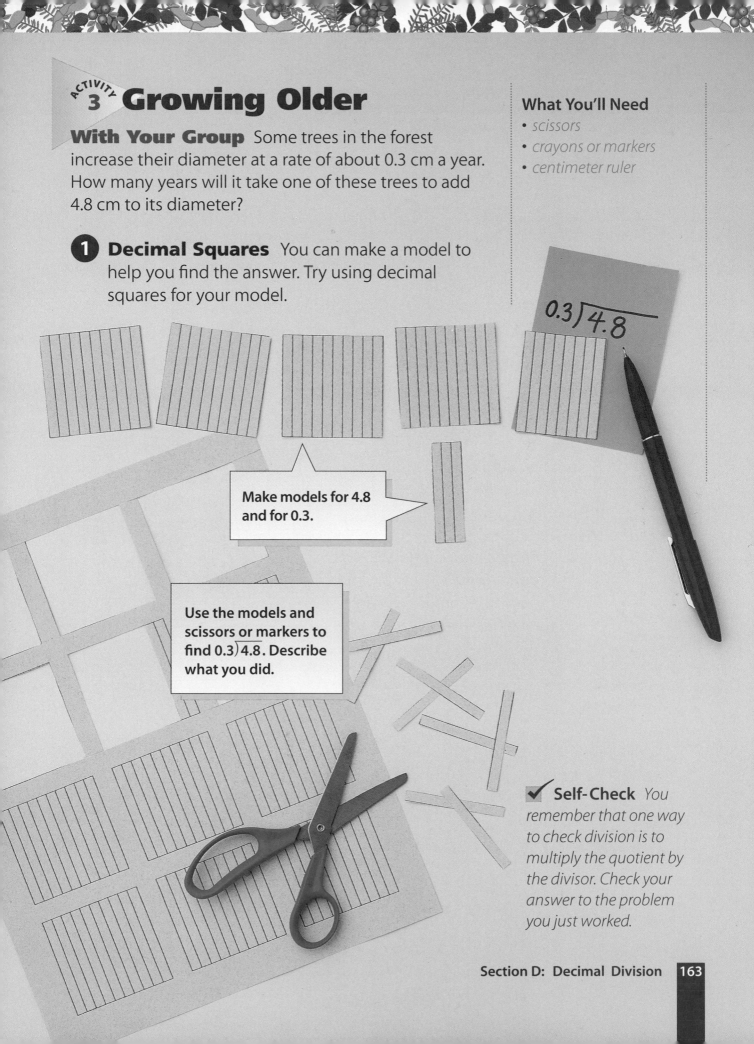

1 Decimal Squares You can make a model to help you find the answer. Try using decimal squares for your model.

> Make models for 4.8 and for 0.3.

> Use the models and scissors or markers to find 0.3)4.8. Describe what you did.

What You'll Need
- *scissors*
- *crayons or markers*
- *centimeter ruler*

$0.3\overline{)4.8}$

✔ **Self-Check** *You remember that one way to check division is to multiply the quotient by the divisor. Check your answer to the problem you just worked.*

2 Metric Model Describe how you could use a centimeter ruler and paper to divide 4.8 by 0.3.

3 Hundredths' Model What happens when you divide with hundredths? Show a model to help you divide 1.75 by 0.25.

  a. How would you represent hundredths?
  b. Describe how you would find the answer.
  c. Compare your model with that of other groups. How are the models the same? How are they different?

a. 0.4) 6.4

b. 0.5) 3

c. 1.2) 4.8

d. 0.25) 3.4

4 Model These Use models to help you answer these problems.

Take a Hike

With Your Group   Plan a hike on the part of the Appalachian Trail that runs through the Shenandoah and Great Smoky national parks. Use the information on these pages.

When you estimate with division, see that the divisor and the dividend are numbers that divide easily.

1   You plan to hike 18.5 km a day. How many days will it take to walk from Mount Katahdin to Moxie Bald Mountain? How would you estimate the answer?

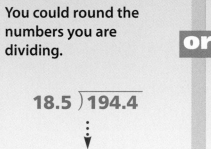

You could round the numbers you are dividing.	**or**	You could use numbers that are easy to divide and that are close to the original numbers.
$18.5\overline{)194.4}$		$18.5\overline{)194.4}$
↓		↓
$20\overline{)190}$		$20\overline{)200}$

a. Which way lets you make a quick mental estimate more easily? Explain.

b. About how many days will the hike take?

2   Between Moxie Bald Mountain and Grafton Notch you must cross a river. You might average 12 km a day. Estimate how long this hike will take.

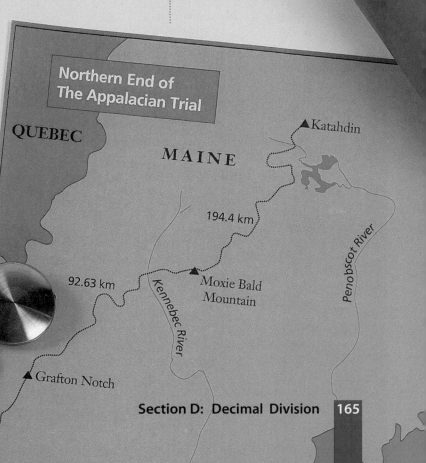

Northern End of The Appalacian Trial

QUEBEC

MAINE

▲ Katahdin

194.4 km

Penobscot River

92.63 km

Kennebec River

▲ Moxie Bald Mountain

▲ Grafton Notch

3 Your friends made a similar trip. They kept track of their big expenses. Use their expense record to help you plan your trip.

Expenses

Sleeping bags	49.85
Cabin rental	54.25
Laundry	12.25
Meals	146.76
Film	18.09
Guidebooks	26.43
Transportation	287.80

a. One night's cabin rental was $7.75. Describe how you can estimate the length of your friends' trip.

b. One friend said they paid an average of $30 a day for food. Do you think this is correct? Explain.

c. Altogether, about how much should you plan to spend for transportation, meals, and cabin rental per day?

Do You Remember?

Try It!

Divide. Show how to check your work.

1. $2.2 \div 0.2$ **2.** $3.6 \div 0.3$ **3.** $5.2 \div 4$ **4.** $42 \div 3$ **5.** $7.2 \div 0.4$

By what number would you multiply to get a whole number? Describe the pattern.

6. 0.0003   **7.** 0.03   **8.** 0.033   **9.** 0.33   **10.** 3.03

Think About It

11. Explain in writing how a quotient changes when you multiply only the divisor by a factor.

Decimal Data

In a recent year 188 moose were living on Isle Royale. Think about how you could find the average number of moose in a square kilometer if their range was about 77.5 km².

ACTIVITY 1 Find the Pattern

With Your Group   You have divided by decimals, using models to help you. Now you will discover how to divide by decimals without models. Noticing patterns will help you start.

1   Look at the examples below.

$$2)\overline{6} \quad 4)\overline{12} \quad 6)\overline{18} \quad 8)\overline{24}$$

    a. What pattern do you find among these divisors and dividends?

    b. What is the quotient in the first example?

    c. What do you notice about the other quotients?

2   Now look at these examples and describe the pattern. How is it the same as the one above? How is it different?

$$2)\overline{6} \quad 20)\overline{60} \quad 200)\overline{600}$$

3   Write a generalization to describe what happens when you multiply the dividend and the divisor by the same number.

When you learn a new skill, like dividing by a decimal, you build on old skills. List three things you always check when you finish a division problem.

ACTIVITY 2 Divide It Up

With Your Group How can the pattern you found in Activity 1 help you divide by a decimal?

1 Use what you have learned about powers of ten to complete this pattern.

$$175 = 1 \times 175$$
$$175 = 10 \times 17.5$$
$$175 = 100 \times n$$
$$175 = 1{,}000 \times n$$

2 How has the pattern from Step 1 been used to rewrite this division?

$$17.5\overline{)154} \longrightarrow 175\overline{)1{,}540}$$

a. Where did the zero in the dividend come from? Remember, 154 = 154.0.

b. Do you think both divisions have the same answer? Why or why not?

c. Use your calculator to find out.

3 Now you are ready to make a plan to find the approximate number of moose per square kilometer. After you divide, share your method and your answer with the class.

$$77.5\overline{)188}$$

square kilometers   moose

Isle Royale
National Park

72 Kilometers Long
5 to 14 Kilometers Wide

188 Moose
on 77.5 square Kilometers

12 Timberwolves

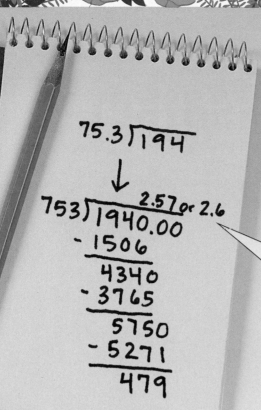

4 What did you do with the remainder? Here is how one person worked a similar division.

75.3)194

↓

2.57 or 2.6
753)1940.00
-1506
4340
-3765
5750
-5271
479

> **You round decimals like you round whole numbers.**
>
> 2.5**7**
>
> └── **5 or greater**
>
> **2.57 rounds to 2.6 to the nearest tenth.**

5 Describe how you would continue the division to find the quotient to the nearest hundredth.

6 Now try your plan to divide a decimal by a decimal. Explain the steps you would follow.

5.8)18.27

7 Try using your plan for 0.6)0.025.

   a. Multiply to check your answer.
   b. What do you need to be very careful about in this particular problem?

8 Now try your plan on these divisions.

   a. 8)4   **b.** 0.75)0.035
   c. 4.5)23.75   **d.** 2.8)3,928

9 Share your plan with other groups. How are their plans like yours?

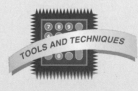

TOOLS AND TECHNIQUES

To make a calculator divide to a certain place, press

Fix *1 for tenths,*
Fix *2 for hundredths, and so on.*

Farmers' Market

Solve these problems about some natural products you might get at a farmers' market. Use what you know about dividing decimals.

Fall Fruit

1 A basket of apples costs $2.35. How many whole baskets did you buy if you got $3.55 back in change from a $20 bill?

2 There are about 2,150.42 in.^{3} in a bushel basket. If an average apple is 22.3 in.^{3}, how many apples will the basket hold?

3 A bushel of apples produces about 3.59 gallons of cider. About how many bushels of apples would it take to make 6.5 gallons of cider?

4 Washington, Michigan, and New York together grow a total of about 101,000,000 bushels of apples per year. What is the average apple production for each state? Round your answer to the nearest million.

Bees and Honey

5 One beekeeper got 188.2 pounds of honey from 4 hives. What was the average production per hive?

6 One family used 0.75 pounds of honey in one week. How many weeks would it take them to use a jar of honey that weighed 5.5 pounds?

Sap to Syrup

7 About 150 L of sap from a sugar maple tree makes 2.5 L of maple syrup. How much sap will it take to make 100 L of maple syrup?

8 An average tree produces about 1.25 L of sap in one hour. About how many hours does it take the tree to produce 150 L?

9 How many trees would it take to produce 150 L of sap in 24 hours?

10 Five liters of maple syrup cost $57.95. If you sell that syrup in small jars that hold 0.75 L each, how much would each jar cost?

Looking Back

Choose the right answer. Write *a, b, c,* or *d* for each question.

1. About how far will this wheel roll after 34 turns?
   a. 64.3 m
   b. 967.3 m
   c. 20.5 m
   d. 10.2 m

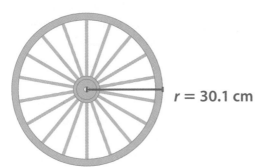

$r = 30.1$ cm

2. How many turns will this wheel make to travel 1 km?
   a. 5,290
   b. 529
   c. 5.29×10^3
   d. 52,900

3. How many turns will the wheel make in 1,000 km?
   a. 5.29×10^1
   b. 529×10^3
   c. 52,900
   d. $52.9 \times 100,000$

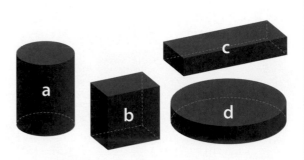

4. Which container can hold the greatest volume of seeds?
   a. $d = 18$ cm, $h = 24$ cm
   b. $h = 18$ cm, $w = 18$ cm, $l = 12$ cm
   c. $h = 6$ cm, $w = 36$ cm, $l = 12$ cm
   d. $d = 36$ cm, $h = 12$ cm

5. If the total volume of one container is about 6,000 cm³, which of these could be its dimensions?
   a. $d = 12$ cm, $h = 72$ cm
   b. $h = 18$ cm , $w = 12$ cm , $l = 24$ cm
   c. $d = 18$ cm, $h = 24$ cm
   d. $h = 50$ cm, $w = 20$ cm, $l = 6$ cm

6. If cylinder a in item 4 is a silo full of grain worth $3,964.99, how much is $\frac{1}{4}$ of the grain worth?
   a. $158.60
   b. about $1000
   c. $2,973.74
   d. about $160

7. If there is an average of 233 ants in 1 m^2 of prairie, about how many are in 1,000 m^3?
   a. 2.33×10^3
   b. 23,300
   c. two million, three hundred and thirty thousand
   d. 2.33×10^5

8. Which of the following is not equivalent to $4\frac{8}{25}$?
   a. 4.32
   b. $1\frac{108}{25}$
   c. $4\frac{16}{50}$
   d. 4.108

9. In which expression is the order of operations used correctly?
   a. $5.34 + 6.19 \times 42 = 484.26$
   b. $5.34 + 6.19 \times 42 = 265.32$
   c. $98.6 \div (0.36 + 0.34) = 140.86$
   d. $98.6 \div 0.36 + 0.34 = 140.86$

10. If a bean plant grows 17.4 cm each day, how many days will it take to grow 2 m?
    a. 3.4 days
    b. 1.5 days
    c. 34 days
    d. 11.5 days

11. Which of the following expressions is not equal to 0.092?
    a. $0.0276 \div 0.3$ **b.** 0.46×0.2
    c. $516.12 \div 561$ **d.** $3.312 \div 36$

12. If you can buy 300 U.S. dollars with 560.45 Italian lire, how many dollars can you buy with 1 lira? Use your calculator or mental math to answer.
    a. $1.87
    b. $0.43
    c. about $2
    d. about one half

Check Your Math Power

13. Give at least three different sets of dimensions for a rectangular prism with a volume of 160 cm^3.

14. Can a square peg with a diagonal of 16 mm fit through a round hole with a radius of 9 mm? Draw a picture to help explain your answer.

15. Explain in writing why dividing a decimal by a decimal sometimes gives you a whole number. When might you expect this to happen?

MODULE 3 **Investigations**

Waste Watch

Trash ruins a beautiful landscape. Some communities even use the land to store trash. They store garbage in areas called sanitary landfills. Find out how much landfill your trash takes up.Then design a way to remind people to produce less trash.

Investigation A **Mega Dumpster**

1

2

About how much trash does your family produce in a day? Tell how you can find out.

How much trash does your family throw out in a year?

3 How much trash does your town produce? First find a yearly average for your group. How can you find the population of your community?

4 Design and draw an imaginary trash can big enough to hold your town's yearly trash. Use a calculator to help you.

5 Design a new trash can to hold the amount of trash each household should throw out daily to reduce the total volume. Explain your design.

Keep in Mind

Your drawings will be judged by how well you do the following things.

☐ How well do you show what you know about volume formulas and decimal multiplication to help you solve the problem?

☐ How well do you check your numbers by estimating to see whether they make sense?

☐ How clearly do you show and explain your designs and your thinking?

Today about $\frac{4}{5}$ of all garbage in the United States goes to landfills. Only about $\frac{1}{10}$ is recycled. But landfill area is running out, and the amount of garbage is growing.

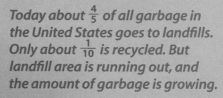

Investigation B — Garbage History

Research and compare different recycling systems. Gather data and make a double-bar graph that compares this data. For example, how much do Americans recycle per year today compared with 20 years ago? How much trash does Japan recycle compared with the United States? You might find data on specific materials: glass, aluminum, paper. You might make a spreadsheet on a computer or gather information from a computer network. Show the graph and write your findings.

Investigation C — Trash Mountain

Find out the yearly volume of trash your town produces. Then work out a way to show the size of this "mountain" of trash. Research to find a way to compare its size with the size of a famous national or local landmark. Design a poster that uses this comparison to show people how much trash they produce.

Let's Get Growing!

Do you fit into the clothes you wore in fifth grade? in fourth grade? Probably not—you've grown since then. Living things grow. Nonliving things can grow too. For instance, this picture shows growth by repeating a simple computer process. In this module, you'll explore growth, growth patterns, and how to predict growth. So let's get growing!

SECTION
A

Growing and Shrinking in Steps

SECTION
B

Growing and Shrinking Shapes

SECTION
C

Growing Pyramids and Cones

SECTION
D

Other Ways to Grow

Growing Evidence

Explore growth patterns and watch your own knowledge grow. Observe the growth of a plant or a crystal and collect data to find the growth patterns.

1 Make a List

Get together as a class and list things that grow. Include living things, such as plants and animals, and nonliving things, such as crystals and flames.

Put a penny a day in a bank and watch your savings grow.

As plants grow taller, their leaves grow larger.

2 Compare the Growth

Which items on your list grow slowly? Which grow quickly? Try to describe different growth patterns.

Tree rings and shell spirals are evidence of growth.

3 Show Growth

Make a collage that shows how an item has grown, or write a story that describes growth.

Investigations Preview

Learn several ways to make numbers grow. Explore ways to describe growth and ways to predict it.

All the King's Corn (pages 192–193)

You will use patterns to show how quickly numbers grow by doubling. You will also use the patterns to predict how numbers grow.

Way to Grow! (pages 238–240)

How tall is a typical sixth grader? eighth grader? You will collect data, find average heights, and make a scattergram to find the growth pattern of a typical sixth grader.

LESSON 1 Step by Step

LITERATURE

A wise man in India has invented the game of chess. In exchange for the game, he asks for a reward.

What shall I give you?" questioned the monarch. "Ask me anything you like, and you shall receive it, to the half of my kingdom."

"I want neither gold nor jewels," said the old man. "All I ask is that your Majesty shall give me one grain of corn for the first square on the chessboard, double that for the second square, double that again for the third, and so on—that is, I am to have one, two, four, eight, sixteen, and so on up to the sixty-fourth square; simply that, and nothing more."

"Of course you can have that," replied the King; "but it is nothing for what you have done. Let me add a hundred lacs of rupees?"

"No, your Majesty," said the old man, modestly; "I am grateful for your generosity, but give me only the corn that I ask for and I shall be content."

"Very well," replied the King; and, calling his treasurer, he told him to count up the number of grains.

"I must ask your Majesty to send them to me," added the wise man; and to this the King agreed, although he could not understand, he said, why the old man could not take so small a reward with him.

From "King Kaid of India"
from *The Victorian Readers,* Fifth Book

x 2

ACTIVITY 1 Piles of Corn

With Your Group King Kaid thought the wise man's request was a very small one. What do you think? You can use counters to show how great the reward was for the first six squares.

1 On a sheet of paper make a 3 × 2 grid. Label the squares 1–6. Place counters in the squares to show how many grains of corn the wise man requested for each square.

2 Record the growth of the reward in a chart like the one below.

3 Show how the corn would increase if the king added 2 grains of corn from one square to the next instead of doubling the corn.

What You'll Need
• *counters*

Predict what will happen if the starting number, the number you multiply by, and the number you add are all 1. What did you find when you checked?

Square 1	Square 2
Square 3	Square 4
Square 5	Square 6

Square	×2	+ 2
1	1	1
2	2	
3	4	
4		
5		
6		

ACTIVITY 2 Growth in Four Steps

With Your Partner Get ready to explore growth with larger numbers. Choose a number from 3 to 9.

Extend the patterns from Activity 2 for six more steps. Describe your results.

1 **Add** your number to 1. Now add your number to the new sum. Repeat until you have four sums. Record each sum in a chart.

$$1 + 3 = 4$$
$$4 + 3 = 7$$
$$7 + 3 = 10$$
$$10 + 3 = 13$$

2 **Multiply** 1 by your number. Multiply that product by your number. Repeat until you have four products. Record each product in your chart.

$$1 \times 3 = 3$$
$$3 \times 3 = 9$$
$$9 \times 3 = 27$$
$$27 \times 3 = 81$$

$$3 = 3^1$$
$$9 = 3 \times 3 = 3^2$$

3 **Compare** the sums and the products. Do your numbers grow faster using addition or using multiplication? Explain.

4 **Write** the factors for each product in expanded form. Use your partner's chart from Step 3. Then think back to what you've learned about using exponents to write powers of ten. Write the factors for each product, using exponents.

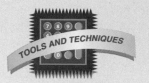
TOOLS AND TECHNIQUES

ᴬᶜᵀᴵᵛᴵᵀʸ 3 **Power Drawing**

With Your Partner   A graph can help you see how fast the numbers in your pattern can grow.

1   The graph below shows growth by 3. Answer these questions about the graph.
   a. Which points show growth by addition?
   b. Which points show growth by multiplication?
   c. How does the graph help you compare growth patterns?

2   Draw your own graph to show growth by 4. (Hint: Label the Growing Number axis by fives.) Plot each sum, then plot your products. How does the graph for growth by 4 compare with the graph for growth by 3?

You can use a spreadsheet to make growth patterns. Then use the graphing function to have your computer make graphs of the patterns.

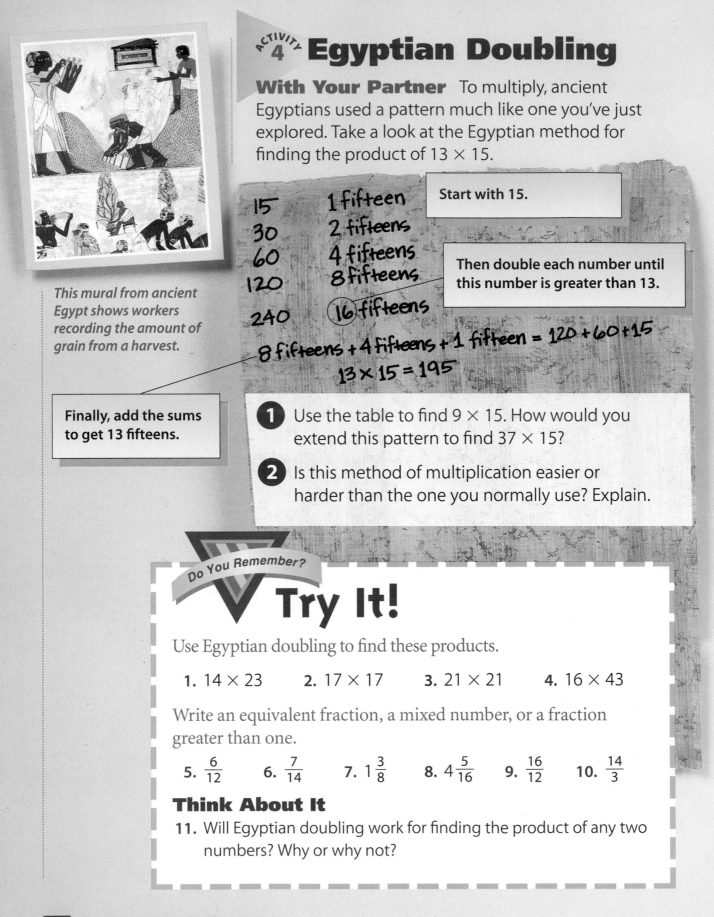

ACTIVITY 4 Egyptian Doubling

With Your Partner To multiply, ancient Egyptians used a pattern much like one you've just explored. Take a look at the Egyptian method for finding the product of 13 × 15.

This mural from ancient Egypt shows workers recording the amount of grain from a harvest.

```
15      1 fifteen
30      2 fifteens
60      4 fifteens
120     8 fifteens
240    (16) fifteens

8 fifteens + 4 fifteens + 1 fifteen = 120 + 60 + 15
           13 × 15 = 195
```

Start with 15.

Then double each number until this number is greater than 13.

Finally, add the sums to get 13 fifteens.

1 Use the table to find 9 × 15. How would you extend this pattern to find 37 × 15?

2 Is this method of multiplication easier or harder than the one you normally use? Explain.

Do You Remember?

Try It!

Use Egyptian doubling to find these products.

1. 14 × 23   **2.** 17 × 17   **3.** 21 × 21   **4.** 16 × 43

Write an equivalent fraction, a mixed number, or a fraction greater than one.

5. $\frac{6}{12}$ **6.** $\frac{7}{14}$ **7.** $1\frac{3}{8}$ **8.** $4\frac{5}{16}$ **9.** $\frac{16}{12}$ **10.** $\frac{14}{3}$

Think About It

11. Will Egyptian doubling work for finding the product of any two numbers? Why or why not?

Target Time

Add or multiply—either way, the numbers grow. Use what you've learned about growth patterns to get from the starting number to the target number.

ACTIVITY 1 Growing in Steps

With Your Group   Use three numbers to play a target game. Take only the number of steps allowed.

1 **Look at the table.** Try to reach each target by adding the same number at each step. Then try to reach the target by multiplying by the same number at each step.

Starting Number	Number of Steps	Target Number
1	4	81
1	3	64
10	2	1,000

Growing by Addition

1 21 41 61 **81**

2 **Record each step.** Tell how you reached each number on the way to the target number.

Growing by Multiplication

1 ? ? ? **81**

185

CONNECT AND COMMUNICATE

In Your Journal Write a letter that explains the target game to a friend. Tell what you did to reach the target number. Include some starting numbers and target numbers so your friend can play the game too.

3 **Aim for any number.** Some numbers work more easily than others. How can you work with numbers that do not give whole-number sums or products? Use your calculator to try this example:

1 to 20 in 5 steps

Growing

1

? ? ? ?

20

4 **Discuss your methods.**
- What method worked best for your group? Did you make an estimate and then check it?
- How precise was your answer?
- Did anyone find an exact answer?

Use your calculator to find sums and products.

too big 5   too small 4

²ᴬᶜᵀᴵⱽᴵᵀʸ Shrinking in Steps

With Your Class Now play the target game with a starting number greater than the target number. Remember to use the same number and operation at each step.

1 What operations can your group use to shrink a number? How can these operations help you get from 27 to 8 in 3 steps?

2 Now try shrinking these numbers. Explain how you reached the target.

    a. 10 to 2 in 4 steps
    b. 28 to 4 in 3 steps
    c. 243 to 1 in 5 steps

3 Is it easier to figure out patterns for growing numbers or for shrinking them? Explain your answer.

Use compatible numbers to help you make an estimate.

Keep a record of the numbers you try. See how close you can get.

 CONNECT AND COMMUNICATE

How can you use this activity to show that subtraction and addition are inverse operations?

4 Did you think of using multiplication to shrink a number? Try multiplying $\frac{1}{3}$ and 27. How is multiplying by $\frac{1}{3}$ like dividing by 3?

5 You may have noticed that $\frac{1}{3} \times 3 = 1$.

Any two numbers whose product is 1 are **reciprocals** of each other. How might you find the reciprocal of $\frac{2}{3}$? Use the clues below to help you.

> To find this number, think about what must be true of any fraction equal to 1.

$$\frac{2}{3} \times \boxed{} = 1$$

Do You Remember?

Try It!

For Exercises 1–4, reach the target number in the required number of steps. Tell what operation you used.

	start	target	steps
1.	3	5	8
2.	7	189	3
3.	16	1	4
4.	27	1	3

Write the reciprocal. Then list the reciprocals in increasing order.

5. $\frac{5}{9}$ 6. $\frac{9}{16}$ 7. 7   8. 1

9. 23   10. $\frac{5}{3}$ 11. $\frac{8}{5}$ 12. $\frac{3}{2}$

Think About It

13. Is the reciprocal of a whole number always a fraction? Write a short explanation.

One-Step Shrinking

A number can grow in one step by being multiplied by itself. The product is a square number or a perfect square.

Be Here or Be Square

On Your Own Use what you already know about arrays to explore perfect squares.

1 There are 64 items in the array on this page. Because the array is a square array, 64 is a perfect square.

2 Write a multiplication sentence that describes the array.

3 The product is the square number. The factor that is multiplied by itself is called the **square root.** The symbol for square root is $\sqrt{\ }$, so you can write $\sqrt{64} = 8$.

> The square root is the number of items on one side of a perfect square array.

How would you use drawings of square numbers to help you estimate the square root of a number that isn't a perfect square?

Perfect Square

Square Root

What You'll Need
- grid paper
- ruler

4 Find all of the perfect squares from 1 to 100. Use counters if you want. Make a table showing the perfect squares and their square roots.

ACTIVITY 2 Imperfectly Square

With Your Partner You can see that perfect squares and square roots grow. Use a graph to help you see the growth pattern.

1 On grid paper, plot the square roots you found in Activity 1.

Perfect Square	Square Root
1	1
4	2
9	3

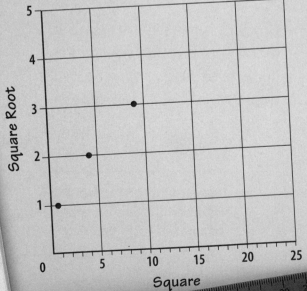

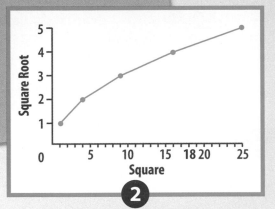

2

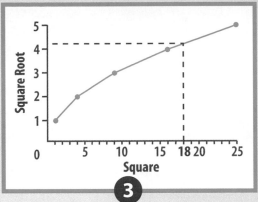

3

Connect the points to form a curve. You can use your graph as a visual tool to estimate the square root of 18. Find 18 between the perfect squares 16 and 25.

Draw a line to the curve from 18. Then draw a line from the curve to the vertical axis. Estimate the square root of 18.

4 Multiply your estimate by itself. What do you need to do to come closer to the actual square root of 18?

$$25 > 18 > 16$$
$$\sqrt{25} > \sqrt{18} > \sqrt{16}$$
$$5 > \sqrt{18} > 4$$

You can use the $\sqrt{}$ key on your calculator to quickly find the square root of any number.

Do You Remember?

Try It!

Estimate the square root to the nearest tenth. Use multiplication to check your estimate.

1. 41   **2.** 32   **3.** 79   **4.** 90

5. 5   **6.** 63   **7.** 50   **8.** 60

Find the area.

9. 3 / 3   **10.** 2 / 9   **11.** 4

Think About It

12. What perfect squares can you use to estimate the square roots for Exercises 1–3? Explain.

All the King's Corn

LITERATURE

The king's treasurer was the first to sound the alarm about the wise man's reward.

The treasurer went away, but after an hour or two he returned in the greatest consternation.

"Have you sent the old man his reward?" asked King Kaid.

"No, your Majesty," replied the treasurer; "it is impossible. He has asked for more than the value of your kingdom."

"What do you mean?" demanded the King severely, looking greatly astonished.

"Why, your Majesty, to give one grain for the first square, two for the second, four for the third, and so on to the sixty-fourth, means that he is to have 18,446,744,073,709,551,615 grains. Not a thousandth part of this corn exists in the world."

From "King Kaid of India"
from *The Victorian Readers*, Fifth Book

Imagine that you are King Kaid's treasurer. You may want to warn the king about how large the reward will be.

1 Choose one of these three questions to answer.

a. How many corn grains will be placed on the 40th square?

b. Which is the 1st square on which there will be more than 1 million grains of corn?

c. By which square will the wise man have received more than 1 million grains of corn?

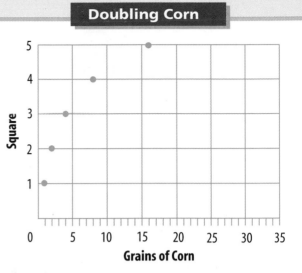

Doubling Corn

2 Decide how to find the number. Will a graph help? Will you need a chart? Will you need to multiply or add or both?

3 Write a step-by-step plan for finding the number. Present your results to the class. Be sure that you can answer at least one of the questions.

Step 1: Find pattern for squares 1–10.

Step 2:

Ask Yourself

☐ How can I use what I already know to find out how much corn will be placed on a specific square?

☐ Is there a simpler way to find how much corn is delivered than by doing all the multiplication?

☐ How can a graph help me find when there will be 1 million grains?

☐ How can a picture show what I learned?

☐ How can I apply what I learned to everyday life?

LESSON
4

Squaring Off

You have discovered patterns in the ways numbers grow and shrink. Like numbers, shapes grow and shrink in patterns.

ACTIVITY
1 **Squares in Squares**

With Your Partner Use ordinary paper to discover size and shape patterns. Explore how changes in the length of a square's side affect its area.

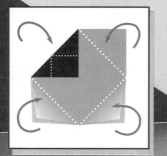

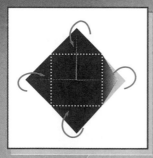

1 Begin with a square piece of paper. Fold the corners of the paper in toward the center to make a second, smaller square. Use the picture to help you.
   a. How does the area of the second square compare with the area of the first?
   b. How can you use a fraction to compare the areas?

2 Make a third square by folding in the corners of the second square. Use a fraction to record how the areas of the second and third squares compare.

ACTIVITY OPTION

3 Continue making smaller squares.
   a. How many times did you fold the square?
   b. What fraction of the first square is the final square?

Try folding a regular hexagon or an equilateral triangle to find fraction patterns. Share results and methods with the class.

 ACTIVITY 2 Countdown

With Your Group Try the Squares in Squares activity on grid paper.

1 Draw a 16 × 16 square on grid paper. What is the area? What is the perimeter? Write each in a chart.

2 Find the midpoint of each side of the square. Connect the four midpoints to form a second, smaller square. Fill in its area on the chart.

3 Repeat Step 2 over and over until you get a 1-cm square. Add each area to the chart.

What You'll Need
- *grid paper*
- *centimeter ruler*

Square	Side	Perimeter	Area

4 Write in the side and perimeter measures of the third, fifth, seventh, and ninth squares in your table.

5 Once you know the area of a square, you can use square root to estimate the length of each side. Estimate the perimeters of the remaining squares and write them in your table. Measure to check your estimates.

In Your Journal Multiply a fraction less than 1 by a series of whole numbers. What happens? Use this information to explain why multiplying two fractions less than 1 results in a product smaller than either factor.

ACTIVITY 3 **Multiplying Fractions**

With Your Partner The squares from the last activity can help you build your number sense about fractions. First take a look at what happens when you try the midpoint activity with an equilateral triangle.

How can you show that the area of the red triangle is $\frac{1}{4}$ the area of the green triangle?

How can you show that the area of the blue triangle is $\frac{1}{4}$ the area of the red triangle?

You can use multiplication to show that the area of the blue triangle is $\frac{1}{16}$ the area of the green triangle. Multiply numerators. Multiply denominators.

$$\frac{1}{4} \times \frac{1}{4} = \frac{1}{16}$$

1 Write multiplication sentences with fractions to show the area of four squares from Activity 2. Each sentence should show the area of the squares as a fraction of the area of the largest square.

2 Find the product of each pair of factors shown at the right. Write the product in simplest terms. A fraction is in simplest terms if the numerator and denominator have no common factors. For example,

$$\frac{1}{2} \times \frac{2}{3} = \frac{2}{6} = \frac{1}{3}$$

a) $\frac{1}{2} \times \frac{1}{4}$ b) $\frac{1}{3} \times \frac{2}{3}$

c) $\frac{3}{8} \times \frac{1}{4}$ d) $\frac{4}{4} \times \frac{1}{2}$

Try It!

Write each product in simplest terms.

1. $\frac{1}{3} \times \frac{1}{3}$ 2. $\frac{1}{2} \times \frac{2}{5}$ 3. $\frac{2}{3} \times \frac{3}{4}$

4. $\frac{3}{8} \times \frac{5}{6}$ 5. $\frac{1}{10} \times \frac{5}{8}$ 6. $\frac{4}{5} \times \frac{7}{8}$

Find the perimeter or circumference of these shapes.

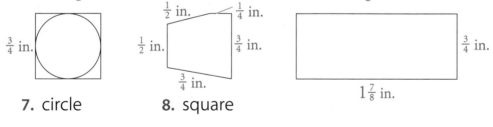

7. circle   8. square

9. pentagon   10. rectangle

Think About It

11. One student did Exercise 2 this way: $\frac{1}{\cancel{2}_1} \times \frac{\cancel{2}^1}{5} = \frac{1}{5}$. How might this method help you? With which other items above could you use it?

LESSON 5 Area Exploration

Tiles come in many beautiful shapes and colors. What shapes do you see in this photograph of ancient Roman tiles? How do you think you could find the area of these shapes?

What You'll Need
- *bendable straws*
- *grid paper*

ACTIVITY 1 The "Squish" Factor

With Your Partner Use four bendable straws to see how the perimeters and areas of rectangles and parallelograms are related.

1 Make a rectangle with the straws. Place the rectangle on grid paper. Trace the rectangle. Find the area of the rectangle by counting squares inside the shape.

2 "Squish" the rectangle to form a parallelogram with no right angles. Trace around the parallelogram. Compare the perimeters and areas of the two shapes. Explain any differences.

3 Squish the straws again. Find the area and perimeter and compare them with those of the other shapes. Discuss your findings with the class.

ACTIVITY
2 **Try Angles**

With Your Partner How could you find the area of a parallelogram without using graph paper? Use your own method and compare your method and answers with those of your classmates.

1 Cut a parallelogram out of a piece of paper. Using a pair of scissors, experiment with ways to turn the parallelogram into a rectangle.

2 Explain how you can use what you know about finding the area of a rectangle to find the area of a parallelogram.

REASONING AND PROBLEM SOLVING

How could thinking of a parallelogram as a combination of smaller shapes help you estimate its size?

What You'll Need
• *scissors*

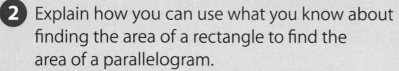

Section B: Growing and Shrinking Shapes 199

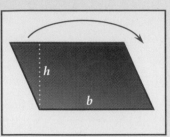

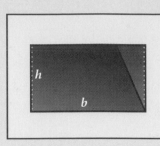

How can you use this diagram to help you explain that the formula for finding the area of a parallelogram is A = bh?

What You'll Need
- *Tracing Tool or tracing paper*
- *scissors*

ACTIVITY 3

Area of Triangles

With Your Partner You've discovered how to find the area of a parallelogram. Use this knowledge to help you discover how to find the area of a triangle.

1 Fold a piece of paper in half. Cut a triangle from the center of the paper. You should now have two congruent triangles.

2 Make a parallelogram. What do you know about finding the area of a parallelogram that can help you find the area of one of the triangles?

3 Write a formula for finding the area of a triangle in terms of base and height. Draw a picture to show how your formula works.

4 Use the dimensions shown to find the areas of the triangle and parallelograms.

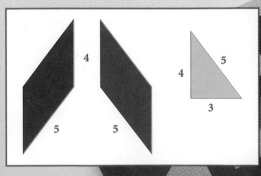

5 Using the areas found in Step 4, find the total area of the shapes on the incomplete tile. What is the area of the blank section?

6 Place a piece of paper over the page and trace the incomplete tile. Complete the tile, using the given pattern. How many triangular shapes will you use? How many purple shapes will you use?

Do You Remember?

Try It!

The dimensions listed below are those of parallelograms. Find the area. Then find the base and height of a triangle with the same area.

1. $b = 5, h = 6$ **2.** $b = 11, h = \frac{7}{8}$ **3.** $b = 5\frac{1}{3}, h = 12$

4. $b = 2, h = 2$ **5.** $b = \frac{2}{3}, h = 3$ **6.** $b = 1, h = 2$

Find each sum or difference. Write it in simplest terms.

7. $3\frac{4}{5} + 6\frac{7}{10}$ **8.** $\frac{5}{4} - \frac{7}{12}$ **9.** $12\frac{1}{2} - 4\frac{2}{3}$

10. $99\frac{1}{4} + 9\frac{1}{6}$ **11.** $\frac{5}{7} + \frac{7}{5}$ **12.** $7\frac{3}{5} - 6\frac{1}{2}$

Think About It

13. Find the perimeter of a rectangle with the same base and height as the parallelogram in item 1. Is the perimeter of the parallelogram greater than or less than that of the rectangle? Explain.

Mixed Multiplying

$3\frac{1}{3}$ ft

$2\frac{1}{2}$ ft

You are going to make a doormat in your art class. Find out how much material you will need to make a mat that measures $2\frac{1}{2}$ ft by $3\frac{1}{3}$ ft.

ACTIVITY 1 **Go Array**

With Your Group Use what you know about multiplying fractions to help you find the area of your doormat. Work with your group to find a solution. Share your solution and strategy.

With Your Partner Use the array on the next page to help you think about this question.

1 The array shows that there are four parts of the product. What are they?

2 Many students make the mistake of just multiplying 2×3 and adding the product to the product of $\frac{1}{2} \times \frac{1}{3}$. Use this array to explain why that method does not work.

3 Now use what you have learned to draw and label your own array to show $1\frac{3}{4} \times 2\frac{1}{3}$.

How can you use the Distributive Property of Multiplication to help you find how many square feet of material are needed to make the mat?

2×3

3

$\frac{1}{3}$

2

$2 \times \frac{1}{3}$

$\frac{1}{2} \times 3$

$\frac{1}{2}$

$\frac{1}{2} \times \frac{1}{3}$

DRAWING TO LEARN

Create a drawing that shows why you can solve the multiplication problem on the right by using fractions greater than 1.

ACTIVITY 2 Fraction Action

On Your Own There's an easier way to multiply mixed numbers than by drawing arrays. First change each mixed number to a fraction greater than 1. Then use what you already know about multiplying fractions. How would you use this method to find the mat's area?

$$2\frac{1}{2} \times 3\frac{1}{3} = \frac{5}{2} \times \frac{10}{3} = \, ?$$

With Your Partner Use the sheet of tangrams your teacher provides to create the shapes on the right. Find the total areas and perimeters of the shapes by using the dimensions on your tangrams. How do the areas and perimeters of the shapes compare? Share your answers and methods with the rest of the class.

ACTIVITY 3 From One to Two

With Your Partner Find out what happens when a fraction between 1 and 2 is multiplied by itself. Use your calculator to help you.

1 Use multiplication to fill in the missing values in this function table.

2 Compare the four sets of numbers in your table. What patterns do you see? How does multiplying mixed numbers compare with multiplying whole numbers?

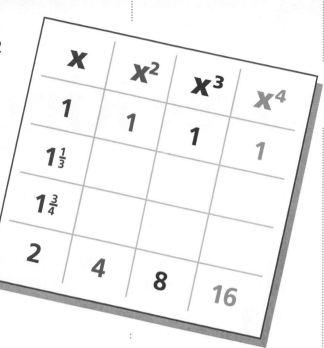

x	x²	x³	x⁴
1	1	1	1
$1\frac{1}{3}$			1
$1\frac{3}{4}$			
2	4	8	16

Do You Remember?

Try It!

Estimate each product. Find exact answers for products between 7 and 9.

1. $11\frac{2}{3} \times \frac{5}{6}$ **2.** $3\frac{3}{4} \times 1\frac{9}{10}$ **3.** $2\frac{1}{3} \times 3\frac{1}{2}$

4. $7 \times 1\frac{1}{3}$ **5.** $\frac{1}{9} \times 79$ **6.** $\frac{99}{100} \times 9$

Use the diagram to help you do Exercises 7–12. Label the following pairs of line segments *parallel*, *perpendicular*, or *neither*.

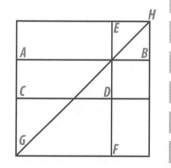

7. $\overline{AB}, \overline{GH}$ **8.** $\overline{CD}, \overline{EF}$ **9.** $\overline{GH}, \overline{GF}$

10. $\overline{AB}, \overline{CD}$ **11.** $\overline{EF}, \overline{AB}$ **12.** $\overline{EF}, \overline{GH}$

Think About It

13. Write a brief description of the strategies you used to estimate the products in Exercises 1–6.

Tree Ring Circus

Plants are the oldest and largest organisms on the planet. Use your math skills to analyze data about these amazing plants.

Trees You may remember from science class that you can find the age of a tree by counting tree rings.

 What is the circumference of this tree slice?

 What is the area of the slice?

 This tree is about 125 years old. What is the average thickness of the tree rings?

 What would the circumference and area of a slice of this tree have been five years ago?

r=6 in.

Creosote Bushes Nicknamed King Clone, a single creosote bush in California is the oldest living thing on earth. The bush grows in huge rings. To find the age of a creosote, researchers use its circumference and average growth rate.

 Some creosote bushes grow about 0.6 mm per year. How old is a creosote if its radius is 6.5 m?

 King Clone is estimated to be 11,700 years old. What is the area of a slice of this tree?

Quaking Aspen A single plant near Salt Lake City, Utah, looks like an entire forest. Nicknamed Pando, Latin for "I spread," the largest organism in the world consists of 47,000 tree trunks with a single root system.

Average Yearly Rainfall
Salt Lake City, Utah = 38.89 cm
Anchorage, Alaska = 38.61 cm
California Desert = 4.14 cm

7 What is the average monthly rainfall in Salt Lake City, Utah?

8 What is the average monthly rainfall in the California desert?

Check Your Math Power

9 Pando averages 98 ft^2 of land per trunk. How many acres does Pando cover in all? (Hint: An acre is 43,560 ft^2.)

10 How might you find the perimeter of this quaking aspen leaf? Share your method and answer with the class.

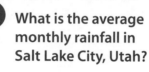

LESSON 7 Pyramid Volume

In Mexico stand giant stone buildings constructed between 700 and 1,300 years ago. They were built by the Toltecs or people they influenced. What growth pattern do you see in the building below?

What You'll Need
• *cubes*

ACTIVITY 1 ▶ Build a Pyramid

With Your Group Construct a model in the style of a Toltec building and find its volume.

This structure, built by either the Toltecs or the Maya, is near Chichen Itza, Mexico. It stands about 100 ft tall and has a square base that measures about 180 ft on each side.

1 **Make a model of a Toltec building** from cubes. Begin with one layer. Then add a 2-by-2 base. Add more layers until the base is 6 by 6. Record your data in a table like the one shown on the next page.

2 Fill in the table for models with up to 10 layers. Complete the last column for rectangular prisms with the same heights and bases as the models.

3 Analyze the patterns in your table.
   a. What is the relationship between the height in layers and the area of the base?
   b. What pattern of growth does the area of the base show?
   c. How do the last two columns compare? Describe any pattern you notice.

Try making a model of a Toltec building out of clay. How can you measure the volume of the clay you use to make your model?

Layers	Area of base (square units)	Volume of model (cubic units)	Volume of prism (cubic units)
1	1	1	1
2	4	5	

What's a Pyramid?

With Your Partner Over 4,000 years ago the Egyptians built some of the largest buildings ever constructed, the **pyramids.** Compare the prisms shown on this page with the pyramids on the next. Then write a definition of a pyramid. In your definition, describe the base, the sides, and the top of a pyramid.

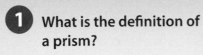

1 **What is the definition of a prism?**

The largest of the pyramids near Giza, Egypt, stands 450 ft tall and has a square base that measures 756 ft on each side.

a. How are the tops of pyramids alike?

b. Are the bases of all pyramids the same shape? Explain.

c. How many faces can a pyramid have? Explain.

With Your Class Discuss what makes a shape a pyramid.

3 One student decided that a pyramid is a space figure with four or more faces. The base can be any polygon. The other faces are triangles. How does this definition compare with yours?

4 If you could pull a slice out of a pyramid, what shape would it be? What determines the size of the shape? What would the third slice look like?

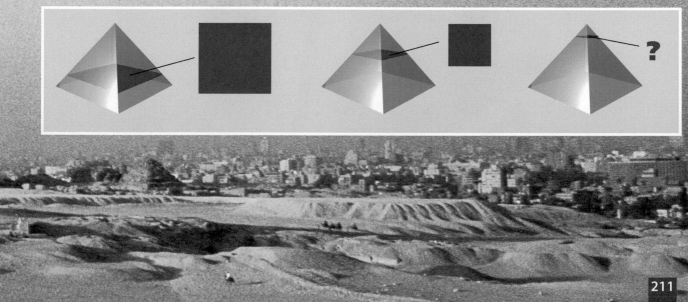

211

Pyramids and Cubes

With Your Partner If a pyramid and a prism are the same height and have bases of equal area, which has a greater volume? How can you estimate how much greater? Try either this activity or Activity 4 to find out.

What You'll Need
- *Geometry Tool or protractor*
- *inch ruler*
- *scissors*
- *tape*
- *rice or sand*

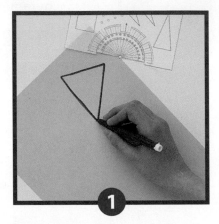

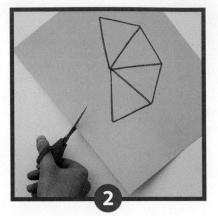

① Make a 50° angle with the protractor on your Geometry Tool. Make each side of the angle $3\frac{1}{16}$ in. Draw a segment connecting the ends of the sides to form a triangle.

② Form the pattern shown above by making three more triangles congruent with the first one. Cut out the pattern. Fold and tape it into a pyramid with an open base.

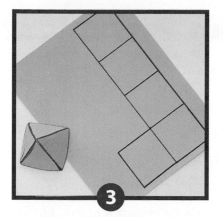

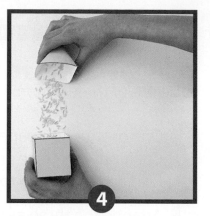

③

Draw five $2\frac{1}{2}$-in. squares in the pattern shown. Cut out the pattern and fold it into a cube without a top. Check that the bases and the heights of the pyramid and the cube are the same.

④

Fill the pyramid with rice. Pour the rice into the cube. Repeat until the cube is full. How much greater in volume is the cube than the pyramid? Compare results with your classmates.

✔ **Self-Check** *If a cube and a pyramid have the same volume and bases with the same area, how do their heights compare? Explain how you know.*

With Your Class Write a formula for finding the volume of a pyramid. Use *h* to represent the height of the pyramid and *B* for the area of the base. How does the formula differ from the one for volume of a cube?

ACTIVITY 4 Cubes from Pyramids

What You'll Need

- *Geometry Tool or protractor*
- *construction paper*
- *scissors*
- *tape*

With Your Partner Explore how to make a cube out of three pyramids.

1 On construction paper draw the shape on the left. Cut it out and trace and cut two more copies of it. Fold and tape each to form a pyramid.

2 Arrange the three pyramids to make a cube. How can you use your results to write a formula for the volume of a pyramid?

3 Compare your formula with your classmate's formulas. Discuss any differences.

Do You Remember?

Try It!

Use the formula $V = \frac{1}{3} Bh$ to find the volume of each pyramid.

1. $B = 28$ in.^{2}, $h = 15$ in. **2.** $B = 40$ in.^{2}, $h = 8$ in.

3. $B = 14.5$ in.^{2}, $h = 32.4$ in. **4.** $B = 7\frac{1}{4}$ in.^{2}, $h = 30\frac{1}{6}$ in.

5. $B = 30$ in.^{2}, $h = 8\frac{4}{5}$ in. **6.** $B = 50$ in.^{2}, $h = 1.9$ in.

Find the products that are greater than 10.

7. 9×0.14 **8.** 2×5.3 **9.** 9×0.8

10. 15×0.94 **11.** 20×0.42 **12.** 37×0.42

Think About It

13. Sketch and show the dimensions of three different rectangular pyramids with volumes of 100 in.^{3}

Cone Volume

From party hats to ice cream cones, you can find items everywhere in the shape of a **cone.** Explore what makes a cone different from a cylinder.

ACTIVITY 1 What's a Cone?

On Your Own A cone is a space figure with a circular base and one vertex. Explain which of the items shown are cones and which are not. How do you know? Share your ideas with your class.

ACTIVITY 2 Cones to Cylinders

With Your Class Discuss how a cone and a cylinder with the same height and bases of the same area compare in volume. Is the relationship the same as between the volumes of pyramids and prisms? Write a formula to find the volume of a cone. Use *V* for the volume, *h* for the height, and *B* for the base area.

DRAWING TO LEARN

Look at the shapes pulled from the pyramid on page 209. Sketch a cone and the shapes you can pull from it.

Section C: Growing Pyramids and Cones 215

Volume CITY

Volume and Strategy

With Your Group Volume City is a game for two to four players. Use what you know about the volume of cones, pyramids, and cylinders to help you play.

What You'll Need
- *gameboard*
- *squares of paper*
- *cube labeled 1–6*
- *game pieces*
- *scissors*

1 Set up the gameboard. Place a square of paper on each floor of each building.

2 The first player rolls a number cube and moves that number of spaces. Players can move back or forth along a pathway or up or down in a building.

What shapes are the buildings shown on the gameboard?

3 When you land on a floor with a square of paper, figure out the volume of the building from that floor to the top. A flag at the top of each building tells the height of the building. In each building the distance between floors is the same. How can you find the distance from each floor to the top?

4 If you figure the volume correctly, claim the square of paper. Players take turns until all papers are claimed. The player with the most points wins.

Do You Remember?

Try It!

$h = 10$ in.

Which cones have the same volume as the cylinder shown?

$B = 90$ in.^{2}

1. $B = 90$ in.^{2}, $h = 20$ in.
2. $B = 90$ in.^{2}, $h = 30$ in.

3. $B = 50$ in.^{2}, $h = 18$ in.
4. $B = 60$ in.^{2}, $h = 20$ in.

5. $B = 100$ in.^{2}, $h = 27$ in.
6. $B = 180$ in.^{2}, $h = 15$ in.

Find the sum or difference.

7. $4.82 + 6.79$
8. $9.11 - 4.76$
9. $5.2 - 3.56$

10. $18.234 + 14.767$
11. $27.843 - 26.2$
12. $9.7 - 1.24$

Think About It

13. Describe the relationship between the dimensions of a cylinder and a cone that have equal volumes.

Solving Equations

You have explored formulas to find the volume of a pyramid or a cone. Other formulas can help you study other quantities and patterns.

ACTIVITY 1 Number Sentences

With Your Class An **equation** is a type of number sentence that uses the equals sign to show that two quantities are equal.

1 Some equations include variables, letters that can stand for any number. An **open sentence** includes one or more variables. A **closed sentence** includes only numbers. Classify each of the following sentences as open or closed.

$$25 + 136 = 161 \qquad 6 + 7 = 8 + 5$$

$$254 - y = 248 \qquad 6z - 3 = 45$$

$$1\tfrac{1}{2} \times 4\tfrac{3}{4} = 7\tfrac{1}{8} \qquad 16 \times \tfrac{1}{2} = n$$

$$15.6 \div c = 3.9 \qquad 5a = 3a + 8$$

2 Any number that makes an open sentence true is a **solution** for the equation. For each open sentence above, replace the variable with these numbers: 2, 4, 6, 8. Write the solution for each.

CONNECT AND COMMUNICATE

In Your Journal Explain why formulas for volume and area are examples of equations.

ACTIVITY 2 Planet Patterns

With Your Partner In the 1700s scientists noticed a growth pattern in the distances of planets from the sun. The equation describing this pattern is:

$$d = (4 + 3n) \div 10$$

In this equation *d* stands for the distance measured in astronomical units (AU). One AU is the distance from the sun to Earth. For the first five planets and the ring of tiny planets known as asteroids, the value for *n* is in the set {0, 1, 2, 4, 8, 16}. Use the equation and the values for *n* to find the distance in AUs of planets from the sun.

To help you find the numbers that make an equation true, think of an equation as an if . . . then sentence. In 3x = y, if x is 1, then y is 3.

TOOLS AND TECHNIQUES

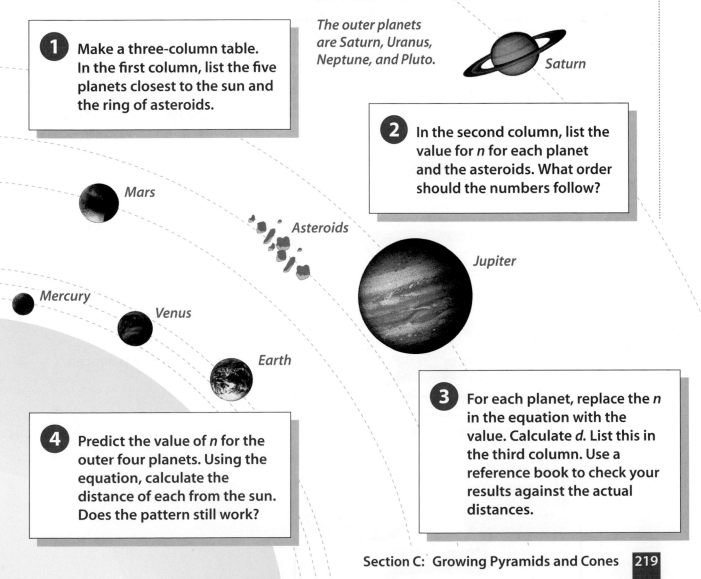

1 Make a three-column table. In the first column, list the five planets closest to the sun and the ring of asteroids.

The outer planets are Saturn, Uranus, Neptune, and Pluto.

Saturn

2 In the second column, list the value for *n* for each planet and the asteroids. What order should the numbers follow?

Mars

Asteroids

Jupiter

Mercury

Venus

Earth

3 For each planet, replace the *n* in the equation with the value. Calculate *d*. List this in the third column. Use a reference book to check your results against the actual distances.

4 Predict the value of *n* for the outer four planets. Using the equation, calculate the distance of each from the sun. Does the pattern still work?

Section C: Growing Pyramids and Cones   **219**

^{ACTIVITY}3 Balancing Act

With Your Class You can use what you know about properties to solve equations. Find the height of a pyramid with a volume of 40 in.³ and a base with an area of 10 in.²

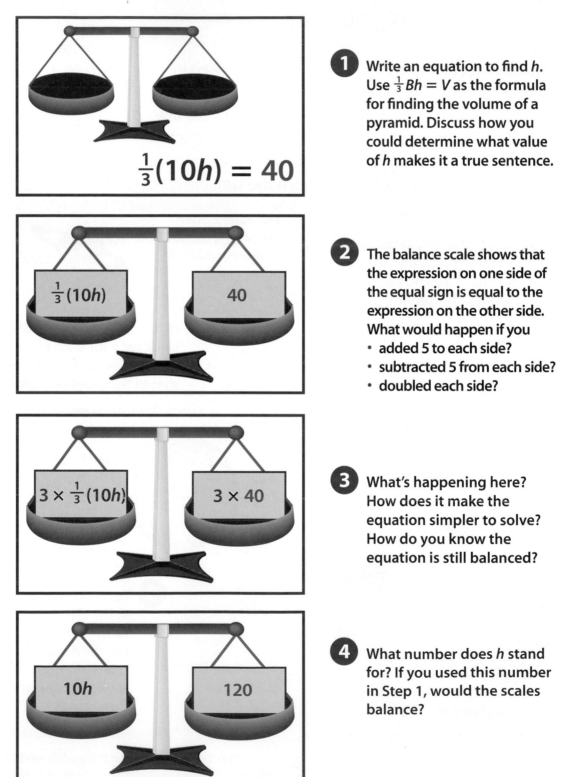

$$\frac{1}{3}(10h) = 40$$

1 Write an equation to find *h*. Use $\frac{1}{3}Bh = V$ as the formula for finding the volume of a pyramid. Discuss how you could determine what value of *h* makes it a true sentence.

$\frac{1}{3}(10h)$ 40

2 The balance scale shows that the expression on one side of the equal sign is equal to the expression on the other side. What would happen if you
- added 5 to each side?
- subtracted 5 from each side?
- doubled each side?

$3 \times \frac{1}{3}(10h)$ 3×40

3 What's happening here? How does it make the equation simpler to solve? How do you know the equation is still balanced?

$10h$ 120

4 What number does *h* stand for? If you used this number in Step 1, would the scales balance?

With Your Partner

Write three equations. Trade with your partner. Draw a balance scale showing your partner's equations. Explain how you could make each equation simpler to solve. Describe a situation that each equation might represent.

To gain skill in working with equations, try making a simple equation more complex. Show how to make $x = 7$ into $(x + 9) \div 6 = (7 + 9) \div 6$.

Do You Remember?

Try It!

What would you do to each side of the equation to make it easier to find the solution?

1. $a - 607 = 231$ 2. $6b = 258$ 3. $c \div 8 = 24$

4. $149 + d = 372$ 5. $9m - 15 = 12$ 6. $19 + 8 = 3x$

7. $y + 7.2 = 9.1$ 8. $18 = 4z$ 9. $\frac{3}{4} - \frac{1}{4} = 2n$

Estimate each quotient. Find an exact answer for quotients between 40 and 60.

10. $6 \div 0.11$ 11. $10 \div 0.2$ 12. $40 \div 1.7$

13. $5 \div 2.3$ 14. $60 \div 0.9$ 15. $160 \div 3.9$

Think About It

16. Describe the steps you would take to solve $y + 15 = 4y - 3$.

LESSON
10

Line Segments

Trees, sixth graders, and line segments have growth patterns that do not always match addition or multiplication patterns. Get ready to explore these other growth patterns.

ACTIVITY
1 **Triangular Numbers**

With Your Partner How does the total number of segments grow as you add points to a line segment?

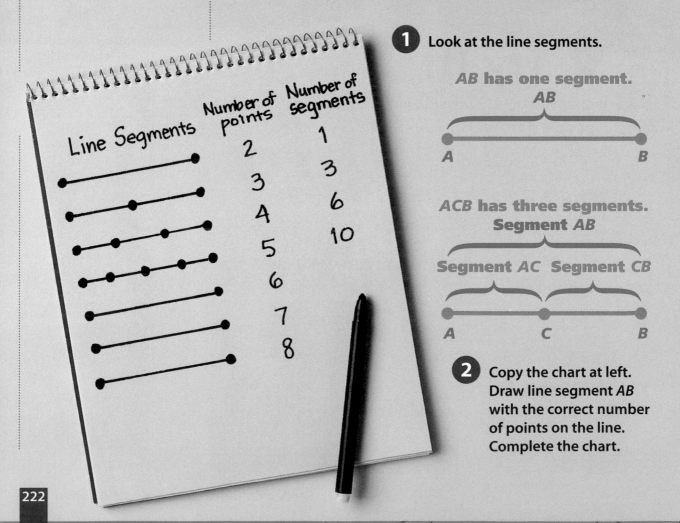

Number of points	Number of segments
2	1
3	3
4	6
5	10
6	
7	
8	

1 Look at the line segments.

AB has one segment.

A —————————— B

ACB has three segments.
Segment *AB*

Segment *AC*   Segment *CB*

A ———— C ———— B

2 Copy the chart at left. Draw line segment *AB* with the correct number of points on the line. Complete the chart.

With Your Group The bowling pins below form a triangle. How do the numbers in the triangle compare with the number of line segments in the chart?

10

6

3

1

You can also use drawing to explore the pattern of triangular numbers. Try extending this pattern:

3 Suppose you wanted to know how many segments are in a line segment with 42 points. How could you find out without drawing or labeling the line segments?

a. Do you see a pattern in the numbers?
b. How does each number in the series differ, from the next.

ACTIVITY 2 Division of Fractions

With Your Partner You can also use line segments to learn about division of fractions.

1 Use the ruler below to do $2 \div \frac{1}{4} = ?$ two ways.

    a. Think, "How many $\frac{1}{4}$-in. segments are in 2 in.?"

    b. Think, "How many $\frac{1}{4}$-in. segments are in 1 in.?" Why can you multiply to find the number of segments in 2 in?

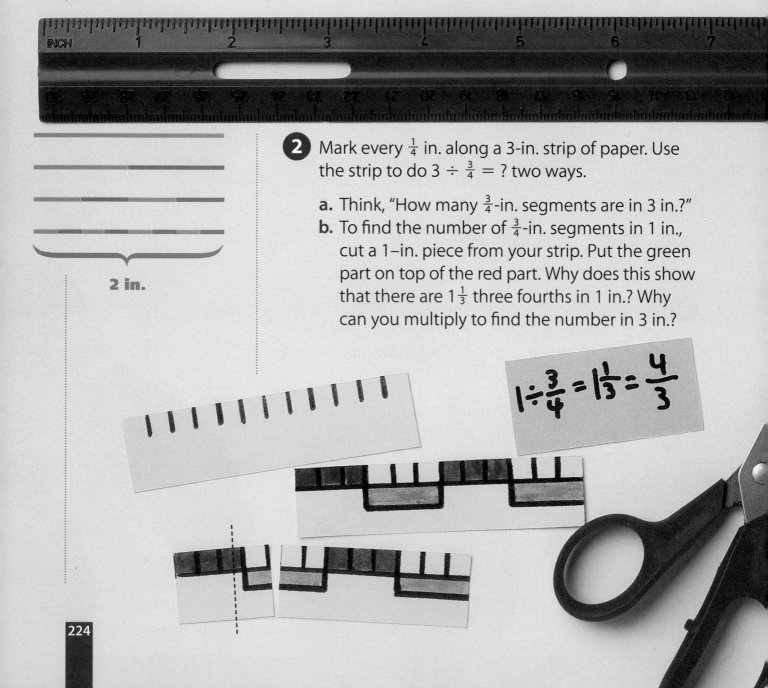

2 in.

2 Mark every $\frac{1}{4}$ in. along a 3-in. strip of paper. Use the strip to do $3 \div \frac{3}{4} = ?$ two ways.

    a. Think, "How many $\frac{3}{4}$-in. segments are in 3 in.?"

    b. To find the number of $\frac{3}{4}$-in. segments in 1 in., cut a 1–in. piece from your strip. Put the green part on top of the red part. Why does this show that there are $1\frac{1}{3}$ three fourths in 1 in.? Why can you multiply to find the number in 3 in.?

$$1 \div \frac{3}{4} = 1\frac{1}{3} = \frac{4}{3}$$

3 How can you use the information in Step 2 to explain why $3 \div \frac{3}{4} = 3 \times \frac{4}{3}$?

   a. How many $\frac{3}{4}$-in. segments are in $3\frac{3}{4}$-in.? Explain how you got your answer.

   b. How many $\frac{3}{4}$-in. segments are in the 12-in. ruler? Find the answer three ways.

✔ **Self-Check** *In Lesson 2 you saw that dividing by a number is the same as multiplying by its reciprocal. How can you use that fact to help you divide by a fraction?*

$3\frac{3}{4}$ in.

Do You Remember?

Try It!

Find each quotient. Write your answer in simplest terms.

1. $2 \div \frac{1}{10}$ **2.** $2 \div \frac{1}{20}$ **3.** $3 \div \frac{3}{5}$ **4.** $\frac{15}{16} \div \frac{3}{2}$

5. $2 \div \frac{1}{5}$ **6.** $3 \div \frac{6}{5}$ **7.** $\frac{1}{2} \div \frac{8}{5}$ **8.** $3 \div \frac{12}{5}$

Tell which of the following length units would be appropriate to measure the objects: km, m, cm, or mm.

   9. an apple   **10.** a pencil point   **11.** a mountain

   12. a desk   **13.** a tennis ball   **14.** your height

Think About It

15. Write the quotients from Exercises 1–8 in order from least to greatest. Describe any pattern you find.

LESSON (11) Fibonacci Numbers

In the 1100s Leonardo Fibonacci used a number pattern to describe the growth of rabbit populations. The first numbers in Fibonacci sequence are shown below. Since Fibonacci's time, people have discovered that the Fibonacci numbers describe many patterns in nature, including the spiral shapes of parrot beaks, pine cones, nautilus shells, and even some galaxies.

1, 1, 2, 3, 5, 8, 13, ?, ?, ?

ACTIVITY 1 Fantastic Fractions

With Your Group See if you can name the next three numbers in the series above. Then use the numbers to make some remarkable fractions.

1 What can you say about any three consecutive numbers? How can you find any number, *n*, in the series?

2 Use the first six Fibonacci numbers to make the fractions shown in the notebook.

3 Divide the first fraction by the second fraction.

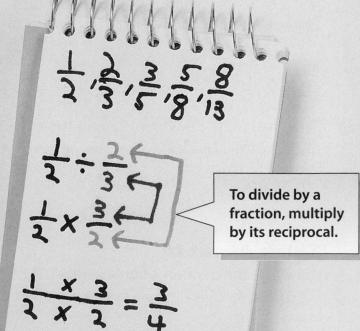

$$\frac{1}{2}, \frac{2}{3}, \frac{3}{5}, \frac{5}{8}, \frac{8}{13}$$

$$\frac{1}{2} \div \frac{2}{3}$$

$$\frac{1}{2} \times \frac{3}{2}$$

To divide by a fraction, multiply by its reciprocal.

$$\frac{1}{2} \times \frac{3}{2 \times 2} = \frac{3}{4}$$

4 Now divide the second fraction by the third, the third by the fourth, and so on. What pattern do you see in the quotients?

5 Tell whether you think the pattern will continue. Test your prediction. Use your calculator to divide these Fibonacci fractions.

In Your Journal Write a note to a friend describing the pattern you found in your own fractions.

$$\frac{1,597}{2,584} \qquad \frac{2,584}{4,181} \qquad \frac{4,181}{6,765}$$

ACTIVITY 2 **Personal Fibonaccis**

With Your Partner Try using your own fractions to make a pattern.

1 Pick two numbers–for example, 4 and 7.

first number 4
second number 7
third number 4+7=11

2 Use the numbers to make a series of five increasing numbers.

4, 7, 11, 18, 29, . . .

3 Use consecutive numbers from the sequence to make at least four fractions.

$$\frac{4}{7}, \quad \frac{7}{11}, \quad \frac{11}{18}, \quad \frac{18}{29}, \ldots$$

4 Divide each fraction by the next one.

$$\frac{4}{7} \div \frac{7}{11} = \frac{4}{7} \times \frac{11}{7}$$

5 Describe any pattern you see in the quotients.

$$\frac{44}{49} \qquad \frac{126}{121}$$

To show that a number is a repeating decimal, write a bar over the numbers that repeat.

$\frac{1}{3} = 0.\overline{33}$

$\frac{8}{9} = 0.\overline{88}$

$\frac{6}{7} = 0.\overline{857142}$

What You'll Need
- *centimeter ruler*
- *11 in. × 17 in. paper*

ACTIVITY 3 Fraction to Decimal

With Your Partner Like any fraction, a Fibonacci fraction is a way of representing division. For example, $\frac{1}{2} = 2)\overline{1.0}$, giving 0.5.

1 Divide to find the decimal form of these fractions.
   a. $\frac{2}{3}$ **b.** $\frac{3}{5}$ **c.** $\frac{5}{8}$ **d.** $\frac{34}{55}$

2 Place the fractions into two groups: (1) decimals that terminate, or end, and (2) decimals that repeat.

3 Use your calculator to explore patterns in the decimal form of fractions that have denominators of 7, 9, or 11.

ACTIVITY 4 Draw a Spiral

With Your Partner Use what you know about rectangles, squares, and diagonals to draw a spiral.

1 Draw a 377 mm × 233 mm rectangle on your sheet of paper. Draw another line to make a square with sides of 233 mm.

2 Draw a diagonal from the lower left corner of the rectangle to the upper right corner of the square.

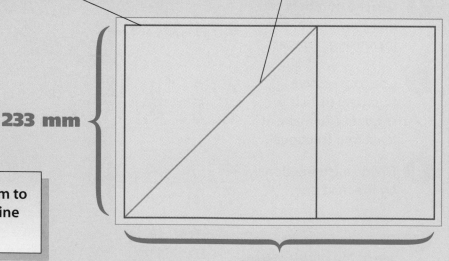

233 mm

Use 1 cm = 10 mm to help you draw a line 377 mm long.

377 mm

144 mm

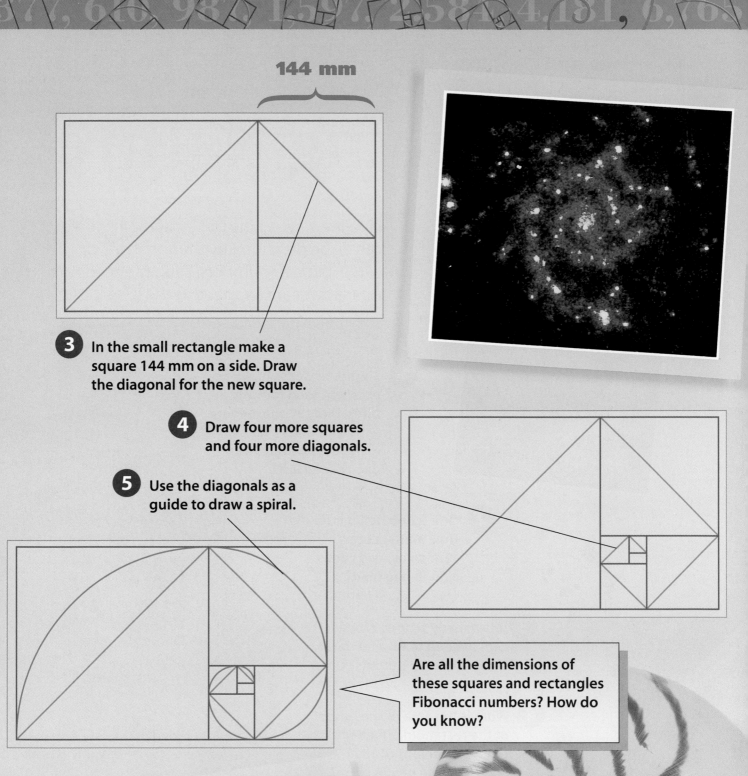

3 In the small rectangle make a square 144 mm on a side. Draw the diagonal for the new square.

4 Draw four more squares and four more diagonals.

5 Use the diagonals as a guide to draw a spiral.

Are all the dimensions of these squares and rectangles Fibonacci numbers? How do you know?

Exercises and Problems

Spiraling Nature

Pipeline waves, pine cones, and pineapples can all be described by the spiral drawn with Fibonacci numbers. Even the seeds on a sunflower are arranged in these spirals!

1 Sunflower seeds make an excellent food for wild birds. Birds at one feeder eat $1\frac{3}{4}$ pounds a day. How many days will a 25-lb bag of seed last?

2 One scoop holds $\frac{3}{8}$ lb. How many scoops of sunflower seeds does a 50-lb bag hold?

3 How many scoops of seeds are needed to fill a feeder that holds $2\frac{1}{2}$ pounds?

4 What is the area of the base of the rectangular feeder that has a height of 18 in and a volume of 528 cu in.?

5 What is the volume of a cylindrical birdfeeder that has a radius of $1\frac{1}{2}$ in. and a height of 14 in.?

6 Five pineapples will serve 11 people. How many pineapples will you need to serve your class? Explain your answer.

7 Estimate the number of $4\frac{1}{4}$ lb pineapples that can be shipped in a box that holds 24 lb.

8 An art project calls for 13 pine cones cut in quarters. How many quarters are there.

9 One pine cone weighs about $\frac{5}{16}$ lb. How many whole pine cones are in a 6 lb carton if the carton itself weighs $\frac{1}{2}$ lb?

10 Trace the nautilus shell. Sketch a set of rectangles, squares, and diagonals like those on pages 228–229 to show how Fibonacci numbers can describe the shell.

Section D: Other Ways to Grow **231**

LESSON (12) Growing Green

You've explored several growth patterns. Some plants, like pine trees, grow in two different ways. Pine cones grow in spirals, while the trees grow vertically.

ACTIVITY 1 Two Feet, Tree Feet

With Your Partner You know that as a tree gets older, it grows taller. But how tall will a tree be when it reaches 30 years old? In the next activity, you will use a graph to study a tree's growth pattern.

1 The graph shows the average growth of three kinds of trees. How tall do you think each tree will be in five more years? Explain.

Average Growth of Pines and Firs:

Bristlecone pine: one to four in. a year throughout lifetime

Douglas fir: four to six in. a year to four feet, 12 to 18 in. a year till maturity

White pine: 12 in. a year to ten years, 24 to 36 in. a year to forty. 12 in. a year until harvest

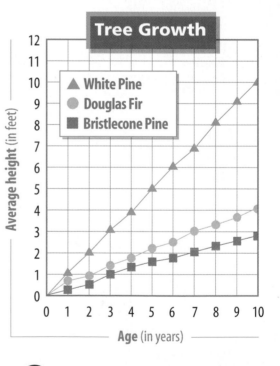

Tree Growth

▲ White Pine
● Douglas Fir
■ Bristlecone Pine

Average height (in feet) vs. Age (in years)

2 Use the data at left to show the growth pattern of each kind of tree to age 30. Decide how you will graph 12 to 18 in. a year.

3 Describe any patterns you see. Use the graph to estimate the height of each kind of tree at age 15. How does this estimate compare with your prediction? Explain.

ACTIVITY 2 My, You've Grown

With Your Partner Of course, graphs can help you see patterns in human growth too.

1 Use the data in the chart below to make two graphs. Both boys and girls are about 49 in. tall at age 8.

2 Tell whether the growth spurts look like growth by addition or by multiplication.

3 Estimate where you are on the graph. How could you estimate what your height will be in three years?

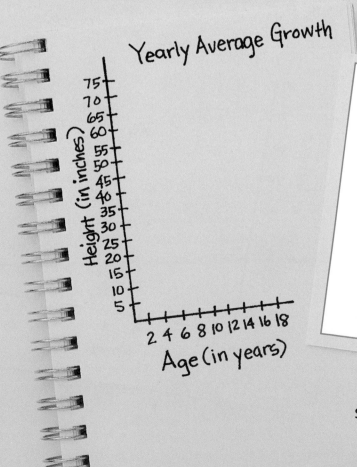

Yearly Average Growth

Average growth per year, ages 9 to 18, in inches		
Age	Female	Male
9	$1\frac{1}{2}$	$1\frac{1}{4}$
10	$2\frac{1}{2}$	$1\frac{1}{4}$
11	$2\frac{1}{4}$	2
12	$2\frac{1}{4}$	3
13	3	$2\frac{1}{2}$
14	$2\frac{1}{2}$	$2\frac{1}{2}$
15	$1\frac{1}{2}$	$2\frac{1}{2}$
16	$\frac{1}{4}$	2
17	0	2
18	0	2

ACTIVITY 3 Feet and Height

With Your Class The graphs in Activities 1 and 2 helped you see a growth pattern. Graphs can also help you see if there is a pattern at all. Make a scatterplot to see if height and shoe size are related.

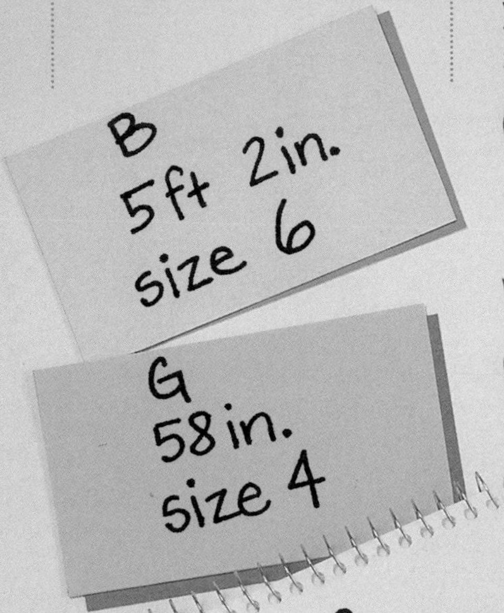

1 Write your height and your shoe size on a slip of paper. Write B for boy or G for girl. Place all paper slips in a box.

With Your Group

2 Take 20 slips of paper from the box. Record the data in a chart and place the slips back in the box.

3 Use the data in your chart to make a scatterplot. Decide if the points of the scatterplot look as if they are in a line.

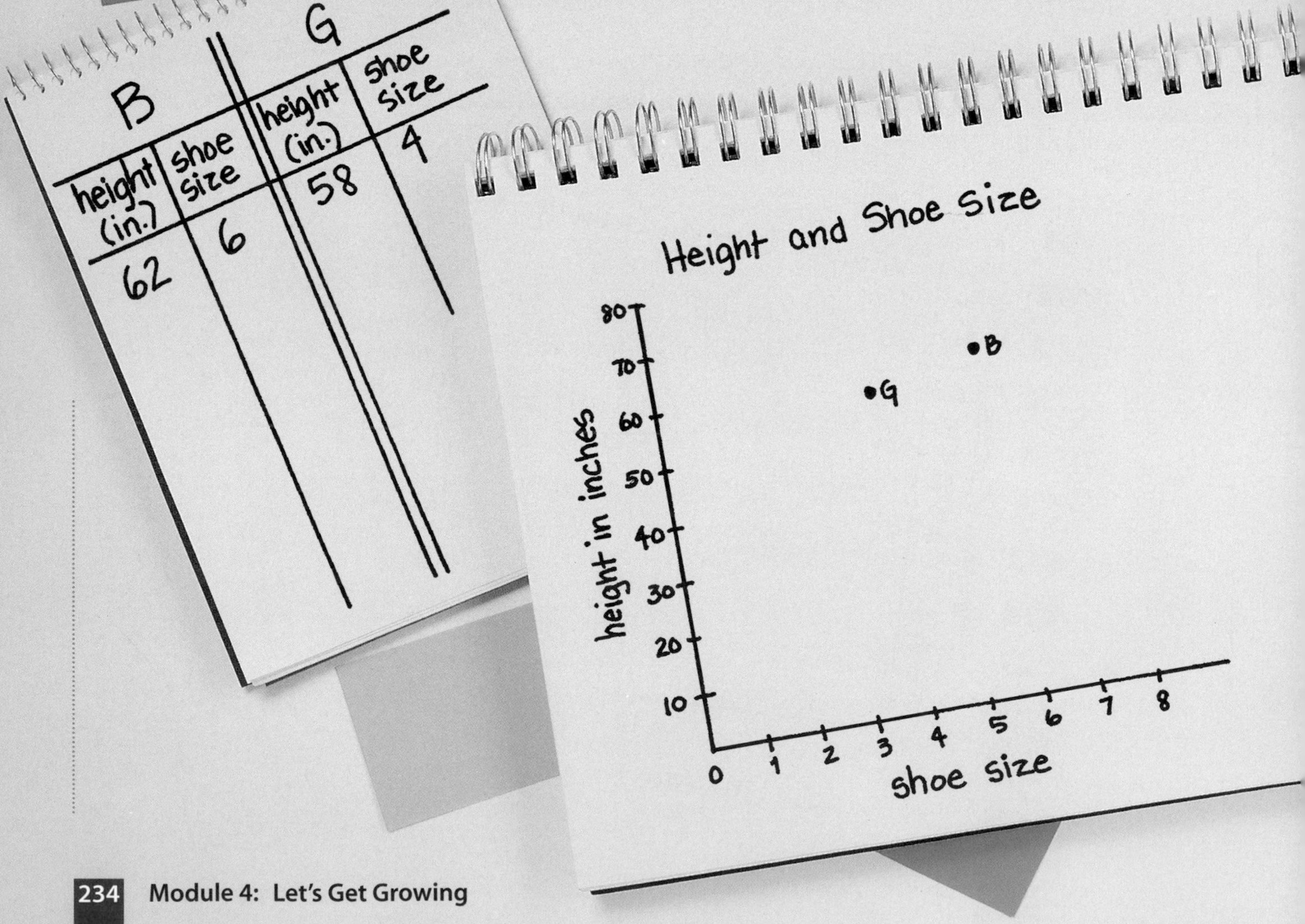

B
5 ft 2 in.
size 6

G
58 in.
size 4

B		G	
height (in.)	shoe size	height (in.)	shoe size
62	6	58	4

Height and Shoe Size

4 Compare your data with the data graphed by another group. What conclusions can you draw about height and shoe size? Explain.

What do you think the graph would look like if you graphed actual foot length rather than shoe size? Explain.

Do You Remember?

Try It!

Describe what you think these graphs would look like.

1. growth of a city's population
2. temperature of iced tea in sunshine
3. the number of dollars in a savings account if you withdrew $2 one week, $4 dollars the second week, $8 the third week and so on
4. growth of a puppy to an adult dog

Solve each equation.

5. 42 in. = y ft
6. s dm = 100 cm
7. $19\frac{1}{2}$ yd = t ft

8. 3,000 m = j km
9. h qt = 168 oz
10. 14 mi = k yd

Think About It

11. Which of the Exercises 1–4 has a graph that shows how a number shrinks? Explain.

Looking Back

Choose the right answer. Write *a, b, c,* or *d* for each question.

1. The square root of 73 is between which two numbers?

   a. 0 and 1
   b. 4 and 5
   c. 8 and 9
   d. 12 and 13

2. Which pattern includes 100?

   a. 1, 2, 4, 8, . . .
   b. 1, 3, 5, 7, . . .
   c. 1, 4, 9, 16, . . .
   d. 1, 5, 9, 13, . . .

3. In which would you multiply each side of the equation by 3 to find the solution?

   a. $\frac{n}{3} = 62 - 5$
   b. $3n = \frac{14}{6}$
   c. $n - 3 = 12 + 6$
   d. $3 + n = 32 \times 4$

4. Which pair of expressions have the same difference?

   a. $4b - 2b$ and $5b - 3b$
   b. $9b - 4b$ and $5b - 1b$
   c. $9b - 8b$ and $9b - 7b$
   d. $7b - 5b$ and $8b - 5b$

5. What does $\frac{3}{8} \times \frac{5}{8}$ equal?

   a. $\frac{3 \times 5}{8}$
   b. $\frac{3 \times 8}{8}$
   c. $\frac{3 \times 5}{8 \times 8}$
   d. $\frac{3 \times 8}{8 \times 5}$

Use the diagram of the pyramid to answer item 6.

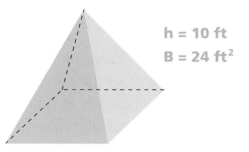

h = 10 ft
B = 24 ft²

6. What is the volume of the pyramid?

   a. 480 ft³
   b. 240 ft³
   c. 120 ft³
   d. 80 ft³

7. Which equals $4(9 - 2) + 3$?

   a. $(4 \times 9) - 4(2 + 3)$
   b. $4(9 - 2 + 3)$
   c. $(4 \times 9 - 4 \times 2) + 3$
   d. $4(9 - 2) + 4 \times 3$

8. What is the product of $1\frac{3}{4} \times 3\frac{1}{3}$?

   a. $5\frac{5}{6}$ b. $3\frac{1}{4}$
   c. 6   d. $4\frac{3}{4}$

9. What is the quotient of $4 \div \frac{2}{5}$?

   a. 5   b. $1\frac{3}{5}$
   c. 20   d. 10

10. What does $19 \div \frac{3}{8}$ equal?

    a. $19 \times \frac{8}{3}$ b. $\frac{19}{3} \times \frac{1}{8}$
    c. $19 \times 3 \div 8$ d. $19 \div 8 \times 3$

Answer items 11 and 12 based on the diagram of the parallelogram.

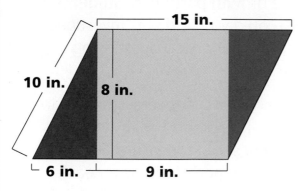

15 in.

10 in.

8 in.

6 in.

9 in.

11. What is the area of the red triangle?

    a. 48 in.^{2}
    b. 24 in.^{2}
    c. 20 in.^{2}
    d. 16 in.^{2}

12. What is the area of the parallelogram?

    a. 120 in.^{2}
    b. 72 in.^{2}
    c. 150 in.^{2}
    d. 60 in.^{2}

Use the diagram of the cone to answer item 13.

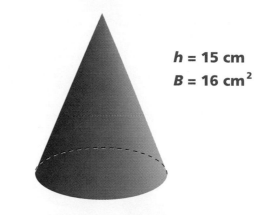

$h = 15$ cm
$B = 16$ cm^2

13. What is the volume of a cone twice as tall as the one shown?

    a. 240 cm^3 b. 160 cm^3
    c. 60 cm^3 d. 80 cm^3

14. Which are Fibonacci numbers?

    a. 13, 21, 34
    b. 34, 57, 90
    c. 148, 239, 387
    d. 626, 737, 848

Check Your Math Power

15. Sketch and label a pyramid and a cone with the same volume but with different bases.

16. List the seventh number in the pattern 3, 4, 6, ... Explain your answer.

17. Sketch and label the dimensions of two different parallelograms that each have an area of $9\frac{3}{8}$ in.^{2}

MODULE 4 Investigations

Way to Grow!

Investigation A How Kids Grow

What is the growth pattern for students in your school? How could you find out? Investigate growth patterns with your group by studying a variety of students.

1 **Measure** the heights of several students in different grades. Decide how many students in each grade you should measure. Find the median, mean, and mode heights for each grade. Choose a way to organize your data.

2 **Analyze** your data. Look for growth patterns. Describe any pattern you find. Is it an addition or a multiplication pattern? How can you show the pattern clearly?

3 **Predict** height based on your data. How tall would you expect a student in grade 7 to be? In grade 8? In grade 9?

4 **Write** a report summarizing your data. Explain why you presented it as you did and what conclusions you reached. Tell how it compares to the average data on page 233.

Keep in Mind

Your report will be judged by how well you do the following things.

☐ How accurately do you gather, record, and report your data?

☐ Do you present the data in a way that shows growth patterns?

☐ How clearly do you present your conclusions? How well does your data support the conclusions?

Investigation B Plant Growth

If you want to predict how tall a plant will be after growing for 60 days, you need to know how fast that plant usually grows. With your group or class, determine the growth pattern for a plant.

1 Choose one type of plant to grow. Use pots or jars of varying sizes. Once the plant sprouts, measure its height every other day for 20 days.

2 Combine the results from all the groups on a large graph. How would you describe the growth? How can you use your data to predict how your plant will grow?

3 Compare the quantity of dirt or volume of water in each container. Explain whether the volume of the container influences the growth pattern. of your plant.

Ongoing Investigation Tessellating Triangles

You've made tessellations with equilateral triangles. Now extend your investigation to isosceles and scalene triangles. To make your patterns, you can use your Geometry Tool or draw your own triangles. Add your tessellations to your portfolio. Also include a note describing the strategies you used. Do all triangles tessellate?

MODULE 5

Step Right Up

Have you been to an amusement park, carnival, or fair and gone home with some souvenirs? Perhaps these souvenirs were tiny or oversized models. In this unit you'll learn about the relationship between fractions, decimals, and percents and between one quantity and another.

SECTION A

Exploring Ratios

SECTION B

Representing Ratios

SECTION C

Predicting with Proportions

SECTION D

Estimating with Percents

The Big and Small of It

Have you ever seen tiny sneakers on a key ring, a giant hat, or a large hand signaling "We're number one!"? How closely do miniature or oversized items resemble the real thing?

1 Look Closely

Choose a classroom object, such as a pencil, a marker, your shoe, or your hand. Look at the object closely. Notice how long and how wide it is. Does it have any special features?

2 Draw It

Draw the object so that the picture is twice as big as the object. Then draw the object so that the picture is half the object's size.

3 Compare

How did you make your drawing twice as big as the actual object? Did you double the length and the width? What would happen if you doubled only one?

Word Bank
- **equivalent ratio**
- **percent bar**
- **proportion**
- **rate**
- **ratio**
- **unit rate**

Investigations Preview

Learn how to use ratio, proportion, and percent bars. With these skills you can explore why ratio is important and design a successful carnival game.

Fun-house Mirrors (pages 272–273)

How does a fun-house mirror work? Knowing ratios will help you understand how they show objects out of proportion.

Come One, Come All (pages 286–288)

How would you design a carnival game?
Use what you learn about ratios to plan a carnival game and predict how often people will win it.

LESSON 1 What's in the Mix?

What makes a carnival fun? Is it the mixture of games and rides? Maybe it's the mixture of sounds in the music. It could be the mixture of water, sugar, and lemon juice in the lemonade. How can you study these mixtures?

ACTIVITY 1 **Matching Mixes**

With Your Class Each bag pictured below holds a different mixture of brown sugar and white sugar. Analyze the bags. If you want, try this activity with three bags, each containing 12 teaspoons of sugar—but different amounts of brown and white sugar in each.

What You'll Need
- *3 plastic bags*
- *brown sugar*
- *white sugar*
- *measuring spoons*

1 Arrange the bags from darkest to lightest. How does the amount of each kind of sugar change the color?

A

2 Discuss how you decided to arrange the bags. What does the order suggest about how much brown sugar and how much white sugar each bag holds? Estimate the amount of each type of sugar in each bag.

Imagine what a larger bag would look like if it had 2 cups of brown sugar and 1 cup of white sugar. Discuss whether the unit of measure makes any difference in ratios.

3 If one bag includes 2 teaspoons of brown sugar for each teaspoon of white sugar, how much brown sugar is in the bag?

4 Discuss how you would write comparisons of the amount of brown sugar and white sugar in each bag.

ACTIVITY 2 Comparing Colors

With Your Partner Can you order other color mixtures? Do either Exercise 1 or 2 below.

1 Find five or more different shades of green. With your partner, order them according to the amount of blue and yellow in each.

2 Make four mixtures using different amounts of two colors of paint or food coloring. Have your partner order them according to the amount of one of the colors.

Which would be darker, 5 drops of blue with 3 drops of yellow or 2 drops of blue with 2 drops of yellow?

ACTIVITY 3 Ratio Draw

With Your Partner In many carnivals people buy all ride tickets at one booth. Though all tickets cost the same, some rides require several tickets. You can use a **ratio,** a comparison of two quantities, to analyze how to use tickets.

1 Which of these are ratios? Explain.
8 tickets for $10
6 tickets for Tuesday
3 tickets for 1 ride

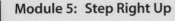

2 There are three ways to write a ratio of 2 tickets to 1 ride. Write three other ratios in three different ways.

How is 2:1 different from 1:2?

2 to 1

2:1

$\frac{2}{1}$

3 The roller coaster costs 5 tickets. Imagine you bought 10 tickets at the carnival. The picture in the notebook shows a way to represent the relationship.

a. Draw a picture to show how you might use 18 tickets for 2 rides that cost 6 tickets each. Label your drawing to show ratios.

b. Draw and label a picture showing 10 tickets used for 3 rides that cost 3 tickets each.

DRAWING TO LEARN

Draw a picture to show how 16 students for every 2 chaperones differs from 15 students for every 2 chaperones.

Explain whether 5 rides per hour and 1 hour per 5 rides *give the same information. Would you use them to solve different problems?*

4 You have 16 tickets. You want to go on 2 rides. One ride costs 3 tickets. The other costs 2 tickets.
  a. Show three ways of using up all of your tickets on these rides.
  b. How many extra tickets would you need to buy to go on each ride the same number of times? Explain.

Do You Remember?

Try It!

Write the ratio in a different way. Draw a picture like the example on page 247 to show the ratio.

1. 6 to 2

2. $\frac{12}{2}$

3. 17 to 3

4. 6:3

5. 13 to 3

6. $\frac{9}{3}$

Write >, <, or =.

7. $\frac{3}{8}$ ■ $\frac{6}{16}$

8. $\frac{9}{8}$ ■ $1\frac{1}{4}$

9. $\frac{3}{4}$ ■ $\frac{5}{8}$

10. $\frac{7}{4}$ ■ $1\frac{3}{4}$

11. $\frac{2}{5}$ ■ $\frac{4}{10}$

12. $2\frac{2}{5}$ ■ $\frac{12}{5}$

Think About It

13. If the ratios in Exercises 3–6 showed the number of tickets to rides, which ride would be most expensive? Explain.

Make That Ratio

Besides offering lots of food and rides to entertain you, carnivals sometimes have games to play. Here's a game that uses ratios.

ACTIVITY 1 The Trait Challenge

With Your Partner In this activity use ratios with shapes in geometry.

1 Select eight or more shapes on your Geometry Tool to trace and cut out. Some of the shapes may be the same and some may be different.

What You'll Need

- *Geometry Tool or shapes to trace*
- *scissors*
- *colored paper or crayons*

249

Try using base ten blocks or pattern blocks to play the game.

 Place the cut-out shapes edge to edge to create new shapes. For example, you could use two triangles to make a square. Create five other shapes, such as parallelograms or hexagons. You may need to cut out more shapes. Describe each new shape in writing and by using ratios.

 Trade shapes and descriptions with another pair of students. Based on the descriptions, try to make the same new shapes.

4 Compare your description of each relationship with the other pair's. Are they the same?

Look at the picture. What is the ratio of triangles to squares? of squares to triangles? Why does order in these ratios matter?

5 Use relationships you and your partner have described. Make multiple versions of each pattern. Two ratios that represent the same relationship are **equivalent ratios.** Sketch at least one equivalent ratio for three of your patterns.

What is the ratio of triangles to squares?

Is the ratio of triangles to squares 2:1 or 4:2? Explain.

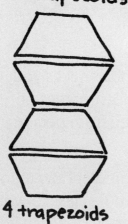

2 trapezoids   1 hexagon

$\frac{2}{1}$

$\frac{4}{2}$

4 trapezoids   2 hexagons

ACTIVITY 2 Sign down the Line

With Your Group At some amusement park rides signs tell you how long you will probably have to wait in line. Discuss how ratios help parks determine estimated time in line. Then use ratios to estimate time in a classroom activity.

1 Write the ratio of the number of people waiting at the first sign to the number of minutes they will be waiting.

People	20	40	60
Minutes	15	x	y

15 MINUTE WAIT

30 MINUTE WAIT

45 MINUTE WAIT

Explain how the number sentence $\frac{20}{15} = \frac{40}{x}$ describes the wait at the second sign. Write a number sentence for the wait at the third sign.

TOOLS AND TECHNIQUES

Just as you can write a fraction in simplest terms, you can write a ratio in simplest terms. What other numbers can you use to write the ratio 10 to 2?

2 Record the number of seconds it takes your group to write their first and last names on a sheet of paper that is passed from person to person.

3 Use this amount of time to predict how many seconds it would take the whole class to write their names on a sheet of paper. How can you describe this as a ratio?

With Your Class Make a chart showing each group's time and the group's estimate of the total class time. Then send a sheet of paper through the class for each person to sign. Record the total time. Which prediction was closest? Discuss how groups made their predictions.

CONNECT AND COMMUNICATE

In Your Journal When during the school day do you stand in line? Describe the situation. How could you use ratios to estimate the length of time you might have to wait?

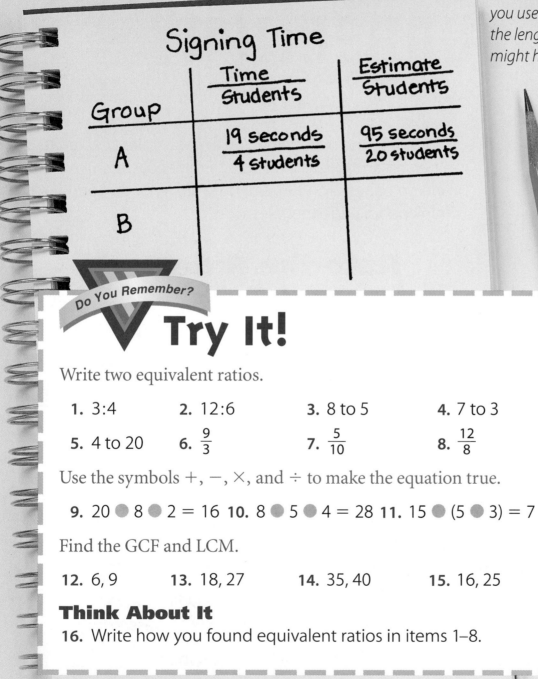

Signing Time

Group	Time / Students	Estimate / Students
A	19 seconds / 4 students	95 seconds / 20 students
B		

Do You Remember?

Try It!

Write two equivalent ratios.

1. 3:4   **2.** 12:6   **3.** 8 to 5   **4.** 7 to 3

5. 4 to 20   **6.** $\frac{9}{3}$ **7.** $\frac{5}{10}$ **8.** $\frac{12}{8}$

Use the symbols $+$, $-$, $\times$, and $\div$ to make the equation true.

9. 20 ● 8 ● 2 = 16   **10.** 8 ● 5 ● 4 = 28   **11.** 15 ● (5 ● 3) = 7

Find the GCF and LCM.

12. 6, 9   **13.** 18, 27   **14.** 35, 40   **15.** 16, 25

Think About It

16. Write how you found equivalent ratios in items 1–8.

SECTION B Representing Ratios

LESSON 3

What's the Connection?

Someone once said, "You enter a roller coaster as a person and exit as a dishrag." Roller coasters, like the one on pages 255–256, can be scary. Why do you think people ride them?

ACTIVITY 1 Rate the Rides

With Your Class What other rides do you think people like? Use the survey below to discover which carnival ride is the class favorite.

In France people call this ride a carrousel. It is known as a roundabout in England. In the United States it is called a merry-go-round.

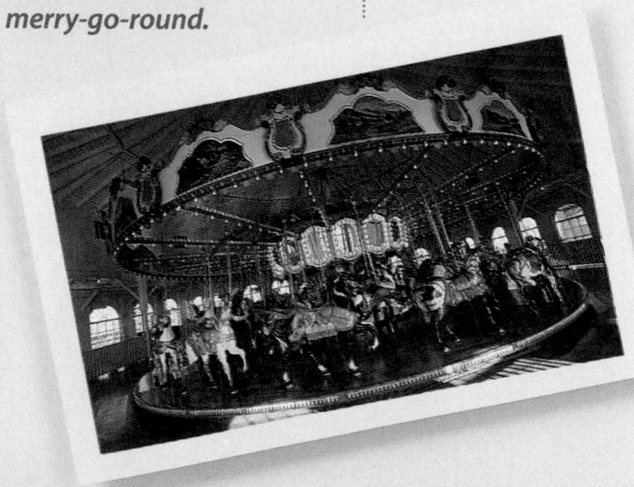

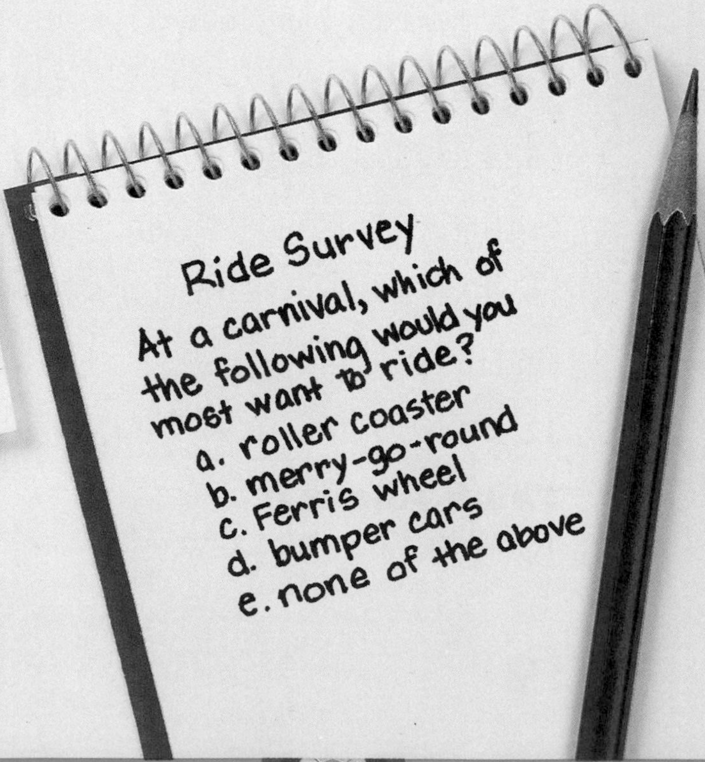

Ride Survey
At a carnival, which of the following would you most want to ride?
a. roller coaster
b. merry-go-round
c. Ferris wheel
d. bumper cars
e. none of the above

With Your Partner Use the data from your class survey to create a pictograph. You may want to combine data with another class.

A ratio can represent information in two ways. Some ratios compare part of the data with the whole amount. Others compare one part with another part. Write two examples of each, using your pictograph.

What is the ratio of people to symbol?

Sixth Grade Survey Results

Roller coaster	🎢🎢🎢🎢🎢
Merry-go-round	🎢🎢
Ferris wheel	🎢🎢🎢
Bumper cars	🎢🎢🎢🎢
None of the above	🎢

🎢 = 3 people

What is the ratio of people who like the Ferris wheel to the total number of people surveyed?

What is the ratio of those who like roller coasters to those who like bumper cars?

After completing your pictograph, redraw it using a different people-to-symbol ratio. Share your pictographs with the class. Discuss whether pictographs show ratios better than bar graphs and line graphs.

The Fair's Wheel

People have been riding wheels at fairs for over 300 years. In 1893 George Ferris, Jr., designed a wheel ride. Since then the ride has been called the Ferris wheel.

1 The tall wheel on the right had 10 individual seats. Write the number of possible passengers per ride as a ratio.

2 In the picture on the right, the ride in the lower left corner has 8 individual seats. Write two ratios comparing it with the tall wheel.

This drawing was made by a traveler in Turkey in 1620.

This wheel was at the Saint Bartholomew Fair in England in 1728.

3 Write the ratio of passengers to each seat for the wheel shown on the left.

4 Look at the wheel on the left. Estimate the total number of passengers per ride as a ratio. How did you make your estimate?

5 In the 1870s, a wheel 20 feet in diameter cost $400. One that was 30 feet in diameter cost $600. How do the ratios compare?

6 George Ferris's wheel had 36 cars that seated 60 people each. The ride was 20 minutes long. Estimate how long you would have waited to ride the wheel if you were 4,000th in line.

The Ferris wheel's first appearance was at the 1893 World's Columbian Exposition in Chicago.

7 People paid 50 cents to ride the first Ferris wheel. How much money was collected for one ride with a full load of people? Use the information given in Exercise 6.

8 Suppose 1,453,611 people rode the Ferris wheel in 9 weeks. Show as a ratio how many people rode per week.

9 Draw a Ferris wheel with a ratio of passengers to total seats of 12 to 3.

10 Sketch two different Ferris wheels that could each hold up to 18 passengers per ride.

257

LESSON 4 Renaming Ratios

Fun House! Games! Food Tent! Carnivals often use banners to attract the crowd's attention. Banners do not always have words. Sometimes they are just colorful designs that catch the eye. Complete Activities 1 and 2. Then do Activity 3 or 4.

ACTIVITY 1 Create a Banner

What You'll Need
- *grid paper*
- *crayons or markers*
- *ruler*

On Your Own Create and design a banner to share with your class. How do you want your banner to look? Do you want it to show your cultural background?

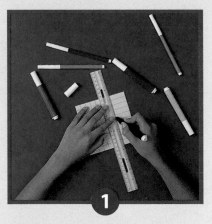

1

Draw a square and divide it into 100 equal parts. Choose three colors to use for your design. Use one color in exactly 30 squares.

2

30 : 100

3

Use your other two colors to fill in the rest of your banner. You may want to leave some squares not colored.

Write ratios to show how much of each color you used compared with each other color. What is the ratio of each color to the total number of squares?

✔ **Self-Check** *How can you change a fraction to a decimal? One way is to find an equivalent fraction with a denominator of 10 or 100. Explain how this method can help you find the percent.*

4 How else can you represent the amount of each color in your banner? Make a chart with three columns. Write your ratios of each color to the whole as fractions. Then write each ratio as a decimal and as a percent.

REASONING AND PROBLEM SOLVING

If you had only 50 squares in your banner, how would the ratios of one color to the whole change?

What You'll Need
- *2 cubes labeled 1–6*

ACTIVITY 2 Quick Conversions

With Your Group Find out how to write any ratio as a fraction, decimal, or percent.

1 Make a chart like the one at left with at least ten rows.

2 Roll number cubes to create a ratio. Write a fraction that is less than or equal to 1. Then write an equivalent decimal.

3 To write a number as a percent, why is it helpful to first write the fraction or the decimal as hundredths? Complete the row by writing the percent.

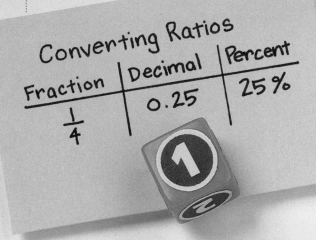

Converting Ratios

Fraction	Decimal	Percent
$\frac{1}{4}$	0.25	25%

With Your Partner Make a chart like the one below. Draw at least ten rows. Fill in one number in each row. Exchange charts with your partner and complete. Check all the conversions with a calculator.

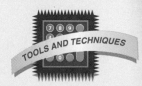

TOOLS AND TECHNIQUES

Calculator Some calculators can change fractions to decimals. If yours does not, divide the numerator by the denominator.

Ratio Conversions

Fractions	Decimals	Percents
	0.05	
$\frac{2}{5}$		
		100%
$\frac{2}{3}$		
	0.75	
		35%

ACTIVITY 3 Match-up

With Your Group Find out how well you can match various representations of the same number.

1 Each player selects a different number between 0 and 1. Players write their number as a decimal, percent, fraction, and ratio on separate cards.

2 Collect the cards and mix them up. Arrange them face down.

What You'll Need
• *cards or slips of paper*

Players may want to add another step to the game. If they turn over a percent or a fraction, they have to correctly draw it on a hundredths' square before they can add it to their cards.

3 The first player turns over two cards. If they represent the same number, the player keeps them and continues. If not, the player turns the cards face down. The next player begins. Whoever collects the most cards wins.

Targeting one

What You'll Need
- *gameboard*
- *game pieces*

ACTIVITY 4 Slide and Convert

With Your Group How well can you convert one type of ratio to another? In this game the winner is the first person to collect and add or subtract numbers to get 1.

1 Take turns dropping your game pieces onto the board. If your game piece lands on more than one number you can choose which to use.

262

2 Read the number your game piece lands on. State two numbers that are equivalent to it. Write the numbers on a chart.

3 Announce when you think that the numbers in your chart can be added or subtracted to make exactly 1. Use your calculator to check your work. If you did not reach exactly 1, start again from 0.

Replay Targeting One. Instead of trying to reach 1, target a different number.

Do You Remember?

Try It!

Match the first number to all of its fraction, decimal, percent, or ratio equivalents in the group.

1. $\frac{1}{4}$, 0.4, 25%, $\frac{4}{100}$ 2. 2:5, $\frac{2}{10}$, 0.40, $\frac{2}{5}$ 3. 75%, $\frac{75}{1}$, 3:4, $\frac{9}{12}$

4. 2:3, 75%, $\frac{3}{2}$, $\frac{2}{3}$ 5. 1.5, 15%, $\frac{1}{15}$, 3:2   6. 40%, $\frac{40}{100}$, 4:10, $\frac{2}{5}$

For each pair of numbers, choose the greater number and write it in words. Then round the lesser number to the nearest tenth.

7. 63.21, 63.121   8. 7.85, 7.701   9. 9.2, 9.11

10. 2.841, 2.481   11. 6.054, 6.54   12. 3.21, 3.29

Think About It

13. Write a rule explaining how to convert a fraction into a decimal and percent.

Carnival Grab Bag

Have you ever bought or won something at a carnival? Answer the questions below. Some of the information you will need is in the picture.

1 Each carnival ticket costs $1.75. How many tickets can you buy for $35.00?

2 What is the ratio of height to depth for the popcorn box?

3 What is the volume of the popcorn box?

4 How many popcorn boxes will fit into a carton 98 cm long, 20 cm wide, and 43 cm high?

5 The popcorn box holds 0.5 g of popcorn per cubic centimeter. What is the mass for all of the popcorn in the box?

6 What metric unit of measure would you use to record the mass of a floating duck like the one shown?

14 cm

5 cm

21.5 cm

delicious nutritious

fresh

POP CORN

POP CORN

DELICIOUS

Net Weight 1.25 OZ.
Net Volume 70 Cu.In.
Reorder Size No. 3-E

ADMIT ONE

7 A game operator started a carnival with 1,000 prize bears. During the first three days, people won 154 bears, 264 bears, and 312 bears. Estimate how many bears were left after three days.

8 What is the volume of the fish tank?

7 cm

22 cm

9 A carnival was open for 7 hours. On average, 145 tickets were sold per hour at $1.75 each. Estimate how much money was received in 5 days.

10 The first-prize bear is bigger than the second-prize bear by a 4:3 ratio. If the second bear is 6 inches tall, how tall is the first-prize bear?

87th Street
CARNIVAL
Corner of 87th and Buena
March 4 – 5

Check Your Math Power

11 A tank 8.5 cm high, 10.5 cm wide, and 13 cm deep holds 25 floating ducks. Sketch three different tanks, each of which has double the capacity and holds 50 ducks.

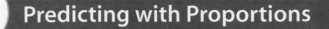

LESSON
5

What's Next?

At a carnival you never know what you will see next. When working with numbers, though, you can make good predictions.

ACTIVITY
1 **4 to 1 and More**

With Your Class In the pictures below, which numbers will make equivalent ratios? Another name for a pair of equivalent ratios is a **proportion.**

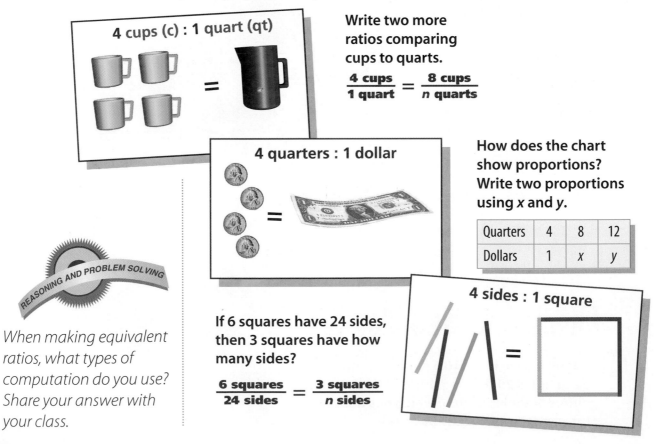

4 cups (c) : 1 quart (qt)

Write two more ratios comparing cups to quarts.

$$\frac{4 \text{ cups}}{1 \text{ quart}} = \frac{8 \text{ cups}}{n \text{ quarts}}$$

4 quarters : 1 dollar

How does the chart show proportions? Write two proportions using x and y.

Quarters	4	8	12
Dollars	1	x	y

REASONING AND PROBLEM SOLVING

When making equivalent ratios, what types of computation do you use? Share your answer with your class.

If 6 squares have 24 sides, then 3 squares have how many sides?

$$\frac{6 \text{ squares}}{24 \text{ sides}} = \frac{3 \text{ squares}}{n \text{ sides}}$$

4 sides : 1 square

ACTIVITY
2 Jar Ratios

With Your Group You can use ratio and proportion to compare capacity and weight.

① Create a chart like the one below, comparing all the jars. Write a proportion for each comparison.

DRAWING TO LEARN

For each picture on page 266, draw at least two more pictures to show equivalent ratios.

Comparing Jars		
Jars	Capacity (in fluid ounces)	Weight (in ounces)
$\frac{A}{B}$	$\frac{14}{21} = \frac{2}{3}$	$\frac{16}{2} = \frac{2}{3}$
$\frac{A}{C}$	$\frac{14}{28} = \frac{1}{2}$	

Which measurement on the cards below represents the capacity? the weight?

A.

B.

C.

D.

14 fl oz
16 oz

21 fl oz
24 oz

28 fl oz
32 oz

42 fl oz
48 oz

② Is the ratio between the capacity of two jars the same as the ratio between weights? Explain.

③ Do you think the ratios in Exercise 2 would change if the jars held a different food? Explain your prediction.

④ Choose one of these activities to complete.
   a. Use labels from different containers. Make a chart showing capacity and weight ratios.
   b. Use information in the Tool Kit. Make a chart showing equivalent ratios for other units of capacity and weight.

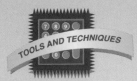
How can you use your chart to figure out how many lemons you would need to serve 20 people?

ACTIVITY 3 Measure to Measure

With Your Group Imagine making lemonade for a carnival. Your recipe requires 9 lemons to make lemonade for 15 people. Make a graph and a chart showing how many lemons you would need to serve 15, 30, 45, and 60 people. Or make a graph and chart for an ingredient in a recipe you bring from home.

Describe the set of points you get when you complete your graph.

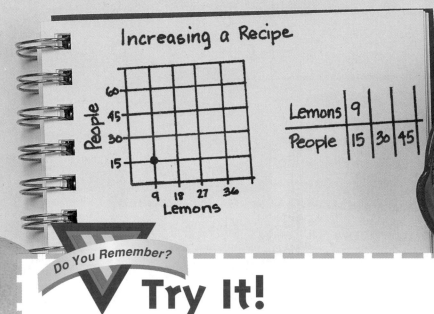

Increasing a Recipe

Lemons	9		
People	15	30	45

Do You Remember?

Try It!

Choose the two ratios that make a proportion. Explain your choices.

1. 2:5, 3:6, 1:2   **2.** 1:4, 2:10, 25:100   **3.** 1:2, 1:3, 3:9

4. 7:3, 28:2, 21:9   **5.** 14:6, 3:7, 7:3   **6.** 3:5, 5:7, 6:10

Write the prime factorization for each number.

7. 36   **8.** 81   **9.** 144   **10.** 68   **11.** 64

Think About It

12. Describe how you chose the equivalent ratios in Exercises 1–6.

Roller Coaster Rates

Up and up the roller coaster climbs. Suddenly, down it goes—but your heart rate soars.

ACTIVITY 1 And the Beat Goes On

With Your Partner Investigate your heart rate. A **rate** is a ratio that compares different types of quantities.

1 Place your fingers on your wrist. Apply pressure until you feel a beat. Count the number of beats in 15 seconds. This is your heart rate.

$$\frac{18 \text{ beats}}{15 \text{ seconds}} = \frac{72 \text{ beats}}{60 \text{ seconds}}$$

2 Estimate what your heart rate will be for 1 minute. Take it and write the results as a proportion.

What You'll Need
- *stopwatch or watch with second hand*

CONNECT AND COMMUNICATE

Explain whether each is or is not a rate.
- *1 m/30 minutes*
- *200 mg/500 mg*
- *3 for $1.00*
- *1 cm: 1 second*
- *14 points per game*
- *12 feet total*

List rates you often use.

269

Survey the heart rates of people older or younger than you. Is there a relationship between age and heart rate? Write a report about your findings.

What You'll Need
• *bottle with cap*

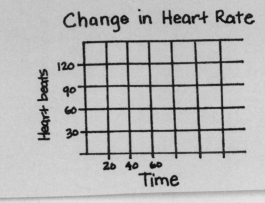

Change in Heart Rate

3 Jog in place for 20 seconds. Take your pulse and graph the result. Now jog for 40 seconds. Measure and graph your heart rate. What will your pulse be after 1 minute? Check your prediction.

4 Discuss how to predict what your heart rate will be after exercising for 30 minutes. Will the rate increase proportionally?

²ACTIVITY Rolling Faster

With Your Group Speed is one type of rate comparing distance and time. What units are used in speed limits? Explore the speed of a rolling bottle.

1 Make an incline with books. Roll a bottle down the incline. Time how long the bottle rolled. Measure how far it went. Record your data in a table. Repeat with the bottle half full of water and then completely full.

2 How does changing each rate to inches per second make comparing them easier? Rates in which quantities are compared with 1 are called **unit rates**. Write the rates as unit rates.

3 Draw a bar graph to compare the unit rates. Which bottle speed was fastest?

✓ **Self-Check** *Explain how you would change 28 feet/4 seconds to a unit rate.*

With Your Class Make a chart to record the rates for the bottles each group studied.

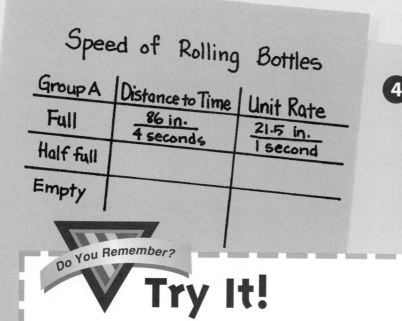

Speed of Rolling Bottles

Group A	Distance to Time	Unit Rate
Full	86 in. / 4 seconds	21.5 in. / 1 second
Half full		
Empty		

4 How do your unit rates compare? How can you explain any differences?

Do You Remember?

Try It!

Change only the ratios that are rates to unit rates.

1. $120 per 2 hours   **2.** 300 g/700 g   **3.** 1 m/45 minutes

4. 33 rotations per 90 seconds   **5.** 46 heartbeats/6 heartbeats

Solve the exercises with answers greater than $\frac{1}{2}$.

6. 34% + 13%   **7.** 0.84 − 0.39   **8.** 0.75 − 0.06

9. 0.25 + 1.34   **10.** $\frac{7}{14} \times \frac{4}{16}$ **11.** $\frac{3}{4} \times \frac{9}{12}$

Think About It

12. Explain how you could write more than one unit rate for one of Exercises 1–5.

Investigation

Fun-house Mirrors

What's wrong with the reflection in a mirror in a carnival fun house? Are the ratios in the reflection the same as those in the real object? What happens when you re-create an image with ratios that are not equivalent?

1 **Create or find an image** to re-create. In pencil, draw a square grid on top of the image. Number the squares in order.

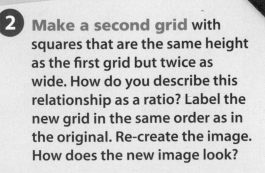

2 **Make a second grid** with squares that are the same height as the first grid but twice as wide. How do you describe this relationship as a ratio? Label the new grid in the same order as in the original. Re-create the image. How does the new image look?

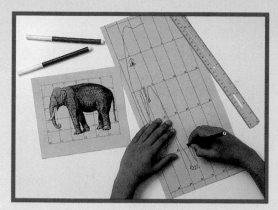

3 **Make a third grid** that will change the proportion of your image. Re-create your image. Use ratios to compare all of your grids. Explain what you discover.

4 **Change the proportions** of a geometric figure, such as a parallelogram or a hexagon. Analyze how the shape changes. How do the angles differ? How much does the area increase or decrease? Share your results with your class.

Ask Yourself

☐ What images will be easier than others to re-create at varying ratios?

☐ Can you imagine what each picture will look like before you re-create it?

☐ How does sketching a grid help you re-create the image?

☐ How would you explain why each picture looks as it does?

☐ How do your pictures compare with those of your classmates?

LESSON 7 Carnival Percents

Have you ever heard a calliope? It's a musical instrument that uses air and pipes to make energetic sounds to advertise circuses and carnivals. What kind of music do you connect with games, rides, and festivals?

LITERATURE

The sounds of a circus are loud and lively. As you read this poem, ask yourself what mood the writer is trying to create.

Sawdust is the earth
        and from it spring
        great poles that hold
        a canvas sky
                and in it fly
                bright, whirling stars,
                wheeling and spinning
                while a moon sweeps by.
Leap from that earth, would I,
Open my arms, take wing,
Soar in that sky, would I,
Out where calliopes sing.

"Circus"
by Felice Holman

Calliopes were first built in the 1850s and were designed to be heard for several miles.

ACTIVITY 1

Visualizing Percents

With Your Class In a circus calliope, the sounds come from the vibration of air in long metal pipes. The sounds of many musical instruments depend on the length of pipes or of strings. Explore the math of making various sounds.

In Your Journal Music and mathematics have been linked since ancient times. Describe some ways that you see the connection between music and math.

> **Each musical note is named by a letter from A through G.**

A B C D E F G A

1 Compare the lengths of the two A strings. Write the ratio as a fraction and a decimal.

2 Predict how long the next B string would be. Discuss how you made your prediction. How long would the next D string be? What would the length of the next A string be?

What You'll Need
- *8 matching glass jars*
- *spoon*
- *pitcher of water*

REASONING AND PROBLEM SOLVING

Why is having matching jars important?

Name That Tune

With Your Class With various levels of water and air in glass jars, you can create sounds that have different pitches. Some sounds can be high and others can be low.

1 Place eight glass jars of the same kind and size on a table. Fill the jars with varying amounts of water.

2 Gently tap the jars with a spoon to hear the sound they make. Put the jars in order from lowest to highest pitch.

3 Estimate what percent of each jar is filled with water. Now estimate the percent of each jar that is filled with air. Label the percent of air in each jar.

4 What is the sum of the percents of air and water in each jar?

5 Suppose you filled a glass with water. Then you drank 35% of the water. What percent of water would be left? Write a number sentence showing this.

In Your Journal You can sketch the glass jars and picture the percent of air in each. How would you show the glass jar that has the lowest pitch?

Try It!

Draw a glass to show each percent of air.

1. 75%	**2.** 66%	**3.** 15%	**4.** 10%
5. 22%	**6.** 40%	**7.** 85%	**8.** 33%

Find the area.

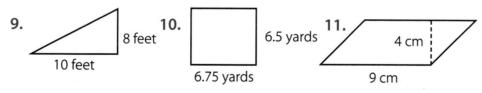

9. 8 feet, 10 feet

10. 6.5 yards, 6.75 yards

11. 4 cm, 9 cm

12. What is the area of a 4-inch-by-1.5-inch rectangle?

13. What is the area of a 5.2-mile square?

Think About It
14. Explain how drawing helped you visualize percents.

Playing with Estimates

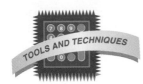
Use percents that you know to help you estimate other percents. How does knowing that 25% is $\frac{1}{4}$ help you estimate 30% of a number?

ACTIVITY 1 Find the Unknown

With Your Class At one game booth at a school fair, you use bean bags. You get a prize if you knock down 22% of the targets as they move. In 2 minutes there are 42 moving targets. Think about ways to estimate 22% of 42.

1 Choose the method you like or make up one of your own. A **percent-bar** model can help.

2 How can you use the same methods to answer other questions? Suppose you hit 54% of the targets. About how many did you hit?

How can thinking about fractions help? What is about $\frac{1}{4}$ of 42?

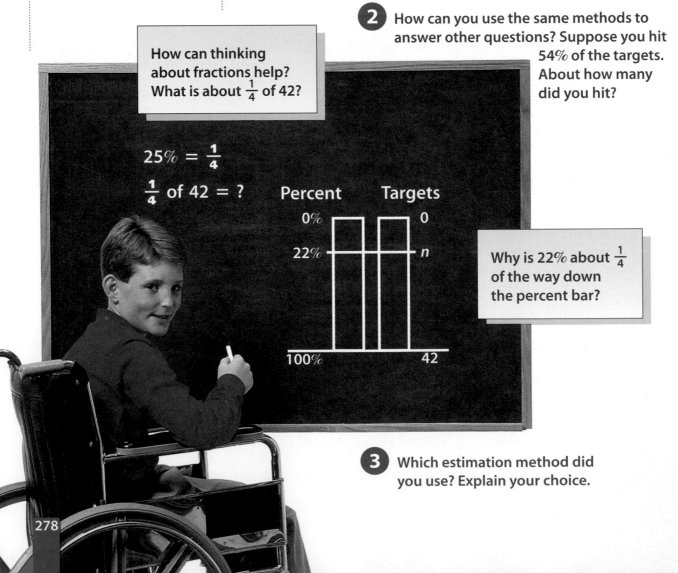

$25\% = \frac{1}{4}$

$\frac{1}{4}$ of 42 = ?

Percent	Targets
0%	0
22%	n
100%	42

Why is 22% about $\frac{1}{4}$ of the way down the percent bar?

3 Which estimation method did you use? Explain your choice.

4 Suppose 65 people are waiting in line to ride the bumper cars. Only 20 people at a time can get on the ride. What percent is that?

• What does 20 represent? If you like, show this number on a percent bar.
• Estimate the percent. Check. Is your answer reasonable?

5 Write a problem that could be solved using this percent-bar model.

✓ **Self-Check** *How does knowing that 100% is the whole help you check answers to percent exercises?*

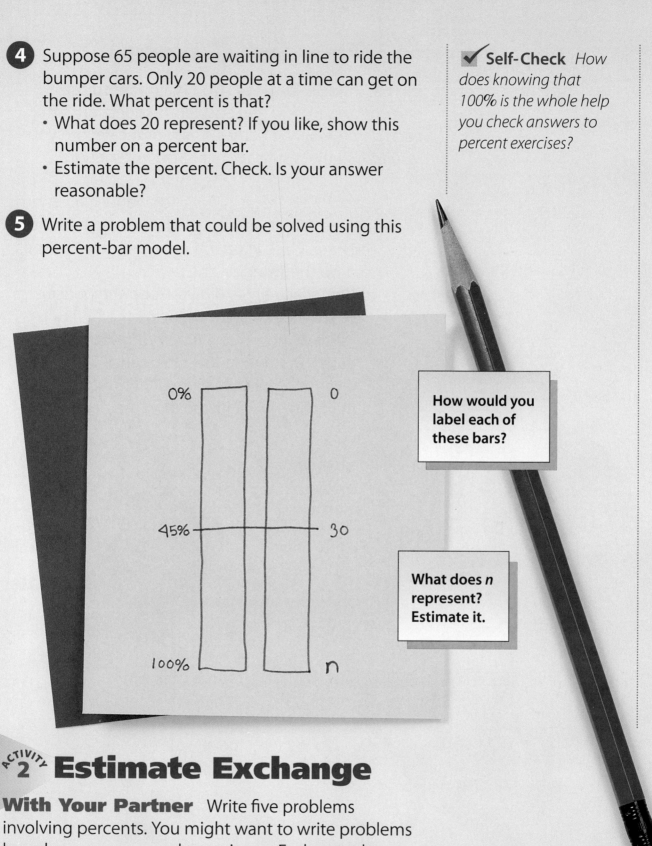

How would you label each of these bars?

What does *n* represent? Estimate it.

ᴬᶜᵀᶦᵛᶦᵀʸ 2 Estimate Exchange

With Your Partner Write five problems involving percents. You might want to write problems based on your personal experience. Exchange the problems and estimate the solutions.

ACTIVITY 3 **Percent Games**

With Your Partner You may want to use percent bars to help you answer the questions after each game. Play the games in any order. Record your results. Use the results to make your estimation.

Loop the Pencil Tie a foot length of string into a circle. Have your partner hold a pencil on the floor. Place your arm on a desk. Try 10 times to drop the string on the pencil.

a. How many times did you loop the pencil? What is the percent of success?

b. Estimate how many times you would need to drop the string to loop the pencil 50 times.

c. If you dropped the string 80 times, about how many times would you loop the pencil?

Capture the Clips Place five paper clips on a desk. Using an opened clip, try to pick up each clip. You have ten seconds per clip.

a. How many paper clips did you pick up? What percent of all the clips was this?

b. If you had 20 paper clips and ten seconds per clip, how many paper clips do you estimate that you could pick up?

Play the Capture the Clips game with various sizes of paper clips. You might also try using your other hand to pick up the clips. How do these changes affect the results?

Drop the Popcorn Hold 25 kernels of popcorn. While standing, drop the kernels onto a sheet of a paper on the floor. Count how many kernels land on the paper.

a. What percent of the kernels landed on the paper?

b. Estimate how many kernels would land on the paper if you dropped 500 kernels.

c. About how many kernels would you need to drop to get 100 on the paper?

Estimate Fair

Across the country, state fairs attract millions of visitors yearly. Use percent bars to help you answer these questions about the 1993 Indiana State Fair. In items 1–5, round all data to the nearest thousand.

1 About what percent of the total attendance was on the day with the largest attendance?

2 Explain whether more or less than 50% of the visitors came on weekends.

3 Of the people who attended the first two days, about what percent attended on the opening day?

4 About 24% of the people who attended the fair were under the age of 18. Estimate this number.

5 About 39% of the fairgoers visited exhibits and 16% went on rides or played games. How many more people visited exhibits than went on rides or played games?

Swine Barn

Playground

Fair Office

Horse Barns

Daily Attendance

Wednesday	48,600
Thursday	28,588
Friday	79,283
Saturday	86,703
Sunday	70,646
Monday	37,255
Tuesday	40,038
Wednesday	63,201
Thursday	36,582
Friday	52,901
Saturday	80,549
Sunday	65,578
Total	689,924

Source: Indiana State Fair Board

Tractor Competition Area

Mini Indy Speedway

Antique Tractor Building

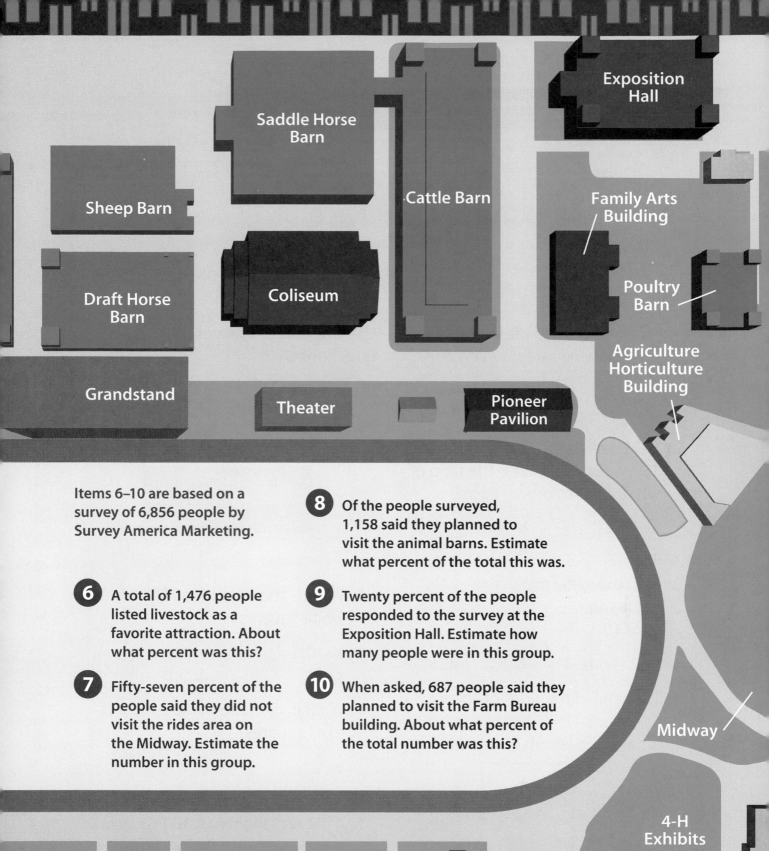

Saddle Horse Barn

Sheep Barn

Cattle Barn

Exposition Hall

Family Arts Building

Draft Horse Barn

Coliseum

Poultry Barn

Agriculture Horticulture Building

Grandstand

Theater

Pioneer Pavilion

Items 6–10 are based on a survey of 6,856 people by Survey America Marketing.

6 A total of 1,476 people listed livestock as a favorite attraction. About what percent was this?

7 Fifty-seven percent of the people said they did not visit the rides area on the Midway. Estimate the number in this group.

8 Of the people surveyed, 1,158 said they planned to visit the animal barns. Estimate what percent of the total this was.

9 Twenty percent of the people responded to the survey at the Exposition Hall. Estimate how many people were in this group.

10 When asked, 687 people said they planned to visit the Farm Bureau building. About what percent of the total number was this?

Midway

4-H Exhibits

Natural Resources Building

Exhibit Building

Minizoo

283

Looking Back

Choose the right answer. Write *a, b, c,* or *d* for each question.

1. The ratio 3:5 is expressed by all of the following *except* which one?

   a. 0.6   b. $\frac{9}{15}$
   c. $\frac{5}{3}$ d. three to five

2. In 3 dozen eggs, 21 are white and 15 are brown. What is the ratio of white eggs to brown eggs?

   a. 15:21   b. 7:5
   c. $\frac{36}{21}$ d. $\frac{5}{12}$

3. Find the value of *a* in the following:
   $2a = 10$

   a. 2   b. 3   c. 5   d. 6

4. The ratio of the sides of square *B* to square *A* is $\frac{3}{1}$. If side $a = 2$ m, what is the length of side *b*?

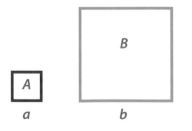

   a. 6 m   b. 9 m   c. 4 m   d. 36 m

Use the grid to answer questions 5–7.

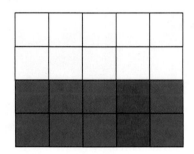

5. What is the ratio of red squares to white squares?

   a. 10:1   b. $\frac{2}{20}$
   c. $\frac{1}{5}$ d. 5:1

6. What is the ratio of blue squares to all squares?

   a. $\frac{8}{1}$ b. 2 to 5
   c. 8 to 12   d. $\frac{1}{5}$

7. If the rectangle had 100 squares in the same proportion, how many squares would be blue?

   a. 8   b. 20
   c. 40   d. 50

8. Which expresses 1.5?

   a. 1:5   **b.** 5:20

   c. $\frac{3}{6}$ **d.** $\frac{27}{18}$

9. Which is equivalent to 112:14?

   a. 8:1   **b.** $\frac{125}{1,000}$

   c. 1:8   **d.** 12

10. A graduating class is about 25% of the school. The school has 308 students. About how many students are in the graduating class?

   a. 4×300 **b.** 25×300

   c. $300 \div 25$ **d.** $300 \div 4$

11. Which five numbers have a mean of 25 and a median of 30?

   a. 25, 30, 31, 32, 33

   b. 10, 19, 30, 31, 35

   c. 15, 20, 25, 30, 35

   d. 26, 27, 28, 29, 30

12. Which is closest to 72% of 268?

   a. 72:268   **b.** $\frac{3}{4} \times 268$

   c. $268 \div 4$ **d.** 8×268

13. Which statements are true about $2a + 5a = 21$?

   a. The solution is 7.

   b. $a = 3$

   c. The equation has no solution.

   d. None of the above

14. Which is a unit rate?

   a. 7:1   **b.** 14 to 21

   c. $\frac{5}{6}$ **d.** 9 to 4

Check Your Math Power

15. Two similar rectangles have sides in a ratio of 7 to 1. The perimeter of the smaller rectangle is 60 m. Find the dimensions of the two rectangles.

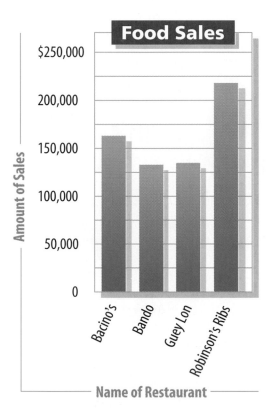

The graph above shows food sales for several restaurants at a food festival in Chicago in 1992. Use the graph to do Exercises 16–17.

16. Do you think mean, median, mode, or range would best describe the sales of a typical restaurant? Explain your thinking.

17. Use the data in the graph to create a pictograph.

MODULE 5 Investigations

Come One, Come All

Schools and communities sometimes hold carnivals to raise money. Using ratios, you can predict how much money a carnival might make. Choose Investigation A, B, or C to do.

Investigation A Carnival Games

1 Make a carnival game. Ask five or more people to play it. For your sample group, estimate the ratio of players to winners. Decide whether the same ratios work as the group increases.

2 Decide how much you will charge for tickets. How much will you spend on prizes? How can you estimate the profit for any size of carnival?

3 Make a presentation summarizing your data for the game. Show how it applies to a class carnival, a school carnival, and a neighborhood carnival.

Data on Ring Toss

	People to players	Players to winners	Sales to cost of prizes
Sample group	10:8	8:2	$12.00 : $4.00
25 people	25:20		
200 people			
1,000 people			

Keep in Mind

Your presentation will be judged by how well you do the following things.

☐ Do you use ratios to show your information?

☐ Do you use math to justify your estimations based on the data you have?

☐ Do you accurately adjust your information for carnivals of various sizes?

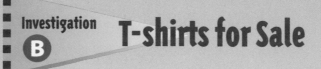

Investigation B — T-shirts for Sale

Create a T-shirt to sell at a carnival. Design a symbol or a slogan to use on it. Then make the shirt in three sizes that are proportional to each other. Make a shirt for souvenir dolls, one for young children, and one for adults.

Computer Option Sketch your T-shirt design using a computer drawing program. How can you scale the size of your design to make it proportional to the size of the shirt? How can ratios help you?

Investigation C — Food Tent

Plan a food stand for a carnival. Identify five foods to serve. Take a survey to find out what items are most popular. What percent of people at a carnival are likely to buy each item? Estimate the cost of preparing one serving of each food. Use ratios to decide how much of each item to prepare for a school carnival and a neighborhood carnival.

Carnival Food Survey

Food	Number of people who would buy it	Percent of people who would buy it
Burritos	HHT IIII	
Tortilla chips	II	36%
Churros	HHT	

In the News

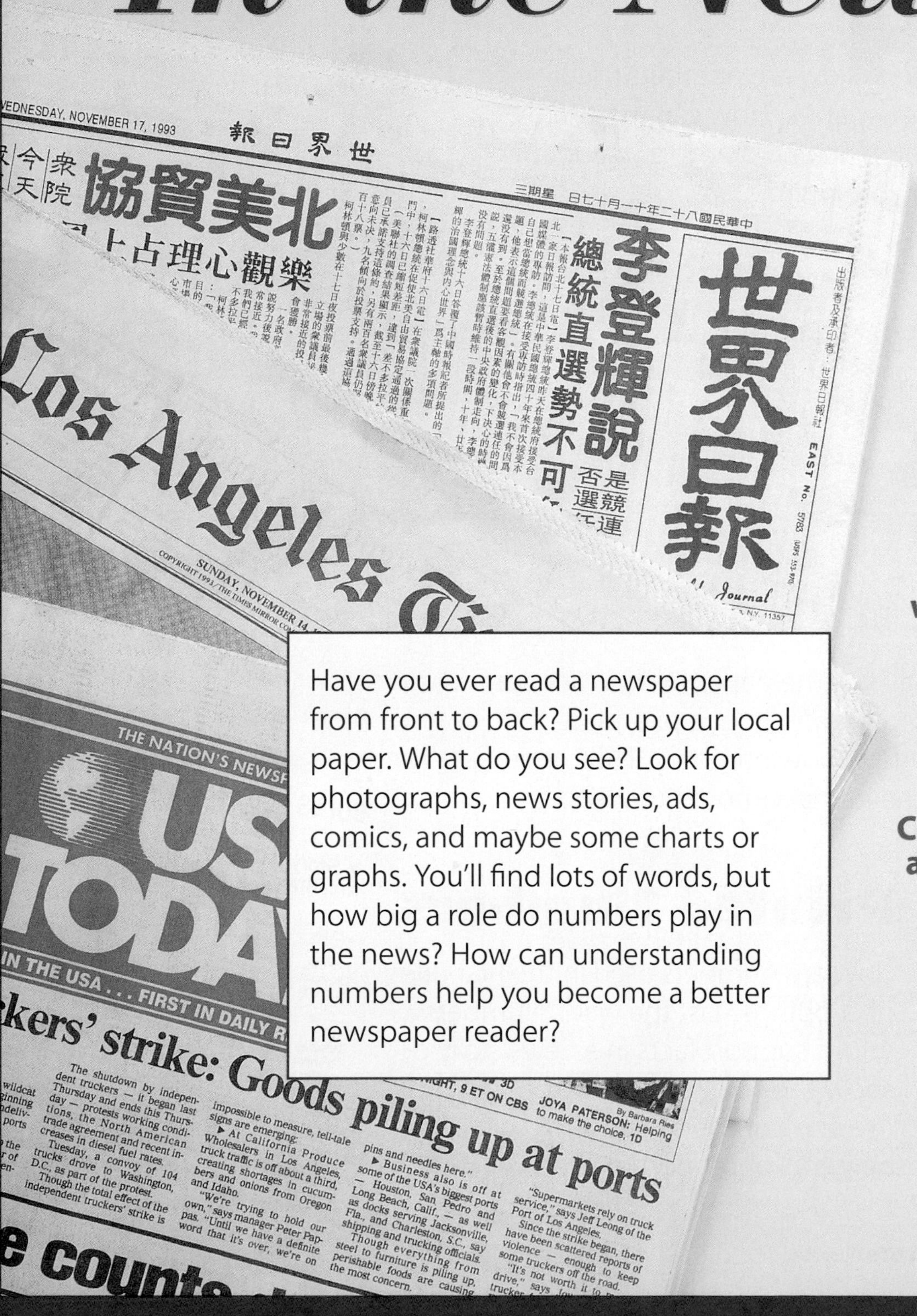

Have you ever read a newspaper from front to back? Pick up your local paper. What do you see? Look for photographs, news stories, ads, comics, and maybe some charts or graphs. You'll find lots of words, but how big a role do numbers play in the news? How can understanding numbers help you become a better newspaper reader?

SECTION
A
Comparing Ratios

SECTION
B
Computing with Percents

SECTION
C
Charts, Graphs, and Functions

SECTION
D
Solving Inequalities

Numbers as News

How are numbers used in the newspaper? How can they help you plan and design a newspaper of your own?

1 Sort It Out

Cut out parts of the paper, such as articles, comics, and graphs. In one pile, place the clippings that show numbers. In another pile, put the items without numbers.

2 Printed Numbers

How are numbers used in the first pile of clippings? List the ways. Numbers might support facts in a news story or show the results of a sports match. Are any numbers used as percents or proportions?

BULLS 106, H

▶ Story, 1C
ATLANTA (80)

	min
Wilkins	29
Willis	34
Koncak	23
Blaylock	33
Augmon	21
Ehio	2
Ferrell	1
Lang	
Whatley	
Graham	
Keefe	
Grace	
TOTALS	

Percentages
2-7, .286 (
rebounds:
Lang 2, Gr
Augmon 3
Steals: 12
2, Ferrell,
CHICA(

Regional
rankings
MIDWEST
1. Cleveland
  St. Ignatius (10
2. Wheaton (Ill.)
2. Warrenville S
  (Mich.) King
  Grant

MONEYL
A QUICK READ ON THE TOP MONEY NE

DOW UP: The Dow Jones ind
points Monday to 3647.90. The N
rose 3.22 points to 766.21. The yield
bonds held at 6.20% (story, right).
three-month Treasury bills remained a
fell $2.30 to $374.80 an ounce. Light swe
38 cents to $16.71 a barrel on the N.Y.
today, the Nikkei average fell 503 points, or
midafternoon (12:30 a.m. ET). (Market Sc

CABLE DEAL: Meredith Corp. wants
telephone company or bigger cable comp
money-losing cable operation, CEO Jack Re
year, Meredith's magazine business had its r
year, but its cable unit isn't expected to be
three or four years. Rehm says the company
sell its cable operations but won't rule out a
systems serve 127,000 customers.

TELEMARKETING FRAUD: State
law enforcement agencies are joining force:
telemarketing fraud schemes that swindle abou
a year, Federal Trade Commission Chairman

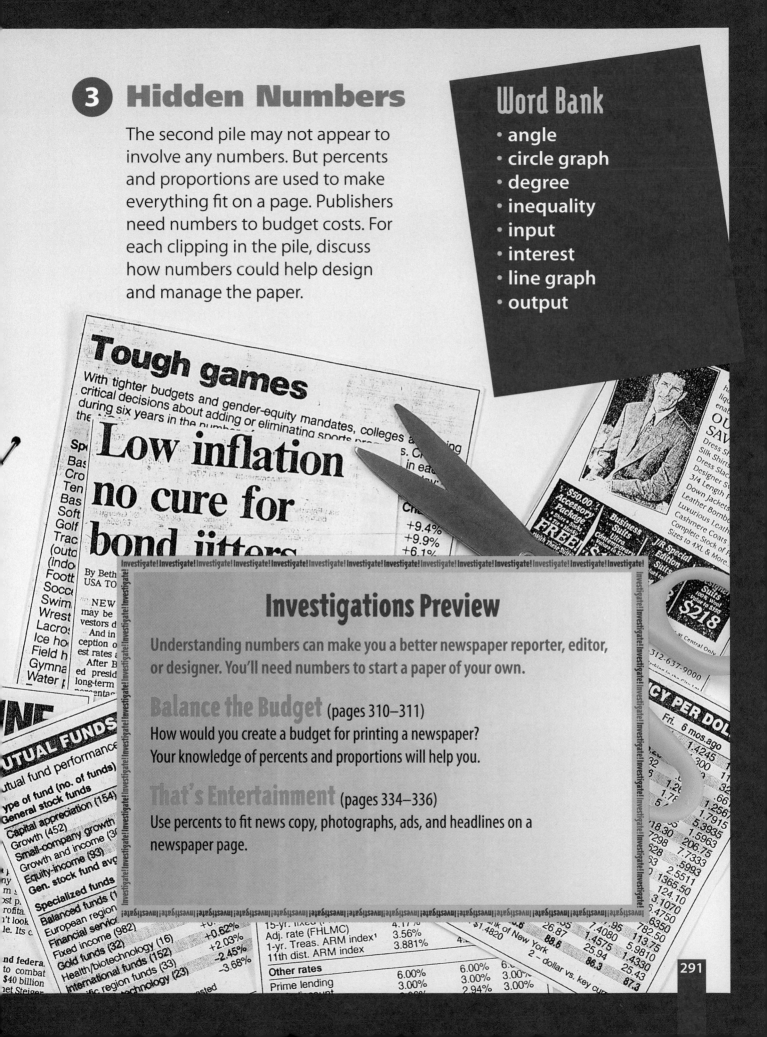

③ Hidden Numbers

The second pile may not appear to involve any numbers. But percents and proportions are used to make everything fit on a page. Publishers need numbers to budget costs. For each clipping in the pile, discuss how numbers could help design and manage the paper.

Investigations Preview

Understanding numbers can make you a better newspaper reporter, editor, or designer. You'll need numbers to start a paper of your own.

Balance the Budget (pages 310–311)

How would you create a budget for printing a newspaper?
Your knowledge of percents and proportions will help you.

That's Entertainment (pages 334–336)

Use percents to fit news copy, photographs, ads, and headlines on a newspaper page.

LESSON 1 Be a Sport

Do you read the sports pages? Sometimes they have stories about outstanding athletes. One of them was Satchel Paige, a great pitcher in baseball. He started in the Negro Leagues at a time when African Americans could not play in the major leagues.

ACTIVITY 1 Play by Play

With Your Partner Look at this record of the American Negro League from the first half of the 1929 season. Your job is to write the standings in order from first to sixth place.

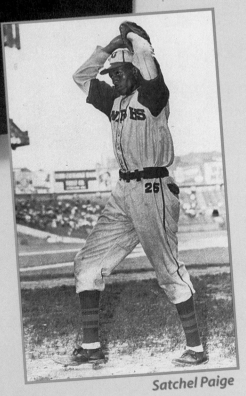

Satchel Paige

American Negro League

Team	Wins	Games Played
Bacharach Giants	11	31
Baltimore Black Sox	24	35
Cuban Stars (East)	6	22
Hilldale	15	35
Homestead Grays	15	28
Lincoln Giants	22	33

Source: *Invisible Men* by Donn Rogosin

1 Why is it easy to compare the wins-to-games ratios for the Baltimore Black Sox and Hilldale?

2 The Homestead Grays won 15 of their 28 games, or $\frac{15}{28}$. The Lincoln Giants won $\frac{22}{33}$ of theirs. How would you compare these ratios? Try it.

3 One way to compare ratios is to write them as equal ratios with common denominators. Who has the better record, the Stars or the Giants?

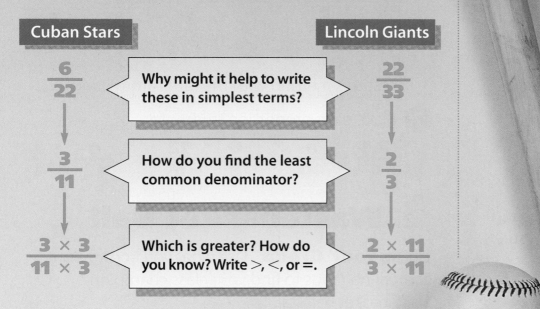

Cuban Stars

$\dfrac{6}{22}$

Why might it help to write these in simplest terms?

$\dfrac{3}{11}$

How do you find the least common denominator?

$\dfrac{3 \times 3}{11 \times 3}$

Which is greater? How do you know? Write >, <, or =.

Lincoln Giants

$\dfrac{22}{33}$

$\dfrac{2}{3}$

$\dfrac{2 \times 11}{3 \times 11}$

4 These ratios are being compared by finding common denominators. Look for a pattern that will lead to a short cut for comparing ratios.

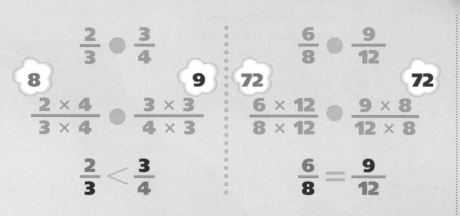

$\dfrac{2}{3} \bullet \dfrac{3}{4}$

8 **9**

$\dfrac{2 \times 4}{3 \times 4} \bullet \dfrac{3 \times 3}{4 \times 3}$

$\dfrac{2}{3} < \dfrac{3}{4}$

$\dfrac{6}{8} \bullet \dfrac{9}{12}$

72 **72**

$\dfrac{6 \times 12}{8 \times 12} \bullet \dfrac{9 \times 8}{12 \times 8}$

$\dfrac{6}{8} = \dfrac{9}{12}$

Describe the short cut you found. Use your short cut to compare $\frac{2}{3}$ and $\frac{3}{5}$. Share your method with the class.

5 Now rank the American Negro League teams from best record to worst. Explain how you compared the ratios.

TOOLS AND TECHNIQUES

Thinking about the relationship between the products that are across from one another may help you compare ratios.

Write a rule for deciding whether two ratios make a proportion.

What You'll Need

• *wastebasket or other container*

6 Look at the way this student decided which ratios make a proportion. What did the student do?

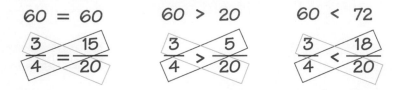

$$60 = 60 \qquad 60 > 20 \qquad 60 < 72$$

$$\frac{3}{4} = \frac{15}{20} \qquad \frac{3}{4} > \frac{5}{20} \qquad \frac{3}{4} < \frac{18}{20}$$

Test this method with the ratios from page 293.

7 Make each proportion true.

$$\frac{2.5}{4} = \frac{n}{40} \qquad \frac{6}{8} = \frac{12}{n} \qquad \frac{n}{12} = \frac{3}{4}$$

ACTIVITY 2 **Wastebasket Ball**

With Your Group Use what you know about comparing ratios to find your class champion wastebasket ball star.

1 Crumple a piece of paper into a ball.

2 Stand about 10 ft from a wastebasket or another container. Try to get the paper into the basket.

3 Take as many tries as the month of your birthday.

4 Write a ratio for the number of baskets you made to your total number of throws.

5 Use the generalizations you made to compare the ratios in your group.

6 Compare the ratios of all the players in your class. Who is the champion?

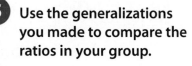

Do You Remember?

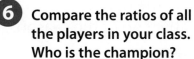

Try It!

Use the four numbers to write two ratios. Which ratio is greatest?

1. 2, 3, 4, 5   **2.** 2, 4, 7, 8   **3.** 1, 3, 5, 7

4. 2, 5, 6, 9   **5.** 7, 8, 10, 12   **6.** 5, 10, 15, 20

Use the two numbers to write a ratio. Then write an equal ratio.

7. 5, 7   **8.** 6, 8   **9.** 10, 12   **10.** 12, 15

Think About It

11. How did you compare the ratios in Exercises 1–6?

LESSON 2 *Team Spirit*

When you work with proportions and percents, you can often write an equation to represent a situation. Knowing how to solve an equation can help you make predictions.

ACTIVITY 1 ▸ The Soccer Season

With Your Partner In Lilburn, Georgia, a soccer team called the Storm has won 3 of its last 5 games. The season has 10 games. You can use this information to predict the number of games the team will have won by the end of the season.

1 How could you use equal ratios to solve the problem? How could setting up a proportion help you?

$$\frac{3}{5} = \frac{n}{10}$$

2 You can write the proportion this way. Why?

$$5n = 30$$

3 How could you find n? You used a balance scale to solve equations before. How can that help you now?

✔ **Self-Check** *How would you solve $60 = 4n$?*

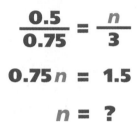
Messy Numbers

With Your Partner The proportion $\frac{3}{5} = \frac{n}{10}$ was easy to solve mentally. Think about how using a simpler problem can help you solve proportions like the one below.

$$\frac{0.5}{0.75} = \frac{n}{3}$$

$$0.75n = 1.5$$

$$n = \ ?$$

1 Why might thinking about the simpler problem $2a = 8$ help you solve $0.75n = 1.5$? What is the value of n?

2 Choose three of the boxed numbers and a variable to set up a proportion like the one below. Trade with your partner and solve. Check each other's work.

$$\frac{2.4}{0.8} = \frac{n}{4}$$

$$0.8n = 9.6$$

$$n = 12$$

3.2	4	2.4
0.8	0.16	0.02

REASONING AND PROBLEM SOLVING

How would cross products help you solve this problem?

$$\frac{1}{2} = \frac{n}{6}$$

What You'll Need
- *index cards or slips of paper*

Solve It!

With Your Partner Think about how you can use a simpler problem to help you play this game.

1 Make two different sets of 12 cards. Each card in set A shows a ratio that has a decimal. Each card in set B shows a ratio that has a variable.

2 Place the sets face down in two piles.

3 Flip the top cards. Solve the proportion. If your partner finds that you are right, you get a point. The person with the most points wins.

Set A

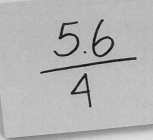

$$\frac{5.6}{4}$$

Set B

$$\frac{n}{2}$$

ACTIVITY OPTION

Make ten pairs of cards. In each pair, one card is a proportion with a variable and the other is the answer. Place the cards face down. Find matching pairs.

Do You Remember?

Try It!

Use the four numbers to write a proportion.

1. 2, 3, 4, 6   **2.** 4, 15, 5, 12   **3.** 1.8, 0.2, 3, 27

4. 9, 1, 3, 3   **5.** 3, 1, 1.5, 2   **6.** 3.5, 4, 7, 8

Use a percent-bar model to estimate.

7. 25% of 60   **8.** 40% of 110   **9.** 75% of 80

10. 20% of 40   **11.** 10% of 50   **12.** 60% of 120

Think About It

13. Is there a different proportion for Exercise 1? Explain in writing.

High Achiever

What put Lauren Wolfe's name in the news? Wrestling! As a sophomore at Okemos High School in Michigan, she's the only girl on her school's team.

ACTIVITY 1 Wrestle with Numbers

With Your Partner At one point in 1993, Lauren had a 13–9 record. If she kept that pace, what would you expect her record to be for the year if she has a total of 47 matches?

1 Set up a proportion to help you answer the question. How many matches has Lauren had? What is her wins-to-matches ratio so far?

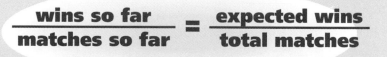

$$\frac{\text{wins so far}}{\text{matches so far}} = \frac{\text{expected wins}}{\text{total matches}}$$

2 What is the total number of matches for the year? How will you solve the proportion?

DRAWING TO LEARN

Draw a percent-bar model and set up a proportion to estimate the percent of matches Lauren won.

Hands Down

Lauren competed with wrestlers from other schools. Use models and write proportions to solve these problems.

1 Compare the wins-to-meets ratios for the teams in 1992. Who had the best record?

2 Which team had the best record in 1993? Determine the order of finish from first to last.

3 Look at Charlotte's record for 1993. If they win at the same rate as in 1993, how many meets would you expect Charlotte to win in 1994 if they have 27 meets?

4 Estimate the percent of meets that Okemos won in 1992 and in 1993. Which was the better year for Okemos? How do you know?

1992 High School Wrestling Standings

Team	Wins	Meets
Okemos	4	14
Lakewood	11	15
Charlotte	6	15
Eaton Rapids	22	22

1993 High School Wrestling Standings

Team	Wins	Meets
Okemos	5	16
Lakewood	7	18
Charlotte	10	18
Eaton Rapids	31	32

5 Another team won 60% of its 20 meets in 1992. Where would it be in the standings for these teams?

6 Look at Lakewood's record in 1992. Was their wins-to-meets ratio for 1993 better or worse? Explain.

7 Look at the 1992 standings. Which teams did better in 1993 than they did in 1992?

8 Use a percent-bar model to estimate each team's winning record in 1993.

9 Suppose a team needs 5 more wins to break the school record. If the team wins at an 80% rate, what is the least number of meets it must have to break the record?

10 Use statistics from district teams or your favorite professional teams to determine the percent of games each team has won. Write a short paragraph about the teams and their standings.

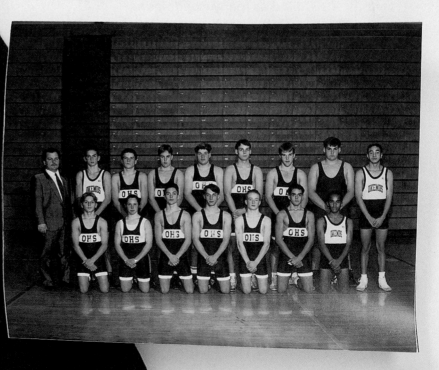

LESSON
4 *Looking at Ads*

Percents are everywhere! One place to find percents is advertisements. Many ads show percents off, or discounts. Other ads may show only a sale price. To be a smart consumer, you need to know what percents mean and how to use them.

What You'll Need
• *newspaper sections with ads*

ACTIVITY 1 **Great Savings?**

With Your Group Use your number sense as you explore percents.

1 Look at a local newspaper. Find as many examples as you can of percents used with money.
   a. Share your examples with other groups.
   b. Discuss what you think the percent in each case means.

2 Look at these ads. Which of your ads are like them? Which are different? Explain.

25% OFF!
CDs from $10–$14
This Week Only!

50% off! on instamatic cameras!

70% OFF!
BIKE HELMETS
ORIGINALLY $30–$75

3 How much would you save on a $60 backpack? Explain how you know. How could you figure out the sale price?

4 You want to buy a jacket. In the ad below, is $100 the amount you would spend or save? Suppose the jacket you like costs $200. Would you get 60% off? How do you know? What percent would you save?

save **25%**

Today only!

Backpacks

Originally $24 to $98

LUNCHEON SPECIAL

PITA POCKET, CHICKEN, LETTUCE, TOMATO, SPROUTS, VEGETABLE SOUP, BEVERAGE

$4.95

PLUS 15% TIP AND 5% TAX

Jacket Sale
Save up to 60%
Now $100!
Regular $125–$250

5 Look at the luncheon special. Will it be more or less than $6 when you include taxes? How do you know?

6 Do you think finding 20% of the meal is the same as finding 5% and 15% of the meal? Explain.

7 Choose two ads your group brought in. Write questions using percents and dollar amounts. Trade questions with another group and solve.

ACTIVITY OPTION

In your group write three ads using percents and dollars. Ask other groups how they would find the savings for each ad.

ACTIVITY 2 Smart Shopping

With Your Partner Your number sense can help you estimate with percents.

1 Yolanda drew this percent-bar model to find the sale price of a calculator that originally cost $15. Estimate the discount and sale price.

28% Off!
on calculators!
Original price $15

BIG SAVINGS!
80% OFF
On all hardcover books
Regular price $9.60 – $48.00

The percent bars can also help you find an exact number.

2 Use the numbers on either side of the bars to write a proportion. Solve the proportion to find the discount and the sale price.

3 Draw a percent-bar model for a $24.50 book on sale at 80% off. Estimate the discount.

✔ **Self-Check** *You get a bill from the restaurant. The bill includes a 7.5% sales tax. Is that the same as 75%? Explain.*

4 Write and solve the proportion. What is the discount? What is the sale price?

5 Look at the shoe ad and percent-bar model.
  a. Why is $44 across from 100%?
  b. Where did $15.40 come from?
  c. Write and solve a proportion to find the percent.
  d. Rewrite the shoe ad so that it uses percents.

How does knowing that $25\% = \frac{1}{4}$, $50\% = \frac{1}{2}$, and $75\% = \frac{3}{4}$ help you draw and estimate with a percent-bar model?

6 Why is it easy to find the price at Sporty Goods? What is the sale price at BOARDS? Would you buy your skateboard at BOARDS or Sporty Goods? Explain.

What You'll Need

- *newspaper and magazine ads*
- *index cards*
- *spinner marked 5%, 10%, 25%, 30%, 50%, and 75%*

REASONING AND PROBLEM SOLVING

There is a 50% sale on sneakers. The sale price is $35 per pair. What is the original price?

Sales, Sales, Sales

With Your Group Find 20 ads in a newspaper or a catalog. Cut them out and paste them on cards for this game. Read these steps for playing the game.

1 Choose a card.

2 Spin the spinner. Use the percent from the spinner to find the discount on your item.

3 Name the sale price of the item. If your group finds your answer correct, you get a point.

4 Take turns until all cards are chosen at least once. The first person who gets ten points wins the game.

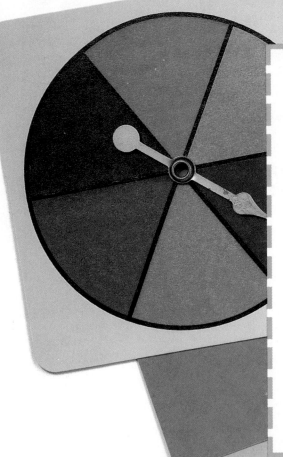

Do You Remember?

Try It!

Find the amount of the discount. Then find the sale price.

1. 15% off $35   **2.** 60% off $15

3. 85% off $145   **4.** 40% off $27

5. 75% off $70   **6.** 30% off $58

Write products that are greater than 5 but less than 10.

7. $2\frac{2}{3} \times 2\frac{4}{6}$ **8.** $\frac{7}{8} \times \frac{9}{4}$ **9.** $1\frac{3}{4} \times 4$

10. $\frac{4}{3} \times 12$ **11.** $1\frac{1}{8} \times 28$ **12.** $\frac{12}{8} \times \frac{35}{6}$

Think About It

13. Write two ways to solve Exercises 1–6.

Misleading Ads

Your job is to screen advertisements to be published in your newspaper. You want to protect your paper's reputation, so you need to make sure the ads are not misleading to your customers.

ACTIVITY 1 Understanding Ads

With Your Partner Suppose the ads below are sent to your paper. Could they mislead customers?

1 Is the sale price for cat food lower than the regular price? Explain.

2 Why would customers find the ad for the photo albums misleading? Do you actually save 25%? Explain.

CAT FOOD ON SALE!
20
CANS FOR $5.00
REG. PRICE: 6 FOR $1.56

Save 25%!
Off List Price Photo Albums
Retail: $10.60 List: $12.00

110% GUARANTEE!
If you find a lower price at a different store, we'll give you 110% of the difference in price.
If you find a lower price at any store, we'll refund the difference.

3 What is unusual about the ad on the left? Is 110% really guaranteed? What does "110% of the difference in price" mean? Explain.

4 Choose one of these ads. Rewrite it so that it doesn't mislead your customers.

In Your Journal *Explain why graphs need to start at 0 and continue at regular intervals.*

How We've Grown!

With Your Partner Graphs are used in some advertisements. They too can be very misleading. Look at the ad below.

1 When you first saw this ad, what did you think? Look at the bars. About how many times taller is the bar that shows bike sales in year 4 than the bar for year 1?

2 Were the sales in year 4 that many times greater than the sales in year 1? How do you know?

3 Why do you think this graph is misleading? Why do you think the Better Built Bikes people like the ad this way? How could you change the ad to make it clearer?

See How We've **Grown!**
Buy a Better Built Bike!

4 Draw a new ad for Better Built Bikes. Explain why your ad is better.

On Your Own Advertisers can also use circle graphs to their advantage. The chart below shows the results of a survey of people's favorite fruit drinks.

Fruit Drink Preferences

Peppy Orange	**40%**
Tingling Lime	**25%**
Peach Fizz	**10%**
No difference	**25%**

People Prefer Peppy!

Peppy Orange
Peach Fizz
Tingling Lime

Peter Plum, owner of Peppy Orange, made this graph.

5 What percent does each section of the circle graph represent?

6 How does Peter Plum make the data look better for Peppy Orange in the circle graph?

Do You Remember?

Try It!

Compute the percents. Circle the greatest amount.

1. 25% of 200   **2.** 55% of 120   **3.** 90% of 20

If a number is divisible by 3, find the prime factorization.

4. 64   **5.** 48   **6.** 36   **7.** 72

Find the least common multiple (LCM).

8. 18, 4   **9.** 12, 8   **10.** 15, 4   **11.** 16, 6

Think About It

12. How did you find the answers to Exercises 1–3? Explain in writing.

DRAWING TO LEARN

You want to advertise your newspaper. To compare the paper's success with the others in town, draw a circle graph so that it works to your advantage.

Your paper	*45%*
Local paper	*30%*
No difference	*25%*

MODULE 6 **Investigation**

Balance the Budget

What do you need to start a newspaper? Lots of things, and they can be costly! Some parent-teacher groups will help pay for school newspapers. But first you need to tell them how much everything will cost.

1 How would you plan a budget for a newspaper? First list the things you might need.

Items	Cost per issue	Percent of total cost
Computer and software		
Photo copying	$120	
Camera		
2 rolls film		
Film developing		
Supplies (paper, tape, scissors, pencil)	$20	

310

2 You want to have eight pages per issue. About how much would it cost to produce one issue at 500 copies per issue? Research the costs.

3 Calculate the percent of your total budget that each item will cost.

4 Write a letter to a parent-teacher group, explaining your budget proposal. Include a graph that shows how money will be spent. Explain why you have the best price or tell how you could save more money.

Percent of total cost for photocopying

$$\frac{\text{cost for photocopying}}{\text{total cost}} = \frac{n}{100}$$

Proposal will include:

Circle graph with percents

Letter

Ask Yourself

☐ Which items on your list might the school provide for free? Which would you need to include in the budget?

☐ What will you do to find out how much your items cost?

☐ What will you do if you find more than one cost per item?

☐ Do your costs, when changed to percents, total 100% of the budget?

☐ How does your presentation compare with the budgets other students planned?

Favorite Comic Strips

If you were a newspaper editor, which comic strips would you publish? The graph below shows comic strips that some fifth and sixth graders like best. Answer the questions about the survey.

Survey of Favorite Comic Strips

Number of Readers

30		27	
25			
20			
19			
15			14
10			
5	3		

Peanuts Garfield Calvin & Hobbes Ziggy

Comic Strips

Source: Fifth and sixth graders, Greeley School, Chicago

1 Did about 22% of the people surveyed vote for *Ziggy*? Explain.

2 What percent of the people surveyed prefer *Calvin & Hobbes* in their newspaper?

3 What is the mean number of votes each comic strip got?

4 Which comic strips have more fans than the mean? Which have fewer?

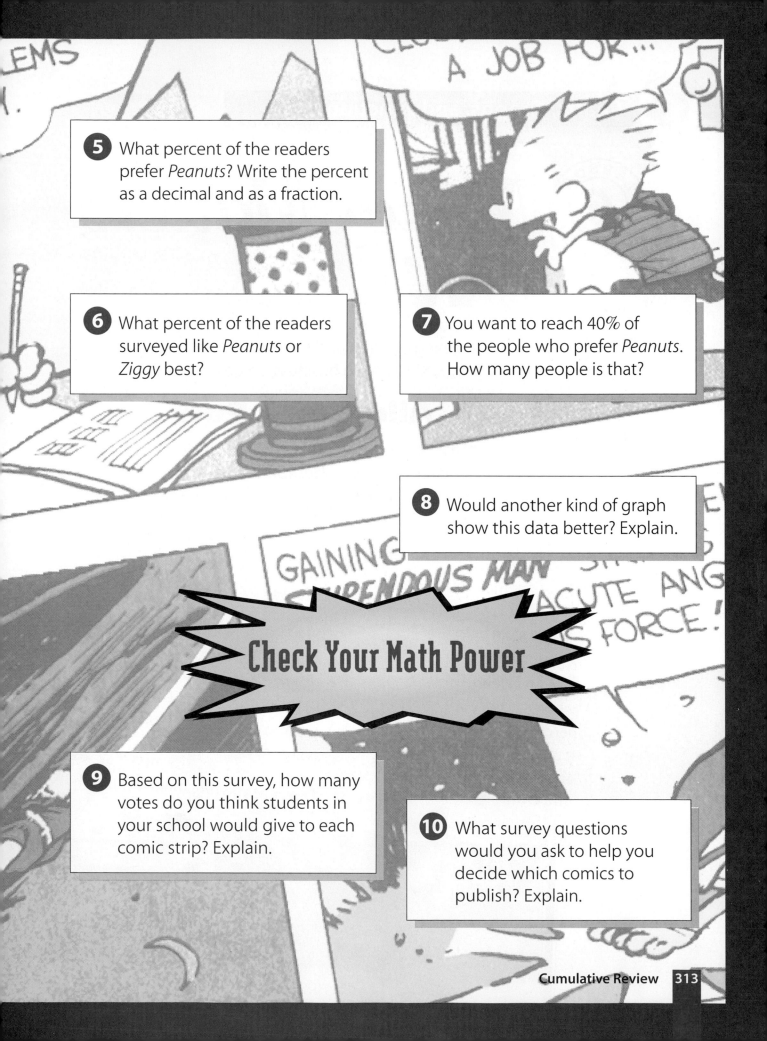

5 What percent of the readers prefer *Peanuts*? Write the percent as a decimal and as a fraction.

6 What percent of the readers surveyed like *Peanuts* or *Ziggy* best?

7 You want to reach 40% of the people who prefer *Peanuts*. How many people is that?

8 Would another kind of graph show this data better? Explain.

Check Your Math Power

9 Based on this survey, how many votes do you think students in your school would give to each comic strip? Explain.

10 What survey questions would you ask to help you decide which comics to publish? Explain.

LESSON 6 · *Money Matters*

Would a student newspaper have a business section? Think about it. More and more businesses are targeting children and teens as their spending power grows. Kids are big business, so be aware!

ACTIVITY 1 · Allowance Power

With Your Partner This article describes subscribers to *Sports Illustrated for Kids*. Proportions and equations can help explain the data below.

The magazine was launched in January 1989 and its current subscription base has climbed to 800,000 boys and girls. The median age for the magazine's readers is listed as 11.1, 78 percent male and 22 percent female. Subscription offers are targeted to both parents and children.

A 1990 subscriber study conducted by the magazine shows that 67 percent of the readership is below age 13, 35 percent of readers save each issue, 57 percent get a weekly allowance that averages $3.94 a week and 79 percent have a savings account.

Source:

Direct Marketing magazine

1 How many subscribers are there? How many subscribers are boys? How many are girls? You can use proportions to look at this data another way.

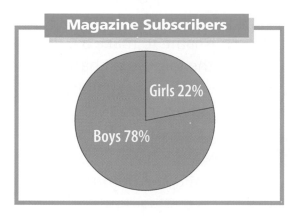

Magazine Subscribers

Girls 22%

Boys 78%

$$\frac{78}{100} = \frac{n}{800,000}$$

> **What question will the proportion help you answer?**

2 From the article, list the number of magazine subscribers, the percent below age 13, the percent with allowances, and the average weekly allowance.

> **What proportions can you write from the data you listed? What questions do the proportions answer?**

3 If you advertised in the magazine, why might you want to know the average amount of money subscribers could spend each year? How could a proportion help you solve the problem?

TOOLS AND TECHNIQUES

Figure the average amount of money available to subscribers with allowances. Check your answers with a calculator.

NOVEMBER 1993

U.S.A. $2.50 CANADA $2.95

Sports Illustrated FOR **KiDS**

GOAL RUSH!

SAN FRANCISCO 49ER QUARTERBACK STEVE YOUNG

The Savings Angle

REASONING AND PROBLEM SOLVING

Suppose children earned the same amount of money but saved 10% more in 1991. How would your estimates of the angle measures change? Explain.

With Your Partner In ancient Babylonia people used a number system based on 60. The Babylonians were the first people to divide a circle into 360 parts. You can do the same to make a **circle graph** for the information in the following chart. The chart shows how much money American children ages 4–12 earned, spent, and saved in one year.

In the Piggy Bank	
National Total, 1989 (in millions of dollars)	
Income	8,642
Spending	6,002
Savings	2,640

Source: *American Demographics*

1 Copy the circle graph below. How can you estimate the measure of each angle in the graph?

How do you think the circle graph below relates to the chart?

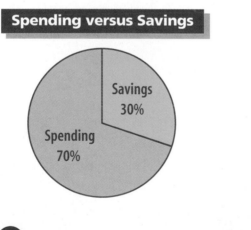

Spending versus Savings

Savings 30%

Spending 70%

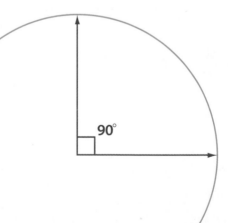

90°

2 A right angle measures 90 degrees (°). How could you use a 90° angle to find a 45° angle? Trace the drawing at right and sketch your answer. Then sketch the angles for 15°, 30°, and 75°.

3 Now think about two right angles together. How many degrees are in this straight angle? How do you know?

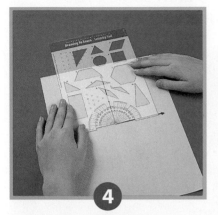

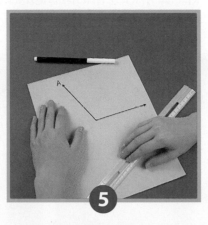

4

Explain how you would decide the number of degrees in four right angles. Sketch and label four different angles between 270° and 360°. Use the protractor on your Geometry Tool to check your angles.

5

Now draw an angle for each of the following: 110°, 145°, 190°, and 250°. Label the angles *A, B, C,* and *D*. Trade angles with your partner to check.

Notice that there are two scales on the protractor. How can you use your number sense and what you know about angle measure to decide which scale to read?

Ancient Babylonian civilization existed from about 4000 to 500 B.C. The Babylonians may have divided a circle into 360 parts because they thought a year had 360 days.

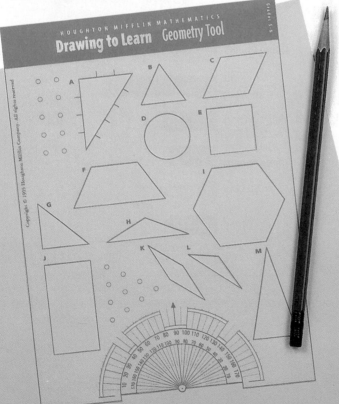

What You'll Need
- *Fraction Tool or compass and ruler*
- *Geometry Tool or protractor*

ACTIVITY 3 Circle Graphs

On Your Own Use the data below and what you know about angle measure to draw some circle graphs. You can also use your own data.

1 Choose one of the percents from the data.

2 Write a proportion to find its angle measure in a circle graph. Why does it help to round your answer to the nearest whole number?

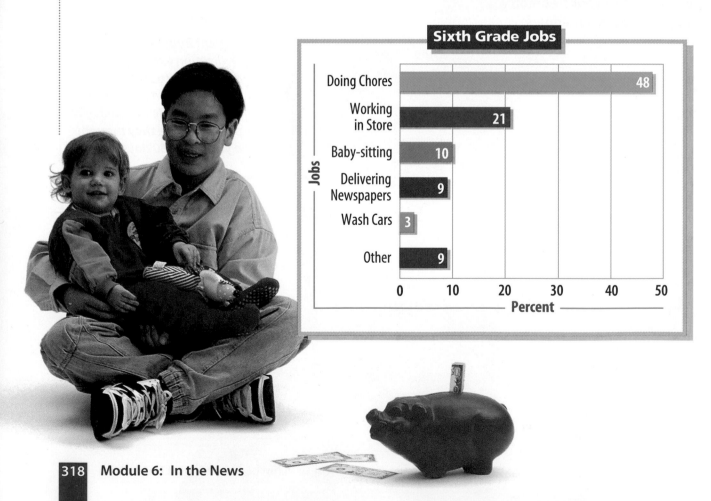

Sixth Grade Jobs

Jobs	Percent
Doing Chores	48
Working in Store	21
Baby-sitting	10
Delivering Newspapers	9
Wash Cars	3
Other	9

x

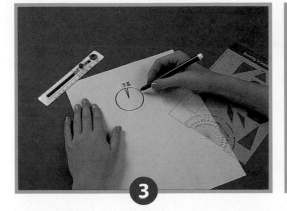

3 Sketch what you think the graph will look like. Then use your Fraction Tool or compass to draw a circle. Mark the center and draw a radius.

4 Use your protractor to find the number of degrees in the first angle. Place it along the radius you drew and line up the centers. Find and mark the angle you need on the circle. Then draw the radius.

5 Now find the angle measures for the other percents. Complete your graph.

Do You Remember?

Try It!

Solve and then draw a circle graph for each of the following.

1. 45% of 60   **2.** 27% of 75   **3.** 7% of 50

4. 16% of 40   **5.** 33% of 90   **6.** 60% of 125

Ali put $10 in a piggy bank in May. Use a line graph to show the contents of the bank each month.

7. June: added $10   **8.** July: took $5

9. August: added $5   **10.** September: took $5

Think About It

11. Write about how you found the percents for Exercises 1–6.

DRAWING TO LEARN

In one classroom 25% of the students read sports stories, 40% read mysteries, and 35% read nonfiction. Describe two circle graphs you can draw with this data.

Earning Interest

Buttons on some cash registers have pictures of items sold. When a button is pushed, an item's price appears. Why must each push on a button be a function?

Have you ever seen ads about **interest** rates? Some people save money in bank accounts because banks pay interest on deposits. Find out what interest means and how it makes money grow.

ACTIVITY 1 The Savings Function

With Your Partner The interest a bank pays on your money is a **function**. A function is a relationship that pairs an **input** with only one **output**.

A function pairs an input with one and only one output.

INPUT $100

4% INTEREST FUNCTION MACHINE

ON

OFF

1 Functions are predictable. If a relationship is a function, you can always tell what the output will be for a given input. Look at these examples. Which are functions? Explain your choice.

a. Input Output

$1 ⟶ $1.50
$2 ⟶ $3.00
$3 ⟶ $4.50

b. Input Output

$1 ⟶ $1.50
$2 ⟶ $3.00
$3 ⟶ $4.50

c. Input Output

$1
$2 ⟶ $3
$3

2 You can use the function table below to predict how much money can be earned in one year at a 5% interest rate. Copy and complete the table.

	Interest Earned					
Deposit	$10	$100	$1,000	$10,000	$100,000	$1,000,000
Interest at 5%	$0.50	$5	$50			

3 Now make your own tables for money deposited at 5.25% and 5.5% interest.

4 *American Demographics* magazine states that children in the United States saved $2,640 million in 1989. If they put the money in one account, how much would it earn at 5%, 5.25%, and 5.5%?

OUTPUT $104

Banks get the money to pay you interest by charging interest when they loan people money. Why would the interest a bank charges on loans be more than the interest it pays on savings?

ACTIVITY 2 Interest Line

With Your Partner Many parents' groups earn money for their schools. Understanding interest can help them invest money wisely and have more buying power later. In a savings account, the interest earned depends on how long the money is in the bank.

1 Suppose your school deposits $100 at 4% interest on January 1. That means if you leave it in the bank for one year, the money earns 4%. How much interest is that?

2 About how long do you think the school would have to keep the money in the bank to earn $2? When would it earn $3?

3 A line graph can help you estimate. How much money will you earn if you keep the money in the bank until September? What if you withdraw it in May?

$100 Deposited at 4% Interest per Year

4 You can also compute the interest for one month. What does the expression

$$\frac{1}{12} \times (4\% \times \$100)$$

tell you? How can you adjust it to find the amount of interest for any month of the year? Plot the interest for at least six dates.

5 Connect the points to make a line graph. What does the line between the points tell you? How do you know?

6 Look for interest rates in your local paper. Choose two rates and show the interest $100 would earn over one year.

Do You Remember?

Try It!

Make a table showing the interest per year for money saved at a 6.25% interest rate. Describe any patterns you see.

1. $75	**2.** $150	**3.** $225	**4.** $300
5. $375	**6.** $450	**7.** $525	**8.** $600

Find *n* in the equation $2a + (4b - 3c) = n$. Which exercise has the greatest value for *n*?

9. $a = 3.1, b = 4.75, c = 1.25$ **10.** $a = 4.8, b = 3.4, c = 2.2$

Think About It

11. How could you find the interest for six months in Exercises 1–8?

LESSON 8
City Life

Your newspaper's living section might include interesting stories about people. In *The Young Landlords*, some teens buy an old building for $1. Monthly bills and other problems start adding up, so the group decides to plan a street fair to raise money.

LITERATURE

Mr. Pender, the accountant, explains to Paul and his friends why they won't make much profit from the building.

Your insurance is equal to a little more than the cost of one and a half apartments. It would be foolish to try to operate a building without insurance. Normal wear and tear, if Mr. Darden does most of the minor repairs, can be kept at one half of one apartment over the cost of the apartment Mr. Darden lives in. Otherwise the cost would be closer to three and one-quarter apartments. Repairs caused by vandalism"—Mr. Pender looked up at us carefully when he said this—"comes to one apartment. That leaves a total profit of one apartment. So what you can expect to earn—that is, if you don't make any improvements in the building, nothing major breaks down, vandalism does not increase, all the apartments are rented and the rent is paid—is the equivalent of one apartment's annual rent."

From *The Young Landlords*
by Walter Dean Myers

ACTIVITY 1 Fund Raiser Figures

On Your Own Suppose the teens need to raise at least $400 to pay bills and have some money left over. To make sure the street fair is successful, they need to think of it as a business.

1 Evaluate the number sentence below by finding values for the variables. Which value do you know?

Item	Expense
Food	$100
Band	$ 75
Ticket/poster printing	$ 25
Booth rental	$ 25

$$t \quad - \quad e \quad \geq \quad \$400$$

Ticket sales for the fair | minus | expenses must be | greater than or equal to | $400.

2 Open sentences with $>$, $<$, $\geq$, $\leq$, or $\neq$ are **inequalities.** You solve them the same way you solve equations. Why must ticket sales be $625 or more?

3 Now price the tickets. Try charging $5 for each adult and admitting children for free.

$5a \geq \$625$ a = number of adults

How many adults must come at $5 per ticket? How do you know?

4 You think 100 adults will come. If an adult's ticket is $4 and a child's ticket is half price, how many children must come? Why does the number sentence below represent the problem?

$4a + 2c \geq \$625$ c = number of children

TOOLS AND TECHNIQUES

Many businesses use computer spreadsheet programs to help them organize their budgets. How could a spreadsheet help you with your fundraiser?

Street Fair

Section D: Solving Inequalities   **325**

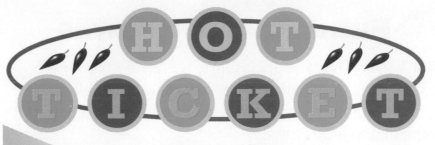

HOT TICKET

ACTIVITY 2 Spending Spree

With Your Group At the street fair, tickets are used as money. In this game, you start with 200 tickets. Solve inequalities to spend as few tickets as possible.

What You'll Need
- *gameboard*
- *spinner*
- *cube labeled 1–6*
- *game pieces*

1 Roll the number cube. Move that number of spaces. The space you land on is the expression you'll solve.

2 Spin the spinner. The symbols = , >, and < tell you how to solve the expression. Solve for *n*.

3 Keep score as you subtract *n* from your total number of tickets. Take turns playing.

> **Hint**
>
> Try to subtract the lowest number possible from your score. If your answer is > *n* or < *n*, choose a number that will help you spend the least number of tickets.

4 You can challenge incorrect answers. As a penalty for a wrong answer, a player must subtract the correct number and give 5 tickets to the challenger.

5 If your value for *n* is greater than your score, get extra tickets to finish your turn. Tickets come in books of 20. If you take 40 tickets, every player must take 40 tickets.

CONNECT AND COMMUNICATE

Explain why number sentences like f < 0.15 × 1,500 and n > 14 are called inequalities. What name do we give to "equalities"? Write an example.

6 You don't need to roll an exact number to reach Finish. When a player finishes, the remaining players complete the round. The player with the most tickets left wins.

✓ **Self-Check** *Keep a list of all the inequalities your group solved during the game. Swap lists with another group to check.*

REASONING AND PROBLEM SOLVING

If you needed more money to advertise a street fair, how could you convince the group to plan to spend more money? How would a bigger ad budget affect the ticket price?

ACTIVITY 3 Ad Rate Roundup

With Your Group The teens have planned $200 for an advertising campaign. How can they get the best ad for the money?

1 Research ad rates for at least two local papers. List the rates for different sizes of ads and for ads in the weekday and Sunday editions.

2 Compare the rates in terms of ad size and days of publication. Choose the best deal. Tell the class which kind of ad you chose and why. Show your equations and inequalities.

Do You Remember?

Try It!

Find the value for *n*. Circle the greatest value that you find.

1. $6n \geq 300$ **2.** $9n < 630$ **3.** $12n \geq 360$

4. $7n < 50$ **5.** $5n = 2.5 \times 8$ **6.** $2n + 45 \geq 225$

Complete and then write an equal ratio for each.

7. ■ qt in 6 gal   **8.** ■ pt in 4 qt

9. ■ c in 2 gal   **10.** ■ pt in 20 c

11. ■ qt in 6 gal   **12.** ■ c in 12 qt

Think About It

13. How did you solve Exercise 3? Write your answer.

Critic's Choice

If you held a food-festival fund raiser, you'd want to know which booths were most popular. A survey might help you. How would you show the results?

ACTIVITY 1 Fund Raiser Follow-up

With Your Group The scattergrams below show how two sets of data relate to each other. You can use them to draw conclusions.

Responses to Vegetarian Food

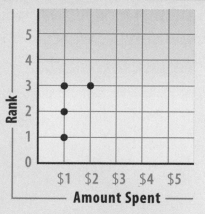

Rank / Amount Spent

Responses to Japanese Food

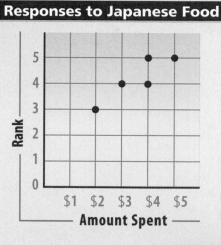

Rank / Amount Spent

1 What relationships do you see between the money a person spent and the rank he or she gave the food? What conclusions might you draw?

2 What responses might be added that would change your conclusions? Explain.

ACTIVITY OPTION

Survey 20 people about the kinds of food they would sell at a food festival. Ask them how much money they think people would spend at each booth. Choose a way to report your results. Show any relationships between the data.

	Thai	Greek	Italian
Person 1	★★★ $ $	★★ $ $ $	★★★ $ $ $
Person 2	★★ $ $ $	★★★★ $ $ $	★★ $ $ $ $
Person 3	★★★★ $ $	★★★ $ $	★ $ $ $ $

Rank ★ Poor	★★★★★ Excellent
Cost $ Inexpensive	$ $ $ $ $ Expensive

3 What relationships, if any, can you see between the amount of money a person spent at a booth and the rating he or she gave it? How could a scattergram help?

4 If you were planning another food festival, would you keep the same booths? Why? What changes, if any, would you make?

Italian: Ziti

Thai: Pad Thai

Greek: Gyros

 2 **Design a Survey**

With Your Group Use the topic below or one of your own as you survey at least 25 classmates. Then choose the best ways to show your data.

1 Ask people to give their first and last choice of five fund raisers, such as a street fair, car wash, bake sale, talent show, or book sale.

2 Ask questions that will help you decide which fund raiser to choose.

3 Make comparisons. Show how you used percents and proportions to make your recommendations.

Try two different kinds of graphs to show your results. Does one work better than the other? Explain.

Street Fair: $\dfrac{16}{40}$ people

$$\dfrac{16}{40} = \dfrac{n}{100}$$

Do You Remember?

Try It!

Six people bought bagels at a bake sale and ranked them from 1 to 5, 5 being best. Show their answers in a scattergram.

	1	2	3	4	5	6
Bought	4	2	3	1	1	5
Rank	2	5	3	4	3	2

Does the mean, median, or mode describe the score highlighted among the test scores shown below? Explain

7. 75, 80, 75, 79, **75**

8. 90, **95**, 100, 100, 90

9. 75, 65, 80, **75**, 80

10. 87, **87**, 99, 100, 87

11. 88, 85, 88, 90, **88**

12. 68, 93, 83, 75, **86**

Think About It

13. Explain how you set up the scattergram for Exercises 1–6.

Looking Back

Choose *a*, *b*, *c*, or *d* for each question.

1. Which ratios are equal?

   a. $\frac{2}{3}$ and $\frac{5}{8}$ **b.** $\frac{20}{24}$ and $\frac{3}{4}$

   c. $\frac{7}{35}$ and $\frac{3}{15}$ **d.** $\frac{11}{16}$ and $\frac{14}{25}$

2. Which ratio is greater than $\frac{4}{5}$?

   a. $\frac{2}{3}$ **b.** $\frac{25}{40}$

   c. $\frac{9}{12}$ **d.** $\frac{7}{8}$

3. Which proportion can you write for $\frac{5}{6} = \frac{n}{12}$?

   a. $5n = 60$ **b.** $6n = 60$
   c. $48n = 6$ **d.** $5n = 72$

4. You have $12. You spend $7 and give $4 to a friend. You find $3, then lose $1. How much is left?

   a. $5   **b.** $13
   c. $3   **d.** $11

5. A football team gained 12 yd, lost 15 yd, then gained 6 yd. How many yards did they gain in all?

   a. 3   **b.** 21
   c. 27   **d.** 9

6. Find the equation in which $n = 12$.

   a. $8n = 72$ **b.** $120n = 360$
   c. $15n = 180$ **d.** $10n = 84$

Use the ads for Exercises 7–8.

7. Which equation shows the discount for Video World?

   a. $0.30 \times 20 = n$ **b.** $0.25 \times 18 = n$
   c. $20 \div 30 = n$ **d.** $30 \times 20 = n$

8. What is the difference in the sale prices at the two stores?

   a. $0.50   **b.** $4.50
   c. $6.00   **d.** $1.50

Use the graph for Exercises 9–11.

Favorite Pets

9. Fifty people answered the survey. How many of them prefer dogs?

  a. 15   **b.** 29
  c. 25   **d.** 9

10. Use a protractor to find the angle measure for the percent of cat lovers.

  a. 72°   **b.** 90°
  c. 40°   **d.** 120°

11. Find the angle measure for the percent of people who prefer either fish or dogs.

  a. 225°   **b.** 162°
  c. 75°   **d.** 198°

12. Which is the value of n in the inequality $25n \leq 100$?

  a. $n \leq 25$ **b.** $n \leq 90$
  c. $n \leq 4$ **d.** $n \leq 10$

13. Solve the expression $3(6 + 5) + 2$.

  a. 25   **b.** 39
  c. 35   **d.** 16

14. Fifty adults pay $5 each for tickets, and 150 children pay $2.50 each. Which expression shows how to find the total sales?

  a. $(150 \times \$5) + (50 \times \$2.50)$
  b. $(\$50 \times 250) + (\$1.50 \times 23)$
  c. $(50 \times \$5) + (150 \times \$2.50)$
  d. none of the above

15. What is the function rule for these inputs and outputs?

Input	0.5	1	2	3	4	25	100
Output	5	6	8	10	12	54	204

  a. $3n + 3$ **b.** $2n + 4$
  c. $n + 6$ **d.** $0.05n - 2$

Check Your Math Power

16. Write a function rule, such as $5n - 1$. Make a chart that shows at least five inputs and outputs for your rule.

17. Explain why you think a circle graph is or is not the best way to display the Favorite Pets data from Exercises 9–11. What changes, if any, would you make?

18. Survey your class about its favorite subject. Make a graph for your data and show how you used percents and proportions to draw conclusions.

MODULE 6 Investigations

That's Entertainment

You're an editor for your school's new newspaper! Your first assignment is to plan a page in the entertainment section. Choose an investigation to get you started.

Investigation A — Design a Page

1 List at least four items, such as movie reviews or ads, to go on your page. Decide what percent of space in the columns each item should take up.

2 Make a graph to show how you would divide the space on the page.

Book Section

Book review   40%
Author profile   30%
Chart   15%
Photo   10%
Ads   5%

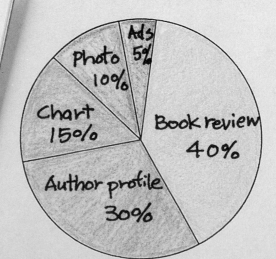

3 Plan your page. Make sure you have a $\frac{1}{2}$-in. border on all sides. Divide the space inside the border into equal columns, with a $\frac{1}{4}$-in. space between columns.

4 Find the total length of your columns in inches. Use your knowledge of proportions to change the percents in your graph to inches in a column.

5 Use your proportions to help you set up the page. Label each item with its name and percent.

Photo
10%

Vol. 4, No. 1

★ The G

Horace Greele

Gre

By Aleksan

G
Academic O
Olympics is a
kids who kno
poems and
Olympics invo
the elementary

The
involved in we
more) and recit
the children had
them which was
in today's music
there was a limit
upper grades had

essays, t

Modernizes

By Leonard Peplinski

Greeley School ha
telephone

Keep in Mind

Your page will be judged by how well you do these things.

☐ How well do you show your understanding of percents when you use a graph?

☐ How well do you show your knowledge of proportions when you decide how many inches of space each item will need?

☐ How clearly do you show on your page the amount of space each item will take up?

Investigations **335**

Investigation B — Survey Your Page

Take a readership survey! Find out what students want to read most in the entertainment section of the school paper. Collect your data and show the results in a graph. Then use the data to design a page that reflects what students said they wanted to read. Explain to the class how you made the graph and how you decided where to place each item.

Ongoing Investigation — Tessellating Pairs

Try making tessellations using pairs of regular polygons. For example, you might try octagons and squares. How many different ways can you find to tessellate with pairs of shapes? Are there any pairs that won't work? Add your tessellations and notes to your portfolio.

Shaping Your World

Bounded by walls, floors, and ceilings, space can be made in any shape and size imaginable. We need spaces to work and to sleep, spaces in which to gather together, and private corners in which to think by ourselves. People always find new ways to design spaces to fit their needs. In this module, you will explore how to use geometry to shape space. Then you will design a space that people of all ages can share.

SECTION **A**

Shaping a Space

SECTION **B**

Giving an Idea Shape

SECTION **C**

Beautiful Math

SECTION **D**

Designing Solutions

Planning to Build

Architects are people who design buildings. Contractors construct the buildings from the architects' plans. Why do you think architects need to be very specific when describing buildings on paper? What do you think architects need to know?

1 Naming Space

How is a school different from a house? Make a list of different kinds of buildings. What are they used for? Who uses them? What shapes and sizes are the spaces inside? How do private spaces and public spaces differ? How do their shapes and sizes fit their purposes?

How would living in a round room be different from living in a square room? What problems might you have with your furniture?

How do you think a computer helps an architect work?

- angle of rotation
- arc
- congruent
- corresponding angles
- corresponding sides
- curve
- diagonal
- regular polygon
- similar figures
- skew lines

2 The Tools of Space

How do you think measurement and geometry help architects and contractors design and build buildings?

Investigate! Investigate! Investigate! Investigate! Investigate! Investigate! Investigate! Investigate! Investigate! Investigate! Investigate! Investigate! Investigate! Investigate!

Investigations Preview

You will learn to describe, define, and construct different kinds of shapes. This will help you build real bridges and design places for all to share.

Building Bridges (pages 368–369)
Knowing how shapes function will help you design a working bridge out of paper.

Over the Wall (pages 398–400)
How would you design the inside of a room that people of all ages could share? Use what you learn about shapes, patterns, and networks to help you plan a space.

LESSON 1 Get the Point

CONNECT AND COMMUNICATE

Why is a line written $\overleftrightarrow{AB}$, a line segment $\overline{AB}$, and a ray $\overrightarrow{AB}$?

When architects design buildings, they are shaping space. Each drawing an architect makes begins with a **point.** Then geometry provides the building blocks used to shape space.

ACTIVITY 1 Shapes Down Under

With Your Partner Use the Sydney Opera House and Exercises 1–5 to explore what you know about geometry.

windows

1 Look at line segment *AB* ($\overline{AB}$). Why is this a line segment and not a line? What do the *A* and *B* refer to?

Diagram of the west side of the Sydney Opera House

2 An arc is part of a circle. Where are arcs used in the drawing? How can you use letters to name different arcs so you can tell them apart?

This is the east side of the Sydney Opera House in Sydney, Australia. Designed by the Danish architect Jørn Utzon, it was built between 1957 and 1973.

3 An **angle** is made of two **rays** that share a common endpoint, or **vertex**. Name all the vertexes in one set of windows.

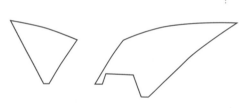

4 These two shapes are **congruent** to two pieces of the roof. Trace one and place it over the diagram. What does *congruent* mean?

5 A **plane** is a flat surface that goes in all directions infinitely. How could you use sheets of paper to show that the wall and the ground are not in the same plane in any building?

ACTIVITY
2 Shaping Up

With Your Partner Design the face of a building. Label ten line segments and shapes in your drawing. Then list them.

What You'll Need
- *crayons or markers*
- *Tracing Tool or ruler*

Between the Lines

On Your Own Lines may be parallel or perpendicular or neither. In your journal, either describe where on pages 340–341 you find parallel and perpendicular line segments or identify them on your drawing from page 341. Some line segments may neither intersect nor run parallel because they are not in the same plane. These are called **skew lines.** Why can skew lines not be perpendicular? Explain your answer.

Are these lines in the same plane? How do you know?

Do You Remember?

Try It!

Draw each figure.

1. $\overleftrightarrow{AB}$ **2.** $\overrightarrow{CD}$ **3.** $\overline{AB}$ **4.** *point A* **5.** $\angle ABC$

Find the area of a 4.2-m-wide rectangle if the length is one of the following.

6. 3.3 m **7.** 0.6 m **8.** 9.5 m **9.** 0.2 m **10.** 7.4 m

Think About It

11. Explain in writing how the items in Exercises 1–3 are similar and different.

✔ **Self-Check** *Are all intersecting lines perpendicular? Explain.*

Describe a Shape

Architects may start with points, lines, and angles. But only when the three come together to form polygons does a building start to take shape. In this lesson you will see that the more closely you look at a shape, the more you can say about it.

A plane figure is a shape whose points all lie in one plane. Which of the figures below are plane figures?

ACTIVITY 1 Define a Curve

With Your Group Curves are figures you can draw without lifting your pencil off the paper. Look at the chart below and decide why each figure belongs to its category.

1 Why are all these figures curves?

2 Which of the curves are not closed curves? Explain.

3 In which of these figures do segments intersect?

4 Which of these figures are made of only line segments?

5 Draw five more examples for each category. Then write a definition for each category.

Curves
Curves
Closed Curves
Simple Closed Curves
Polygons

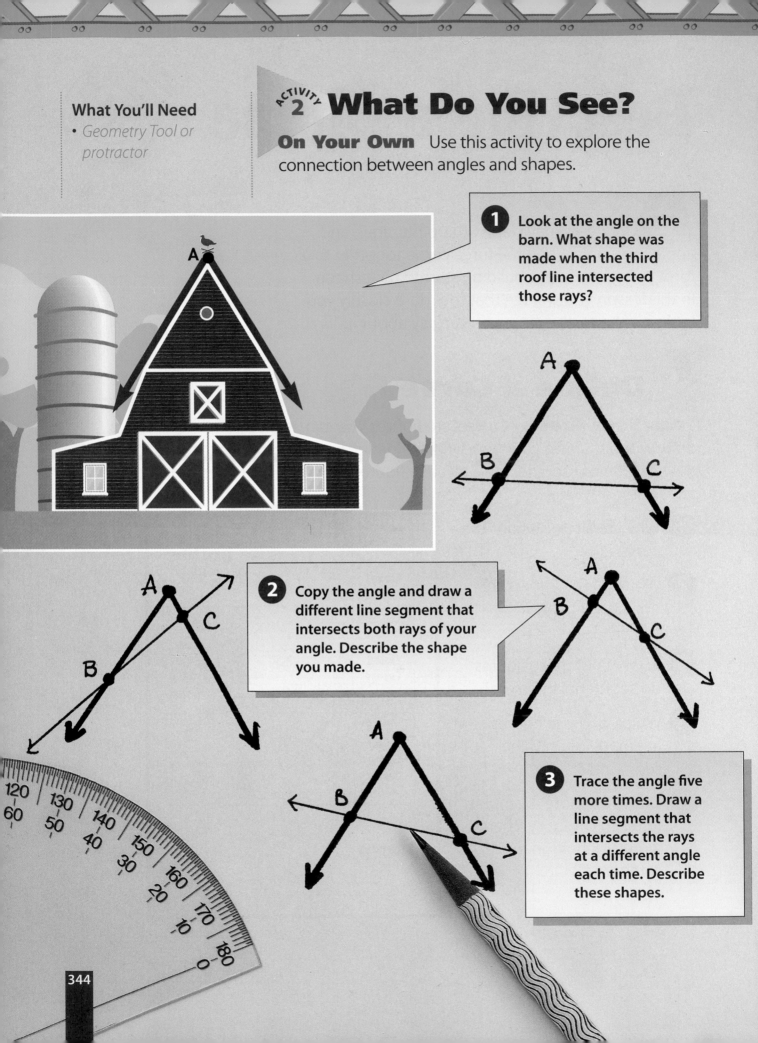

What You'll Need
- *Geometry Tool or protractor*

ACTIVITY 2 What Do You See?

On Your Own Use this activity to explore the connection between angles and shapes.

1 Look at the angle on the barn. What shape was made when the third roof line intersected those rays?

2 Copy the angle and draw a different line segment that intersects both rays of your angle. Describe the shape you made.

3 Trace the angle five more times. Draw a line segment that intersects the rays at a different angle each time. Describe these shapes.

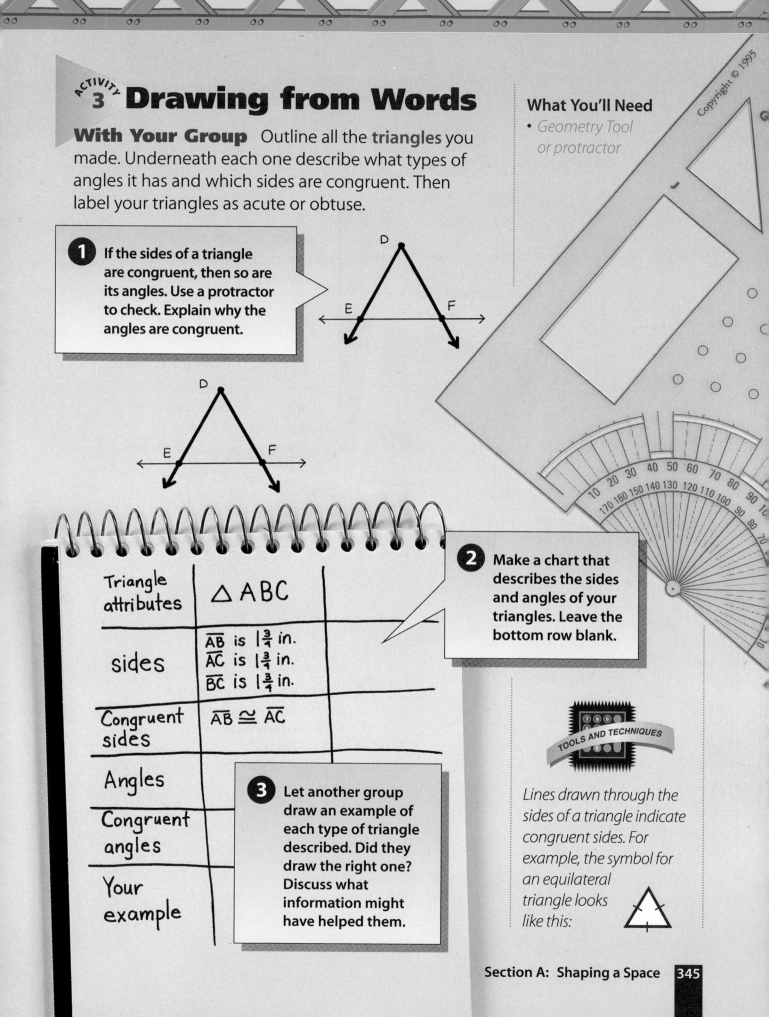

^{ACTIVITY} 3 Drawing from Words

What You'll Need
• *Geometry Tool or protractor*

With Your Group Outline all the **triangles** you made. Underneath each one describe what types of angles it has and which sides are congruent. Then label your triangles as acute or obtuse.

1 If the sides of a triangle are congruent, then so are its angles. Use a protractor to check. Explain why the angles are congruent.

2 Make a chart that describes the sides and angles of your triangles. Leave the bottom row blank.

Triangle attributes	△ ABC
sides	$\overline{AB}$ is $1\frac{3}{4}$ in. $\overline{AC}$ is $1\frac{3}{4}$ in. $\overline{BC}$ is $1\frac{3}{4}$ in.
Congruent sides	$\overline{AB} \cong \overline{AC}$
Angles	
Congruent angles	
Your example	

3 Let another group draw an example of each type of triangle described. Did they draw the right one? Discuss what information might have helped them.

TOOLS AND TECHNIQUES

Lines drawn through the sides of a triangle indicate congruent sides. For example, the symbol for an equilateral triangle looks like this:

Section A: Shaping a Space 345

ACTIVITY 4 Define and Refine

With Your Group Try this activity to see how precise a definition for a triangle you can write.

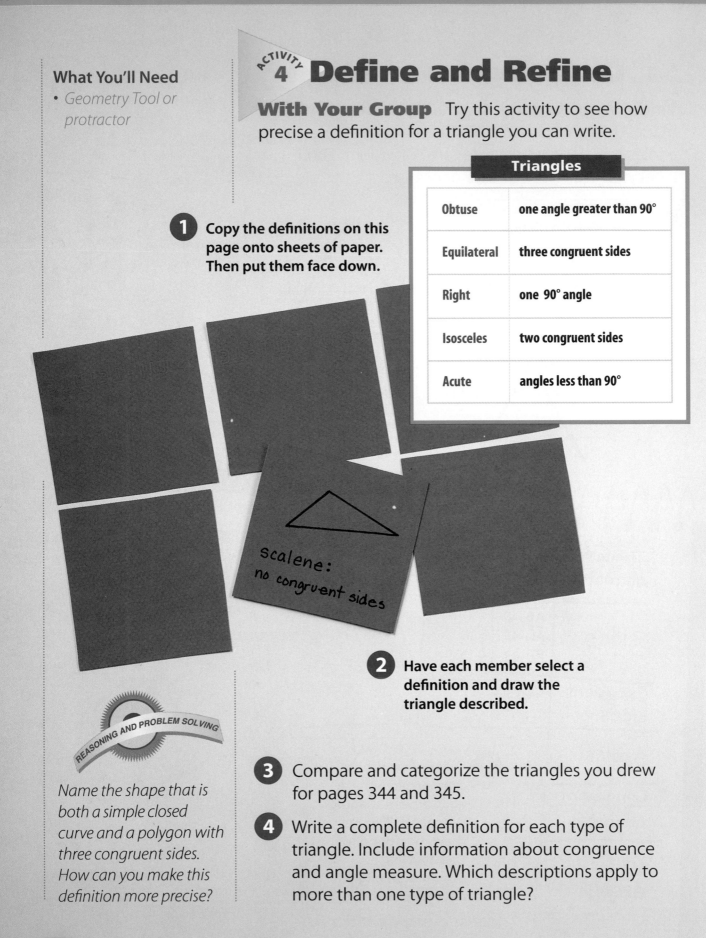

Triangles	
Obtuse	**one angle greater than 90°**
Equilateral	**three congruent sides**
Right	**one 90° angle**
Isosceles	**two congruent sides**
Acute	**angles less than 90°**

1 Copy the definitions on this page onto sheets of paper. Then put them face down.

scalene: no congruent sides

2 Have each member select a definition and draw the triangle described.

REASONING AND PROBLEM SOLVING

Name the shape that is both a simple closed curve and a polygon with three congruent sides. How can you make this definition more precise?

3 Compare and categorize the triangles you drew for pages 344 and 345.

4 Write a complete definition for each type of triangle. Include information about congruence and angle measure. Which descriptions apply to more than one type of triangle?

ACTIVITY 5 The Big Picture

What You'll Need
• *index cards*
• *scissors*
• *string*
• *hanger*
• *crayons or markers*
• *straws*

On Your Own Use what you know about curves, closed curves, polygons, and triangles to make a geometry mobile that shows how shapes are related.

 1 On cards show examples of curves, closed curves, open curves, and polygons. Write a definition on the back of each card.

2 Where should you attach a card labeled *Triangles*? Add it to your mobile.

3 Cut out examples of different kinds of triangles, label them, and hang them from the mobile.

With Your Group Compare your mobile with mobiles of other students. Describe any differences you see. Explain any changes you think you need to make to your mobile. Revise your mobile, if necessary, and draw a diagram of it in your journal.

What You'll Need

- *scissors*
- *ruler*

DRAWING TO LEARN

Draw a right triangle. Explain how you could use it as a guide to help you draw both obtuse triangles and acute triangles.

ACTIVITY 6 # Pick Up the Pieces

With Your Partner Divide a sheet of paper into six triangles. Cut them out and give them to your partner to reassemble. Have your partner describe the kinds of triangles that fit in each space. Then switch roles and solve your partner's puzzle.

Exchange your puzzles with another pair of students. Give them all 12 pieces from both puzzles and see whether they can solve them.

Do You Remember?

Try It!

Describe each triangle below.

1.   2.   3.   4.   5.

Find the circle's other measurements so you have circumference, radius, and diameter.

6. $r = 12.3$ cm   **7.** $d = 42$ cm   **8.** $C \approx 15.7$ cm
9. $C \approx 17.27$ cm   **10.** $d = 37$ cm   **11.** $r = 5$ cm

Think About It

12. Why can't an equilateral triangle be an obtuse triangle?

What's Your Angle?

Angles play an important role in architecture. A 90° angle can be seen in most corners, and a 180° straight angle can be seen on most floors. What angles do you see in the structure below? Which angles share a vertex? Put together, angles can make things stand up!

ACTIVITY 1 A Matter of Degrees

With Your Partner Look at the diagram and answer the questions.

1 Why is a **straight angle** a good name for an angle that, like ∠FAB, measures 180°?

2 Can you combine two obtuse angles to make a right angle? Explain.

3 Which pairs of angles together can make a straight angle?

4 Find ∠BAC. Which point is the vertex? Explain.

5 Can two acute angles make a right angle? Show it.

In Your Journal Search out angles in other structures in your world. Draw and describe them. Where do you find pairs of angles that make right and straight angles?

What You'll Need
- *Geometry Tool or protractor*

ACTIVITY 2 Sum of the Angles

With Your Partner Look at one of the triangles you made for page 348. What would you estimate the sum of the angles in your triangle to be? Try to find out!

1 Tear off two corners.

2 Rearrange the three pieces so that they form a straight angle. What is the sum of the angles?

3 Reassemble the triangle and measure the angles. What is their sum? Will the sum of the angles of any triangle be the same? How do you know?

ACTIVITY 3 Missing Angles

With Your Partner Look at the large picture on the next page. Use what you know about the sum of the angles in any triangle to find the measures of any missing angles in a triangle. Then write an explanation of how you found each.

CONNECT AND COMMUNICATE

In Your Journal Describe how different triangles are alike. Is there a triangle the sum of whose angles would be greater than or less than 180°? Explain.

350 **Module 7: Shaping Your World**

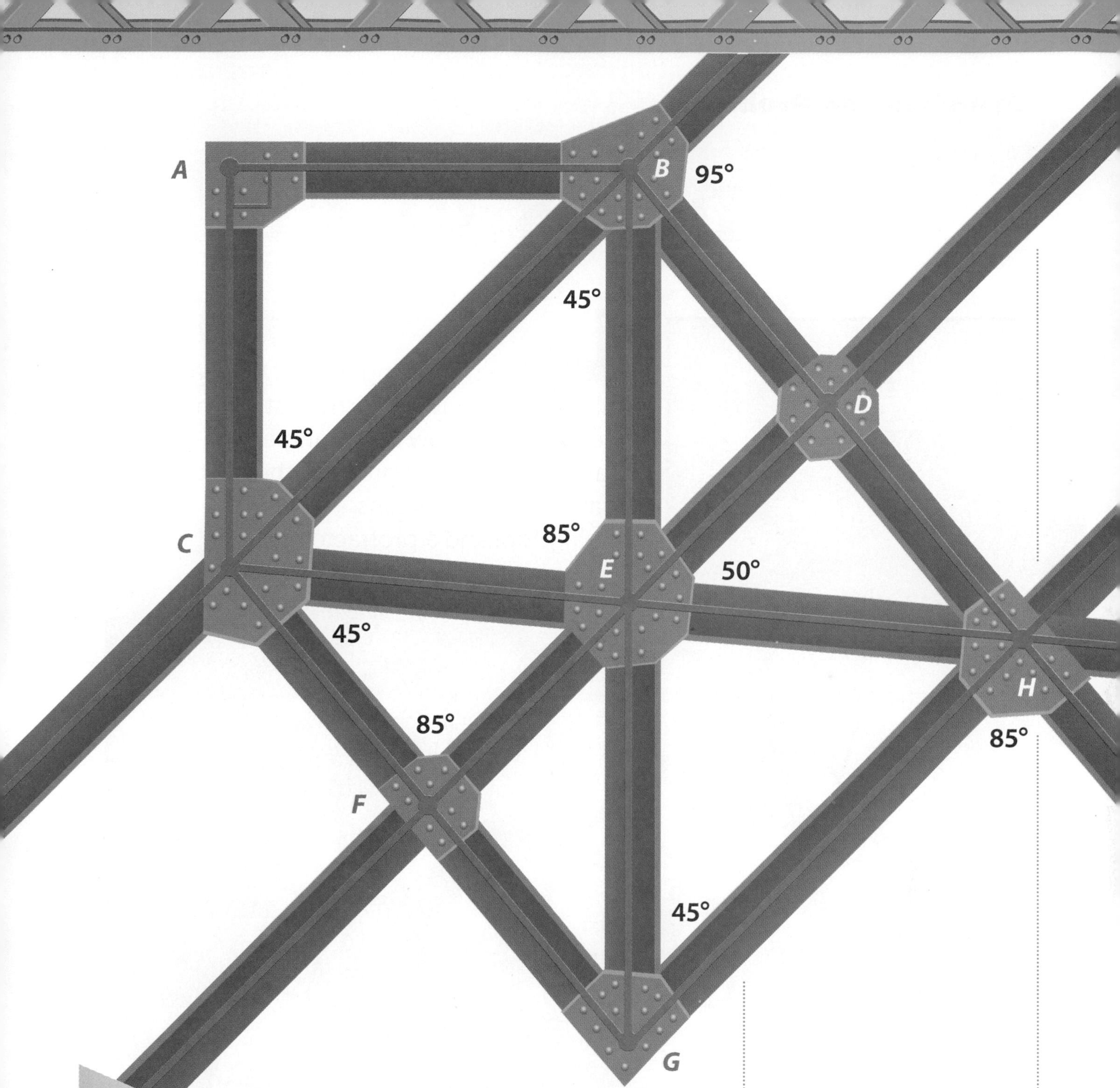

A

B 95°

45°

45°

C

45°

D

85°

E

50°

45°

85°

H

85°

F

45°

G

ACTIVITY 4 **Different Angles**

With Your Partner Draw and label a structure like the one above, using different kinds of triangles. Measure and label two of the three angles for each triangle. Then exchange drawings with your partner and find the missing angles. Does your partner work the same way you do? Describe your process.

What You'll Need
• *Geometry Tool or protractor*

Section A: Shaping a Space 351

Triangles of Light

Look at the ceiling of the National Gallery of Art. It is full of interesting shapes. Use what you know about angles and triangles and the diagram on the next page to answer the questions. You may use your Tracing Tool and a protractor.

The East Building of the National Gallery of Art in Washington, D.C., was designed by American architect I. M. Pei.

1 If a triangle has one angle that measures 75°, can one of the other two angles measure 110°? Explain your answer.

2 Name three angles that together form a straight angle.

3 Name two angles that together form a right angle.

4 Name two pairs of triangles that appear to be flips of one another.

5 Does the diagram show that triangles *CGE* and *BDC* are congruent? Explain how you found out.

6 Explain one way to find out if ∠ *ACH* and ∠ *FCH* are congruent.

7 Describe a way to prove that the sums of the measures of the angles in triangles *EFG* and *CGE* are equal.

Some of the pieces of glass that appear to form the triangles in the picture you see are really pointing outward toward the sky.

8 If you think of triangle *ABC* as the base of a three-dimensional figure, what kind of figure are the points *A, B, C,* and *D* part of?

9 On the actual ceiling, are the triangles *ABD* and *ACD* in the same plane? How do you know?

10 Think of your answer to Exercise 8. Describe another way to think of the figure, using a different triangle for the base.

LESSON 4

Name That Shape

Look at the chart of common polygons on this page. Where do you see these shapes in the classroom? How are they being used?

Shapes are the tools architects work with to design spaces. Using shapes correctly requires knowing about all their different characteristics. Therefore, having a good definition for each shape is important.

ACTIVITY 1 Building Blocks

With Your Class How many examples of each polygon in the chart can you find in this Japanese office building? Describe where you find each one.

How many different names do you know for this polygon?

A quadrilateral is a four-sided polygon. How many different quadrilaterals can you find?

The Shibuya Higashi T Building on page 355 is a small office building in the middle of Tokyo designed by architect Kisho Kurokawa. Completed in 1989, this building is made of many different materials: concrete, granite, metal, and glass.

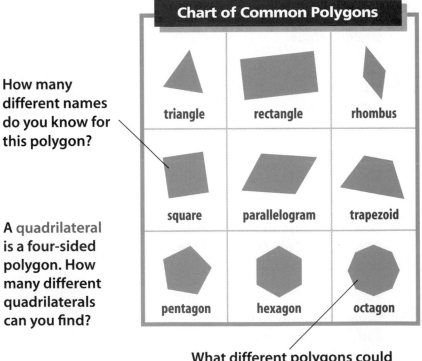

Chart of Common Polygons

triangle	rectangle	rhombus
square	parallelogram	trapezoid
pentagon	hexagon	octagon

What different polygons could you break this shape into?

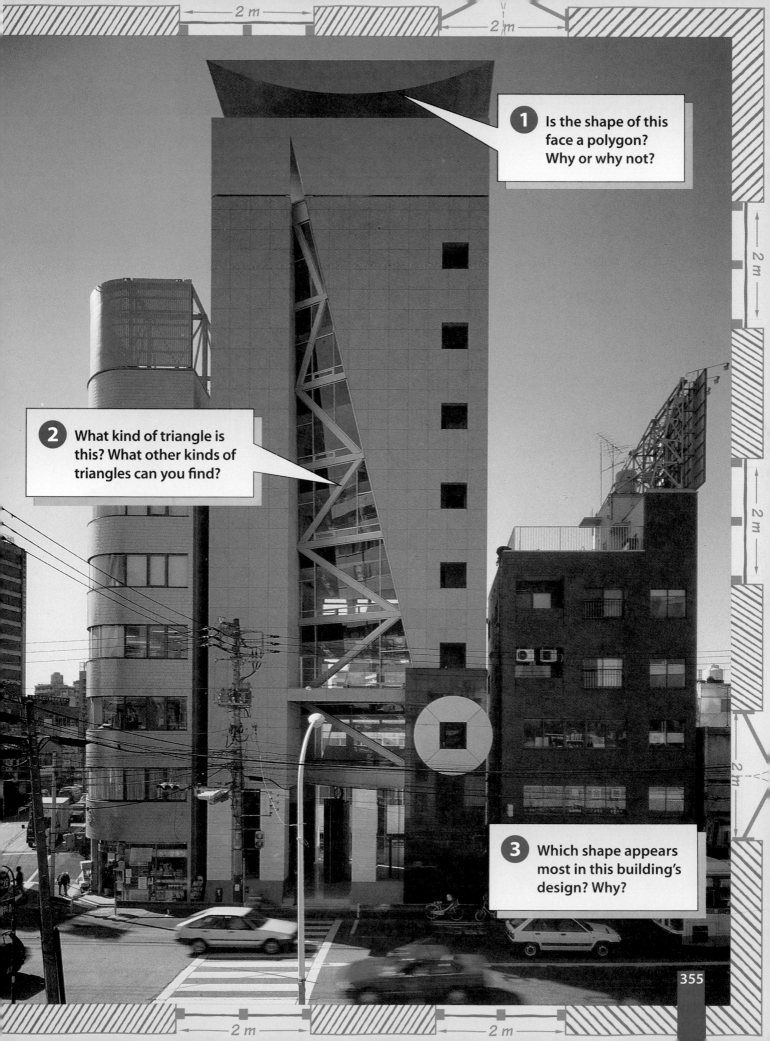

355

What You'll Need
- *scissors*
- *straws*

2 Regular Shapes

With Your Partner Use what you know about congruence and angles to explore polygons. First cut some straws into pieces.

1 With your straws make several 3- to 10-sided polygons. Sketch them. Repeat this step, using only straws cut in half.

2 On your sketches circle the polygons with all sides and angles congruent. Why do you think these shapes are called regular polygons? Write a definition for a regular polygon in your journal.

2 m

2 m

2 m

2 m

ACTIVITY 3 ▶ Drawing Diagonals

With Your Partner A **diagonal** is a line segment that connects two vertexes but is not a side. Use diagonals to help find the sum of the angles of any polygon.

What You'll Need
• *Geometry Tool or protractor*

1 Use your Geometry Tool to make five different 4- to 10-sided polygons.

2 Draw as many diagonals as you can in each polygon without letting any intersect. What shapes do these diagonals form?

diagonal

3 Use what you know about the sum of the angles of triangles to estimate the sum of the angles of each polygon. How can you test your estimate?

*2 triangles
Each has 180°.
How many degrees altogether?*

REASONING AND PROBLEM SOLVING

HOU...

Drawing to Learn Geometry Tool

Grades 5–6

A B C

D E

F

G

H I

J K L

What is the relation of the number of sides of a polygon to the number of diagonals in it that do not intersect? How many diagonals do not intersect in a 12-sided polygon?

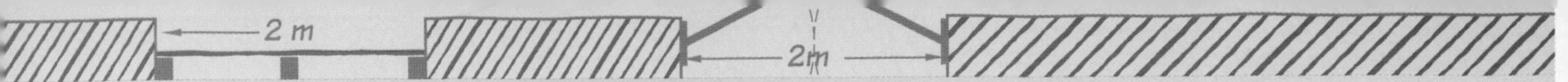

What You'll Need

- *straws*
- *tape*
- *pipe cleaners*
- *scissors*

ACTIVITY 4

Straw Structures

With Your Group Use straws and tape or pipe cleaners to make the tallest structures you can in ten minutes. Divide your group in half. Have one half build with only triangles. Have the other group build using other shapes. Which structure stands up best? Why?

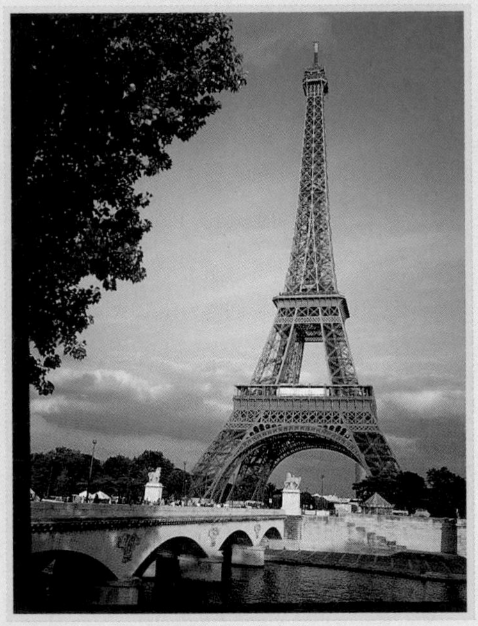

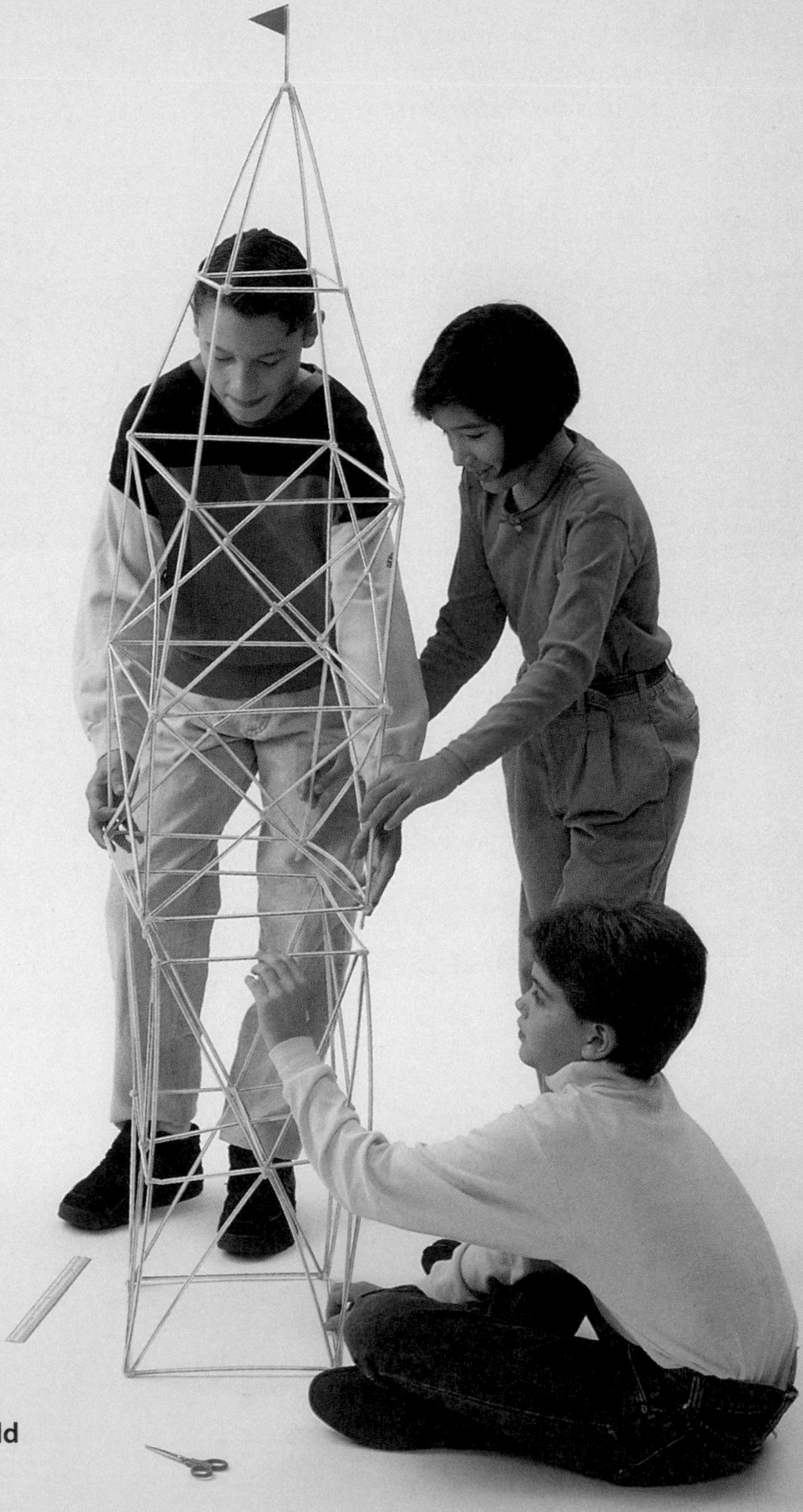

TOOLS AND TECHNIQUES

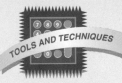

Throughout history, architects have depended on triangles to make structures strong. When the 300-m Eiffel Tower in Paris, France, was completed in 1889, it was the tallest structure in the world.

ACTIVITY 5 ▶ Standing Firm

With Your Partner Try this activity to explore the strength of shapes.

1 Cut congruent strips of cardboard. Use paper fasteners to make a 4- to 10-sided polygon. Can you move the sides of this figure?

2 Make a different 4- to 10-sided polygon. Can you move its sides? Why or why not?

3 Add strips of cardboard to your polygon until it becomes rigid. Test strips in different positions. Which positions allow you to use the fewest strips? Collect data on the shapes your classmates use.

4 Based on this data, which polygon do you think is the most rigid? How did you find your answer? Test your generalization by making this shape with cardboard strips.

CONNECT AND COMMUNICATE

In Your Journal Write a definition of a rigid figure. Explain what makes a figure rigid and why you think it is important for architects to understand.

Section B: Giving an Idea Shape 359

To check your definitions, draw quadrilaterals that are not on your list.

ACTIVITY 6 Drawing Fours

On Your Own Sketch one example of each kind of quadrilateral shown on page 354. Label them. Under each sketch write the letters of all the statements that apply:

a. has at least one pair of parallel sides
b. has at least one pair of parallel and congruent sides
c. has at least one pair of parallel and congruent sides and all right angles
d. has all congruent and parallel sides and all right angles

parallelogram
a, b

rectangle

trapezoid
a

square

Write a definition for each kind of quadrilateral, and then use what you know to add them to your mobile.

ACTIVITY 7 Shape a Dictionary

On Your Own Fold ten pieces of paper in half and fasten them in the middle to make a book. On each page, draw an example of a different common polygon. Label each shape and write as complete a description as possible. Think about all the attributes of line segments, angles, and shapes as you write.

What You'll Need
• *paper fasteners or stapler*
• *Geometry Tool or protractor*

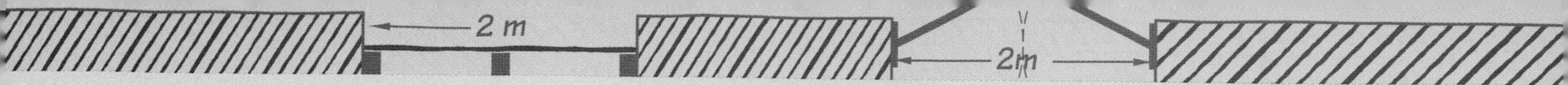

With Your Group Copy a description from your shape dictionary on the bottom half of a piece of paper. Attach several pieces of paper as shown below. Have each group member draw a picture of your description, then fold back their page. If they did not draw the polygon you described, discuss how to improve your definition.

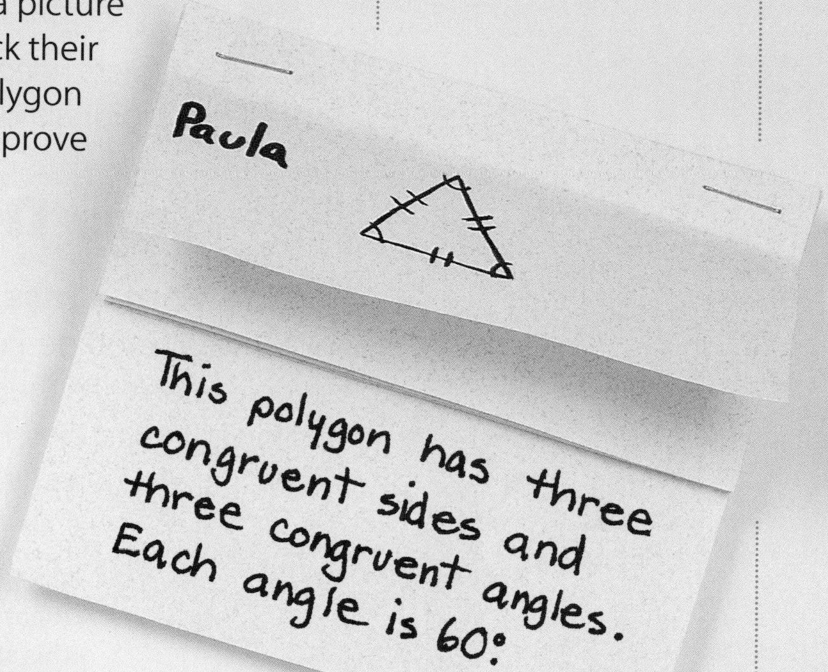

Paula

This polygon has three congruent sides and three congruent angles. Each angle is 60°.

Try It!

Match the words with the drawings below. There may be more than one answer for each. Write the letter(s) for each exercise.

1. polygon **2.** rectangle a. 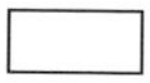 ▭ b.  ⌂ c. 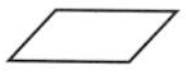 ▱

3. quadrilateral **4.** trapezoid d. 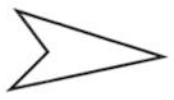 ▷ e. ◻ f. 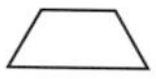 ⬡

5. parallelogram **6.** square g.  ▱ h.  ⬡ i. 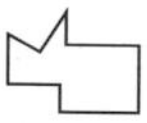 ⬟

Trace and measure the angles below with your Tracing Tool or a protractor. Extend the rays to make them easier to measure.

7.  **8.** 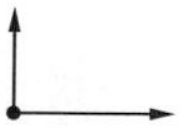 **9.**  **10.**  **11.**

Think About It

12. Write about how you used the definitions of polygons to help you answer Exercises 1–6.

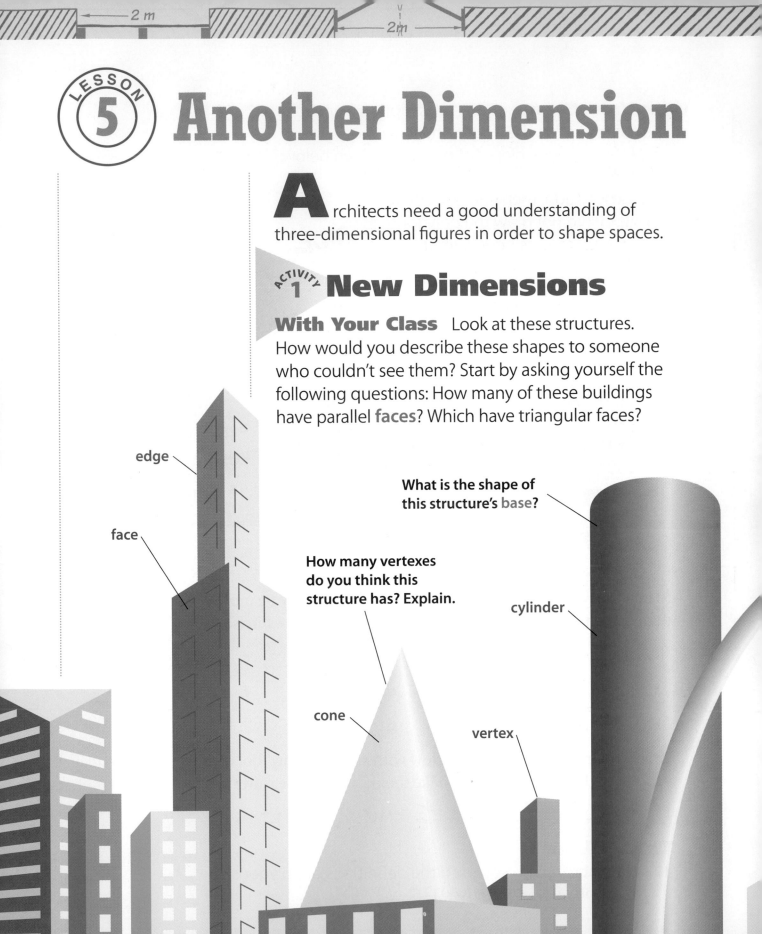

LESSON 5 Another Dimension

Architects need a good understanding of three-dimensional figures in order to shape spaces.

ACTIVITY 1 New Dimensions

With Your Class Look at these structures. How would you describe these shapes to someone who couldn't see them? Start by asking yourself the following questions: How many of these buildings have parallel **faces**? Which have triangular faces?

edge

face

What is the shape of this structure's base?

How many vertexes do you think this structure has? Explain.

cylinder

cone

vertex

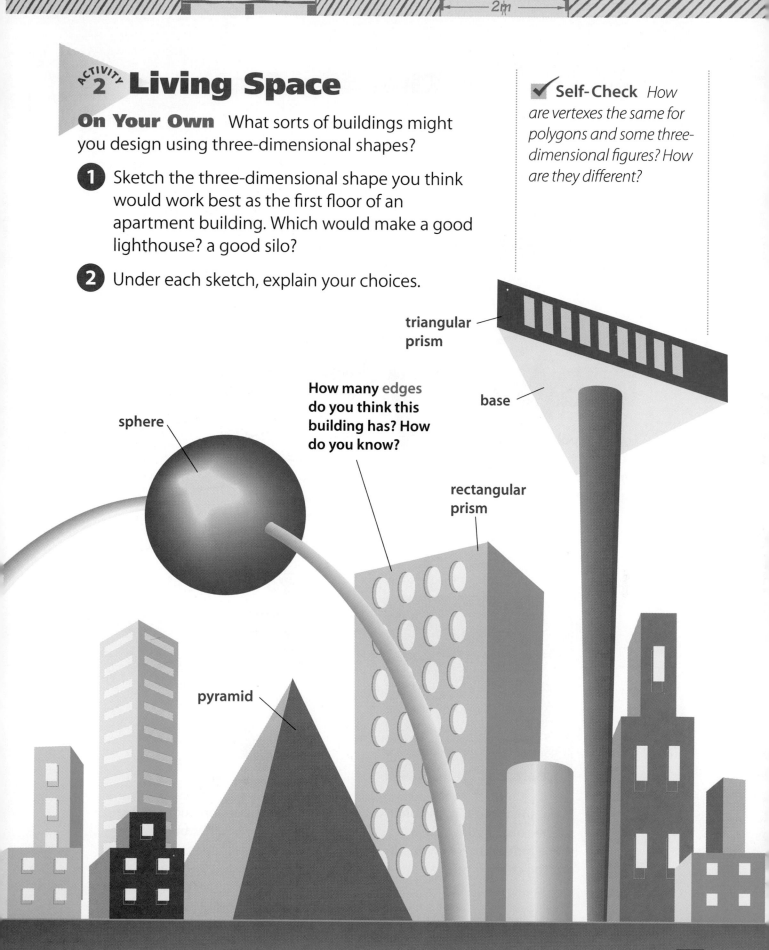

ACTIVITY 2 Living Space

On Your Own What sorts of buildings might you design using three-dimensional shapes?

1 Sketch the three-dimensional shape you think would work best as the first floor of an apartment building. Which would make a good lighthouse? a good silo?

2 Under each sketch, explain your choices.

✔ **Self-Check** How are vertexes the same for polygons and some three-dimensional figures? How are they different?

2 m

2 m

triangular prism

base

sphere

How many edges do you think this building has? How do you know?

rectangular prism

pyramid

What You'll Need

- *straws*
- *tape*
- *grid paper*
- *scissors*

^{ACTIVITY} **3** ▶ **Charting Precision**

With Your Group Use your dictionary of shapes to help you understand and describe three-dimensional shapes. Complete Steps 1–3 in any order you choose.

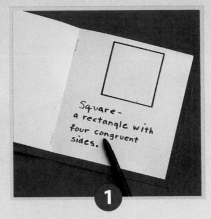

Square– a rectangle with four congruent sides.

1

For each polygon in your dictionary, write down all the three-dimensional shapes that have it as a base.

Shape of base	Cube	Cylinder
Number of flat faces	square	
Shape of faces	6	
Number of congruent edges		
Number of congruent angles		
Kinds of angles		

2

Make a chart like this one for each three-dimensional shape. Be sure to include your own categories.

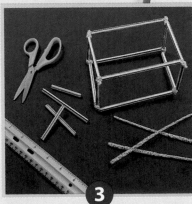

3

Make the three-dimensional shapes out of straws. Use these models to help you fill out the chart.

4

What shapes on pages 362 and 363 have you not built? Why? Add those shapes and any new categories to your chart. Can you make these shapes out of paper? straws? Explain.

ACTIVITY 4 · You're the Contractor

With Your Group Fold the chart you made in Activity 3 so that the shapes' names are hidden.

1 Exchange your chart for another group's. Use their chart to draw nets of the shapes described. Remember, a net is a pattern that folds into a three-dimensional shape. Draw as many different kinds of nets as you can.

2 Cut out and assemble your nets. Discuss the results. For which items were you able to construct more than one net? What other categories might have made your job easier? Add these categories to your chart.

With Your Class Make a master chart using all the groups' lists. Select which categories help define shapes in the most precise way. Then fill it out.

What You'll Need

- *Geometry Tool or protractor*
- *scissors*
- *tape*

CONNECT AND COMMUNICATE

In Your Journal Explain what you think makes a good definition for any given shape.

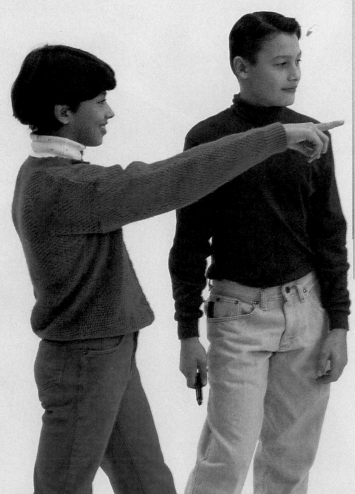

Three-dimensional Shapes and Their Attributes

	Cone	Cube	Sphere
Shape of faces			
Number of flat faces			
Number of right angles			
Shape of base			

What You'll Need
- *models of three-dimensional figures from Activity 3*
- *Geometry tool or protractor and ruler*
- *scissors*
- *tape*

ACTIVITY 5 # Raising Shapes

With Your Group Most buildings are made of simple three-dimensional shapes. Design several buildings based on the nets you made. Consider how each building will be used and how it relates to the others.

Present your designs and plans to the class. Describe what kinds of buildings they are and who would be most likely to use them. Then explain how you used each model and why the shape suited its purpose.

You may want to combine simple three-dimensional shapes into more complex shapes.

This housing complex, Habitat '67, was designed for Montreal's Expo 67 by Canadian-Israeli architect Moshe Safdie.

ACTIVITY 6 Back to the Books

On Your Own Sketch the three-dimensional shapes in your dictionary. Choose how you will show the shapes on your two-dimensional paper. Label and define each shape. Then compare your definitions and drawings with those of other group members.

TOOLS AND TECHNIQUES

Architects use computers to make scale models of their buildings. Print out a number of congruent shapes and assemble them into three-dimensional figures.

Do You Remember?

Try It!

Draw Venn diagrams to classify the shapes below in at least two different ways.

1. octagon
2. cone
3. triangular prism
4. quadrilateral
5. circle
6. rhombus
7. pyramid
8. trapezoid
9. pentagon
10. rectangular prism
11. closed curve
12. polygon

Think About It

13. Explain how you decided to classify each shape.

Investigation

Building Bridges

Bridges have to be strong enough for cars, trucks, and trains to cross them. Geometry shows bridge designers how to provide the strength and structure needed to bear such loads. In this investigation you will use what you know about geometry and rigid figures to build a 2-ft-long bridge by using nothing but paper and tape. The bridge should be able to stand on its own. You will need to make it strong enough to roll a spool of thread or a small toy car across it.

1 Test different shapes for strength. Use the one that you think will provide your bridge with the most rigid structure.

Ask Yourself

- ☐ What makes a shape rigid?
- ☐ Which shapes have the greatest strength?
- ☐ What can I do to make my shape stronger?
- ☐ How can I explain why my bridge supports the object?
- ☐ Does my bridge work? Why or why not?

2 Demonstrate your bridge to the class. Explain why you used the shapes you did, how you thought of your idea, and why your design provides enough support for the spool or car.

Section B: Giving an Idea Shape **369**

Ancient Architects

The Anasazi, an ancient cliff-dwelling Native American people, built this remarkable structure over 750 years ago.

Mesa Verde National Park

Utah | Colo.

Ariz. | N. Mex.

Visit the Cliff Palace at Mesa Verde National Park in Colorado.

1 Name and record as many different two- and three-dimensional regular shapes as you can find among the ruins.

2 The walls of the structure are perpendicular to the ground. What is their angle of measure?

3 The buildings are divided into rooms. What is the area of one of the rooms? What would you need to know to estimate the area of the whole structure?

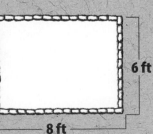

6 ft

8 ft

4 How could archeologists estimate the range of volume of a typical room if the walls are between 5 ft and 6 ft high?

5 The building is set in a crescent-shaped alcove 325 ft long and 89 ft wide at its deepest point. Use what you know about the size of the rooms to estimate a range of possible perimeters of the entire structure.

6 Dug into the floor of the cave are *kivas* (underground multi-purpose ceremonial rooms) 15 ft in diameter. If the walls are about 6 ft high, then what would be the volume of a room?

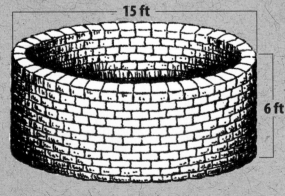

15 ft

6 ft

7 Describe at least four different planes you see in the photograph and identify where they intersect.

Check Your Math Power

The structure is actually a group of connected buildings where as many as 200 people lived at once.

8 Small rectangles cut out of the walls served as doors. Sketch three different doors in an 8-ft-by-6-ft wall. What fraction of the whole wall are the doors?

9 How can you use fractions in at least four different ways to describe the cliff structure shown above?

10 Make a sketch of one of the 8-ft-by-6-ft rooms. Label and describe the angle measures in the room.

LESSON 6 Measured Parts

When architects tell contractors what to build, they describe shapes and the dimensions of those shapes. When you design a building, you'll decide which measurements look and work best.

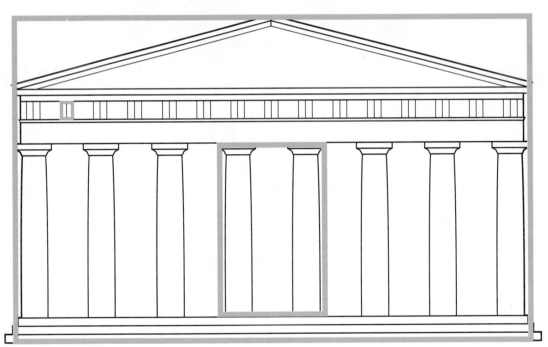

Diagram of the Parthenon

What You'll Need
- *Tracing Tool or centimeter ruler*

ACTIVITY 1 Drawing on the Past

With Your Partner Find the ratio of length to width for all the gold rectangles in the diagram of the Parthenon of ancient Greece. Measure to the nearest millimeter. Use your calculator to change each ratio to a decimal. What do all the ratios have in common?

Rectangles with the ratio 8 : 5 have been used throughout the history of architecture. This ratio is known as the **Golden Ratio.** How do the ratios you found compare with the Golden Ratio?

✓ **Self-Check** *Predict the dimensions of a rectangle three times larger than the rectangle around all the columns.*

The Parthenon was built around 447–432 B.C. This temple was designed with the same ratio throughout.

²ACTIVITY Changing History

With Your Partner Make a scale drawing of the diagram of the Parthenon on page 372.

1 What scale would you use to make a sketch of the Parthenon at twice the size of the diagram? half the size?

2 How would your drawing change if your scale was three times larger? How about four times as small?

3 Choose a scale. Then use your ratio to make a scale drawing of the Parthenon.

With Your Class Dimensions can change the way a space functions. What problems would the ancient Greeks have had if the Parthenon had been only 4 m wide and 100 m long? What results would changes in the dimensions of your classroom have?

What You'll Need
• *centimeter grid paper*
• *Tracing Tool or centimeter ruler*

ACTIVITY OPTION

Measure some rectangles in your classroom or in your school. Which use the Golden Ratio?

What You'll Need
- *grid paper*
- *ruler*
- *scissors*

ACTIVITY 3 **Homegrown**

On Your Own Throughout history, people have lived in many different kinds of houses. Make a sketch of the house in the story below. Then use what you've learned to design a floor plan for a house that two families can live in.

1 The base of your house is 80 ft × 60 ft. Use grid paper to make a scale drawing of the floor.

LITERATURE

Meet Pattie Ridley Jones, an African American girl growing up in the 1880s. You'll also find out how shapes make houses.

Papa built our house. It was shaped like a capital L lying down on its side. Well no, to tell you the truth, it was more like three L's sandwiched together—the back porch, and the front porch, and the house in the middle. It was made of wood mostly, but right at the corner of the front bedroom, there was a big brick chimney that started on the ground and went way up taller than the house.

From *Childtimes: A Three-Generation Memoir*
by Eloise Greenfield and Lessie Jones Little
with material by Pattie Ridley Jones

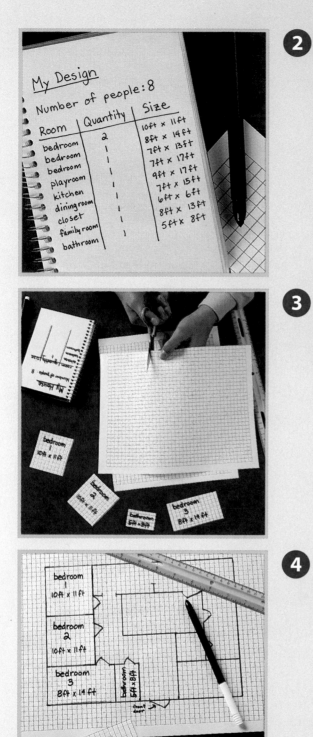

2 Decide what rooms to have in your home. How many people will live there? What will be the main activities in each room? Choose dimensions for each room.

3 On grid paper draw the rooms to scale. Cut them out and label them. Arrange them on the floor plan of the house.

4 Mark all the doors in your house. What must you keep in mind as you decide where the doors go?

TOOLS AND TECHNIQUES

Use string to outline the actual sizes of the rooms in your house or the classroom floor. This should help you make final decisions about size and dimensions.

5 What changes would you make in your house if you were designing it for families that like to spend a lot of time together? Look at others' floor plans to get ideas about how you might change yours.

The longhouse was the traditional dwelling of Native Americans of the Iroquois nation until the 1800s. Each longhouse served several family groups.

The house I designed has 1,350 square feet with

6 Write a paragraph explaining your decisions.

Try It!

Give sets of lengths and widths for rooms with each given area. Describe a purpose each is suited for.

1. 100 m² **2.** 72 m² **3.** 12 m² **4.** 600 m² **5.** 10 ft²

Estimate. If the product is greater than 1, find the exact answer.

6. $\frac{3}{4} \times \frac{2}{5}$ **7.** $1\frac{1}{2} \times \frac{2}{3}$ **8.** $\frac{8}{4} \times 5$ **9.** $\frac{9}{7} \times \frac{7}{9}$ **10.** $3 \times 4\frac{5}{6}$

Think About It

11. How did you use factoring to find dimensions in Exercises 1–5? Explain in writing.

In Я Reflection

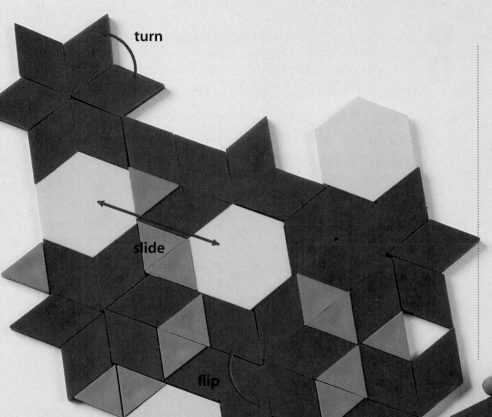

turn

slide

flip

CONNECT AND COMMUNICATE

In Your Journal Record examples of symmetry, flips, and slides you see around you. How many buildings can you find that have the door in the center? How does this relate to symmetry?

ᴬᶜᵀᴵᵛᴵᵀʸ 1 Around and About

With Your Partner Slides, flips, and turns are ways of moving shapes to form patterns. Look at the examples and write a definition for each. Then use polygons from your dictionary of shapes to make a pattern that uses flips, slides, and turns for the floor tiles in one room of your house.

What You'll Need
- *Tracing Tool or ruler*
- *crayons or markers*

Section C: Beautiful Math 377

What You'll Need
- *Tracing Tool or ruler*

DRAWING TO LEARN

How many lines of symmetry can you find on a square? on a regular octagon or a circle? How can you use what you know about symmetry to add to your definitions of polygons?

In the early 1600s in what is now northern India, Mumtaz Mahal died. Her husband, the Mogul Emperor Shah Jahan, had the Taj Mahal built as his and her burial place.

ACTIVITY 2 In Perfect Balance

With Your Partner The Taj Mahal uses flips to create symmetry. You know a **line of symmetry** divides a figure into two congruent halves. Choose one of these two activities to complete.

1 Make a diagram to show what you find.

2 Design a building that uses symmetry in its face and its floor plan. Describe how you used slides and flips to create symmetry and list all the ways in which your building is symmetrical.

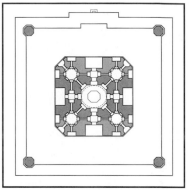
Floor plan of the Taj Mahal

Which angles and lines are congruent? Use your Tracing Tool or ruler to tell.

Do slides and turns also show symmetry? Explain.

ACTIVITY 3 Round and Round

With Your Partner An architect needs to describe the **angle of rotation,** or number of degrees a shape is turned, so someone else can follow the plan.

1 Trace an equilateral triangle. Label its vertexes. Rotate and trace the triangle. Line up the edges as you go until you meet your original shape. What shape did you make?

2 Estimate how far the triangle was turned each time. Use your protractor to check your answer.

Architect R. Buckminster Fuller designed geodesic domes like the one above. The domes use polygons for the faces. Fuller designed the one that housed the United States exhibit at Expo 67 in Montreal in 1967.

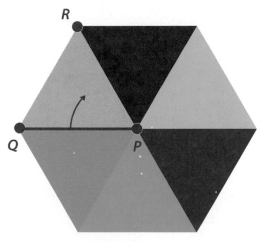

a. Which color panel is a 180° turn of the yellow panel around point *P*? Explain how you know.

b. Which color panel shows a 240° turn of the yellow panel around point *P*?

c. Which kind of triangle could you rotate to make an octagon? How far would you need to rotate it each time?

You know there are 360° in a circle. How could you use this information to find the angle of rotation, or turn, of a regular polygon?

With Your Partner Draw your own tile pattern using turns of 90°, 180°, and 270°.

One Brick at a Time

Italy   Iraq

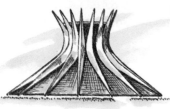

Brazil   Nigeria   Japan

The buildings shown are from all over the world and from different historical periods. Nevertheless, their architects used the same mathematical tools to design them. The drawings show the top and front of each building. Use what you've learned to answer five questions in any order you choose.

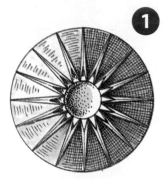

1 **Brasília Cathedral Dome**
Brasília, Brazil, 1960
Make diagrams of the Brasília Cathedral Dome to show its symmetry. Describe any turns you see and measure the angle of rotation.

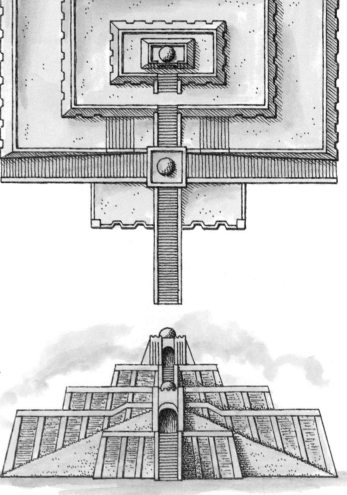

2 **Ziggurat at Ur**
Ur, now Iraq, c. 2125 B.C.
Use diagrams to show any symmetry, flips, slides, and turns you see in the ziggurat at Ur. Measure any angles of rotation.

3 Use a ruler to describe the ratio of length to height of the ziggurat.

4 **Castel del Monte**
Bari, Italy, c. 1200
Diagram the Castel del Monte to show its symmetry. Describe any flips, slides, and turns and measure the angle of rotation of any turns.

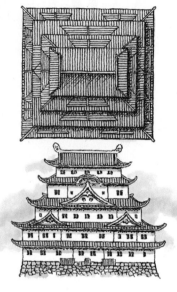

5 **Nagoya Castle**
Nagoya, Japan, 1612
Describe any symmetry you see in the Nagoya Castle. Are any flips, slides, and turns used in the castle? Where?

6 Assuming you know the scale to which the floor plan of the castle was drawn, describe how you would find the area of the actual building.

7 **Central Mosque**
Kano, Nigeria, 1951
Describe what is symmetrical and what is not symmetrical about this drawing of the Kano Mosque.

8 How would you alter one of these buildings to make it completely symmetrical or nonsymmetrical?

9 Design a building using one polygon and flips, slides, and turns. Include 90°, 180°, and 270° turns.

10 Choose one building on these pages and describe how it uses triangles.

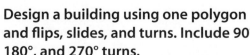

Section C: Beautiful Math **381**

LESSON
8

Imagining Spaces

How do you think a community center gets built? In many cities the local government first describes the kind of building it wants. Then architects submit their designs. As you'll see, the real work begins with analyzing how the building will be used.

ACTIVITY
1 **Reviewing the Plan**

With Your Class Read the letter on the left. Then make a list of the information you will need before you can begin to design a building.

MAYOR

The mayor's office has decided to build a public recreation center for the senior citizens and young people of the community. The building will be constructed in the downtown area on a piece of land that is 150 ft wide by 200 ft long.

The center will serve as the home to the city's new *Seniors Helping Juniors* tutorial program. The center will be a space where older and younger people get together to share ideas, work on projects, and socialize.

Your plan should include spaces for the following uses:

1 auditorium   6 artists' studios
1 gymnasium   6 music practice rooms
2 locker rooms   4 bathrooms
2 lounges   3 storage rooms
5 classrooms   12 closets
1 computer room   2 drinking fountains

The building must be wheelchair accessible and cannot be more than two stories high. Your plan should include an estimate of your building materials costs.

We look forward to seeing your design.

ACTIVITY 2 Making Plans

With Your Group Review the different building materials and their prices on the sheet below. Then brainstorm design ideas. Make several sketches of your structure and, as a group, select your favorite one. Keep in mind the following:

- Your design should meet the needs of both senior citizens and young people.
- You must include an estimate of the cost of the building materials you will be using.

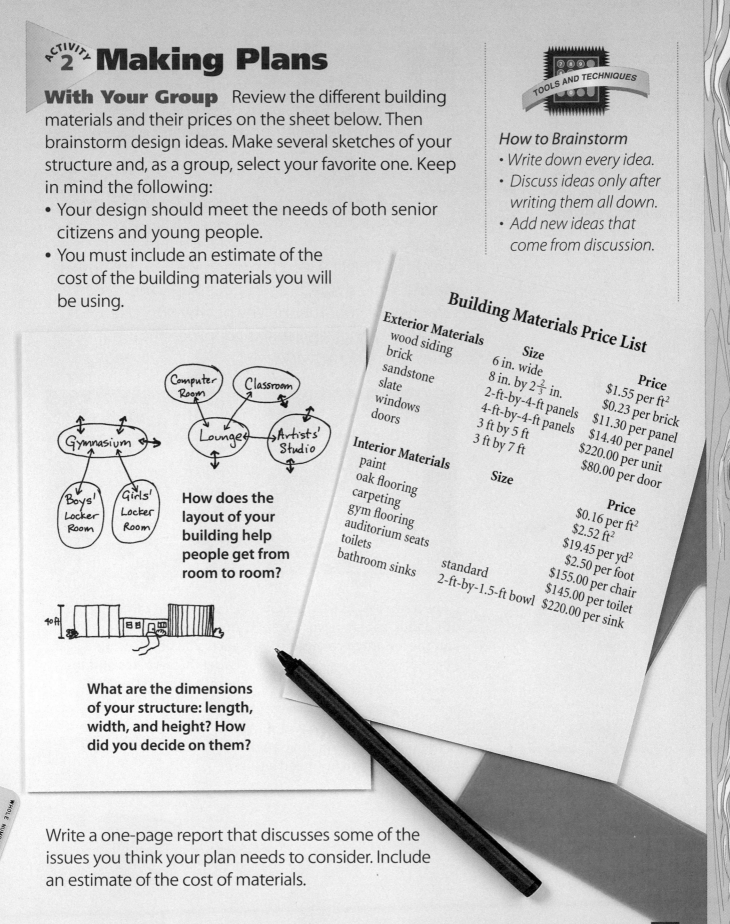

How to Brainstorm
- *Write down every idea.*
- *Discuss ideas only after writing them all down.*
- *Add new ideas that come from discussion.*

Building Materials Price List

Exterior Materials

	Size	Price
wood siding	6 in. wide	$1.55 per ft²
brick	8 in. by 2⅔ in.	$0.23 per brick
sandstone	2-ft-by-4-ft panels	$11.30 per panel
slate	4-ft-by-4-ft panels	$14.40 per panel
windows	3 ft by 5 ft	$220.00 per unit
doors	3 ft by 7 ft	$80.00 per door

Interior Materials

	Size	Price
paint		$0.16 per ft²
oak flooring		$2.52 ft²
carpeting		$19.45 per yd²
gym flooring		$2.50 per foot
auditorium seats		$155.00 per chair
toilets	standard	$145.00 per toilet
bathroom sinks	2-ft-by-1.5-ft bowl	$220.00 per sink

How does the layout of your building help people get from room to room?

What are the dimensions of your structure: length, width, and height? How did you decide on them?

Write a one-page report that discusses some of the issues you think your plan needs to consider. Include an estimate of the cost of materials.

How could you estimate the length, width, and height of a building without measuring? One way is to estimate how many times one unit can be repeated. How else could you estimate size?

Striking Similarities

On Your Own Another way to estimate size is to look at an object with a similar shape. **Similar figures** are the same shape, but not necessarily the same size. Can they be congruent? Why or why not? Use what you know about similar and congruent figures and ratios to do this activity.

What You'll Need
- *Geometry Tool or protractor*
- *Tracing Tool or ruler*
- *dot paper*
- *crayons or markers*

1 Draw a small right triangle on dot paper. Label the vertexes and the length of each side.

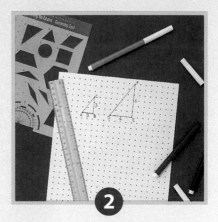

2 Draw a similar triangle by doubling the measure of each side of the original. Label the vertexes and the length of each side.

How could you draw two similar triangles just using dot paper? Why would you not need a ruler?

REASONING AND PROBLEM SOLVING

How could you decide whether two figures are congruent if the only tool you have is a protractor?

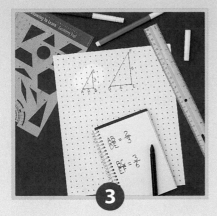

3

Find pairs of **corresponding sides**. Write the ratio of the lengths in the first triangle to the lengths in the second triangle. What do you notice about the ratios?

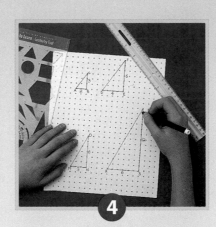

4

Draw two more similar right triangles using a different equivalent ratio. What do you notice about the angles in your triangles?

In Your Journal Describe how you could determine whether two figures are similar.

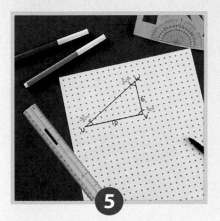

5

Draw a different triangle. Then measure its angles and record the lengths of its sides.

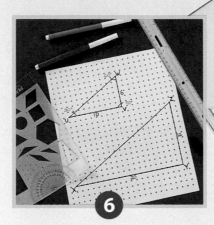

6

Use an equivalent ratio for the lengths of the corresponding sides to draw a similar triangle. What do you notice about **corresponding angles** in your similar triangles?

With Your Partner Extend what you've learned about similar triangles to other polygons. Choose the shape you want to explore and have your partner see whether your figures are similar. Then switch roles and check your partner's work.

What You'll Need

- *Tracing Tool or ruler*

ACTIVITY 4 Ancient Shadows

With Your Class Ancient Babylonians and Egyptians found that they could estimate the height of an object by looking at the length of its shadow. How do you think they did this?

1 Measure the length of the shadow cast by the building.

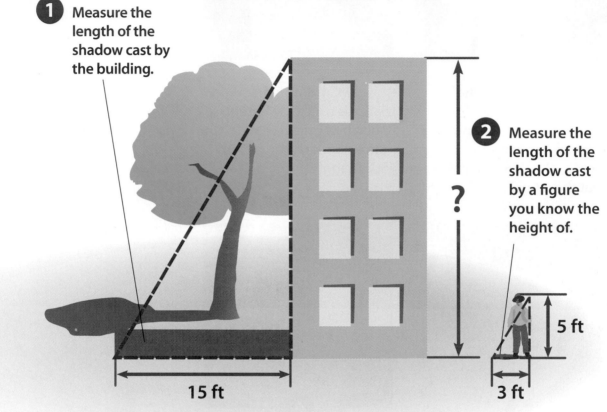

2 Measure the length of the shadow cast by a figure you know the height of.

?

5 ft

15 ft

3 ft

ACTIVITY OPTION

Go outside and measure your shadow and the shadows of at least three buildings. Now estimate their height. When you show your calculations, include sketches of the buildings.

3 If you measure both your shadow and the building's shadow at the same time of day and you know your height, explain how you can use similar figures to find the building's height.

4 Discuss why the shadow makes a triangle. How can you write ratios and use proportion to find the height of the building? How could you use the shadow from a yardstick stuck in the ground to compare with the shadow from the building? Explain your answer in your journal.

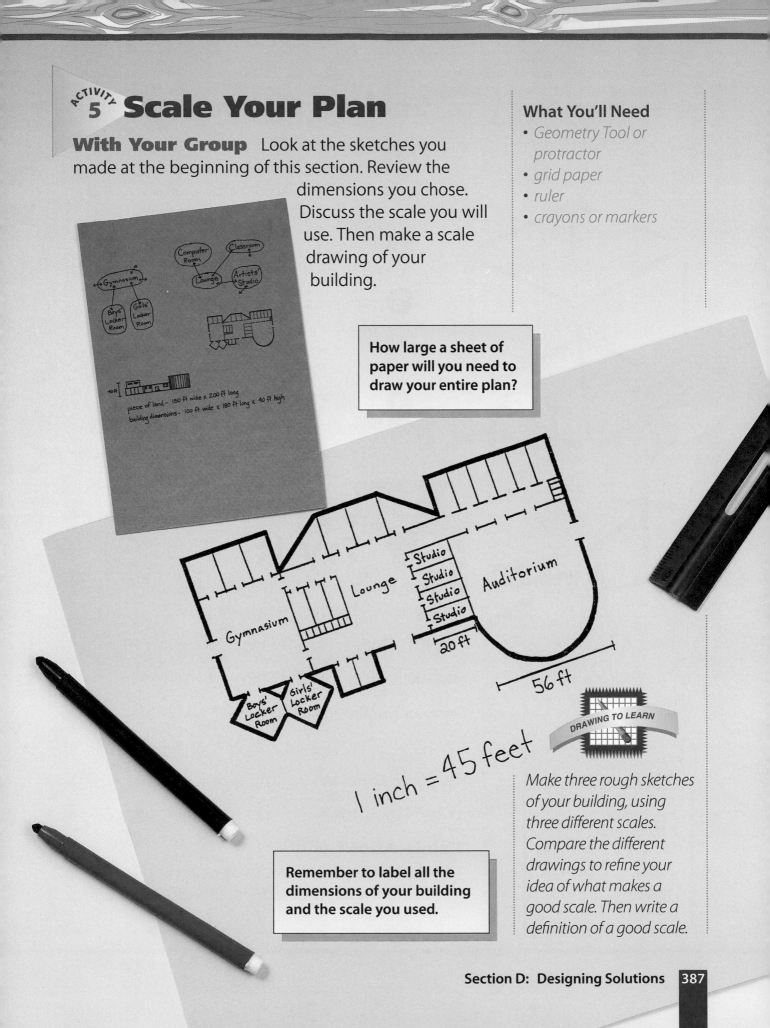

ACTIVITY 5 ▸ Scale Your Plan

With Your Group Look at the sketches you made at the beginning of this section. Review the dimensions you chose. Discuss the scale you will use. Then make a scale drawing of your building.

How large a sheet of paper will you need to draw your entire plan?

piece of land– 150 ft wide x 200 ft long
building dimensions– 100 ft wide x 180 ft long x 40 ft high

Gymnasium

Boys' Locker Room   Girls' Locker Room

Lounge

Studio
Studio
Studio
Studio

20 ft

Auditorium

56 ft

DRAWING TO LEARN

1 inch = 45 feet

Remember to label all the dimensions of your building and the scale you used.

Make three rough sketches of your building, using three different scales. Compare the different drawings to refine your idea of what makes a good scale. Then write a definition of a good scale.

What You'll Need

- ruler
- straws
- tape
- scissors

Scale a Space

With Your Partner The proportions you used with your scale drawings involved length and width. When a scale model is three-dimensional, the dimension of height must also be proportional.

1 Build a three-dimensional figure out of straws.

2 Make two more models of your figure. Make one proportionately larger than the original, the other proportionately smaller. Name the ratio you use.

3 Trade figures with another set of partners. Determine the proportions they used and explain how you did this.

Do You Remember?

Try It!

Name an object for which the scale given is appropriate if drawn on notebook paper.

1. 40 ft : 1 in.　　**2.** 5 ft : 1 in.　　**3.** $\frac{1}{8}$ in. : 10 in.

4. 100 ft : $\frac{1}{2}$ in.　**5.** 2 ft : 1 in.　　**6.** 1 in. : 5 in.

Solve for r in the equations below.

7. $12r \times 2r = 216$　3　　　**8.** $2r \times 8r = 64$　2

9. $20r \times 7r = 140$　1　　　**10.** $8r \times r = 128$　4

11. $9r \times 3r = 108$　2　　　**12.** $10r \times 2r = 500$　5

Think About It

13. Why is the scale in Exercise 3 not appropriate for drawing a building 16 ft tall and 20 ft wide?

✔ **Self-Check** *Match the object with the scale that would allow you to draw it on a sheet of notebook paper.*

Object	Scale
house	1 ft = 3 in.
birdhouse	15 ft = 1 in.
doghouse	1 ft = $\frac{1}{4}$ in.
10-story building	1 ft = 1 in.

Making Spaces

Architects must know what it costs to construct buildings. The outside, or **surface area,** of a three-dimensional shape is the sum of the areas of its faces. How does surface area let you estimate building costs?

ACTIVITY 1 On the Surface

On Your Own How could you find the surface area of a rectangular prism? A net can help you figure it out. Use nets to find the surface area for shapes a–c, or design your own solution.

What You'll Need
- *centimeter grid paper*

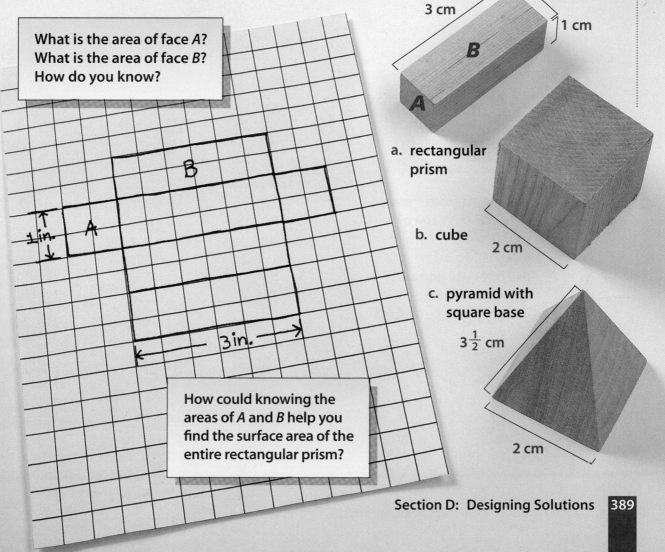

**What is the area of face *A*?
What is the area of face *B*?
How do you know?**

B

A

1 in.

3 in.

How could knowing the areas of *A* and *B* help you find the surface area of the entire rectangular prism?

3 cm

1 cm

1 cm

B

A

a. **rectangular prism**

b. **cube**   2 cm

c. **pyramid with square base**

$3\frac{1}{2}$ cm

2 cm

Section D: Designing Solutions   **389**

What You'll Need
- *floor plan of your community center*
- *construction paper or cardboard*
- *tape, paste, or glue*
- *scissors*
- *ruler*

ACTIVITY
2 Estimating Cost

With Your Group   Use what you know to figure out your building's surface area. Decide what materials will be used on the outside of your building. What will it cost to use these materials?

1 Use your scale model as a guide to begin making a three-dimensional model.

2 Will the outside of your structure be made of more than one kind of material? How can you use what you know to estimate the costs of covering your structure?

3 Do you need to make adjustments to your plans?

390

With Your Group Estimate how much it would cost to paint the outside of your building. Which surfaces would you need to cover? How much money would you save by using brick and not painting the outside? Explain.

CONNECT AND COMMUNICATE

In Your Journal Explain how you could use surface area to figure out how much paint to buy to paint your classroom.

Building Materials Price List

Exterior	Size	Price
wood siding	6 in. wide	$1.55 per ft^2
brick 8 in.	8 in. by $2\frac{2}{3}$ in.	$0.23 per brick
sandstone	2-ft-by-4-ft panels	$11.30 per panel
slate	4-ft-by-4-ft panels	$14.40 per panel
paint		$0.16 per ft^2

Do You Remember?

Try It!

Refer to the figure on the right. If 1 gal of paint covers 300 ft^2, how many gallons will you need to paint all the surfaces of rectangular rooms having the following dimensions?

1. $a = 10$ ft	$b = 10$ ft	$c = 10$ ft
2. $a = 10$ ft	$b = 50$ ft	$c = 80$ ft
3. $a = 5$ ft	$b = 10$ ft	$c = 5\frac{1}{2}$ ft
4. $a = 12$ ft	$b = 50$ ft	$c = 75$ ft
5. $a = 30$ ft	$b = 5$ ft	$c = 15$ ft
6. $a = 15\frac{3}{4}$ ft	$b = 60$ ft	$c = 80$ ft

Estimate the quotients.

7. $\frac{2}{5} \div \frac{3}{5}$ 8. $\frac{3}{8} \div \frac{1}{4}$ 9. $\frac{2}{3} \div \frac{5}{6}$ 10. $\frac{3}{7} \div \frac{1}{7}$

Think About It

11. How could you use division to check your answers to Exercises 1–3?

LESSON 10 Traffic Flow

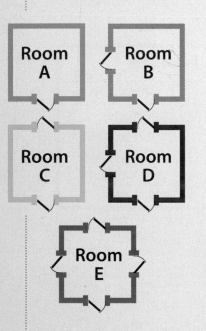

Room A
Room B
Room C
Room D
Room E

What You'll Need

- scissors
- crayons or markers
- gameboard
- spinner

A

n important detail architects must design is the system of pathways, or **network,** that allows people to get from one part of the building to another.

ACTIVITY 1 Networks

With Your Class Look at the rooms on the left. What is the shortest path from room A to room B? How many ways are there to get from room B to room D? Explain. How many ways are there to get from room A to room C? Explain.

ACTIVITY 2 Door to Door

With Your Group Make a network on the gameboard. Choose a door from which to begin. For example, if you start on the green door, you will build a network to the opposite green door.

1 Each player draws a 5-in.-by-3-in. grid on a sheet of paper. Draw rooms A through E on the grid. Use a marker or crayon the same color as your door. Be sure to label each door A through E.

2 Fill the entire grid so that you have three copies of each kind of room. Then cut them out.

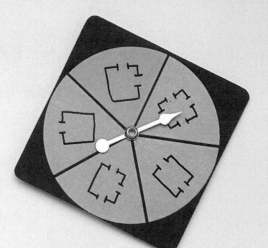

3 Draw each room on the spinner.

4 Spin to decide the order of play. The player who spins the room with the greatest number of doors goes first. Spin again if there is a tie.

5 On each turn, spin. Place a room on the board that matches the room the spinner landed on. Now the other players take their turns.

6 Start at your door. Build a network to the opposite side. You must build door to door to make a clear path to the opposite side.

7 Start over again if you spin room A three times in a row. If your spin blocks your only path, you lose a turn

8 Avoid obstacles, build off other players' paths, or block them. The first player to make a clear path to their other door wins!

On Your Own In your journal write about what you think makes a good network. Describe the issues you think an architect must be aware of when connecting spaces.

ACTIVITY 3 **Prepare to Present**

With Your Group Now that you've studied many of the issues architects face, you are ready to revise your plans and present them to your class. Be sure to appoint a review committee to look at each group's plans.

Draw a traffic plan for your school. Predict the possible networks for getting from the room you are in now to the end of the corridor. Sketch a floor plan and show all the possible routes.

Review all the details of your plan. Then write a report. Discuss how your design addresses the issues of cost, size, materials, flow, and structure. Include a scale drawing of the front of the building and floor plans of the inside. Be sure you have clean copies of your plans.

ACTIVITY 4 Make Your Case

With Your Class Review each group's design. Then take turns presenting your plans to the class. Be sure to explain why you think your design addresses all the concerns of the mayor's office. Use any visuals you think will help convince the class of the strength of your group's design.

In Your Journal *Write about your group's building design and what you learned about geometry and architecture from it.*

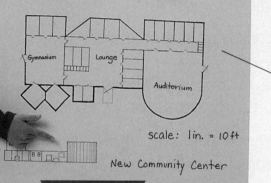

How does your design help people get around the building? Why is a well-designed floor plan important, especially in your building?

Do You Remember?

Try It!

1	2	3	4
5	6	7	8
9	10	11	12
13	14	15	16

Refer to the diagram on the right to find the shortest path between rooms.

1. from 1 to 16   **2.** from 1 to 4   **3.** from 6 to 15
4. from 1 to 3   **5.** from 3 to 4   **6.** from 1 to 7

Find the perimeter of triangles with the following measurements.

7. 4 cm, 5 cm, 6 cm   **8.** 12 ft, 7 ft, 5 ft
9. 20 in., 11 in., 7 in.   **10.** 3 cm, 2 cm, 9 cm

Think About It

11. Where could you add one door on the chart above to make the shortest possible path between 1 and 16?

Section D: Designing Solutions   **395**

Looking Back

Choose the right answer. Write *a*, *b*, *c*, or *d* for each exercise.

Use the diagram below to answer Exercises 1–4.

$\frac{1}{8}$ in. = 4 ft

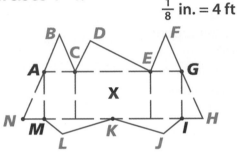

1. Which angles are right angles?

   a. $\angle ABC$ and $\angle CDE$
   b. $\angle EFG$ and $\angle GHI$
   c. $\angle AEJ$ and $\angle ANM$
   d. $\angle AMK$ and $\angle EGI$

2. Which angle is not obtuse?

   a. $\angle CDE$ b. $\angle KLM$
   c. $\angle IJK$ d. $\angle JKL$

3. What is the area of room X?

   a. 24 ft × 36 ft   b. $\frac{1}{2}$ ft × $\frac{3}{4}$ ft
   c. 6 ft × 4 ft   d. 16 ft × 24 ft

4. Which line segments are neither parallel nor perpendicular?

   a. $\overline{AG}$ and $\overline{MI}$ b. $\overline{AM}$ and $\overline{DE}$
   c. $\overline{KH}$ and $\overline{AM}$ d. $\overline{CD}$ and $\overline{DE}$

5. A scalene triangle must have which of these characteristics?

   a. two congruent angles
   b. one 90° angle
   c. no congruent line segments
   d. no obtuse angles

6. What makes a rectangle a special kind of parallelogram?

   a. sum of angles is 360°
   b. two pairs of parallel sides
   c. two pairs of congruent angles
   d. two pairs of right angles

7. A regular octagon must not have which of these attributes?

   a. four pairs of parallel sides
   b. no congruent line segments
   c. divides into 6 triangles
   d. all angles congruent

8. A triangular prism must have which of these characteristics?

   a. a triangular base
   b. three faces
   c. no parallel faces
   d. all congruent edges

9. To make as large a scale drawing as possible on $8\frac{1}{2}$-in.-by-11-in. paper, which scale would you use for a 12-ft-by-15-ft room?

   a. $\frac{1}{4}$ in. = 1 ft   b. $\frac{1}{4}$ in. = 24 in.
   c. $\frac{1}{4}$ in. = 10 in.   d. $\frac{1}{4}$ in. = 3 ft

10. What angle of rotation does the outlined parallelogram show?

   a. 45°   b. 90°   c. 120°   d. 60°

11. Identify the corresponding sides or angles.

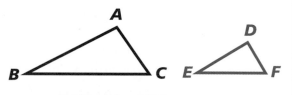

   a. $\angle BAC$ and $\angle EFD$
   b. $\overline{AC}$ and $\overline{DE}$
   c. $\angle ACB$ and $\angle DFE$
   d. $\overline{AB}$ and $\overline{BC}$

12. Which rate is in simplest terms?

   a. 3 gal : 2,100 ft   b. $17 : 51 panels
   c. 11 bricks : 13 ft   d. $48 : 16 yards

13. Which angles added together make straight angles? Complete this function table to find out.

n	20		45	62		135
180° − n		105			90	

14. Find the measure of the other angles in these parallelograms. Use diagrams and number sentences to show your work.

   a. 80°, 100°   b. 42°, 42°
   c. 54°, 126°   d. 90°

Check Your Math Power

15. Draw three different pairs of angles that add up to 90°. Explain how you made your choices.

16. Copy the diagram and find the number of possible networks from A to B.

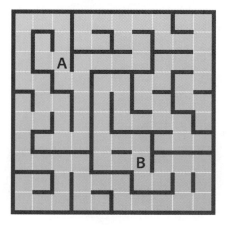

17. Match the room with dimensions you think would function best. Explain your choices.

   school cafeteria   48 in. × 42 in.
   closet   20 ft × 4 ft
   hallway   180 in. × 216 in.
   living room   75 ft × 130 ft

MODULE
7 **Investigations**

Over the Wall

What happens inside your building? outside? How your building is used is affected by who uses it. Choose one of the following investigations to explore how to make your building fit your purpose.

Investigation
A **Moving In**

Choose one room of your community center to furnish. What is it used for? Who will use it? What needs to be in it? How high do your tables and chairs need to be? Find the measurements you need by exploring your world. Then design your own furniture.

What measurements should a chair have in order to fit you? Are they the same measurements as a chair for a young child?

1 **Draw** a floor plan of the room. On the floor plan draw and label the furniture for the room. Then on a separate sheet of paper draw a front view of each piece of furniture. Label each piece, write where it will be used, and give its scale.

2 **Label** your sketches with the measurements of all sides and angles. Label the vertexes and points as necessary.

How high should a cabinet be for a person in a wheelchair?

3 **Describe** the shapes you used in your drawings. Use letters to refer to specific examples. If you used symmetry, describe how. Identify any flips, slides, and turns, and point out examples of congruence.

Keep in Mind

Your report will be judged by how well you do the following things.

☐ How did you use your knowledge of ratio and measurement to help you make specific plans?

☐ Did you include all the measurements and descriptions to accurately describe your furniture?

☐ How clearly do your words and diagrams communicate the furniture you want built?

Investigation B — In the Middle of Things

What community is your community center in? Use what you know to plan the streets, buildings, and parks in the neighborhood around your building. Refer to your drawings to describe why you made the choices you did and identify the math you used.

ledges

flower bed

tomato patch

Planning A Garden

Investigation C — A View with a Room

Even a garden uses geometry. Design a garden that creates personal spaces or public meeting areas. Will you grow vegetables or plant flowers? Make a scale drawing. Then write a description of your garden, using what you know about shapes and patterns.

Computer Option If you have a computer, you can use a drawing program for this investigation. Draw your flower beds and vegetable patches. Move them around to make new gardens. Label congruent line segments, shapes, and angles.

MODULE 8

No Purchase Necessary

Congratulations! You're a winner!

These are words everyone likes to hear. Many contests and drawings give away money and prizes. These contests may seem easy to win—but what are the real chances? How can you tell?

In this module you will explore how to measure your chances of winning. You can use what you learn to help you figure out how likely it is that you will take home a prize.

SECTION A

Exploring Probability

SECTION B

Multiple Events

SECTION C

Using Simulations

SECTION D

Dependent or Independent?

And the Winner Is . . .

Do you think all contests give you the same chance of winning? Should you fix your old bike or expect to win that new one? Find out!

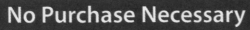

Win a New Bike!

ANNOUNCING THE
GREAT BIKE GIVEAWAY

The **Ultimate RACING BIKE!**

PLUS FREE SAFETY GEAR!

1 Describe the Chance

Choose the sentence below that describes your chance of winning the bike in each case.

a. You are the only person who enters.
b. You don't enter.
c. You and 11,999 other people enter.

- unlikely
- impossible
- certain

Think of how many times you hear words such as *possibly* or *maybe* used to describe the probability, or chance, that something will happen. Make a list of other words that describe probability.

② Flip a Coin

What is the chance of throwing heads? Could you say there is a fifty-fifty chance of throwing tails? The chances of throwing heads or tails are equally likely. Explain what that means.

③ Experiment

When you hold a paper cup at arm's length and drop it, is it likely to land on its top, side, or bottom? Are any of these results certain or impossible? equally likely? How do you know? Make predictions for each result and test them. Share your results. Discuss what the experiment told you about the probability of each result.

Word Bank
- **combination**
- **dependent events**
- **experimental probability**
- **independent events**
- **permutation**
- **probability**
- **simulation**
- **trial**

Investigations Preview

Learn how to measure the size of a chance. Then use mathematical probability to estimate numbers too great or difficult to count and to control the chances of winning a contest.

Tag Team (pages 422–423)
How do ecologists count the number of bees in a hive?
Explore how you can use probability and sampling to solve real problems.

Hidden Talents (pages 446–448)
How would you use math to predict the number of musicians in your school?
Use what you learn about random sampling and simulations.

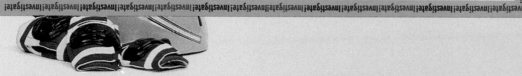

LESSON
1 # Grand Opening

You are in charge of getting customers for a new supermarket that's about to open in your neighborhood. You want to plan some exciting activities and prize giveaways that will get people to come into the store.

ACTIVITY
1 ## Come One, Come All

With Your Class Take a survey to find out the kinds of activities that will attract people to your store.

1 **Plan** your survey.

    a. Brainstorm a list of activities. Write a survey that asks people to choose and rank the activities.

    b. Decide whom to survey. How can you make sure your sample represents the customers the store will have?

    c. Decide how many people to survey. How will you know that you have a large enough sample so that you can draw conclusions?

Activity Survey

Which of these items would make you stop by a new store? Write 1, 2, or 3 beside your top 3 choices.

☐ *Balloons*
☐ *Clowns*

With Your Group

 2 **Predict** which activities will be more likely than others to be chosen.

   a. Is each choice equally likely to attract people to your store? Why or why not?

   b. List your predictions of the three most popular activities.

3 **Conduct** your survey and combine the results from all the groups. How good were you at predicting?

A graph is a good way to display the results of your survey. Make a circle graph, a bar graph, or a pictograph.

4 **Organize** and analyze the results. Present your recommendations to the class.

新張營業

GRAND OPENING

2 **Spin to Win**

With Your Group The supermarket managers need to decide on a spinner to use at the Grand Opening. They want to know the probability, or chance, of giving away the prizes listed on each of the spinners. Each customer gets one chance to spin for a prize.

1 Choose two of these spinners to test. Make a list of all the possible **outcomes,** or results, of spinning each spinner.

A

Balloons | T-shirt
Kite | Groceries

B

Balloons
Groceries

TOOLS AND TECHNIQUES

Trace the spinners with your Fraction Tool. Use a paper clip for a pointer. Hold the paper clip in the center of the spinner with a pencil eraser.

 2 Make some predictions. How many times do you think each outcome will happen in 100 spins?

3 Test your predictions by spinning. Each spin is called a **trial.** Carry out the trials. Record the results of each trial.

4 Write a ratio comparing the number of times each outcome occurred with the number of trials you made. These results of your experiment are called the **experimental probability**.

5 Find the results for 100 trials. Write your results as ratios in fraction form.

If you can write your probabilities in fraction form, do you think you can write the probabilities as decimals? as percents? Justify your reasoning.

Probability for Spinner A

Possible Outcomes	Predictions for 100 spins	Results
balloons	$\frac{25}{100}$	

C

Balloons · T-shirt · Groceries · Tickets

D

Tickets · Balloons · Kite · Groceries · T-shirt

6 How did your results compare with your predictions? Were there any surprises? Why or why not?

Section A: Exploring Probability **407**

On Your Own Think about the probability of some outcomes on spinners A and B.

7 What are the chances that you will get one of these prizes in one spin?

    a. any prize   **b.** a T-shirt

    c. a balloon   **d.** no prize

Write the probabilities as ratios in fraction form. Use simplest terms.

8 Explain in writing why it is said that the probability of certain events is 1, the probability of impossible events is 0, and all other probabilities fall between 0 and 1.

Do You Remember?
Try It!

Based on the results in the chart, write the probability as a fraction.

	10 Spins	
Red	**Blue**	**White**
III	ⅢⅠ	II

1. red   2. blue

3. red or white   4. white

5. not white   6. blue or white

Write the answers in order from least to greatest.

7. $72 \div 5\frac{1}{2}$ 8. $1\frac{1}{3} \div 2\frac{1}{2}$ 9. $2\frac{3}{4} \times 40$

10. $1{,}652 \div 236$ 11. $\frac{1}{3} \times 3\frac{1}{2}$ 12. $4\frac{7}{8} \times 9\frac{1}{3}$

Think About It

13. Draw a spinner that may have given the results shown in the chart. Explain your choice in writing.

This or That?

The manager wants to make a big splash on opening day. She printed the letters for GRAND OPENING on individual cards and placed them in a box. Every customer who pulls out a *G* or an *O* will get a $5 gift certificate.

ACTIVITY 1 A New Game

With Your Partner Find the experimental probability of pulling a *G* or an *O* out of the box.

 Make an organized list, or **sample space,** of all the possible outcomes.

> Sample Space
>
> G, R, A,

What is the ratio of *G*'s to all possible outcomes? What is the ratio of *O*'s to all possible outcomes?

REASONING AND PROBLEM SOLVING

Which letter has the greatest chance of being drawn? Why?

Why do you need to experiment to find the probability of a tack landing on its side when flipped?

What You'll Need
- *spinner*

2 The ratio of outcomes you are looking for to the total number of possible outcomes is the probability. This number describes the chance that something will happen.

$$\text{Probability } (P) = \frac{\text{Number of outcomes you choose}}{\text{Number of possible outcomes}}$$

What is the probability of choosing each letter in *GRAND OPENING*? How do you know?

3 Plan an experiment to test your probability of choosing *G* or *O*. Test your plan. Explain your results to the class.

ᴬᶜᵀᴵᵛᴵᵀʸ 2 What's Your Game?

With Your Partner Make up a game for the store manager to use. First look at this game.

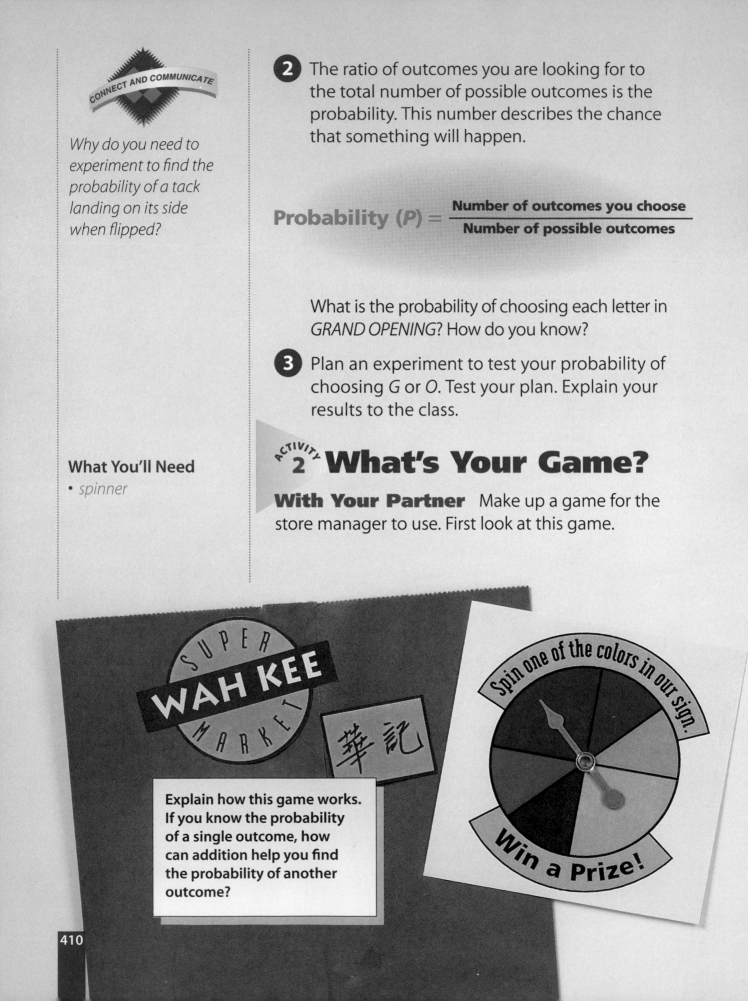

SUPER WAH KEE MARKET 華記

Spin one of the colors in our sign.

Win a Prize!

Explain how this game works. If you know the probability of a single outcome, how can addition help you find the probability of another outcome?

$$\text{Probability of Spinning:} \quad \underset{\text{green}}{\frac{1}{4}} + \underset{\text{blue}}{\frac{1}{4}} \searrow \frac{2}{4} \text{ or } \frac{1}{2}$$

Suppose that in order to win you needed to get red or white or blue. What would the probability of winning be?

1 Make up a game of your own. Write the probability of choosing each outcome. Then find the probability of choosing one outcome or the other—for example, spinning 5 or red.

2 Test the probabilities.

3 Write a letter to the manager explaining why she should use your game.

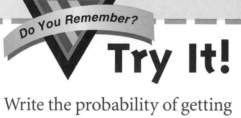

Try It!

Write the probability of getting each outcome in one spin of the spinner.

1. an odd number   **2.** blue or red   **3.** 2

4. red or green   **5.** 1 or 4   **6.** red

Find the value of *n* that makes each proportion true.

7. $\frac{4}{4} = \frac{n}{9}$ **8.** $\frac{5}{8} = \frac{n}{32}$ **9.** $\frac{45}{1} = \frac{n}{3}$

10. $\frac{n}{4} = \frac{13}{26}$ **11.** $\frac{n}{0.2} = \frac{5}{4}$ **12.** $\frac{2.5}{20} = \frac{n}{10}$

Think About It

13. Write how you found the probability for spinning red or green in Exercise 4.

In Your Journal Outline the main points from your letter to the manager. Is your argument persuasive? Do you need to make it stronger? How good are your reasons?

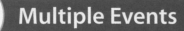

LESSON
③

Chances Are?

You probably often see all sorts of contests. What are your chances of winning one?

ACTIVITY
1 **Winning Numbers**

With Your Class Each Friday a grocery store awards free groceries to someone who is the first to match a winning number. Five cards, each with a number 1 – 5, are put into a box. The store manager picks a card one at a time and displays the first number first, the second number second, and so on. If the numbers are on your grocery receipt in the correct order, you win!

WIN!

A BASKET OF GROCERIES

Match the four numbers on your receipt to this week's combination of four numbers.

THIS WEEK'S WINNING NUMBERS

4 2 3 1

1 Estimate what you think the probability of winning might be.

2 Talk about some of your class's guesses. Talk about which estimates might be the most reasonable.

2 Showing Probabilities

With Your Group You need to find the probability of drawing four digits in a particular order. A good strategy to try is to start with a simpler problem. What is the probability of drawing a 1 and then a 2 when you are choosing from 1, 2, 3?

What You'll Need
- *index cards or thin cardboard*
- *scissors*
- *bag to hold cards*

1 Label three small cards 1, 2, and 3. Put the cards into a bag. Have a group member draw out two of the cards.

2 Keep trying until you get 1, then a 2. How many times did you have to draw? Run several trials. Write the results you found.

3 How many different pairs of two numbers can you draw from the numbers 1, 2, and 3? List them in a sample space.

4 What is the probability of getting a 1 and then a 2?

REASONING AND PROBLEM SOLVING

How many favorable outcomes are there in the 1–3 problem? How can you find the probability of drawing 1, then 3, in a single draw? of drawing 2, then 3?

413

Use four tiles of different colors. Drop the tiles into a bag. Choose a two-color combination and see how many tries it takes for you to pick out those two colors.

5 How does this probability compare with the results of your experiment? Why?

6 Make a **tree diagram** showing all the pairs you can get by drawing two numbers from 1, 2, 3, and 4. How many outcomes are there? What is the probability of drawing 1, then a 2?

> **A tree diagram is a way of showing a sample space. This tree diagram shows the outcomes for drawing two numbers from 1, 2, and 3.**

First Choices	Second Choices	Outcomes
1	2	(1,2)
	3	(1,3)
2	1	(2,1)
	3	(2,3)
3	1	(3,1)
	2	(3,2)

ACTIVITY 3 Counting Outcomes

With Your Group You can figure out numbers of outcomes from tree diagrams.

1 Look at the tree diagram on page 414. How many choices are there for the first number? How many choices are left for the second number? What is the total number of pairs possible?

2 Look at your 1–4 tree diagram. How many choices are there for the first number? for the second number? How many outcomes are there in all?

3 Under the headings below, list the numbers you got from the tree diagrams. What relationship can you see between the number of choices for the first and second number and the total number of outcomes? How can you predict the outcomes without a tree diagram?

Choices for First Number	Choices for Second Number	Total Outcomes

4 Predict the number of possible outcomes. Then choose two experiments and draw tree diagrams to check your predictions.
   a. Draw two numbers out of 1, 2, 3, 4, and 5.
   b. Draw two numbers out of 1–6.
   c. Draw three numbers out of 1–4.

TOOLS AND TECHNIQUES

When there are many choices, finding the probability with pencil and paper can be a long process. Use a calculator to do it faster.

Your Four Contest Numbers:

3 4 2 1

5 Now you can solve part of the problem this lesson began with. You want to know the number of outcomes for drawing four numbers out of 1–5.

- How many choices are there for the first number?
- How many choices for the second number?
- How many for the third and fourth numbers?
- How can you calculate these numbers of choices to find the total number of outcomes?
- What is the probablility of winning?

Do You Remember?

Try It!

Draw a tree diagram.

1. Pick 1 then 3 from the numbers 1–4.
2. Pick red, blue, then green from red, blue, green, and yellow.

Write the total number of outcomes, the number of favorable outcomes, and the probability.

3. Roll a sum of 3 with two 1–6 number cubes.
4. Spin 3's on both of two spinners with equal 1–4 parts.
5. Flip heads on a coin three times in a row.

Estimate by rounding to the nearest hundred.

6. 10% of 8,585   **7.** 30% of 5,100   **8.** 20% of 496

9. 5% of 6,550   **10.** 40% of 22,900   **11.** 75% of 5,250

Think About It

12. How can you find the total number of outcomes without listing a sample space? Use an example from Exercises 1–5 in your written explanation.

Make Arrangements

You are a little closer now to solving the problem of the four numbers drawn from 1 through 5. Do you know whether your four numbers must be in exactly the same order as the winning numbers? Does it make a difference in the probability of winning?

ACTIVITY 1 ▸ How Many Ways?

With Your Group Again, think about a simpler problem first. In how many different ways can you arrange the three soups on sale?

1 List a sample space to show all the different arrangements of the three soups.

SALE!
3 / $2

DRAWING TO LEARN

Instead of using numbers or initials, you may wish to make a drawing of the different arrangements of the three soups.

SALE
SAEL
SEAL

2 Each outcome you listed is a different arrangement, or **permutation.** In a permutation, the order of the outcomes is important.

Is not the same as

3 Draw a tree diagram to show the possible arrangements of soup. How many permutations are there? Outcomes in which order doesn't matter are called **combinations.** How does the number of combinations of three soups differ from the number of permutations? Why are the numbers different?

4 Make a tree diagram or a sample space for each case below. Is the case a permutation or a combination? How can multiplication help you find the number of permutations?

a. arranging the letters *s, a, l, e* to make *sale.*
b. four cashiers going on break two at a time

5 Share your results with the class. Did all groups get the same results? Why or why not?

ACTIVITY 2 Figuring It Out

With Your Group Now you have the tools you need to solve the grocery store giveaway problem.

1 Will it make a difference in probability if the numbers must be in the exact order?

a. Make a tree diagram to show all the permutations. What is the probability that your numbers will be in the same order as the winning numbers?

b. Look at the tree diagram again. Which sets of four numbers are the same if order doesn't matter? Use different colors to circle similar combinations. What is the probability of winning if the order of the numbers doesn't matter?

2 If you were the grocery store manager, which method would you choose if you were giving away a $5 gift certificate? if you were giving away a balloon? Explain your choices.

Your Four Contest Numbers: **2 1 5 4**

Your Four Contest Numbers: **3 5 4 1**

Your Four Contest Numbers: **5 2 4 3**

Your Four Contest Numbers: **4 1 3 2**

Your Four Contest Numbers: **2 3 4 1**

Your Four Contest Numbers: **1 3 5 2**

✔ **Self-Check** *Explain to a partner the difference between a combination and a permutation. Ask your partner to tell you whether your explanation was clear.*

Probing Probabilities

1 What is missing in the sample space at the right? Copy and complete it.

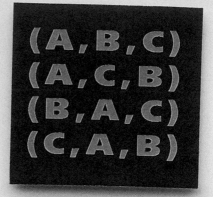

(A, B, C)
(A, C, B)
(B, A, C)
(C, A, B)

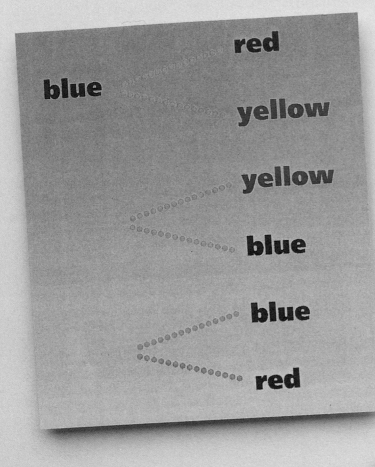

red

blue

yellow

yellow

blue

blue

red

2 What is missing in the tree diagram? Complete it.

3 What numbers would you multiply to find all the permutations of six books on a shelf? How many are there?

4 What questions would you have to ask before you could figure out the probability of winning this contest?

You are a winner if these numbers are drawn

2 7 4 12

5 In how many different orders could you and four friends list your first names?

6 How many possible outcomes are there on each spinner?

7 What is the probability of spinning a 3 on spinner A? on spinner B?

8 What is the probability of spinning 3 on both spinners?

9 How could you find the number of ways of arranging the letters in the word CONTEST?

10 Each one of five people shakes hands with each of the others. How many handshakes are there? Explain how you know.

Investigation

Tag Team

To estimate the number of bees in a hive, ecologists catch and tag a small portion. Then they take a representative sample from the whole hive, and count the number of tagged bees. How do you think this helps them estimate the total population? Use beans as bees to figure out how this works.

These bees are tagged with bar codes, just as in the supermarket! This ensures that the same bees don't get counted twice.

1 Pour 2 cups (c) of beans into a bowl. Take a handful and mark each bean. Count and record the number of beans you mark.

2

Mix the marked beans with the total beans. Then take a handful. Use this as your sample.

3

Find the ratio of marked beans to total beans in your sample to estimate the probability of choosing a marked bean from the bowl.

4

Is your handful representative of the whole bowl? Why or why not? Repeat the experiment until you feel confident in your prediction.

5 Write a report on your experiment. Include each ratio and probability you found, as well as the number of beans you predicted and the actual number.

Ask Yourself

☐ What do you know about probability that can help you solve this problem?

☐ How can you use what you know to find the information that is missing?

☐ Can you model the problem with a diagram? an equation?

☐ Does your answer make sense?

☐ How can this model be used in a real-life situation? How does the size of your sample make a difference?

6 Describe how you could apply this model to estimate the number of animals in each group given below:
• bass in a lake
• wild horses in Arizona
• seals in Alaska
• bison in Wyoming

Section B: Multiple Events **423**

Market Makeover

To increase sales at her corner grocery, Mrs. Olivia plans to redesign the store. Look at the current floor plan to help answer these questions.

1 How many acute angles and how many obtuse angles can you find in this floor plan? Show an angle less than 70° and an angle greater than 110°.

2 How many different ways could you arrange the four displays in the window?

3 Shelves cost $120 each. Mrs. Olivia can get 25% off if she buys 50 or more. She needs only 38 shelves. Will she save money by buying 50?

4 The original sandwich counter cost $145. A new one will cost $188.50. What percent did the price increase?

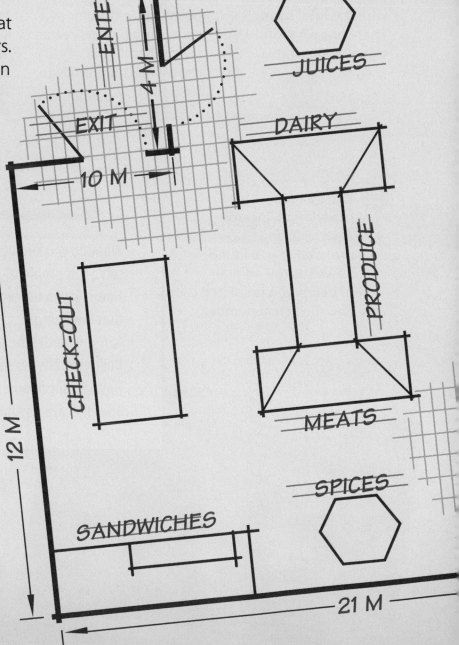

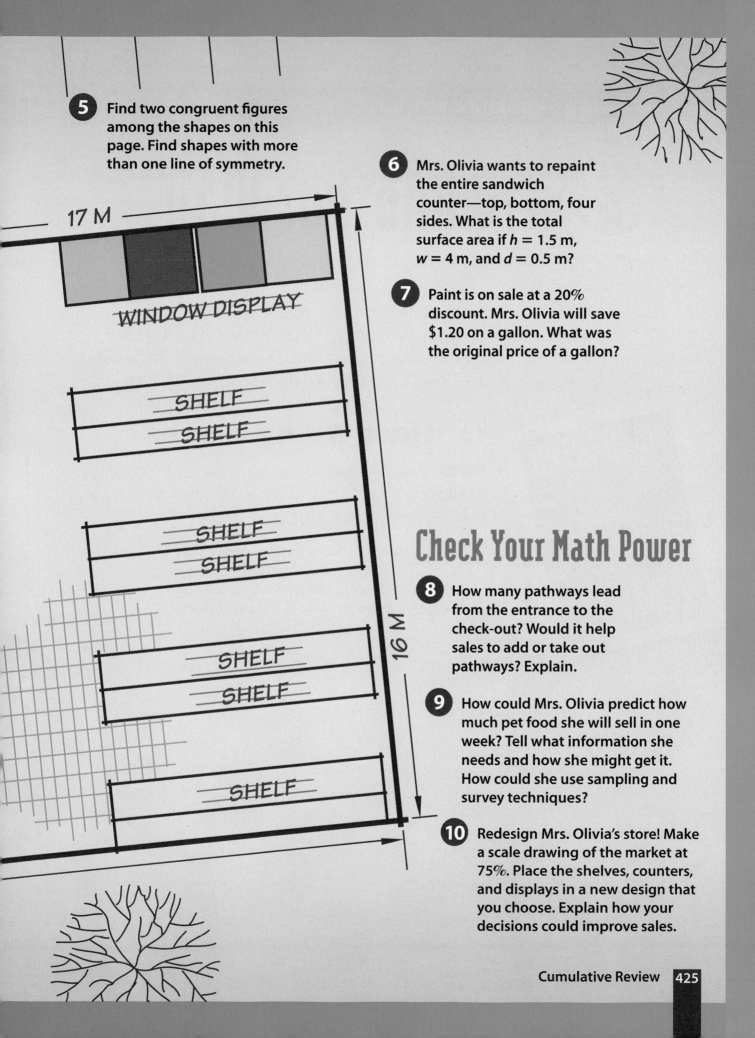

5 Find two congruent figures among the shapes on this page. Find shapes with more than one line of symmetry.

17 M

WINDOW DISPLAY

SHELF
SHELF

SHELF
SHELF

SHELF
SHELF

SHELF

16 M

6 Mrs. Olivia wants to repaint the entire sandwich counter—top, bottom, four sides. What is the total surface area if $h = 1.5$ m, $w = 4$ m, and $d = 0.5$ m?

7 Paint is on sale at a 20% discount. Mrs. Olivia will save $1.20 on a gallon. What was the original price of a gallon?

Check Your Math Power

8 How many pathways lead from the entrance to the check-out? Would it help sales to add or take out pathways? Explain.

9 How could Mrs. Olivia predict how much pet food she will sell in one week? Tell what information she needs and how she might get it. How could she use sampling and survey techniques?

10 Redesign Mrs. Olivia's store! Make a scale drawing of the market at 75%. Place the shelves, counters, and displays in a new design that you choose. Explain how your decisions could improve sales.

LESSON 5 Try Another Way

Your local grocery store is selling a new brand of cereal. Each box has a set of trading cards of a popular music group. There are six sets of cards, but the boxes don't tell you which set is in a package.

ACTIVITY 1 How Many Boxes?

With Your Class How many boxes of cereal would you need to buy to get all six sets? more than 6? fewer than 6,000?

1 A **simulation** is an experiment that matches a situation too messy or too difficult to bring about. Why would a simulation help in this case? Discuss how you could create one.

MUSIC STAR

TRADING CARDS

100% Natural
CORN SQUARES

Music Star
Trading Cards
INSIDE

2 One student used A–F to stand for the six sets of cards. She put a card with each letter into a bag. She then drew a card from the bag, recorded it on a checklist, and put it back in the bag before drawing again. For each trial, she found the number of draws needed to get all six sets. Does her simulation match the situation? Why or why not?

How many draws have been made in trial 1? Why are only four sets of cards checked off?

trials	Set of Cards						total draws
	A	B	C	D	E	F	
1	✓		✓	✓	✓		⫼⫼ II
2							
3							

A computer program can generate lists of random numbers you can use in a simulation. Random means that there is an equal chance of getting any number.

What You'll Need
- *cube labeled 1–6, spinner, or slips of paper*

ACTIVITY 2 # Let the Trials Begin!

With Your Group Simulate the cereal problem. Choose one method you discussed in Activity 1.

1 Each group of outcomes that ends in getting all six sets of cards is a trial. Complete at least 20 trials. Discuss these questions before starting.
- Are we sure our chosen method imitates the goal of getting six different sets of cards?
- What equipment will we need?
- How can we keep track of our results?
- What will each group member's role be?

	trial 1	trial 2
A	I	⦸⦸ (HHT)
B	⦸ I (HH I)	I
C	II	III
D	I	
E	III	III
F	II	

number of draws **15**

trials	SET OF CARDS					
	A	B	C	D	E	F
1	✓	✓	✓	✓	✓	✓
2	✓		✓	✓		✓
3						

REASONING AND PROBLEM SOLVING

In what other cases would you have to use simulation to figure out a probability? Explain why other methods you know would not work as well in those cases.

2 After you have finished your trials, summarize your conclusions. What is the best way to show your data? Prepare a report for the class.

3 After each group has reported, discuss how the group results compared. Were any group's results very different from those of the other groups? How would you explain the differences?

4 Average the results of all the groups. How many trials does the average add up to?

5 According to the class average, how many boxes of cereal must you buy to get all six sets of cards? How does this figure compare with the figure each group got? How does it compare with your earlier guess? Which result do you think is the most accurate? Why?

Trial Results

```
                              X
                         X    X
                    X    X    X
          X    X    X    X    X    X
     X    X    X    X    X    X    X    X    X    X
    10   11   12   13   14   15   16   17   18   19
```

Do You Remember?

Try It!

State the probability if it can be found by multiplying. Write *S* if a simulation should be used to find the probability.

1. Two students in a class of 24 were born in the same month.
2. Two 1–6 number cubes are tossed and the sum is 12.
3. Both of the children in a family are girls.
4. Two 1–4 spinners with equal parts are spun and the sum is 7.
5. You and five others check your coats. The coat attendant later hands them back at random. You get the right coat back.

Use estimation to complete. Write $>$, $<$, or $=$.

6. $355 + 675 \, \bullet \, 925$ 7. $540 + 680 \, \bullet \, 1{,}220$

8. $936 - 344 \, \bullet \, 692$ 9. $1{,}290 - 855 \, \bullet \, 445$

10. $240 + 580 - 310 \, \bullet \, 500$ 11. $675 + 220 + 65 \, \bullet \, 970$

Think About It

12. Choose one problem that you marked *S* in Exercises 1–5 above. Explain in writing how you would simulate it.

LESSON 6 Contests

CONNECT AND COMMUNICATE

In Your Journal Describe a contest you entered or wanted to enter. Do you know what the probability of winning was? Write about it in your journal.

Contests seem to be everywhere. Have you ever entered one or thought about entering one?

LITERATURE

People who enter a contest like to think they have a chance of winning. Jonah thinks he has a chance.

A new program was going to be launched next week. The program, an amateur variety show called "Banana Blitz," was to be sponsored by the American Banana Institute. All you had to do to win the thousand dollars was to keep track of the number of times the word *banana* was used in every commercial. There would be six shows, one each Wednesday afternoon at two o'clock. Three commercials to every show.

I got out a pencil and figured it out. Six times three: eighteen. Eighteen commercials to watch, and I'd win a thousand dollars. I read it again. A thousand dollars! And all I had to do was to watch television commercials! . . .

I kept reading the ad: "Get your BANANA BINGO card at your supermarket TODAY! Only one to a customer. WIN A THOUSAND DOLLARS!"

From *Banana Blitz*
by Florence Parry Heide

ACTIVITY 1 · Winning a Contest

With Your Group Discuss these questions and record your answers. Compare your answers with another group's. Did you all agree? Why or why not?

1 What are some things that could affect Jonah's chance of winning the Banana Blitz contest?

2 Why is it easy to determine the probability of winning a contest if there are numbers to match or cards to scratch? Will the probability of winning change if all the numbers or cards are not distributed? Explain.

DRAWING TO LEARN

Design a poster or magazine ad for your contest that will explain the contest rules.

Will the probability of winning be affected if more people or fewer people enter the contest? Explain.

Play
Banana Bingo
Pick up your card at this store and try to **WIN $1,000.**

3 The probability of winning the $1,000 was pretty small. Design two versions of a contest—one with a very great probability of winning and one with a very small probability of winning.

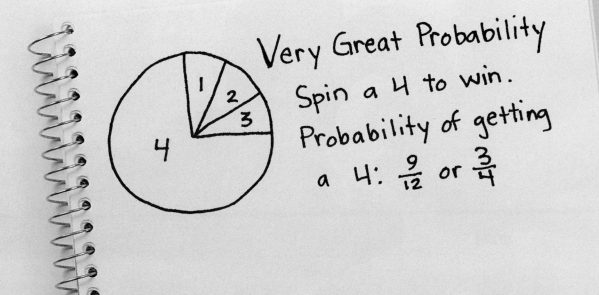

Very Great Probability
Spin a 4 to win.
Probability of getting
a 4: $\frac{9}{12}$ or $\frac{3}{4}$

431

What You'll Need
- *3 spinners*
- *1 coin*
- *beans in 3 colors*
- *bag to hold beans*
- *small cards*

✔ **Self-Check** *What if the probability you find by using one of the methods named here seems wrong? How can you check it?*

Can You Win?

With Your Partner Choose two of the contests on these pages. Use whatever method you wish to figure out the probability of winning each contest you chose.

1 Spin all three spinners once. If you spell *W I N*, you win.

2 Flip a coin four times. If you get four heads in a row, you win.

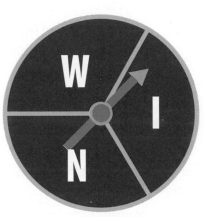

3 The bag has an equal number of red, blue, and green beans. Picking two at once, get two red ones.

432

4 Only the letters *M, U, S, I,* and *C* are used. The order of letters is scrambled in random permutations.

ACTIVITY OPTION

Invent a contest of your own. Challenge members of your group to figure out the probability of winning it.

Do You Remember?

Try It!

Calculate to solve if you can. If you must make a simulation to solve, tell what you would use to get random results.

1. If there were 8 different sets of pictures, how many boxes of popcorn would you need to buy to get them all?
2. How many sets of partners are possible in a class of 25 if order doesn't count? if order does count?
3. What is the probability of correctly answering 7 out of 10 true-false questions by guessing?
4. How many ways can you arrange 6 people in a line?

Change a fraction to a decimal, a decimal to a percent, and a percent to a fraction.

5. 0.40   6. 20%   7. 0.04

8. $\frac{3}{5}$ 9. $\frac{65}{100}$ 10. $\frac{3}{20}$

Think About It

11. How can you increase the accuracy of a simulation? Explain.

LESSON 7 Change the Rules

Ms. Wah has to choose a new contest for the Wah Kee Market. Here are some games she is considering.

Add It Up

1. **Spin two times.**
2. **Find the sum of your two spins.**
3. **A sum of 9 wins.**

ACTIVITY 1 So Who Wins?

With Your Group Read the rules for this game. Find the probability of winning.

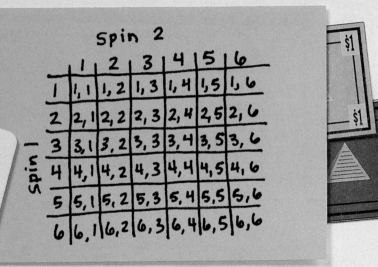

1. Use the chart. It shows all the possible outcomes for two spins.
   a. Which outcomes have the same result?
   b. What is the probability of each outcome?
   c. What is the probability of winning with a sum of 9?

2 Which sum has the greatest probability? What is that probability?

3 Which sums have the least probability? What is that probability?

4 Suppose Ms. Wah decides to change the rules. What are the probabilities of these outcomes?
   a. two odd numbers
   b. two prime numbers
   c. a sum of 14

5 How would you change the game so Ms. Wah doesn't spend too much but customers have a good chance of winning? Share your rules and reasons with the class.

REASONING AND PROBLEM SOLVING

How can arranging the outcomes in an array help you find the total possible outcomes?

- *5 slips of paper, 2 red and 3 white*

ACTIVITY 2 Is It Independent?

With Your Group For another game, Ms. Wah put two red and three white table tennis balls in a bag. Each red ball drawn in two tries earns a point toward a prize. Ms. Wah is testing two sets of rules. Decide whether the probability of winning is the same in each game.

1 Compare games A and B.

    a. What is the probability of getting red on the first try in game A? Is the probability the same for the first draw in game B? How do you know?

    b. In game A, why is the probability of pulling red in the second draw the same as it is for the first draw?

    c. In game B, do you think the probability of pulling red in the second draw is the same as it is for the first draw? Why or why not?

2 Find the probability of pulling two reds in game A. First think about the probability of getting red in each draw. Should you add or multiply to find the combined probability? Why?

WIN BIG!

Get two tries to earn points!

GAME A

After your first draw, return the ball to the box before drawing again.

GAME B

After your first draw, do not return the ball to the box before drawing again.

$$\frac{2}{5} + \frac{2}{5} = \frac{4}{5}$$

$$\frac{2}{5} \times \frac{2}{5} = \frac{4}{25}$$

Does it make more sense for the probability of drawing two reds to be 4 out of 5 or 4 out of 25?

3 Test your thinking by experimenting. In 20 games, is your ratio for drawing two reds closer to $\frac{4}{5}$ or $\frac{4}{25}$? Why do you think that is?

4 Do you have a better chance, a worse chance, or about the same chance of pulling two reds in game A as in game B? Justify your answer.

Why would you not subtract or divide to find the probability?

5 If two events happen and one does not influence the other, these are called **independent events.** Explain why the events in game A are independent.

6 Game B uses **dependent events.** What do you think that means? Have you heard the word *dependent* before? How can its use help you figure out its meaning?

✔ **Self-Check** *You spin two spinners and record the result. Are the two spins independent events? How do you know?*

Section D: Dependent or Independent? **437**

Pick a Path

Pick a Winner

With Your Group Make a chart to help you make choices in the game.

1 Play the game several times.

What You'll Need
- *gameboard*
- *game markers*
- *2 cubes labeled 1–6*

Pick a Path

1. Throw one number cube to find out whether to start on odd or even. Put your game piece on that space.

2. Announce which of the outcomes on the board you will try to get with two number cubes. You have three throws with two number cubes to get the outcome you want.

3. If you get the outcome you announced, move your game piece to that space. Now it's the next player's turn.

4. The first player to get to the finish wins.

Two players may rest on the same space.

TOOLS AND TECHNIQUES

Make a chart that shows the sums of two 1–6 number cubes to help you find probabilities more quickly.

2 How did thinking about the probabilities help you make decisions? How did the chart from Activity 1 help you?

3 Talk about how you might change the game. Think of at least two ways to make it more challenging or more fun.

4 Share your new version with another group.

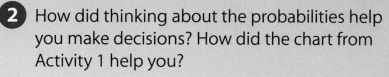

Do You Remember?

Try It!

A   B

Find the probabilities of one spin on these two spinners.

1. two prime numbers   2. two odd numbers
3. a sum of 2   4. 5 on both spinners
5. probability of losing if sums greater than 6 are winners

Which would cost the least?

6. a $35.00 sweater at 25% off
7. a $24.95 radio with 8% sales tax
8. a $49.95 jacket at 50% off

Solve.

9. A bicycle reduced 20% costs $80. What was the original price?
10. A $12.00 tape sells for $9.00. What percent is it reduced?

Think About It

11. For Exercises 1–5 would spinning B first change the probability of any outcome on A? Why or why not?

Everybody Wins

Ms. Wah wants someone like you who knows a lot about probability to help design the best contest yet!

What You'll Need
- *spinner labeled 1–6*
- *spinner labeled 1–8*

ACTIVITY 1 **Making Plans**

With Your Group   Use two spinners like these, the list of prizes, and the chart, to set up a contest.

Prizes		
Number of Prizes	**Prize**	**Cost for Each**
5	**$25 gift certificate**	**$25**
10	**Fruit basket**	**$10**
100	**$5 gift certificate**	**$5**
1,000	**$1 gift certificate**	**$1**

CONNECT AND COMMUNICATE

In Your Journal Explain why the prizes with the highest cost should have the least probability of being won. Why should prizes with the lowest cost have the greatest probability of being won?

1 First, look at the probabilities for doubles. What is the probability of spinning each pair of doubles?

2 Find the probabilities for these pairs of outcomes.
   a. the first spin is 1
   b. any doubles
   c. the spin on B is a greater number than on A

Spinner B

Spinner A	1	2	3	4	5	6	7	8
1	1,1	1,2	1,3	1,4	1,5	1,6	1,7	1,8
2	2,1	2,2	2,3	2,4	2,5	2,6	2,7	2,8
3	3,1	3,2	3,3	3,4	3,5	3,6	3,7	3,8
4	4,1	4,2	4,3	4,4	4,5	4,6	4,7	4,8
5	5,1	5,2	5,3	5,4	5,5	5,6	5,7	5,8
6	6,1	6,2	6,3	6,4	6,5	6,6	6,7	6,8

ACTIVITY OPTION

What if you decided to use sums, differences, or products to determine the outcomes? Make up some rules. Explain how the game would be played and how the prizes would be awarded.

Outcomes	Spinner A Probability	Spinner B Probability	Probability of Doubles
1	$\frac{1}{6}$	$\frac{1}{8}$	$\frac{1}{48}$
2	$\frac{1}{6}$	$\frac{1}{8}$	$\frac{1}{48}$
3	$\frac{1}{6}$		
4			
5			
6			
7			
8			

This student started making a chart to show the probabilities. By completing the chart, what pattern do you see that can help you find each probability?

3 Which outcomes have the greatest probability of being spun? Which have the least? Make up your own rules for the game.

4 Share your recommendations about rules, outcomes, probabilities, and prizes with your class. Discuss which game would be best for Ms. Wah.

What You'll Need
• *3 spinners*

DRAWING TO LEARN

How could you draw spinner B so that it shows equal parts, yet gives each number the same probability of being spun as before?

ACTIVITY 2 More Games

With Your Partner Choose two of these activities.

1. Use spinners A and B. List each event and its probability. Explain how you decided on the probabilities. Test your probabilities by copying the spinners and running 100 trials. Compare your predictions with your results.

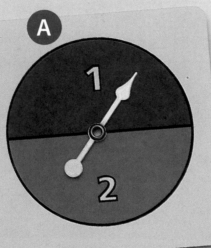

A

B

2 Use spinners A, B, and C. Is the probability of getting three of the same number in one turn the same as the probability of getting three different numbers? Describe how you got your answer.

3 Draw another spinner to use with spinner A so that the probability of spinning a sum of 3 in two spins is $\frac{1}{6}$.

Try It!

List outcomes with these probabilities for 1–6 number cubes.

1. $\frac{2}{36}$ or $\frac{1}{18}$ 2. 0   3. $\frac{4}{36}$ or $\frac{1}{9}$

4. $\frac{1}{36}$ 5. $\frac{1}{4}$ 6. $\frac{1}{3}$

Copy and complete the chart.

	Figure	Faces	Edges	Vertexes
7.	Cube			
8.	Triangular prism			
9.	Rectangular prism			
10.	Square pyramid			
11.	Triangular pyramid			

Think About It

12. How can you use what you know to figure out which events will result in a given probability?

Looking Back

Choose the best answer or answers. Write *a, b, c,* or *d* for each exercise.

1. Which shows dependent events?

   a. Pull three marbles out of a bag, put them back in; pull out the same three marbles.
   b. Pull three marbles out of a bag; roll 3 on a number cube.
   c. Pull one marble out of a bag; keep it and pull another one.
   d. Flip heads 12 times in a row; the next flip is tails.

2. Louie has 3 shirts, 2 pairs of pants, and 2 pairs of shoes. How many different outfits can he make?

   a. 24   b. 6

   c. 12   d. 8

3. On a four-quadrant coordinate grid, which of these sets of points could form a trapezoid if you connect them?

   a. (−3,−4), (−1,2), (3,2), (5,−4)
   b. (−7,1), (−3,−1), (1,−2), (3,−4)
   c. (−2,1), (−2,4), (2,4), (2,1)
   d. (−3,1), (0,−1), (0,−2), (2,−3)

To answer Exercises 4–6, imagine a hat that contains 25 cards numbered 1–25.

4. What is the probability that you will draw the number 23?

   a. $\frac{1}{10}$ b. $\frac{1}{12}$

   c. $\frac{1}{23}$ d. $\frac{1}{25}$

5. What is the probability of drawing an odd number?

   a. $\frac{1}{12}$ b. $\frac{1}{2}$

   c. $\frac{2}{25}$ d. $\frac{13}{25}$

6. What is the probability that you will draw any one of the following numbers: 1, 2, 3, 4, or 5?

   a. $\frac{1}{4}$ b. $\frac{1}{5}$

   c. $\frac{3}{25}$ d. $\frac{2}{25}$

7. What are the chances of throwing a sum of 2 with two 1–6 number cubes?

   a. $\frac{1}{720}$ b. $\frac{1}{360}$

   c. $\frac{2}{12}$ d. $\frac{1}{36}$

Base your answers to Exercises 8–12 on the incomplete tree diagram.

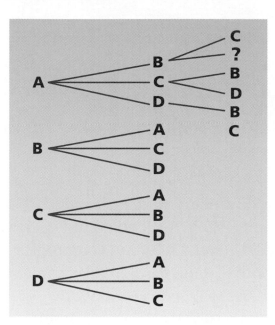

8. How many permutations will there be for the three draws?

    a. 8   b. 12   c. 16   d. 24

9. What will the outcome marked with the question mark be?

    a. (A,B,D)   b. (B,A,D)
    c. (C,B,A)   d. (D,B,A)

10. How many permutations of the outcome (A,B,C) are possible?

    a. 3   b. 6   c. 8   d. 12

11. What is the probability of picking A, B, and C in that exact order?

    a. $\frac{1}{6}$ b. $\frac{1}{12}$ c. $\frac{1}{16}$ d. $\frac{1}{24}$

12. What is the probability of picking A, B, C in uninterrupted order?

    a. $\frac{1}{12}$ b. $\frac{1}{8}$ c. $\frac{1}{3}$ d. $\frac{1}{24}$

Base your answers to Exercises 13 and 14 on the chart below.

Average Temperatures in °F				
City	**Month**			
	Jan.	Apr.	July	Oct.
Sioux Falls, S. Dak.	12.4	46.4	74.0	49.0
Tucson, Ariz.	51.1	64.9	86.2	70.4
San Francisco, Calif.	48.5	54.8	62.2	60.6

Source: *The 1992 Information Please Almanac*

13. Decide which statement is probably true.
    a. The average yearly temperature in Sioux Falls is about the same as in San Francisco.
    b. The average temperature in Sioux Falls in March is between 30° F and 50° F.
    c. Tucson has the smallest yearly range of temperatures.
    d. The average temperature in Tucson is usually 10% higher than in San Francisco.

Check Your Math Power

14. Graph the data in the chart above. Describe the kind of graph you drew and what the graph shows that a chart can't.

15. Explain how you would simulate the following problem. You want to know what grade a student is likely to get on a ten-item true-false quiz if the student guesses all the answers.

Hidden Talents

Do you know how many students in your school play a musical instrument? What kind do they play? Without asking each student, how can you predict this information for the whole school? You can survey a small sample and use what you know about probability to predict results for the larger group.

Investigation A — Design a Survey

1. Write your questions. Do you want yes-or-no answers or write-in responses?

2. Decide how many people you need to survey. Use what you know about probability and choose your sample.
   a. Your first group should be a random sample. What methods can you use to find your random sample?
   b. Group 2 should be a biased sample— a group that has a special interest in your subject. Why would surveying members of the school band be a biased sample?
   c. Can the results from both groups be used to make predictions about the entire school? If not, what could they be used to predict?

3 Conduct your survey and organize your results.

4 Make predictions about the number of students in your school who play musical instruments.

5 Present your results to the class. Use charts and other visual information to show your data. Describe how you used probability to make your predictions.

Keep in Mind

Your report will be judged by how well you do the following things.

☐ How well do you show what you know about probability to help you solve the problem?

☐ How well do you use your results to make predictions?

☐ How clearly do you show and explain your plan and your thinking?

1. Do you play a musical instrument?
   ☐ yes   ☐ no
2. If yes, what kind?
   ☐ guitar   ☐ violin
   ☐ piano/key board

447

Investigation B — Cereal Survey

Use what you have learned about probability and sampling to predict what brands of cereal a grocer should stock for a new store. How could you design a survey to find out what cereals customers will buy?

Pretend the students of your school are the new store's potential customers. Design a survey, choose a sample group, collect and organize data, and make predictions about what brands of cereal the grocer should stock. Can you use your survey to find out how much of each brand to stock? Does it matter who buys the cereal for the family? You can design the survey questions to tell you this information as well.

Ongoing Investigation — Wrapping Up Tassellations

Select items from your tessellation portfolio to demonstrate what you have discovered about tessellations this year. Be sure to include an explanation of how to use angle measure to determine whether or not a shape or pair of shapes will tessellate.

Tool Kit

Contents

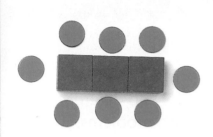

Problem Solving Strategies

Computation Tools

Technology

Data Collection

Drawing to Learn

Measurement

Ways to Solve Problems

On the next few pages, you'll find different strategies, or ways, for solving math problems. Learning these strategies will give you a powerful set of problem solving tools.

Problem

You have square tables for a party. Only one person can sit comfortably on each side. What is the greatest number of people you can seat at 1, 2, 3, 4, 5, and 6 tables if you want the tables to touch on at least one side?

▶ Draw a Picture or a Diagram

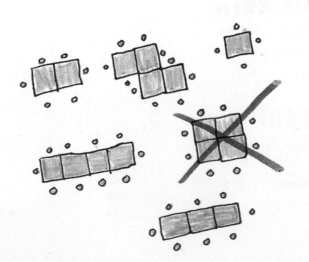

Drawing a picture or diagram can help you solve many problems. You will probably find it helpful to draw a picture when a problem asks you to arrange objects, work with shapes, or compare varying measurements in a space. (See Drawing to Learn on pages 470–471.)

Build a Model or Act It Out

Making a model with objects is another way to find solutions to a problem about arrangements. In this case, you could use blocks to show tables and counters to show chairs. You could move the blocks and counters all sorts of ways to find the best arrangements.

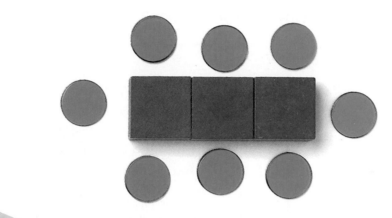

Use a Pattern

You may find a pattern when you are trying to solve some problems. If you do, use the pattern to predict numbers without doing extra calculations. Drawing a picture or making a table can also help you discover the pattern.

Steps

1. **Work through the first several steps of the problem. Drawing a picture often helps.**

2. **Write the numbers in a table and look for a pattern.**

3. **Use the pattern to complete the table.**

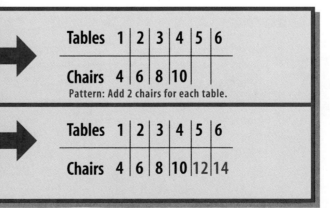

Tables	1	2	3	4	5	6
Chairs	4	6	8	10		

Pattern: Add 2 chairs for each table.

Tables	1	2	3	4	5	6
Chairs	4	6	8	10	12	14

Tool Kit

Problem Solving Strategies

Problem

What is the least number of coins you can use to make 35 cents? What is the greatest number of coins you can use? In how many different ways can you make 35 cents?

Organize Information

Some problems require you to make combinations or arrange data. In these cases, it helps to organize your information in a list, table, chart, or graph.

Write a List Making a list is one way to organize your information. Write down all the possibilities in a planned way.

Make a Table or Chart

If you find yourself writing the same words again and again, organize your information into a table. Making a table will save you time and space.

First you can list all the ways to make 35¢ using just one quarter.

Ways to Make 35¢

Quarters	Dimes	Nickels	Pennies
1	1		
1		2	
1			10
1		1	5
	3	1	
	3		5

Then you can write all the ways to make 35¢ using 3 dimes.

Problem

At the end of a day, you have $2.04 left. You can't remember exactly how much you took out of your home bank that morning. How can you figure it out?

Work Backward

If you have ever lost something, you may have found it by tracing your steps backward. That's exactly how to use the strategy Work Backward. You'll want to use this strategy when you know the endpoint of a problem but not the information that leads to it.

Steps

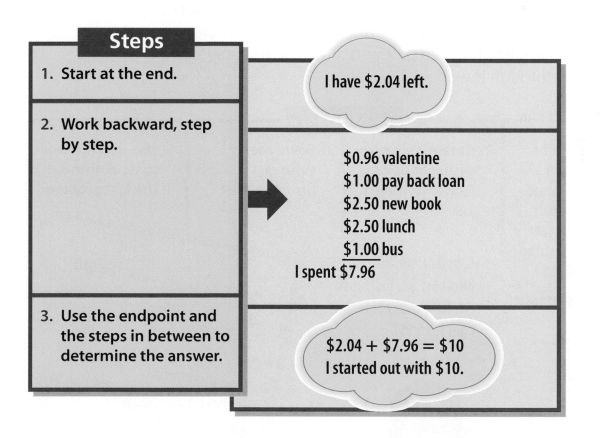

1. **Start at the end.**

   I have $2.04 left.

2. **Work backward, step by step.**

   $0.96 valentine
   $1.00 pay back loan
   $2.50 new book
   $2.50 lunch
   $1.00 bus
   I spent $7.96

3. **Use the endpoint and the steps in between to determine the answer.**

   $2.04 + $7.96 = $10
   I started out with $10.

Problem

A sporting goods store usually sells bats for $8.95. Now they're on sale for $6.98. If balls cost $4.95, how many bat-and-ball sets can you buy with $120?

Use a Simpler or Related Problem

Some problems seem hard because they involve lots of data or large numbers. Unnecessary data also makes problems difficult to solve. In such cases, working a simpler or related problem can show you how to work through the original problem.

Steps

1. Cut out words and numbers you don't need. (In this case, it doesn't matter that bats *used* to sell for $8.95.)

2. Create a simpler problem using "easy" numbers.

3. Solve the simpler problem.

4. Use that method to work through the first problem.

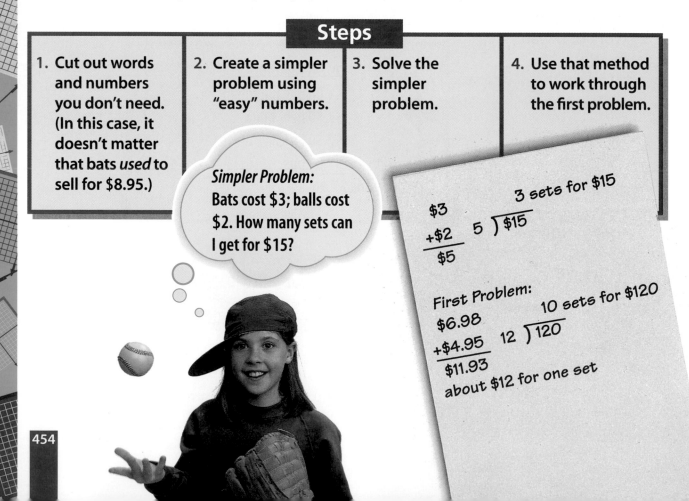

Simpler Problem: Bats cost $3; balls cost $2. How many sets can I get for $15?

$$\begin{array}{r} \$3 \\ +\$2 \\ \hline \$5 \end{array}$$

3 sets for $15

$5\overline{)\$15}$

First Problem:

$$\begin{array}{r} \$6.98 \\ +\$4.95 \\ \hline \$11.93 \end{array}$$

10 sets for $120

$12\overline{)120}$

about $12 for one set

Problem

Find two numbers whose sum is 135 and whose difference is 21. What are they?

Guess and Check

Guess and Check is a strategy that helps you plunge right into a problem. First make a guess at an answer. Then check to see if it works. Use that information to decide if your next guess should be lower or higher.

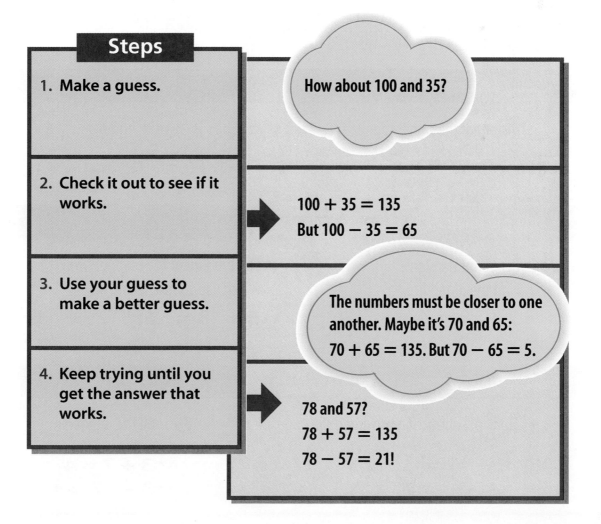

Steps	
1. **Make a guess.**	*How about 100 and 35?*
2. **Check it out to see if it works.**	$100 + 35 = 135$ But $100 - 35 = 65$
3. **Use your guess to make a better guess.**	*The numbers must be closer to one another. Maybe it's 70 and 65:* $70 + 65 = 135.$ But $70 - 65 = 5.$
4. **Keep trying until you get the answer that works.**	78 and 57? $78 + 57 = 135$ $78 - 57 = 21!$

Computing by Steps

Use this part of the Tool Kit to review ways to add, subtract, multiply, and divide. You'll find methods for computing with paper and pencil as well as "in your head."

▶ Paper and Pencil

These methods are helpful whenever you are using paper and pencil to help you compute.

Adding Integers with Same Signs

1 Disregard the signs. Add.

$$^-3 + {}^-7 = ?$$ _(3 + 7 = 10)_

2 Use the sign of both numbers.

$$^-3 + {}^-7 = {}^-10$$

Adding Integers with Different Signs

1 Disregard the signs. Find the difference.

$$5 + {}^-8 = ?$$ _(8 − 5 = 3)_

2 Use the sign of the number from which you subtracted.

$$5 + {}^-8 = {}^-3$$

Subtracting Integers

1 Think of subtracting as adding the opposite.

$$^-3 - {}^-7 = {}^-3 + 7$$ _(7 is the opposite of ⁻7.)_

2 Add the integers.

$$^-3 + 7 = 4$$
$$^-3 - {}^-7 = 4$$

Adding and Subtracting Fractions: Different Denominators

1 Find a common denominator.

$$\begin{array}{r} \frac{1}{4} \\ + \frac{3}{8} \\ \hline \end{array}$$

Multiples of 4: 4, 8
Multiples of 8: 8

8 is a common denominator of 4 and 8.

2 Use the common denominator to write equivalent fractions.

$$\begin{array}{r} \frac{1}{4} = \frac{2}{8} \\ + \frac{3}{8} = \frac{3}{8} \\ \hline \end{array}$$

3 Add. Simplify if necessary.

$$\begin{array}{r} \frac{2}{8} \\ + \frac{3}{8} \\ \hline \frac{5}{8} \end{array}$$

Multiplying by a 2-Digit Factor

1 Multiply by the ones.

$$\begin{array}{r} 46 \\ \times 25 \\ \hline 230 \end{array}$$

5×46

2 Multiply by the tens.

$$\begin{array}{r} 46 \\ \times 25 \\ \hline 230 \\ 920 \end{array}$$

2 tens × 46

3 Add.

$$\begin{array}{r} 46 \\ \times 25 \\ \hline 230 \\ + 920 \\ \hline 1,150 \end{array}$$

Dividing by a 2-Digit Divisor

1 Decide how many digits are in the quotient.

$$23\overline{)378}$$

The first digit is in the tens' place.

2 Estimate the first digit.

$$23\overline{)378}^{\,1}$$

3 Multiply to find the number of tens shared. Subtract to find the tens left.

$$\begin{array}{r} 1 \\ 23\overline{)378} \\ -23 \\ \hline 14 \end{array}$$

14 tens

4 Trade the tens for ones. Share the ones.

$$\begin{array}{r} 16 \\ 23\overline{)378} \\ -23 \\ \hline 148 \\ -138 \\ \hline 10 \end{array}$$

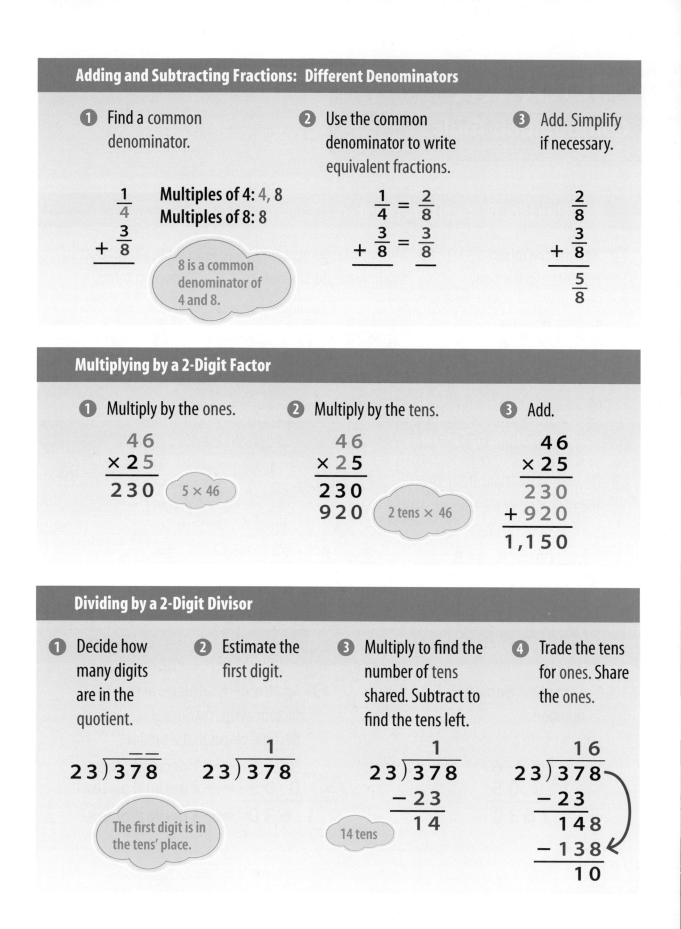

Tool Kit

Computation Tools

Multiplying Fractions and Mixed Numbers

1 Rewrite the mixed number as a fraction.

2 Multiply the numerators. Multiply the denominators.

3 Write the product in simplest terms.

$$\frac{1}{6} \times 1\frac{1}{2} = \frac{1}{6} \times \frac{3}{2}$$

$$\frac{1}{6} \times \frac{3}{2} = \frac{3}{12}$$

$$1 \times 3 = 3$$
$$6 \times 2 = 12$$

$$\frac{3}{12} = \frac{1}{4}$$

Dividing Fractions by Fractions

1 Rewrite as multiplication. Use the reciprocal of the divisor.

2 Multiply.

3 Simplify the product.

$$\frac{3}{4} \div \frac{3}{8} = \frac{3}{4} \times \frac{8}{3}$$

$$\frac{3}{4} \times \frac{8}{3} = \frac{24}{12}$$

$$\frac{24}{12} = 2$$

Multiplying Decimals

1 Multiply as with whole numbers.

2 Add the decimal places in the factors. Write that many decimal places in the product.

$$\begin{array}{r} 32.6 \\ \times\ 0.05 \\ \hline 1630 \end{array}$$

$$\begin{array}{r} 32.6 \\ \times\ 0.05 \\ \hline 1.630 \end{array}$$

32.6 ←— 1 decimal place
× 0.05 ←— 2 decimal places
1.630 ←— 3 decimal places

Dividing Decimals by Whole Numbers

1 Write a decimal point in the quotient.

$$12\overline{)1.14}$$

2 Divide as with whole numbers.

$$
\begin{array}{r}
0.095 \\
12\overline{)1.140} \\
-\ 1\ 08 \\
\hline
60 \\
-\ 60 \\
\hline
0
\end{array}
$$

Write a zero in the tenths' place to show that there are no tenths in the quotient.

Dividing Decimals by Decimals

1 Multiply the divisor to make it a whole number.

$$1.25.\overline{)1.5}$$

$$
\begin{array}{r}
1.25 \\
\times\ 100 \\
\hline
125
\end{array}
$$

2 Multiply the dividend by the same number.

$$125\overline{)1.50}$$

$$
\begin{array}{r}
1.5 \\
\times\ 100 \\
\hline
150
\end{array}
$$

3 Divide as with whole numbers.

$$
\begin{array}{r}
1.2 \\
125\overline{)150.0} \\
-\ 125 \\
\hline
25\ 0 \\
-\ 25\ 0 \\
\hline
0
\end{array}
$$

▶ Mental Math

Doing computation mentally can be faster than writing something down. Here are some strategies you can use for mental math.

Counting On or Counting Back

When you add or subtract numbers, you can count ahead or count back by multiples of ten. Then count ahead or back one number at a time.

Add: 28 + 43

28 . . . 38, 48, 58, 68 . . .
Then count ahead by 3 ones.
68 . . . 69, 70, 71

Subtract: 88 − 32

Start with 88 and count back by 3 tens.

88 . . . 78, 68, 58 . . .
Then count back by 2 ones.
58 . . . 57, 56

Canceling Zeros

If both the divisor and dividend end in zeros, mentally cross out the same number of zeros in each. Then divide.

6,600 ÷ 200 = *n*

Cancel same number of zeros.

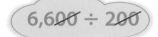

6,600 ÷ 200

Then divide.

66 ÷ 2 = 33

Multiplying Tens

When you multiply by multiples of 10, 100, or 1,000, multiply the nonzero digits. Then supply the zeros in the product.

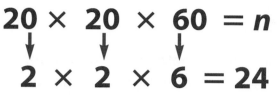

$$20 \times 20 \times 60 = n$$

$$2 \times 2 \times 6 = 24$$

First multiply the factors as if they have no zeros.

$$20 \times 20 \times 60$$

$$24,000$$

Then count the number of zeros in the factors.

3 zeros

Supply the zeros in the product.

Compensation

When you add or subtract, changing one number to a round number can make solving easier. Then change your answer to compensate.

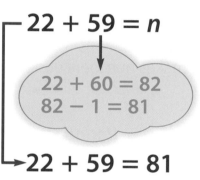

$$22 + 59 = n$$

$$22 + 60 = 82$$
$$82 - 1 = 81$$

$$22 + 59 = 81$$

Add 1 to 59 to get 60. **Subtract 1** from the answer to compensate.

Breaking Apart Numbers

You can break apart numbers to get numbers that are easier to use mentally. Breaking apart numbers in a multiplication problem is one way to use the Distributive Property.

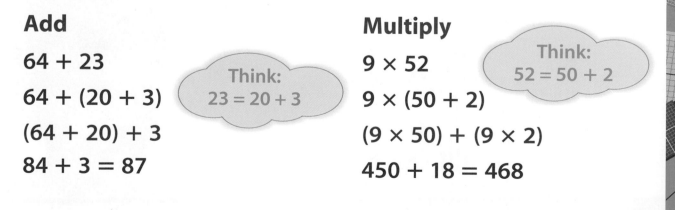

Add

64 + 23

64 + (20 + 3)

(64 + 20) + 3

84 + 3 = 87

Think:
23 = 20 + 3

Multiply

9 × 52

9 × (50 + 2)

(9 × 50) + (9 × 2)

450 + 18 = 468

Think:
52 = 50 + 2

▶ Estimation

Estimation is using mental math to get an answer that's close to the actual answer but not exact. When is it helpful to estimate?

- When an exact answer isn't necessary
- When you want to know if your answer is reasonable
- When there is no way of getting an exact number

Here are four estimation strategies.

Rounding

Rounding makes numbers easier to work with mentally.

Round Whole Numbers
To nearest 100

$$75 \longrightarrow 100$$
$$233 \longrightarrow 200$$

Round Decimals
To nearest whole number

$$\$6.59 \rightarrow \$7$$
$$\$136.98 \rightarrow \$137$$

Round Fractions
To whole numbers

$$2\frac{2}{3} \longrightarrow 3$$
$$5\frac{1}{8} \longrightarrow 5$$

Rounding to Estimate Products

To get a quick estimate of the product, round the factors. Then multiply.

$$19 \times 665$$
$$\downarrow \qquad \downarrow$$
$$20 \times 700 = 14{,}000$$

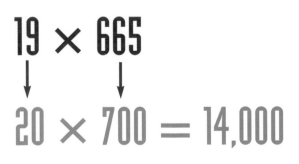

Front-End Estimation

Use front-end estimation to quickly add money amounts.

First group dollars. You get $6.

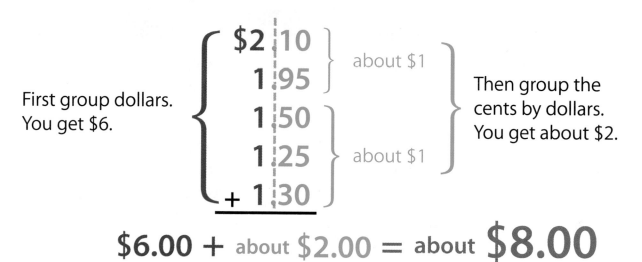

$$\begin{cases} \$2.10 \\ 1.95 \end{cases} \text{about } \$1$$
$$\begin{cases} 1.50 \\ 1.25 \end{cases} \text{about } \$1$$
$$+ 1.30$$

Then group the cents by dollars. You get about $2.

$6.00 + about **$2.00 =** about **$8.00**

Compatible Numbers

Compatible numbers are numbers that are easy to divide. You can use compatible numbers to help estimate quotients and the products of some fractions and whole numbers.

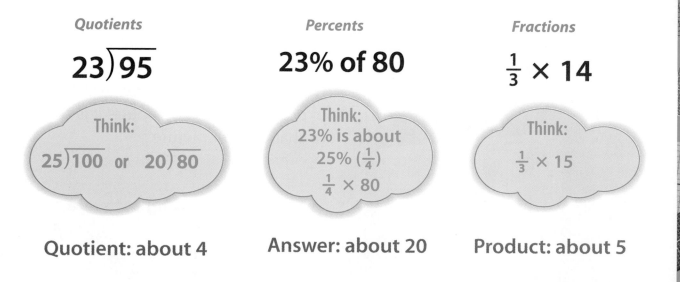

Quotients

$23\overline{)95}$

Think:
$25\overline{)100}$ or $20\overline{)80}$

Quotient: about 4

Percents

23% of 80

Think: 23% is about 25% ($\frac{1}{4}$)
$\frac{1}{4} \times 80$

Answer: about 20

Fractions

$\frac{1}{3} \times 14$

Think:
$\frac{1}{3} \times 15$

Product: about 5

Electronic Tools

Computers and calculators can help you solve problems, calculate numbers, and present work. The trick is in knowing how and when to use them.

▶ Computer

Computers can help you collect, organize, and analyze large amounts of data. With different kinds of software, you can create diagrams, charts, tables, graphs, and pictures.

Software Software programs are the instructions that tell a computer what to do. Drawing programs, spreadsheets, word processing packages, and computer games are all software.

Drawing Programs Pictures can help you solve a problem or explain an idea. Using drawing software is a fun and easy way to make all kinds of pictures. On the computer it is easy to change your picture.

File   Edit   Formula   Format   Data   Options   Window

Drawing Software Uses:

- draw pictures
- make patterns
- illustrate stories
- create floor plans

Spreadsheets/Graphs

Spreadsheets/Graphs Spreadsheet programs are very useful when you are working with lots of numbers. Spreadsheets have columns and rows, like a table. You can enter your own numbers or have the computer calculate them for you. Then you can sort, rearrange, and even graph your information.

Spreadsheet Uses:

- organize budgets
- make tables
- draw graphs

Cost to Feed Animals

	$400	$300	$200	$100	0

Monkeys Flamingos Sea Lions Anteaters Rhino

■ Cost per group

File	Edit	Formula	Format	Data	Options	Window

Sample spreadsheet

	A	B	C	D	E	F	G
1	Cost of Feeding Animals Each Week in Wildlife Park						
2							
3	Animals	Number	Cost/One	Total Cost			
4							
5	Monkey	8	$17.00	$136.00			
6	Flamingo	12	$32.00	$384.00			
7	Sea Lion	4	$11.00	$44.00			
8	Anteater	2	$115.00	$230.00			
9	Rhino	1	$165.00	$165.00			
10							
11	SUM	27	$340.00	$959.00			
12							
13							
14							
15							
16							
17							
18							
19							
20							

The spreadsheet added the total cost.

Databases

Databases With database software you can organize large amounts of data, including words, dates, and numbers. A database is a great place to put survey results because it can sort through all the answers in the survey. For example, for this survey, the database can search for how many boys have pet hamsters or what kind of pet is owned by the most students.

Name	Male/Female	Age	Pets	
1 Mark Ellis	M	11	dog	parrot
2 Sue Linn	F	12	fish	
3 Reggie Brown	M	10	dog	
4 Cassie Houston	F	12	dog	cat
5 Rosa Rodriguez	F	12	hamster	
6				
7				
8				
9				
10				
11				
12				
13				
14				
15				

Database Uses:

- record survey data
- group data into categories

Tool Kit

▶ Calculator

Your calculator may be a little different from the one shown on these pages. Read the instructions that come with your calculator to learn how to use it.

Examples:

Division
This calculator will divide and show the remainder.

$173 \div 15$

173 INT÷ 15 = [___Q___11 ___R___8]

Fractions
This calculator will compute with fractions, change fractions to mixed numbers, and simplify fractions.

$\frac{26}{3} \times \frac{51}{4}$

26 / 3 x 51 / 4 = 1326/12

Ab/c 110⌴6/12

Simp = 110⌴3/6

Simp = 110⌴1/2

Mixed Numbers
This calculator will compute mixed numbers.

$4\frac{1}{5} + 6\frac{3}{8}$

4 + 1 / 5 + 6 + 3 / 8

= 10 23/40

Percents
This calculator will find percents.

What is 40% of 75?

40 % x 75 = 30

Parentheses
This calculator will perform multiple calculations in the order you want.

$2 \times (4 + 5)$

2 x (4 + 5) = 18

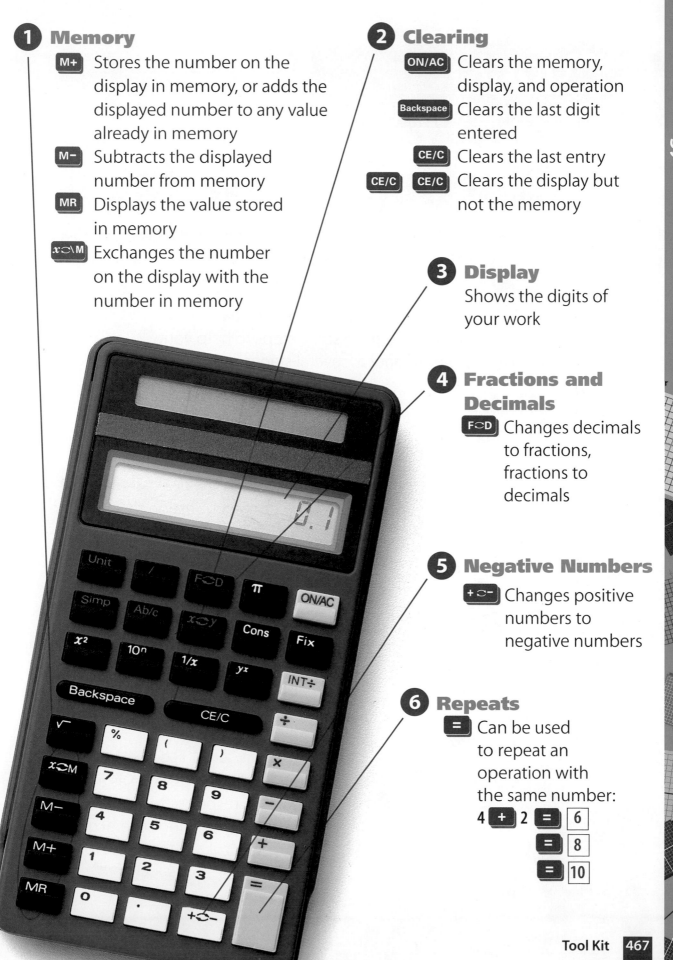

① Memory

M+ Stores the number on the display in memory, or adds the displayed number to any value already in memory

M− Subtracts the displayed number from memory

MR Displays the value stored in memory

x⌒\M Exchanges the number on the display with the number in memory

② Clearing

ON/AC Clears the memory, display, and operation

Backspace Clears the last digit entered

CE/C Clears the last entry

CE/C **CE/C** Clears the display but not the memory

③ Display

Shows the digits of your work

④ Fractions and Decimals

F⌒D Changes decimals to fractions, fractions to decimals

⑤ Negative Numbers

+⌒− Changes positive numbers to negative numbers

⑥ Repeats

= Can be used to repeat an operation with the same number:

4 **+** 2 **=** 6
= 8
= 10

Working with Data

Data refers to facts of all kinds. Numbers, statistics, dates, and responses to interviews are all examples of data. Here are some steps to help you plan and organize data at several stages.

Eight Steps to Good Data Collection

Possible Questions
- How much has my state's population changed?
- How much did our class grow last year?
- What kinds of arrays are found in grocery stores?

Ways to Collect Data
- counting
- measuring
- observing
- researching
- interviewing
- experimenting

1 Begin with a Question
Choose a question that you can answer by collecting data from several people or sources.

2 Plan Your Strategy
Choose a way to collect data. Where will you go for information? What kind of data are you likely to collect? How can you share it?

3 Collect and Record the Data
This could be as simple as a few tally marks in response to a question or as complex as making several graphs.

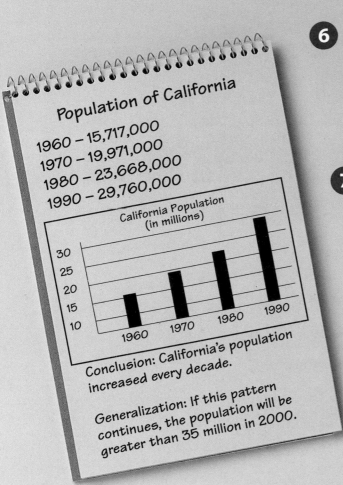

Population of California

1960 – 15,717,000
1970 – 19,971,000
1980 – 23,668,000
1990 – 29,760,000

California Population
(in millions)

30
25
20
15
10

1960   1970   1980   1990

Conclusion: California's population increased every decade.

Generalization: If this pattern continues, the population will be greater than 35 million in 2000.

6 Draw a Conclusion

What does the data tell you about your original question? Does it describe something? Does it allow you to make comparisons?

7 Use Your Conclusion

You may be able to use your conclusion as a basis for a prediction, generalization, or decision.

8 Look Back/Look Ahead

As you look over the results of your data collection, you may want to begin the process again with a related or refined question. Or you may wish to test the theory you developed.

4 Organize the Data

Review and arrange your data. What's the best way to categorize your data?

5 Represent Your Data

What's the best way to display your data? A table? A chart? A graph? Now you're ready to share your results.

How does California's growth compare to that of other states?

469

Drawing as a Math Tool

Drawing can help you discover, understand, and share key concepts in math. Use your Drawing to Learn tools to make a variety of precise shapes and measurements.

Drawing to Discover

Drawing can lead to discovery. For example, if you draw what you know about a problem, you often find the solution. If you draw a chart, you can see how groups of numbers relate. And drawing helps you discover your own creative ideas about math.

As you draw, patterns appear that you might not have noticed otherwise.

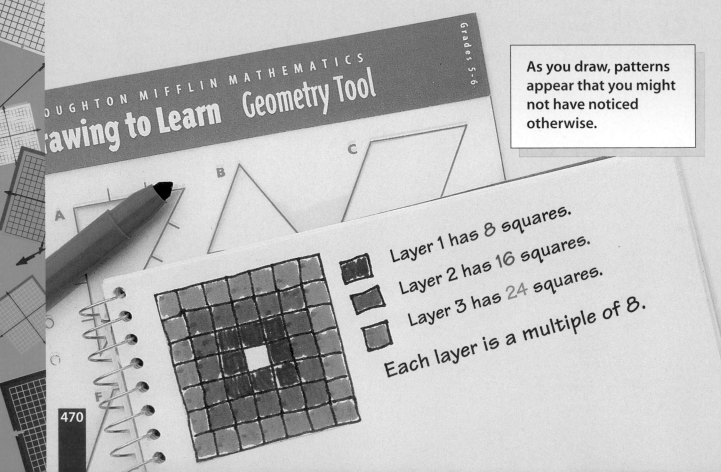

Layer 1 has 8 squares.
Layer 2 has 16 squares.
Layer 3 has 24 squares.
Each layer is a multiple of 8.

Drawing to Understand

To simplify the steps of a process, pick up a pencil and start to draw. Drawing can also help you understand key concepts in math, including the basic computations of adding, subtracting, multiplying, and dividing.

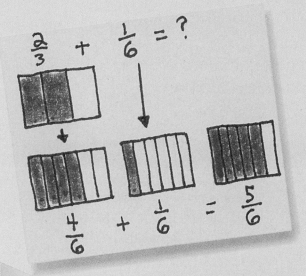

> You can use drawing to create your own system for understanding a key math concept.

Drawing to Share

Pictures, diagrams, graphs—all these are visual ways to share information. You can pack a great deal of data into a drawing.

> People can point to your graph and ask questions or give feedback.

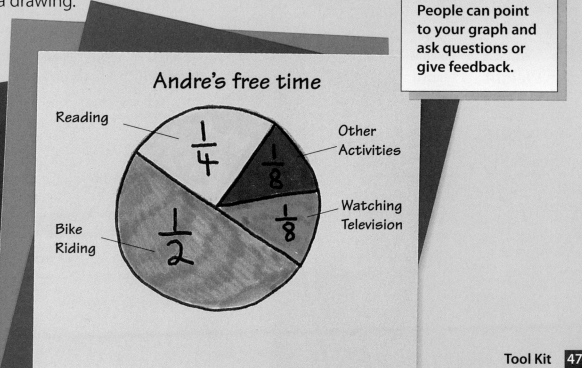

Measurement Tools

The charts on this page identify common measures. Check the glossary and index for more information on specific terms.

Customary	Metric
Length	
1 foot (ft) = 12 inches (in.)	1 centimeter (cm) = 10 millimeters (mm)
1 yard (yd) = 3 feet (ft) or 36 inches (in.)	1 decimeter (dm) = 10 centimeters (cm)
1 mile (mi) = 5,280 feet (ft)	1 meter (m) = 10 decimeters (dm)
	1 kilometer (km) = 1,000 meters (m)
Capacity	
1 cup (c) = 8 fluid ounces (fl oz)	1 liter (L) = 1,000 milliliters (mL)
1 pint (pt) = 2 cups (c)	1 kiloliter (kL) = 1,000 liters (L)
1 quart (qt) = 2 pints (pt)	
1 gallon (gal) = 4 quarts (qt)	
Mass/Weight	
1 pound (lb) = 16 ounces (oz)	1 gram (g) = 1,000 milligrams (mg)
1 ton (t) = 2,000 pounds (lb)	1 kilogram (kg) = 1,000 grams (g)
Temperature	
Fahrenheit	*Celsius*
freezing point = 32° F	freezing point = 0° C
boiling point = 212° F	boiling point = 100° C

Time
1 minute (min) = 60 seconds (s)
1 hour (h) = 60 minutes (min)
1 day = 24 hours (h)
1 week = 7 days
1 year = 52 weeks

Module 6.1 Section A

a **For use with Lesson 1 (pages 4–7)**

Rewrite the survey questions to make them more specific.

1. Do you like sports?

2. Do you like movies?

3. Do you have a hobby?

4. Do you listen to the radio?

b **For use with Lesson 2 (pages 8–12)**

Week	1	2	3	4	5	6	7
Math	76	67	89	92	76	95	80
Science	88	83	72	83	81	75	91

Use the table of test scores above.

5. Make a stem-and-leaf plot of the math scores.

6. Make a stem-and-leaf plot of the science scores.

7. What comparisons can you make?

8. Make a double-bar graph comparing the math and science scores.

9. What conclusions can you make from the double-bar graph?

10. Which type of graph do you think is the most useful for this type of data?

c **For use with Lesson 3 (pages 13–17)**

Attendance for One Game				
Major league teams	A	B	C	D
Paid attendance	34,567	14,032	43,924	27,748

Use the data above for the following:

11. Round the attendance for each team to the nearest thousand.

12. Round to the nearest ten thousand.

13. Give the place value of every 4.

14. What do you need to add to each number to put a 1 in the thousands place?

Module 6.1 Section B

a For use with Lesson 4 (pages 18–21)

Write the greatest number. If it is a fraction greater than one, write it as a mixed number. Write mixed numbers as fractions greater than one.

1. $\frac{5}{4}, \frac{2}{4}, \frac{8}{4}$ 2. $\frac{1}{2}, \frac{9}{2}, \frac{7}{2}$ 3. $\frac{7}{9}, \frac{10}{9}, 1\frac{3}{9}$ 4. $1\frac{1}{3}, \frac{5}{3}, \frac{7}{3}$

Use <, >, or = to make true statments.

5. $1\frac{5}{8} \bullet \frac{15}{8}$ 6. $4\frac{2}{3} \bullet \frac{13}{3}$ 7. $\frac{12}{4} \bullet 1\frac{3}{4}$ 8. $\frac{15}{2} \bullet 7\frac{1}{2}$

b For use with Lesson 5 (pages 22–24)

Choose the equivalent fractions in each group.

9. $\frac{4}{5}, \frac{3}{9}, \frac{5}{6}, \frac{4}{12}$ 10. $\frac{3}{10}, \frac{3}{20}, \frac{6}{10}, \frac{6}{20}$ 11. $\frac{3}{8}, \frac{9}{24}, \frac{12}{36}, \frac{18}{36}$

12. $\frac{7}{9}, \frac{12}{18}, \frac{4}{6}, \frac{14}{36}$ 13. $\frac{11}{12}, \frac{1}{2}, \frac{22}{24}, \frac{33}{45}$ 14. $\frac{9}{16}, \frac{6}{19}, \frac{18}{32}, \frac{12}{36}$

Draw a number line from 0 to 1. Locate the fractions on the number line.

15. $\frac{5}{8}, \frac{1}{4}, \frac{1}{2}, \frac{15}{16}$ 16. $\frac{7}{10}, \frac{3}{4}, \frac{1}{8}, \frac{1}{2}$ 17. $\frac{33}{100}, \frac{1}{4}, \frac{7}{25}$

c For use with Lesson 6 (pages 25–28)

Arrange the decimals in order from least to greatest.

18. 1.05, 1.501, 1.5   19. 0.8, 0.88, 0.0888   20. 10.45, 10.405, 10.4005

21. 2.1, 2.21, 2.201   22. 0.07, 0.70, 0.707, 0.007   23. 4.08, 4.079, 4.401

Use >, <, or = to make true statements.

24. 43.34 ● 43.43   25. 0.35 ● 0.305   26. 9.821 ● 11   27. 0.99 ● 0.9899

d For use with Lesson 7 (pages 29–33)

Draw a percent-bar model.
Estimate the number.

28. 50% of 220   29. 75% of 24   30. 25% of 160   31. 10% of 72

32. 70% of 700   33. 52% of 900   34. 33% of 360   35. 90% of 4,000

Module 6.1 Section C

a **For use with Lesson 8 (pages 36–41)**

Find the mean, median, mode, and range for each set.

1. 34, 56, 14, 17, 34

2. 1, 10, 100

3. 88, 97, 71, 71

4. 1, 1, 2, 4, 2, 3, 4, 5, 2, 6

5. 56, 24, 13, 80, 45

6. 63, 80, 93, 85, 77, 80, 82

Use this box-and-whisker plot to answer Exercises 7–10.

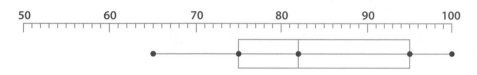

7. What is the range of these test scores?

8. What was the median test score?

9. Between what scores do the test scores for most of the students fall?

10. Explain why or why not you think this was probably a good test?

b **For use with Lesson 9 (pages 42–45)**

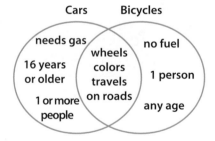

11. Use the Venn diagram to list some things cars and bicycles have in common.

12. Use the Venn diagram to name two differences between cars and bicycles.

13. Where would you write *travels on water?*

14. Draw a Venn diagram and put the following sets of numbers in the appropriate places: set A = { 2, 4, 6, 8, 10, 12} set B = { 3, 6, 9, 12, 15, 18}

15. Draw a Venn diagram and put the following sets of numbers in the appropriate places: set C = { 2, 4, 6, 8, 10} set D = { 1, 3, 5, 7, 9}

16. Describe in words the relationship between the sets C and D.

Module 6.1 Section D

a For use with Lesson 10 (pages 48–53)

Write the opposite of the following.

1. $^-19$ **2.** 11   **3.** $^-100$ **4.** 87   **5.** $^-301$

Write the numbers in order from least to greatest.

6. 11, 3, 28, $^-15$, 17, $^-4$ **7.** 0, $^-5$, 4, 13   **8.** 35, $^-25$, $^-16$, 21

9. $^-1$, $^-4$, $^-31$, 32, 5, 1   **10.** 12, $^-3$, 46, 0, $^-19$ **11.** $^-12$, 3, 0, $^-5$, $^-10$

---

b For use with Lesson 11 (pages 54–59)

Use the coordinate grid, to name the coordinates of each point.

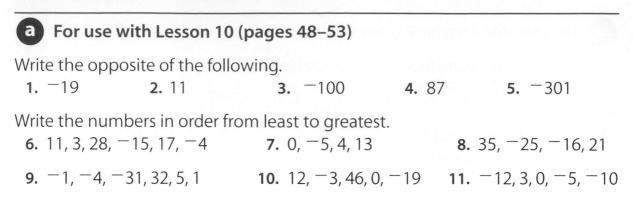

12. A   **13.** B   **14.** C   **15.** D   **16.** E

17. F   **18.** G   **19.** H   **20.** J   **21.** K

Draw a coordinate grid for each set of points. Plot the points and describe the shape formed.

22. (5, 0), (7, 3), (2, 3), (0, 0)   **23.** (1, 1), (3, 2), (5, $^-4$)

24. (0, 0), (0, 6), (6, 0)   **25.** (3, 4), ($^-3$, 4), ($^-5$, $^-4$), (6, $^-4$)

Module 6.2 Section A

a **For use with Lesson 1 (pages 68–73)**

Use the table to answer Exercises 1–3, remembering to consider time zone changes. Consult your math book page 69.

1. How long is the flight from Dallas to Los Angeles?

2. How much longer is it to fly from Los Angeles to Chicago than from Chicago to New York?

Flight Schedule			
From	**To**	**Depart**	**Arrive**
Los Angeles	Chicago	1:35 PM	7:28 PM
Chicago	New York	8:14 AM	11:11 AM
Miami	Dallas	9:55 AM	11:51 AM
Dallas	Los Angeles	11:08 AM	12:03 PM

3. Estimate the total time for a trip from Miami to Los Angeles if there is a 30-minute stopover in Dallas.

Use the table to answer Exercises 4–7.

4. Write an equation for the distance from L.A. to Chicago, then to New York.

5. What property would explain the fact that the reverse distance from New York to L.A. is the same?

Airline Distances		
From	**To**	**Distance**
Los Angeles	Chicago	2,808 km
Chicago	New York	1,191 km
Miami	Dallas	1,786 km
Dallas	Los Angeles	2,005 km

6. Write an expression using the distances in this table to show that the Associative Property applies to distances.

7. Do you think that time for the airline flights is commutative? Explain your reasons.

---

b **For use with Lesson 2 (pages 74–77)**

For Exercises 8–11, let $a = 2.42$, $b = 5.082$, $c = 9.703$. Find the value of n.

8. $a + 2 + b = n$

9. $c - a + 11.67 = n$

10. $2b + a = n$

11. $3c + 3.5043 = n$

Rewrite the expression by combining like variables.

12. $a + 3b + 2a + 4b$

13. $5x - 3y + 9x$

14. $7m + 4n + 5m + 3p + m$

15. $2s + 5t + 4s - 2t + 9s - 3t$

Module 6.2 Section B

(a) For use with Lesson 3 (pages 78–81)

List as many factors as you can, then write *prime* or *composite*.

1. 40
2. 39
3. 47
4. 49
5. 63
6. 71
7. 65
8. 57

Use factor trees to find the prime factorization.

9. 45
10. 32
11. 72
12. 60
13. 54
14. 66
15. 98
16. 70

Use the prime factorization to find at least three composite factors.

17. $2 \times 3 \times 5$
18. $3 \times 3 \times 7$
19. $2 \times 2 \times 3 \times 3$
20. $5 \times 5 \times 7$
21. $2 \times 11 \times 13$
22. $7 \times 13 \times 19$

(b) For use with Lesson 4 (pages 82–85)

List the common factors. Circle the Greatest Common Factor.

23. 25, 45
24. 12, 24
25. 15, 16
26. 30, 40
27. 18, 27
28. 20, 45
29. 21, 42
30. 16, 25
31. 26, 39

List the multiples. Circle the Least Common Multiple.

32. 8, 9
33. 9, 12
34. 6, 15
35. 10, 15
36. 4, 20
37. 7, 34
38. 10, 12
39. 15, 20
40. 12, 18

41. Pick two pairs of numbers from Exercises 23–31. Find the GCF again, this time using the prime factorizations.

42. Pick two pairs of numbers from Exercises 32–40. This time find the LCM using the prime factorizations.

Module 6.2 Section C

a **For use with Lesson 5 (pages 90–93)**

Add or subtract as indicated. Put answers in simplest terms.

1. $\frac{1}{2}$
   $+ \frac{3}{4}$

2. $\frac{2}{3}$
   $+ \frac{1}{4}$

3. $\frac{3}{5}$
   $+ \frac{7}{10}$

4. $\frac{3}{4}$
   $+ \frac{3}{8}$

5. $\frac{5}{6}$
   $- \frac{3}{4}$

6. $\frac{7}{8}$
   $- \frac{1}{3}$

7. $\frac{8}{15}$
   $- \frac{2}{5}$

8. $\frac{7}{10}$
   $- \frac{1}{5}$

9. $\frac{4}{5} + \frac{1}{6}$

10. $\frac{7}{12} - \frac{2}{5}$

11. $\frac{8}{9} - \frac{2}{3}$

12. $\frac{5}{12} - \frac{2}{9}$

13. $\frac{7}{10} + \frac{2}{5}$

14. $\frac{4}{9} + \frac{2}{3}$

---

b **For use with Lesson 6 (pages 94–99)**

Add or subtract as indicated. Put answers in simplest terms.

15. $2\frac{1}{3}$
    $+ \frac{1}{8}$

16. $5\frac{3}{4}$
    $+ 3\frac{3}{5}$

17. $7\frac{1}{5}$
    $+ \frac{3}{8}$

18. $10\frac{2}{3}$
    $+ 8\frac{3}{10}$

19. $2\frac{5}{6}$
    $- 1\frac{1}{4}$

20. $5\frac{3}{8}$
    $- \frac{1}{2}$

21. $6\frac{2}{15}$
    $- 4\frac{2}{3}$

22. $12\frac{7}{8}$
    $- 9\frac{1}{5}$

23. $3\frac{1}{4} - 1\frac{5}{6}$

24. $7\frac{1}{12} - \frac{2}{3}$

25. $4\frac{8}{9} + \frac{2}{3}$

Module 6.2 Section D

ⓐ For use with Lesson 7 (pages 100–104)

Draw a number line to show the answer for each exercise.

1. $^-3 + 4$
2. $^-2 + ^-6$
3. $5 + ^-8$
4. $^-7 + 7$

5. $5 - 6$
6. $^-8 - 3$
7. $10 - ^-1$
8. $^-9 - ^-3$

Add or subtract as indicated.

9. $^-5 + ^-3$
10. $^-1 + 12$
11. $^-8 + ^-4$
12. $^-13 + 7$

13. $9 - 6$
14. $8 - ^-5$
15. $^-2 - ^-3$
16. $^-7 - ^-1$

ⓑ For use with Lesson 8 (pages 105–107)

Use the numbers 1–10 to make an input/output table for each function.

17. Add $^-8$.

18. Add 1.5.

19. Multiply by 2; add $\frac{1}{4}$.

20. Multiply by 5; add $^-3$.

21. Add 10; divide by 2.

22. Add $\frac{3}{5}$; subtract $\frac{1}{2}$.

Use a variable to write a rule for each function. Fill in the missing numbers.

23.
Input	2	4	■	8
Output	4	16	9	■

24.
Input	$^-5$	■	■	2
Output	$^-3$	$^-1$	2	4

25.
Input	2.3	6.5	■	0.72
Output	3.8	■	8.58	2.22

26.
Input	$3\frac{1}{2}$	$2\frac{1}{6}$	$1\frac{1}{6}$	■
Output	$3\frac{5}{6}$	■	$1\frac{1}{2}$	$\frac{11}{15}$

27.
Input	$2\frac{1}{3}$	$1\frac{1}{6}$	$4\frac{5}{12}$	$4\frac{1}{4}$
Output	$1\frac{1}{2}$	$\frac{1}{3}$	■	■

28.
Input	$^-6$	5	1	■
Output	$^-8$	3	■	0

Module 6.3 Section A

a **For use with Lesson 1 (pages 116–121)**

Write in standard form.

1. 8×10^1

2. 8×10^2

3. 8×10^3

4. 8×10^4

5. 1.23×10^3

6. 1.23×10^6

7. 12.3×10^2

8. 12.3×10^4

9. $200 \div 10^1$

10. $200 \div 10^2$

11. $200 \div 10^3$

12. $200 \div 10^4$

13. $16.4 \div 10^1$

14. $16.4 \div 10^2$

15. $164 \div 10^2$

b **For use with Lesson 2 (pages 121–123)**

Use scientific notation to rewrite.

16. 2,000,000

17. 6,000,000,000

18. 90,000,000

19. 800,000,000

20. 435,000

21. 34,000

22. 5,470,000

23. 9,008,000,000

24. 450,100,000

These numbers are in scientific notation. Write in standard form.

25. 2×10^1

26. 2.3×10^2

27. 4.2×10^3

28. 6.8×10^5

29. 8.47×10^3

30. 9.07×10^2

31. 1.65×10^6

32. 5.74×10^4

33. 3.461×10^1

c **For use with Lesson 3 (pages 124–127)**

Change the measurement to meter, gram, or liter.

34. 5 cm

35. 23 dm

36. 430 mm

37. 3,670 mg

38. 6.7 dg

39. 54,000 mL

40. 908 cL

41. 7 dL

Fill in the blank.

42. 34 m = _____ cm

43. 800 mm = ___ cm

44. 6 m = ___ dm

45. 560 g = ___ kg

46. 8 km = _____ dm

47. 200 L = ___ kL

Module 6.3 Section B

a For use with Lesson 4 (pages 128–132)

Use order of operations and/or parentheses to make the answer correct.

1. $4 + 3 \times 2 - 8 = 6$
2. $2 - 8 + 3 - 4 = {}^-13$
3. $2 \times 4 \div 2 + 3 = 10$
4. $6 \times 4 - 5 + 8 = 11$
5. ${}^-4 + {}^-6 + 8 - 10 = {}^-12$
6. $12 \div 2 + 4 + {}^-5 = {}^-3$

b For use with Lesson 5 (pages 133–135)

If each measure is the area of a rectangle, sketch at least one possible rectangle and find its perimeter.

7. 36 m^2
8. 45 m^2
9. 24 m^2
10. 25 m^2

If each measure is the perimeter of a rectangle, sketch at least one possible rectangle and find its area.

11. 24 m
12. 36 m
13. 30 m
14. 42 m

c For use with Lesson 6 (pages 136–139)

Find the area of a rectangle 7.2 m long with the following width.

15. 2.6 m
16. 0.9 m
17. 3.4 m
18. 5.2 m

Use estimation to place the decimal point in the correct place.

19. $5.34 \times 0.6 = 3204$
20. $4.032 \times 0.45 = 18144$
21. $98.6 \times 5.06 = 498916$
22. $72.15 \times 8.03 = 5793645$
23. $13.6 \times 41.09 = 558824$
24. $102.8 \times 3.451 = 3547628$

d For use with Lesson 7 (pages 140–143)

Find the volume of a box with these dimensions.

25. $2 \text{ cm} \times 3 \text{ cm} \times 8 \text{ cm}$
26. $1.4 \text{ cm} \times 2.5 \text{ cm} \times 6 \text{ cm}$
27. $4.6 \text{ m} \times 5 \text{ m} \times 9.1 \text{ m}$
28. a cube with sides of 4 in.
29. $8 \text{ ft} \times 9 \text{ ft} \times 12 \text{ ft}$
30. a cube with sides of 11 km

Module 6.3 Section C

a **For use with Lesson 8 (pages 148–150)**

Find the approximate circumference of the circle using $\pi \approx 3.14$.

1. $r = 12$ cm
2. $d = 16$ m
3. $d = 15$ in.

4. $d = 5$ ft
5. $r = 2.7$ cm
6. $r = 6.3$ in.

Estimate the radius of a circle with the given circumference.

7. 24 ft
8. 48 cm
9. 9 in.
10. 100 m

---

b **For use with Lesson 9 (pages 151–155)**

Find the approximate area of the circle using $\pi \approx 3.14$.

11. $r = 12$ cm
12. $d = 16$ m
13. $d = 15$ in.

14. $d = 5$ ft
15. $r = 2.7$ cm
16. $r = 6.3$ in.

Estimate the radius of a circle with the given area.

17. 27 ft^2
18. 48 cm^2
19. 75 in.^{2}
20. 150 m^2

---

c **For use with Lesson 10 (pages 156–159)**

Find the approximate volume of each cylinder using $\pi \approx 3.14$.

21. $r = 12$ cm, $h = 10$ cm
22. $d = 16$ m, $h = 5$ m

23. $d = 15$ in., $h = 20$ in.
24. $r = 2.7$ yd, $h = 0.5$ yd

Find the volume.

25. If the volume of a cylinder is 500 cm^3, what is the volume of a cylinder with the same base and half the height?

26. If the volume of a cylinder is 200 cm^3, what is the volume of a cylinder with the same base and twice the height?

27. If the volume of a cylinder is 600 cm^3, what is the volume of a cylinder with the same height and twice the radius?

Module 6.3 Section D

a **For use with Lesson 11 (pages 160–166)**

Estimate whether the quotient is greater than one.

1. $3.0 \div 0.4$

2. $0.45 \div 0.9$

3. $0.9 \div 0.3$

4. $0.78 \div 5$

5. $0.37 \div 0.06$

6. $5 \div 0.7$

7. $3.6 \div 0.8$

8. $6.3 \div 0.09$

9. $0.25 \div 0.4$

10. $0.4 \div 0.5$

11. $0.2 \div 0.1$

12. $0.05 \div 0.6$

Find the quotient.

13. $0.4\overline{)4.8}$

14. $0.8\overline{)0.64}$

15. $1.2\overline{)0.36}$

16. $0.13\overline{)3.9}$

17. $0.07\overline{)4.9}$

18. $0.2\overline{)4}$

19. $3\overline{)0.27}$

20. $0.5\overline{)45}$

21. $0.06\overline{)0.24}$

22. $2.5\overline{)2.25}$

23. $0.56\overline{)1.12}$

24. $0.15\overline{)8.1}$

---

b **For use with Lesson 12 (pages 167–171)**

Find the quotient to the nearest hundredth.

25. $34 \div 4$

26. $3.4 \div 0.4$

27. $0.34 \div 0.04$

28. $8.52 \div 0.3$

29. $85.2 \div 0.03$

30. $0.852 \div 3$

31. $4.5 \div 0.25$

32. $0.45 \div 2.5$

33. $0.45 \div 0.25$

34. $0.08\overline{)8.9}$

35. $8\overline{)89}$

36. $0.8\overline{)0.089}$

37. $1.2\overline{)7.8}$

38. $0.12\overline{)78}$

39. $0.12\overline{)0.78}$

40. Describe any patterns you observed by working Exercises 25–39.

Module 6.4 Section A

 a **For use with Lesson 1 (pages 180–184)**

Use your calculator to answer Exercises 1–4.

1. What are the first ten numbers of an addition pattern using 10?

2. Write the first ten numbers of a multiplication pattern using 10.

Exercises 3 and 4 refer to the literature selection on page 180.

3. If the old man requests a dollar the first day, two dollars the second day, and doubles the request each day, in how many days will he have a million dollars?

4. If the old man had started with $3, tripling each day, in how many days would he be a millionaire?

b **For use with Lesson 2 (pages 185–188)**

Tell the operation you would use to reach as close to the target number as possible in the number of steps given.

	Start	Target	Steps
5.	5	50	3
6.	90	5	5
7.	3	243	5
8.	12	100	4
9.	1,000	1	3
10.	10	500	5

c **For use with Lesson 3 (pages 189–191)**

Find the two perfect squares closest to the given number.

11. 45   **12.** 67   **13.** 23   **14.** 89

Estimate the square root to the nearest tenth. Multiply that number by itself and write the result.

15. 45   **16.** 67   **17.** 23   **18.** 89

Module 6.4 Section B

a **For use with Lesson 4 (pages 194–197)**

Write the product in simplest terms.

1. $\frac{1}{2} \times \frac{3}{4}$

2. $\frac{3}{5} \times \frac{2}{9}$

3. $\frac{4}{5} \times \frac{5}{12}$

4. $\frac{5}{8} \times \frac{1}{15}$

5. $\frac{1}{14} \times \frac{7}{8}$

6. $\frac{6}{7} \times \frac{5}{21}$

Write two possible factors for each product.

7. $\frac{1}{2}$

8. $\frac{3}{4}$

9. $\frac{5}{12}$

---

b **For use with Lesson 5 (pages 198–201)**

Find the area of a parallelogram with the following dimensions.

10. $b = 12$ in., $h = 5$ in.

11. $b = 34$ cm, $h = 10$ cm

12. $b = 9\frac{1}{2}$ in., $h = 4\frac{1}{4}$ in.

13. $b = 11.3$ cm, $h = 6.4$ cm

Find the area of a triangle with the following dimensions.

14. $b = 6$ in., $h = 8\frac{1}{2}$ in.

15. $b = 15.4$ cm, $h = 8.2$ cm

16. $b = 14$ in., $h = 3\frac{3}{4}$ in.

17. $b = 32.6$ cm, $h = 8.7$ cm

---

c **For use with Lesson 6 (pages 202–205)**

Estimate the product. Find exact answers for products greater than 10.

18. $9\frac{1}{2} \times \frac{3}{4}$

19. $12 \times 3\frac{1}{3}$

20. $5\frac{1}{2} \times 2\frac{1}{5}$

21. $15 \times 6\frac{1}{2}$

22. $3\frac{3}{5} \times 2\frac{1}{2}$

23. $10\frac{1}{2} \times \frac{3}{8}$

24. $6\frac{2}{3} \times 2\frac{1}{4}$

25. $\frac{5}{12} \times 13\frac{1}{3}$

26. $2\frac{3}{4} \times 2\frac{1}{2}$

27. $20 \times 3\frac{1}{6}$

Module 6.4 Section C

---

a **For use with Lesson 7 (pages 208–214)**

Find the volume of the prism.

1. $B = 12$ in.^{2}, $h = 8$ in.

2. $B = 32$ cm^2, $h = 10$ cm

3. $B = 20$ in.^{2}, $h = 2\frac{1}{3}$ in.

4. $B = 28$ cm^2, $h = 6.5$ cm

Find the volume of the pyramid.

5. $B = 12$ in.^{2}, $h = 8$ in.

6. $B = 32$ cm^2, $h = 10$ cm

7. $B = 20$ in.^{2}, $h = 2\frac{1}{3}$ in.

8. $B = 28$ cm^2, $h = 6.5$ cm

---

b **For use with Lesson 8 (pages 215–217)**

Which cylinder and cone have the same volume? Find the volume.

9. Cylinder: $B = 16$ in.^{2}, $h = 8$ in.; cone: $B = 32$ in.^{2}, $h = 16$ in.

10. Cylinder: $B = 15$ cm^2, $h = 20$ cm; cone: $B = 45$ cm^2, $h = 20$ cm

11. Cylinder: $B = 25$ in.^{2}, $h = 10$ in.; cone: $B = 12\frac{1}{2}$ in.^{2}, $h = 20$ in.

12. Cylinder: $B = 12$ in.^{2}, $h = 8$ in.; cone: $B = 12$ in.^{2}, $h = 24$ in.

---

c **For use with Lesson 9 (pages 218–221)**

Select an operation to solve the equation: addition, subtraction, multiplication, or division. Explain what you would do to solve. You do not need to find the solution.

13. $m - 506 = 125$

14. $12t = 780$

15. $h \div 34 = 45$

16. $w + 50.7 = 329$

17. $y - 908 = 67.3$

18. $\frac{2}{3}b = 12$

Write an equation for each of the following solutions.

19. $n = 10$

20. $a = 4.5$

21. $k = \frac{4}{5}$

22. $r = 22$

23. $c = 110.5$

24. $p = 8$

Module 6.4 Section D

ⓐ For use with Lesson 10 (pages 222–225)

Divide.

1. $4 \div \frac{1}{2}$

2. $\frac{1}{2} \div 4$

3. $\frac{1}{2} \div \frac{1}{4}$

4. $12 \div \frac{1}{3}$

5. $\frac{1}{3} \div 12$

6. $\frac{1}{3} \div \frac{1}{6}$

7. $3 \div \frac{1}{2}$

8. $3\frac{1}{2} \div \frac{1}{6}$

9. $3\frac{1}{2} \div \frac{1}{12}$

10. $\frac{3}{4} \div \frac{1}{4}$

11. $\frac{4}{5} \div \frac{1}{5}$

12. $\frac{4}{3} \div \frac{1}{2}$

ⓑ For use with Lesson 11 (pages 226–231)

Use your calculator to answer Exercises 13–16.

13. Find the decimal equivalents for the Fibonacci fractions, $\frac{1}{2}, \frac{2}{3}, \frac{3}{5}, \frac{5}{8}, \frac{8}{13}$.

14. Starting with 9 and 11, write the next eight numbers in a Fibonacci pattern.

15. Use the numbers from Exercise 14 to make five fractions and find the decimal equivalent of each fraction.

16. Describe any patterns you discover.

ⓒ For use with Lesson 12 (pages 232–235)

Describe what you think the graph would look like.
Make a sketch of each graph.

17. speed of a baseball pitched in a major-league game

18. growth of a newly planted forest

19. growth of the square of a number

20. growth of a number multiplied by $\frac{1}{2}$

Module 6.5 Section A

ⓐ For use with Lesson 1 (pages 244–248)

Write the ratio in a different way. Draw a picture to show the ratio.

1. 1 to 2

2. 4 : 5

3. $\frac{6}{3}$

4. 9 : 3

5. $\frac{5}{2}$

6. 7 to 8

7. $\frac{9}{10}$

8. 2 : 3

9. 4 : 1

10. $\frac{1}{5}$

11. $\frac{3}{2}$

12. 4 to 6

Write a ratio for each picture; be sure to label it.

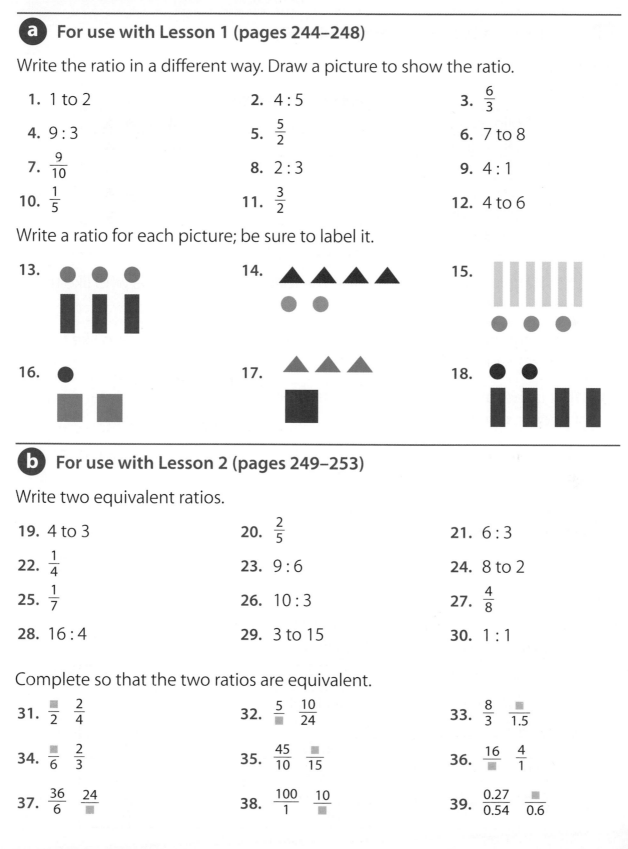

13.

14.

15.

16.

17.

18.

ⓑ For use with Lesson 2 (pages 249–253)

Write two equivalent ratios.

19. 4 to 3

20. $\frac{2}{5}$

21. 6 : 3

22. $\frac{1}{4}$

23. 9 : 6

24. 8 to 2

25. $\frac{1}{7}$

26. 10 : 3

27. $\frac{4}{8}$

28. 16 : 4

29. 3 to 15

30. 1 : 1

Complete so that the two ratios are equivalent.

31. $\frac{\blacksquare}{2}$ $\frac{2}{4}$

32. $\frac{5}{\blacksquare}$ $\frac{10}{24}$

33. $\frac{8}{3}$ $\frac{\blacksquare}{1.5}$

34. $\frac{\blacksquare}{6}$ $\frac{2}{3}$

35. $\frac{45}{10}$ $\frac{\blacksquare}{15}$

36. $\frac{16}{\blacksquare}$ $\frac{4}{1}$

37. $\frac{36}{6}$ $\frac{24}{\blacksquare}$

38. $\frac{100}{1}$ $\frac{10}{\blacksquare}$

39. $\frac{0.27}{0.54}$ $\frac{\blacksquare}{0.6}$

Module 6.5 Section B

ⓐ **For use with Lesson 3 (pages 254–257)**

Use the pictograph to answer the questions.

Sixth Graders' Favorite Rides	
Roller coaster	▲ ▲ ▲ ▲
Merry-go-round	▲ ▲ ▲ ▲ ▲
Ferris wheel	▲ ▲ ▲ ▲ ▲ ▲ ▲
Bumper cars	▲ ▲ ▲
None of the above	▲
▲ = 4 people	

1. What is the ratio of those who like the roller coaster to those who like the bumper cars?

2. What is the ratio of those who like the Ferris wheel to those who like the merry-go-round?

3. What is the ratio of those who like the merry-go-round to the total number of people surveyed?

4. If 40 sixth graders had been surveyed, how many might have said none of the above?

5. If 100 sixth graders had been surveyed, how many might have said the merry-go-round?

ⓑ **For use with Lesson 4 (pages 258–263)**

Use your knowledge of the relationship between fractions, decimals, and percents to find the missing numbers on the chart.

Ratio Conversions		
Fractions	Decimals	Percents
6. ▦	0.4	7. ▦
$\frac{1}{2}$	8. ▦	9. ▦
10. ▦	11. ▦	20%
12. ▦	0.09	13. ▦
$\frac{3}{4}$	14. ▦	15. ▦

Module 6.5 Section C

a **For use with Lesson 5 (pages 266–268)**

Choose the two ratios from each group that make a proportion.

1. 30 : 10, 20 : 5, 12 : 3 **2.** 2 : 6, 4 : 20, 6 : 18

3. 1 : 9, 3 : 15, 6 : 54 **4.** 8 : 2, 6 : 24, 12 : 3

5. 3 : 5, 12 : 20, 10 : 6 **6.** 7 : 5, 10 : 14, 15 : 21

7. 2 : 4, 3 : 6, 1 : 3, 6 : 2 **8.** 5 : 1, 15 : 3, 12 : 4, 10 : 5

9. 6 : 4, 12 : 10, 9 : 6, 6 : 5 **10.** 7 : 21, 9 : 12, 15 : 20, 14 : 28

11. 10 : 4, 8 : 6, 5 : 2, 4 : 3 **12.** 5 : 6, 10 : 12, 15 : 20, 20 : 24

13. Complete the chart and draw a graph that shows the number of apples and servings in a recipe for applesauce.

Apples	6	12	18	24
Servings		8		

14. Use your graph to estimate how many apples you would need for 15 servings.

b **For use with Lesson 6 (pages 269–271)**

Write the unit rate.

15. $200 for 8 hours **16.** 15 beats/10 seconds

17. $500 for 2 weeks **18.** 30 beats/15 seconds

19. 120 miles in 3 hours **20.** 30 miles in 30 minutes

21. 56 points in 4 games **22.** 45 ft/15 minutes

23. 200 rainy days/365 days **24.** 20 in. in 8 hours

25. 150 words/2 minutes **26.** 12 kilometers/2 hours

27. 50 yd in 4.4 seconds **28.** 21 pages in 3 hours

Module 6.5 Section D

a **For use with Lesson 7 (pages 274–277)**

Estimate the percent of the shaded portion of each rectangle.

1. 2. 3.

4. 5. 6.

Draw a rectangle. Then shade it to show the indicated percent.

7. 45%   **8.** 75%   **9.** 30%

10. 10%   **11.** 90%   **12.** 60%

13. 25%   **14.** 100%   **15.** 5%

---

b **For use with Lesson 8 (pages 278–283)**

Show the method you use to estimate the value for *n*. If you use the percent bar model, draw it on your paper.

16. 20% of 80 = *n*   **17.** 50% of *n* = 45   **18.** *n*% of 30 = 10

19. 30% of 90 = *n*   **20.** 75% of 180 = *n*   **21.** 10% of *n* = 50

22. *n*% of 28 = 7   **23.** *n*% of 250 = 5   **24.** 90% of *n* = 180

Write a problem that could be solved using each percent bar model.

25.

26.

Module 6.6 Section A

a For use with Lesson 1 (pages 292–295)

Replace the ● with >, <, or = to make the statement true.

1. $\frac{3}{4} ● \frac{8}{9}$

2. $\frac{7}{12} ● \frac{5}{11}$

3. $\frac{2}{5} ● \frac{6}{7}$

4. $\frac{6}{9} ● \frac{12}{18}$

5. $\frac{4}{5} ● \frac{7}{10}$

6. $\frac{5}{3} ● \frac{4}{9}$

Use the four numbers to write a proportion.

7. 6, 9, 12, 8

8. 3, 12, 8, 2

9. 4, 15, 5, 12

b For use with Lesson 2 (pages 296–298)

Find a value for the variable that makes each proportion true.

10. $\frac{2}{5} = \frac{n}{15}$

11. $\frac{3}{4} = \frac{18}{b}$

12. $\frac{c}{6} = \frac{6}{9}$

13. $\frac{5}{d} = \frac{1}{8}$

14. $\frac{2}{3} = \frac{x}{2.4}$

15. $\frac{4}{9} = \frac{2}{m}$

c For use with Lesson 3 (pages 299–301)

Write a proportion for each exercise, then find the solution.

16. If the ratio of boys to girls is 3 : 4, and there are 12 girls, how many boys are there?

17. If the ratio of teachers to students is 2 : 25, how many teachers for 75 students?

18. If team A has won 3 out of 5 games, how many games have they won out of 25?

19. If Sue's free throw ratio is 4 out of 9, how many tries did it take to make 12 free throws?

20. If Carlos won 12 wrestling matches in 25 meets, what is the ratio of his wins to losses?

21. If the ratio of cars to people is 2 : 3, and there are 150 cars in a parking lot, about how many people are there?

Module 6.6 Section B

a **For use with Lesson 4 (pages 302–306)**

Find the missing information.

	Sixth Graders Favorite Rides			
	Original Price	Sale Price	Discount	Percent of Discount
1.	$12.00	$8.40	$3.60	
2.	$25.50	$21.68		
3.	$45.00			20%
4.		$18.00	$2.00	10%
5.	$40.00		$16.00	
6.		$34.00		15%
7.			$7.50	25%
8.	$68.50			50%
9.	$86.00	$56.00		
10.			$5.40	$33\frac{1}{3}$%

b **For use with Lesson 5 (pages 307–309)**

Find a value for each variable to the nearest tenth.

11. 25% of n = 14.5

12. m% of 45 = 27

13. 40% of 78 = x

14. 5% of 906 = y

15. 90% of b = 40.5

16. p% of 4 = 3

17. 2% of 500 = d

18. 60% of w = 15

19. a% of 12 = 6

20. 1% of 50 = r

21. Use the following data to make two circle graphs. Make one to the advantage of the Super Cereal; make the other showing all the data.

Cereal Choices for Sixth Graders	
Super Cereal	40%
Yummy Cereal	30%
Healthy Cereal	20%
No difference	10%

Module 6.6 Section C

 For use with Lesson 6 (pages 314–319)

Write the number of degrees for each color, then draw a circle graph showing the appropriate divisions.

1. 25% red   **2.** 10% blue   **3.** 45% yellow   **4.** 20% green

Write the percent for each section in these graphs. Use your protractor to measure the angles.

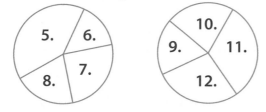

b **For use with Lesson 7 (pages 320–323)**

Find the interest for one year if the interest rate is 5.5%.

13. $100   **14.** $150   **15.** $175   **16.** $535

Find the interest for one year if the interest rate is 6%.

17. $100   **18.** $150   **19.** $175   **20.** $535

21. If the interest rate is 4.25% a year and $250 is deposited, how much interest will be earned after 6 months?

22. If the interest rate is 3.5% a year and $380 is deposited, how much interest will be earned after 4 months?

23. If the interest rate is 7% a year and $800 is deposited, how much interest will be earned after 2 years?

24. Draw a line graph showing the interest earned each month for a year for $450 if the interest rate is 3% a year.

Module 6.6 Section D

a **For use with Lesson 8 (pages 324–328)**

Find at least three values for each variable.

1. $5n > 42$ **2.** $3m < 67$ **3.** $9x > 100$

4. $a + 8 > 12$ **5.** $b - 10 < 5$ **6.** $w - 8 > 10.6$

7. $2h + 3 < 56$ **8.** $7d - 23 > 45$ **9.** $5k - 24 < 403$

10. $3y + 25 > 200$ **11.** $9p + 32 < 100$ **12.** $4n - 45 > 28$

---

b **For use with Lesson 9 (pages 329–331)**

The scattergram shows the result of a survey of sixth graders in which they were asked to rank how important music is to them and the number of hours they spend during a typical day listening to music.

13. Describe the possible relationship between the number of hours a student spends listening to music and the importance that student gives to music.

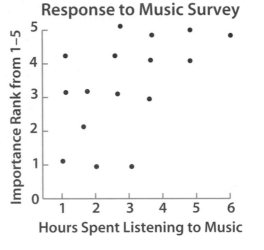

Response to Music Survey

14. Write two more questions that a survey could ask in order to help a radio producer decide what music to play.

15. Use the data to make a scattergram.

Hours Spent Reading	1	2	2	3	3	4	4	5
Importance of Reading	1	2	3	3	4	5	3	5
Respondents	2	1	4	3	2	1	2	1

Module 6.7 Section A

 For use with Lesson 1 (pages 340–342)

Use the diagram to name the parts.

1. at least two lines

2. at least two rays

3. two parallel lines

4. two perpendicular lines

5. at least two angles

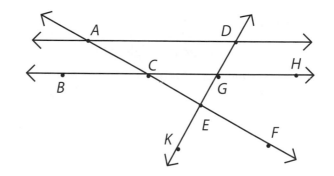

---

b **For use with Lesson 2 (pages 343–348)**

6. Draw a closed curve.

7. Draw a simple closed curve.

8. Explain the difference between a closed curve and a simple closed curve.

9. Draw a right triangle.

10. Draw an acute triangle.

11. Draw an obtuse triangle.

12. Draw an isosceles triangle.

---

c **For use with Lesson 3 (pages 349–352)**

13. If triangle *ABC* has one angle that is 75° and one that is 30°, what is the measure of the missing angle?

14. Draw a triangle with two 45° angles.

15. What is the measure of the missing angle in your triangle?

16. Measure the sides of your triangle. Describe the triangle you drew.

17. Draw a triangle in which all the angles are less than 90°. Give the measure of each angle.

18. Use the diagram at the top of the page. Name two angles that together form a straight angle. Measure each angle. Is the sum 180°?

19. Use the diagram at the top of the page. Find at least two angles that look congruent. Measure them. Were you right? How did you know they were congruent?

Module 6.7 Section B

ⓐ For use with Lesson 4 (pages 354–361)

Use as many of the words and phrases listed in the box as possible to describe each shape.

> right angle, acute angle, obtuse angle, parallel, perpendicular, polygon, regular, congruent, quadrilateral, parallelogram, trapezoid, square, closed curve, triangle, rectangle, isosceles, equilateral, rhombus

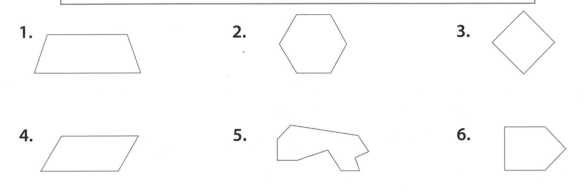

1.   **2.**   **3.**

4.   **5.**   **6.**

7. Drawing diagonals that do not intersect, how many triangles can you make in Exercise 1? What is the sum of the angles in this shape?

8. Drawing diagonals that do not intersect, how many triangles can you make in Exercise 2? What is the sum of the angles in this shape?

9. Drawing diagonals that do not intersect, how many triangles can you make in Exercise 2? What is the sum of the angles in this shape?

10. In Exercise 6 what do you know about the angles?

ⓑ For use with Lesson 5 (pages 362–367)

Sketch a picture of each of the following shapes. Describe the base and the shape of the faces.

11. rectangular prism   **12.** triangular prism   **13.** pyramid

14. cone   **15.** cylinder   **16.** cube

Module 6.7 Section C

 For use with Lesson 6 (pages 372–376)

Use a blank sheet of paper and your Geometry Tool or a ruler.

1. Draw a rectangle 16 cm by 10 cm. What is the area of the rectangle?

2. Name at least two other dimensions that would give you the same area.

3. With a different color pencil draw at least one rectangle with the same area on your paper. What are the new dimensions?

4. Can you draw a square with the same area?

5. What is the area of the biggest square you can fit inside the rectangle from Exercise 1?

6. What is the area of the biggest square you can fit inside the rectangle from Exercise 3?

7. If the measure of its sides is a whole number, what is the biggest square that will fit inside a rectangle with the same area as the rectangle from Exercise 1?

---

b **For use with Lesson 7 (pages 377–381)**

Use your Geometry Tool or a ruler and a protractor.

8. Draw an isosceles right triangle with two sides equal to 4 cm. With the right angle as the vertex, rotate the triangle 90° and draw another triangle. Repeat until you return to the starting point. Describe your results.

9. Draw an isosceles triangle with two sides equal to 4 cm and the angle between them equal to 45°. With the 45° angle as the vertex, rotate the triangle 45°; repeat until you return to the starting point. Describe your results.

10. Repeat the same process but make the vertex angle 40° and rotate 40° each time. Describe your results.

11. Now try it with a 30° vertex angle. Describe your results.

12. What results would you get if the vertex angle was 10°?

Module 6.7 Section D

a For use with Lesson 8 (pages 382–388)

1. If a rectangle has a length of 15 ft and a width of 10 ft, draw a similar rectangle using a scale of 1 in. : 3 ft.

2. Draw another similar rectangle using the scale of 1 in. : 5 ft.

3. What is the ratio between the two rectangles you drew?

4. Draw a third similar rectangle using any scale smaller than 1 in. : 5 ft. What is your scale? What is the ratio between your new rectangle and the rectangle you drew in Exercise 1?

If the shadow of a 5-ft person measures 2 ft, find the height of a building with the following shadows measured at the same time.

5. 10 ft   6. 15 ft   7. 30 ft   8. 45 ft

---

b For use with Lesson 9 (pages 389–391)

Find the surface area.

9. a pyramid with a square base of 5 cm and a triangular side 10 cm high

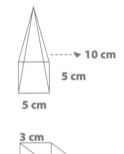

10. a triangular prism with the triangular face 6 cm wide and 4 cm high, and a rectangular side 3 cm × 5 cm

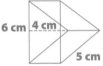

---

c For use with Lesson 10 (pages 392–395)

11. How many two-step paths go from 1 to 5?

12. How many three-step paths go from 1 to 6?

13. How many four-step paths go from 1 to 9?

14. Which square has the most entrances?

15. Which square has the least number of entrances?

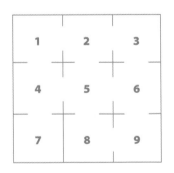

Module 6.8 Section A

a **For use with Lesson 1 (pages 404–408)**

Use spinners A and B to answer Exercises 1–3.

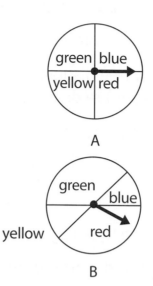

1. What is the probability of green on spinner A?

2. Which results are the most likely on spinner B?

3. Is the probability of yellow greater on spinner A or on spinner B?

Using spinner A, one group had the following results:

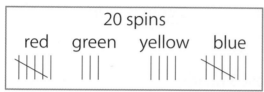

20 spins			
red	green	yellow	blue
卌	|||	||||	卌|

4. What was the experimental probability for red?

5. Are the experimental results for red greater or less than the expected results?

6. What were the experimental results for green?

7. Are the experimental results for green greater than or less than the expected probability?

---

b **For use with Lesson 2 (pages 409–411)**

Consider the word *MATHEMATICS* with one letter on each card.

8. What is the probability of drawing an *M* if all the cards are in a bag?

9. What is the probability of drawing an *S* if all the cards are in a bag?

10. What is the probability of drawing a *T* or a *C* if all the cards are in a bag?

11. What is the probability of drawing a vowel if all the cards are in a bag?

12. What is the probability of drawing a *K* if all the cards are in a bag?

13. If you draw an *A* when all the cards are in the bag, what is the probability of drawing another *A* if you don't return the first *A* to the bag?

Module 6.8 Section B

Exercises 1–3 refer to four cards, each labeled with one of the letters *A*, *B*, *C*, and *D*.

1. Draw tree diagrams to show all the outcomes if all the cards are in a bag and 2 letters are drawn out.

2. What is the probability of drawing an *A* and a *B*?

3. What is the probability of having a *D* as one of the cards?

Exercises 4–7 refer to flipping a coin.

4. Draw a tree diagram to show all the outcomes if a coin is flipped 4 times.

5. What is the probability of flipping 4 heads?

6. What is the probability of flipping at least 3 heads?

7. What is the probability of flipping at least 2 heads?

b **For use with Lesson 4 (pages 417–421)**

8. Using the tree diagram you drew for Exercise 1, what is the probability of drawing an *A* first?

9. Using the tree diagram you drew for Exercise 1, what is the probability of drawing an *A* first and then a *B*?

10. Using *A*, *B*, *C*, *D*, and *E*, list all the combinations of 4 letters.

11. What is the probability of a combination of 4 letters that includes the letters *A*, *B*, *C*?

12. Using *A*, *B*, *C*, *D*, and *E*, list all the combinations of 3 letters.

13. What is the probability of a combination of 3 letters that includes the letters *B* and *C*?

14. Using *A*, *B*, *C*, *D*, and *E*, list all the combinations of 2 letters.

15. What is the probability of a combination of 2 letters that includes the letter *D*?

Module 6.8 Section C

a **For use with Lesson 5 (pages 426–429)**

1. Give the sample space when you roll two cubes numbered 1–6.

2. What is the probability of getting a sum of 7?

3. What is the probability of rolling a 2 on one cube, then a 5 on the other?

4. Is the outcome to Exercise 2 a permutation or a combination?

5. Is the outcome to Exercise 3 a permutation or a combination?

6. Andy, Betty, Clyde, and Dawn have tickets for four reserved seats in a row at a concert. How many different ways can they seat themselves so that Andy and Betty will be next to each other?

7. In order to answer Exercise 6, are you using permutations or combinations?

8. Design an experiment to see how many purchases it might take to get a set of 5 toys if there is a different toy in each box of cereal and an equal number of each kind of toy.

9. What is the probability that it will take only 5 purchases to get a set of 5 toys?

b **For use with Lesson 6 (pages 430–433)**

10. How many sets of partners are possible in a class of 30 students if order doesn't count?

11. How many ways can you arrange 5 people in a line?

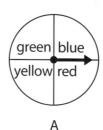

A

12. Which spinner would you choose if in order to win you had to spin green three times out of 5 spins?

13. Which spinner would you choose if in order to win you had to spin each color at least once out of 5 spins?

14. What is the probability of spinning green, then blue in 2 spins?

B

Module 6.8 Section D

a **For use with Lesson 7 (pages 434–439)**

1. If you have one spin on each spinner, what is the probability of getting yellow and green?

2. If you have one spin on each spinner, what is the probability of getting green on at least one spinner?

3. If you have one spin on each spinner, what is the probability of getting the same color on both spinners?

4. If you have to choose one spinner, which spinner would you use if the prize went to the person who spun the same color twice? Why?

5. Design a spinner to use for a game using six colors. Explain your design and the possible outcomes for two spins.

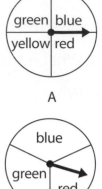

A

B

b **For use with Lesson 8 (pages 440–443)**

6. Make a chart showing all the possible outcomes if you spin the two spinners shown.

7. If you spin both spinners once, what is the probability of spinning the same color on both?

8. If you spin both spinners, what is the probability of spinning yellow on at least one?

9. If you spin both spinners, what is the probability of spinning orange on at least one?

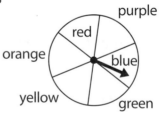

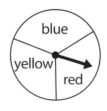

10. Design a two-spinner game that has a very low probability winning combination. Not all sections of the spinner need to be the same size. Identify each fractional part.

Glossary

A

acute angle (p. 346) An angle that measures less than 90°.

angle (p. 341) Two rays that share an endpoint. See ray.

angle of rotation (p. 379) The number of degrees a shape is turned.

arc (p. 340) A part of a circle.

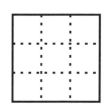

area (p. 133) The number of square units in the surface of a shape.

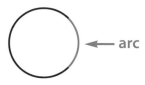

Area is 9 square units.

Associative Property of Addition (p. 73) Changing the grouping of the addends does not change the sum. Example:

$$(4 + 3) + 7 = 14$$
$$4 + (3 + 7) = 14$$
$$\text{so} \quad (4 + 3) + 7 = 4 + (3 + 7)$$

average (p. 139) The quotient found by dividing the sum of a group of numbers by the number of addends.

B

base (of a figure) (p. 156) Either of the two congruent parallel faces of a prism or cylinder. The face of a cone or pyramid opposite the vertex.

base (of a power) One of equal factors in a product. The base in 10^3 is 10.

billion (p. 122) The number equal to 1,000 x 1,000 x 1,000. In standard form, a billion is written as 1,000,000,000.

C

capacity (p. 126) The amount a container can hold.

Celsius (p. 146) The metric temperature scale that has 0° as the freezing point of water and 100° as the boiling point.

centigram (cg) (p. 124) A metric unit for measuring mass. 100 cg = 1 gram

centiliter (cL) (p. 124) A metric unit for measuring capacity. 100 cL = 1 liter

centimeter (cm) (p. 124) A metric unit for measuring length. 100 cm = 1 meter

circle graph (p. 316) A circle divided into parts to show data.

Glossary

circumference (C) (p. 148) The distance around the outside of a circle.

closed sentence (p. 218) A mathematical sentence that includes only numbers.

combinations (p. 418) An arrangement of things in which order doesn't matter.

common denominator (p. 22) A common multiple of the denominators of two or more given fractions. A common denominator of $\frac{2}{3}$ and $\frac{1}{4}$ is 12.

common factor (p. 82) A number that is a factor of two or more given numbers. The common factors of 8 and 12 are 1, 2, and 4.

common multiple (p. 24) A number that is a multiple of two or more numbers. 12 is a common multiple of 2, 3, 4, 6, and 12.

Commutative Property of Addition (p. 72) Changing the order of the addends does not change the sum. Example:

$$7 + 4 = 11$$
$$4 + 7 = 11$$
$$\text{so}\quad 7 + 4 = 4 + 7$$

Commutative Property of Multiplication (p. 77) Changing the order of the factors does not change the product. Example:

$$5 \times 8 = 40$$
$$8 \times 5 = 40$$
$$\text{so}\quad 5 \times 8 = 8 \times 5$$

compatible numbers (p. 187) Numbers that divide easily for use in estimating quotients.

composite number (p. 79) A number that has more than two factors. An example of a composite number is 10.

cone (p. 215) A space figure with a circular base and one vertex.

congruent (p. 341) Having the same size and shape.

corresponding angles (p. 385) The angles at matching vertexes of congruent figures. In the figures below, $\angle B$ and $\angle E$ are corresponding angles.

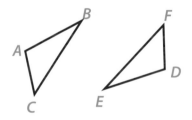

corresponding sides (p. 385) The matching sides of congruent figures. In the figures below, AC and DF are corresponding sides.

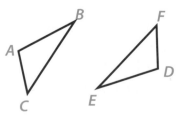

cube (p. 140) A space figure in which all six faces are congruent squares.

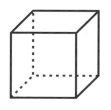

cup (c) (p. 266) A unit of capacity in the U. S. Customary System. 2 c = 1 pint

curve (p. 343) An uninterrupted set of points. The figures below are examples of curves.

cylinder (p. 156) A space figure with circular bases and no corners.

D

data (p. 6) Numbers that give information.

decigram (dg) (p. 124) A metric unit for measuring mass. 10 dg = 1 gram

deciliter (dL) (p. 124) A metric unit for measuring capacity. 10 dL = 1 liter

decimal (p. 26) A number that uses the place-value system and a decimal point. Another way to write fractions with denominators of 10, 100, 1,000, and so on. Examples: 0.2 and 1.75

decimeter (dm) (p. 124) A metric unit for measuring length. 10 dm = 1 meter

degree (°) (p. 317) A unit for measuring angles.

denominator (p. 196) The bottom number of a fraction. It shows the total number of equal parts. The denominator in the fraction $\frac{2}{3}$ is 3.

dependent events (p. 437) Two events in which the result of the first affects the result of the second.

diagonal (p. 357) A line segment that connects two vertexes.

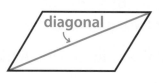

diameter (p. 148) A line segment through the center of a circle that has its two endpoints on the circle.

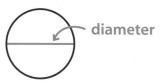

Distributive Property (p. 203) The product of a factor and a sum is equal to the sum of the products. Example:

$$5 \times (3 + 2) = (5 \times 3) + (5 \times 2)$$

dividend (p. 161) The number being divided in division. In 36 ÷ 4 = 9, the dividend is 36.

divisible (p. 309) Capable of being divided without a remainder. Example: 24 is divisible by 3 because 24 ÷ 3 = 8.

divisor (p. 161) The number that divides the dividend in division. In the equation 30 ÷ 5 = 6, the divisor is 5.

Glossary

double-bar graph (p. 9) A graph that uses two bars to compare two sets of data.

E

edge (p. 363) The line segment formed when two faces of a space figure meet.

equation (p. 218) A number sentence stating that two quantities are equal.

equilateral triangle (p. 346) A triangle with all sides congruent.

equivalent fractions (p. 22) Fractions that name the same number. $\frac{1}{3}$ and $\frac{2}{6}$ are equivalent fractions.

equivalent ratios (p. 251) Two ratios that represent the same relationship. $\frac{2}{3}$ is equivalent to $\frac{4}{6}$.

experimental probability (p. 407) The number of times the event occurs divided by the total number of trials in the experiment.

exponent (p.118) A number showing how many times a base is used as a factor. Example: $5^3 = 5 \times 5 \times 5 = 125$

expression (p. 76) A way to write a relationship with numbers and symbols.

F

face (p. 362) A flat surface of a solid.

factor (p. 78) A number being multiplied to obtain a product. In the equation $4 \times 6 = 24$, the factors are 4 and 6.

Fahrenheit (p. 146) The temperature scale that has 32° as the freezing point of water and 212° as the boiling point.

fluid ounce (fl oz) (p. 267) A unit for measuring capacity in the U.S. Customary System. 8 fl oz = 1 cup

formula (p. 200) A rule that is written using symbols. Example: $A = l \times w$

fraction (p. 26) A number that shows parts of a whole unit. $\frac{1}{2}$, $\frac{4}{5}$, and $\frac{5}{8}$ are fractions.

function (p. 106) A special relationship between the members of one group and those of another. For example, in the pairs (2, 5), (4, 7), and (5, 8) the first numbers are related to the second numbers by the rule "add 3."

G

Golden Ratio (p. 373) A ratio of 8 units of length to 5 units of width. Rectangles with the ratio 8 : 5 are used throughout the history of architecture.

gram (g) (p. 124) A metric unit for measuring mass. 1,000 g =1 kilogram

greatest common factor (GCF) (p. 82) The greatest of the common factors of two or more given numbers. The GCF of 12 and 18 is 6.

H

hexagon (p. 250) A polygon with 6 sides and 6 angles.

histogram A bar graph showing frequency data.

hundredth (p. 137) One of 100 equal parts. In the decimal 0.86, the digit 6 is in the hundredths' place.

I

Identity Property of Addition (p. 73) Adding zero to any number gives that number. Example:

$$6 + 0 = 6$$

Identity Property of Multiplication (p. 136) Multiplying any number by 1 gives that number. Example:

$$8 \times 1 = 8$$

independent events (p. 437) Events that have no effect on each other.

inequality (p. 325) A number sentence that states two numbers or quantities are not equal. Examples: $n - 2 > 5$, $6 \neq 3$

input (p. 320) Numbers to which a function is applied.

x	2	5	3	6	← input
$x + 7$	9	12	10	13	numbers

integers (p. 51) The positive numbers 1, 2, 3, . . ., the negative numbers −1, −2, −3, . . ., and zero.

interest (p. 320) Payment for the use of money.

inverse operation (p. 102) One operation that "undoes" another. Addition and subtraction are inverse operations.

isosceles triangle (p. 346) A triangle in which two sides are of equal length.

K

kilogram (kg) (p. 124) A metric unit for measuring mass. 1 kg = 1,000 grams

Glossary

kiloliter (kL) (p. 124) A metric unit for measuring capacity. 1 kL = 1,000 liters

kilometer (km) (p. 124) A metric unit for measuring length. 1 km = 1,000 meters

L

least common denominator (LCD) (p. 93) The least common multiple of the denominators of two or more given fractions. The LCD of $\frac{2}{3}$ and $\frac{1}{4}$ is 12.

least common multiple (LCM) (p. 84) The least multiple, excluding zero, of two or more numbers. The LCM of 4 and 6 is 12.

line graph (p. 10) A graph that uses a line to show change over time.

line of symmetry (p. 378) A line that divides a figure into two congruent halves.

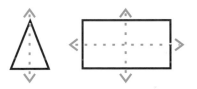

line segment (p. 340) A part of a line with two endpoints, named with two letters. The line segment below is named line segment *AB*.

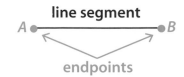

line segment

A •————————————• B

endpoints

liter (L) (p. 124) A metric unit for measuring capacity. 1 L = 100 mL

M

mass (p. 126) In an object, the actual amount of matter that is not subject to the force of gravity.

mean (p. 39) The quotient found by dividing the sum of a group of numbers by the number of addends.

median (p. 38) The middle number in a set of data after the data are arranged in order from least to greatest. Example: In 3, 5, 12, 16, 17, the median is 12.

meter (m) (p. 124) A metric unit for measuring length. 1 m = 100 cm

mile (mi) (p. 71) A unit of length in the U.S. Customary System. 1 mi = 5,280 feet

milligram (mg) (p. 124) A metric unit for measuring mass. 1,000 mg = 1 gram

milliliter (mL) (p. 124) A metric unit for measuring capacity. 1,000 mL = 1 liter

millimeter (mm) (p.124) A metric unit for measuring length. 1,000 mm = 1 meter

million (p. 170) A number equal to 1,000 × 1,000. In standard form a million is written as 1,000,000.

mixed number (p. 20) A number that consists of a whole number and a fraction. $2\frac{1}{2}$ is a mixed number.

mode (p. 38) The number that appears most often in a set of data. Example: In 3, 4, 6, 2, 3, 3, the mode is 3.

N

negative integer (p. 51) An integer less than zero. See *integer*.

network (p. 392) A system of pathways to and from different points.

numerator (p. 196) The top number of a fraction. It shows the number of parts chosen. The numerator in the fraction $\frac{2}{3}$ is 2.

O

obtuse angle (p. 346) An angle that measures more than 90° and less than 180°.

obtuse triangle (p. 346) A triangle with one obtuse angle.

octagon (p. 354) A polygon with 8 sides.

open sentence (p. 218) A mathematical sentence that includes one or more variables.

order of operations (p. 130) A set of rules indicating the order in which operations should be performed if there are several operations to do in an expression.

ordered pair (p. 55) A pair of numbers that shows the location of a point on a grid. The ordered pair for the point on the coordinate grid below is (4, 2).

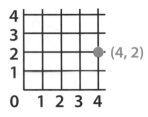

ounce (oz) (p. 267) A unit for measuring weight in the U.S. Customary System. 16 oz = 1 pound

outcome (p. 406) A possible result. Each number or color on a spinner is a possible outcome.

output (p. 320) The numbers resulting from a function being applied.

x	2	5	3	6
x + 7	9	12	10	13

← output numbers

P

parallel lines (p. 72) Lines that are the same distance apart at all points. Parallel lines never intersect.

parallelogram (p. 354) A quadrilateral with opposite sides parallel.

Glossary

pentagon (p. 354) A polygon with five sides.

percent (p. 29) Hundredths written with a % sign. Example: $0.33 = \frac{33}{100} = 33\%$

percent bar (p. 30) A model for working with percent.

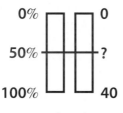

50% of 40 is 20

perimeter (p. 129) The distance around any figure.

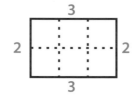

The perimeter is 10 units.

permutation (p. 418) An arrangement of things in a particular order.

perpendicular lines (p. 72) Two lines that intersect to form a right angle.

pi (π) (p. 149) A number that is the ratio of the circumference to the diameter of any circle. Circumference = π × diameter. π ≈ 3.14

pictograph (p. 8) A graph that uses pictures to show data.

plane (p. 341) A flat surface. In a plane, a straight line joining any two points in the surface lies entirely in the suface. The face of a chalkboard represents part of a plane.

point (p. 340) An exact location. Points are usually labeled with capital letters.

positive integer (p. 51) An integer greater than zero. The counting numbers. See integer.

pound (lb) (p. 89) A unit of weight in the U.S. Customary System. 1 lb = 16 ounces

power of ten (p. 119) Any number that can be written as a product of tens. Example: 10,000 is a power of ten because 10,000 = 10 × 10 × 10 × 10.

prime factorization (p. 80) Expressing a composite number as the product of prime factors.The prime factorization of 60 is 2 × 2 × 3 × 5.

prime number (p. 79) A number that has exactly two factors—itself and 1. An example of a prime number is 7.

prism (p. 209) A space figure with five or more faces. Two of the faces, the bases, are parallel and congruent.

probability (p. 402) The chance that something will happen.

proportion (p. 266) Another name for a pair of equivalent ratios.

pyramid (p. 210) A space figure with four or more faces. The base can be any polygon. The other faces of the pyramid are triangles.

Q

quadrant (p. 56) One of the four regions into which the *x*- and *y*-axes divide a plane.

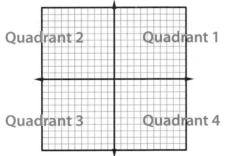

quadrilateral (p. 354) A polygon with four sides.

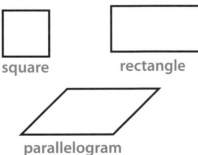

square

rectangle

parallelogram

quart (qt) (p. 266) A unit of capacity in the U.S. Customary System. 1 qt = 2 pints

quotient (p. 161) The answer in division. In the equation 56 ÷ 7 = 8, the quotient is 8.

R

radius (r) (p. 148) A line segment from the center to a point on the circle.

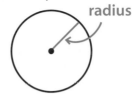

radius

range (p. 38) The difference between the greatest and the least numbers of given data.

rate (p. 269) A special type of ratio that compares different types of quantities.

ratio (p. 246) A quotient of two numbers used to compare one number with the other. Example: 2 bicycles to 3 cars = $\frac{2}{3}$ or 2 : 3 or "two to three."

ray (p. 341) A part of a line with one endpoint. A ray goes on and on in one direction.

ray *RS*

reciprocal (p. 188) Any two numbers whose product is 1. Example: $2 \times \frac{1}{2} = 1$, so 2 and $\frac{1}{2}$ are reciprocals.

rectangle (p. 354) A parallelogram with all angles right angles.

rectangular prism (p. 140) A prism in which the faces are rectangles.

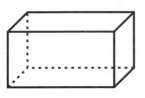

regular polygon (p. 356) A polygon in which all sides are congruent and all angles are congruent.

repeating decimal (p. 228) A decimal in which a sequence of digits repeats endlessly. Examples: 33.33 . . . , 0.257257257 . . .

rhombus (p. 354) A parallelogram with all sides equal.

right angle (p. 316) An angle that measures 90°.

rounding (p. 26) Changing a number to the nearest ten or hundred to make it easier to use. 67 rounded to the nearest ten is 70.

sample space (p. 409) A list of all the possible outcomes of an experiment.

scale (p. 373) The ratio of size in a drawing to actual size.

scale drawing (p. 387) A drawing made by using a scale.

scattergram (p. 329) A graph showing each data item as an ordered pair.

scientific notation (p. 122) A way of writing a number in which one factor is greater than or equal to 1 and less than 10. The other factor is a power of 10.

similar figures (p. 384) Figures that are the same shape but not necessarily the same size.

simplest terms (p. 197) The form in which both terms of a fraction have no common factor greater than one. In simplest terms, $\frac{3}{6}$ is $\frac{1}{2}$.

simplify (p. 96) To write a shorter or easier form of a fraction or expression.To simplify $\frac{8}{12}$, we can write $\frac{4}{6}$ or $\frac{2}{3}$.

simulation (p. 426) An imitation of a problem situation that gives an estimate of the results.

skew lines (p. 342) Lines that do not lie in the same plane.

solution (p. 218) Any number that makes an open sentence true.

sphere (p. 363) A solid that is made up of all the points that are the same distance from one point called its center.

square (p. 354) A rectangle with all sides congruent.

square root (p. 189) When you multiply a whole number by itself, the product is a square number. The number you started with is called the square root. Example: $2^2 = 2 \times 2 = 4$; 2 is the square root of 4.

stem-and-leaf plot (p. 9) A way to show data. Often the tens' digits are "stems" and the ones' digits are "leaves." The plot below shows this data: 20, 29, 31, 42, 45, 48.

stem-and-leaf plot	
2	0 9
3	1
4	2 5 8

straight angle (p. 349) An angle that measures 180°.

← 180°

surface area (p. 389) The sum of the areas of the faces of a space figure.

survey (p. 4) Information gathered by asking questions and recording answers.

symmetry (p. 377) What a figure has when it can be folded so that both parts match.

T

three-dimensional object (p. 140) An object that has the three dimensions: length, width, and height.

trapezoid (p. 354) A quadrilateral with exactly one pair of parallel sides.

tree diagram (p. 414) A picture used to count the way things can be combined.

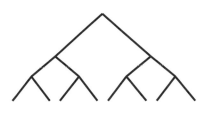

trial (p. 406) Each try in a probability experiment, such as spinning a spinner.

triangle (p. 345) A polygon with three sides.

U

unit rate (p. 270) The ratio of a quantity to 1.

V

variable (p. 76) A letter or symbol that holds a place for a number. In the equation $4 + n = 7$, n is the variable.

Venn diagram (p. 43) A diagram that represents collections of numbers or objects and the members they have in common.

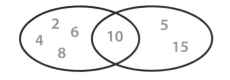

vertex (p. 341) The common endpoint of two rays or two segments. The point where three or more edges of a solid meet.

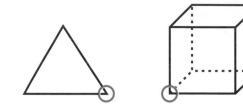

volume (p. 140) The amount of space inside a solid shape.

Zero Property of Multiplication (p. 136) Multiplying any number by zero gives zero. Example: $5 \times 0 = 0$

Index

A

Addition
  algebra and, 76–77, 101, 102–103, 104
  Associative Property of, 73
  calculator activities using, 104
  Commutative Property of, 72
  of decimals, 74–75
  estimating with, 28, 97, 104, 271, 429
  of fractions, 92–93, 262–263, 457
  growing patterns, 182, 183
  Identity Property of, 72
  of integers, 101, 104, 105, 456
  mental math and, 461
  with missing addends, 76–77
  of mixed numbers, 96, 97, 98–99
  with money, 74–75, 76–77
  of percents, 277
  properties of, 72, 73
  of units of measure, 132, 139, 195–196, 204
  of whole numbers, 16–17
Algebra. See also Functions; Proportions, writing and solving.
  balancing equations, 220, 221
  comparing expressions, 76–77
  division and, 107, 219
  equations, writing and solving, 150, 218, 219, 220, 221, 252, 296–297, 311
  formulas and, 129, 133, 140–141, 146–147, 149–150, 151–152, 156–157, 214, 215
  games, 298
  inequalities, solving, 325, 326–327
  integers and, 101, 102–103, 104
  multiplication and, 107, 168, 218
  open and closed sentences, 218
  percents and, 311
  properties and, 72, 73
  variables and, 76–77, 129, 133, 140–141, 146–147, 149–150, 151–152, 156–157, 214, 215, 311, 315
Angle
  acute, 345, 346, 349
  congruent, 341, 345, 356, 378
  defined, 341
  measuring, 350, 351, 352
  obtuse, 345, 346, 349
  right, 349
  of rotation, 379
  sum of, in triangles, 350, 351, 352, 353
Arc, 340
Area
  of circles, 151–152, 154–155
  estimating, 136, 151–152, 390–391
  finding, using scale drawing, 151–152, 154–155
  fractions and, 204, 249–251
  meaning of, 133
  of parallelograms, 198, 199, 200–201
  perimeter and, 134
  of rectangles, 135, 136, 139, 198
  of squares, 194–195, 197
  surface, 157, 158–159, 389, 390–391
  of triangles, 200–201
  using formulas for, 133, 151–152, 157, 158
Arithmetic operations. See also Addition; Division; Multiplication; Subtraction.
  comparing alternative algorithms, 23, 24, 137, 138, 184
  developing and explaining procedures, 101, 104, 162, 168–169, 189, 197, 202–203, 292–293
  order of, 130–131
Arrangements, 417–418, 421
Array 137, 189–190, 202–203
Art. See Curriculum connections.
Assessment. See also Investigations; Review.
  student self-assessment, 14, 31, 43, 59, 69, 84, 94, 103–104, 121, 129, 156, 213, 251, 259, 279, 297, 304, 323, 327, 342, 363, 408, 419, 432, 437
  tasks, 35, 61, 89, 109, 147, 173, 207, 237, 265, 285, 313, 333, 371, 397, 425, 445
Associative Property of Addition, 73, 77

Average, 26–27, 39, 45, 46–47, 63, 170–171, 174–175, 429
Axis, 55

B

Bar graph, 9, 12, 15–16, 30, 48–49, 308, 318–319
  double, 9, 12
Biased sample, 446
Billion, 122

C

Calculator, how to use, 466–467
Calculator activities
  adding integers, 104
  algebra and , 106
  finding area, 157, 158–159
  finding averages, 26, 315
  changing sign key, 104
  checking answers, 104, 191, 315
  common denominators, 93
  computing volume, 158–159
  converting fractions to decimals, 260
  decimals, 26–27, 137, 168
  division, 78, 120–121, 168, 227
  estimation and, 191
  finding factors, 78
  fractions, 227, 260
  functions, 106
  geometry and measurement, 131, 157, 158–159
  integers, 104
  measurement, 131, 157, 158–159
  multiplication, 106, 120–121, 137, 205
  order of operations, 131
  patterns, 120–121, 137, 168, 205, 227
  percent, 260
  pi, 149
  place value and, 26–27
  powers of ten, 120–121
  probability, 415–416
  squares and square roots, 191
  subtracting integers, 104
Capacity, 124–125, 267
Celsius, converting, 146–147
Centimeter, 71, 72–73, 124–125

Index

Index

Index

Index

Acknowledgments

Text (continued from page iv)

Reprinted with permission of Andrews & McMeel. All rights reserved. **90** "Rabbinical Arithmetic" in *A Treasury of Jewish Folktales,* edited by Nathan Ausubel. New York: Crown Publishers, Inc., 1948, 1976. **160** "We Have Grown . . ." from *War Cry on a Prayer Feather: Prose and Poetry of the Ute Indians,* by Nancy Wood. New York: Doubleday and Company, Inc., 1979. Reprinted with permission of the author. **192** From "King Kaid of India," by Arthur Mee in *My Magazine.* Published in *The Victorian Readers, Fifth Book.* Victoria, Australia: The Department of School Education. Extensive efforts to locate the rights holder were unsuccessful. If the rights holder sees this notice, he or she should contact the School Division Rights and Permissions Department, Houghton Mifflin Company, 222 Berkeley Street, Boston, Massachusetts 02116. **274** "Circus" from *The Song in My Head,* by Felice Holman. Copyright © 1985 by Felice Holman. Reprinted with permission of Charles Scribner's Sons, an imprint of Macmillan Publishing Company. **314** From "Consumer Kids: A New Marketing Frontier" by Gary W. Wojtas in *Direct Marketing,* a direct mail advertising magazine published by Henry R. Hoke Jr. and edited by Raymond A. Roel. New York: August 1990. **316** From "Children as Customers" by James McNeal in *American Demographics,* a publication of Dow Jones and Company, Inc. Ithaca, New York: September 1990. **324** From *The Young Landlords,* by Walter Dean Myers. New York: Viking Penguin, a Division of Penguin Books USA Inc., 1979. **374** From *Childtimes: A Three-Generation Memoir,* by Eloise Greenfield and Lessie Jones Little. Copyright © 1979 by Eloise Greenfield and Lessie Jones Little. Reprinted by permission of HarperCollins Publishers. **430** From *Banana Blitz,* by Florence Parry Heide. New York: Holiday House, 1983.

Illustrations

13 Chris Reed. **14** Chris Reed. **54** Reprinted from *The Archaeology Handbook* by Bill McMillon. © 1981 by permission of John Wiley & Sons, Inc. (c). **124–25** Wild Onion Studio. **154–55** Mark Rattin. **255** Barry Wetmore. **256–57** Barry Wetmore. **320–21** Carl Kock. **370** Chris Costello (br). **376** Illustration by Simon Galkin from *America Will Be* in Houghton Mifflin Social Studies by Armento, *et al.* Copyright © 1991 by Houghton Mifflin Company. Reprinted by permission of Houghton Mifflin Company. All rights reserved. **340** Illustration based on elevation drawings courtesy of the Sydney Opera House, Sydney, Australia. **380–81** Chris Costello. **430** Carl Kock.

Photography

Front cover Allan Landau. **Back cover** Sharon Hoogstraten. **i** Allan Landau. **ii–iii** Allan Landau. **vi** Allan Landau (b). **v–vii** Sharon Hoogstraten. **viii–ix** Sharon Hoogstraten. **ix** Allan Landau (b). **x** Allan Landau (bl). **x–xi** Sharon Hoogstraten. **xii–xiii** Allan Landau. **xv** Sharon Hoogstraten. **xvi** © M. C. Escher/Cordon Art, Baarn, Holland. All rights reserved (t, b). **1** Sharon Hoogstraten. **2** Allan Landau. **3** Sharon Hoogstraten. **4–5** Sharon Hoogstraten. **6** Allan Landau (l). **6–7** Sharon Hoogstraten. **7** Allan Landau (l, r). **8–9** Sharon Hoogstraten. **10** Sharon Hoogstraten. **11** © Bob Daemmrich, Tony Stone Worldwide (l, r). **12** © L. Manning, Westlight (l); © Bob Thomas, Westlight (r). **15** Sharon Hoogstraten. **16** Allan Landau. **17** Sharon Hoogstraten. **18** Allan Landau. **19** Allan Landau. **20–21** Sharon Hoogstraten. **22–23** Sharon Hoogstraten. **24–25** Sharon Hoogstraten. **26–27** Sharon Hoogstraten. **28–29** Sharon Hoogstraten. **31** Allan Landau. **32** Oglethorpe University (l). **32–33** Sharon Hoogstraten. **34–35** Sharon Hoogstraten. **35** Brooklyn Museum (tr). **36** Allan Landau (br). **36–37** Sharon Hoogstraten. **38–39** Sharon Hoogstraten. **40–41** Sharon Hoogstraten. **42** Photofest (l). Copyright © by Universal City Studios, Inc. Courtesy of MCA Publishing Rights, a Division of MCA Inc. **43** Sharon Hoogstraten. **44–45** Sharon Hoogstraten. **46–47** Allan Landau. **47** Sharon Hoogstraten (r). **49** Allan Landau. **52-53** Allan Landau. **53** Allan Landau (l, r). **54** Sharon Hoogstraten (l); © Kevin Laubacher, Earthwatch (r). **56–57** Sharon Hoogstraten. **57** Allan Landau (tl, tr, bl, br). **58** Allan Landau (t); Sharon Hoogstraten (bl, bc, br). **62–63** Sharon Hoogstraten. **64** Allan Landau (b). **65** Sharon Hoogstraten; © Kristin Finnegan, Allstock (cl); © Richard Francis, Tony Stone Worldwide (bl); © Mike Surowiak, Tony Stone Worldwide (br); © Pete Saloutos, The Stock Market (tr). **66–67** Sharon Hoogstraten. **68** Allan Landau (l, c, r). **68–69** Allan Landau. **70–71** Sharon Hoogstraten. **71** Allan Landau (tl, tr, bl); Sharon Hoogstraten (br). **74–75** Allan Landau. **79** Allan Landau (tl, tc, tr); Sharon Hoogstraten (b). **80** Aric Attas. **81** Allan Landau. **82** Allan Landau (l, r). **82–83** Aric Attas. **84** Aric Attas. **86–87** Sharon Hoogstraten. **88–89** Sharon Hoogstraten. **91** Sharon Hoogstraten; Allan Landau (l, c, r). **92–93** Aric Attas. **94** Allan Landau. **95** Allan Landau. **96** Allan Landau. **97** Sharon Hoogstraten; Allan Landau (l, r). **98** © Tony Stone Worldwide (t); © John Elk, Tony Stone Worldwide (b). **100** Allan Landau (l, c, r). **100–101** Sharon Hoogstraten. **102–3** Sharon Hoogstraten. **105** Allan Landau. **106** © 1992 Tony Stone Worldwide (tl); © 1992 Thomas Craig, FPG International Corp. (br). **106–7** Aric Attas. **110–11** Aric Attas. **112** Aric Attas. **113** © Joseph Nettis, Tony Stone Worldwide. **114–15** Sharon Hoogstraten. **116** From *Powers of Ten* by Eames and Morrison. © 1982 by Scientific American Library. Reprinted with permission of W. H. Freeman and Company (bl, br). **117** From *Powers of Ten* by Eames and Morrison. © 1982 by Scientific American Library. Reprinted with permission of W. H. Freeman and Company (l, r). **118** From *Powers of Ten* by Eames and Morrison. © 1982 by Scientific American Library. Reprinted with permission of W. H. Freeman and Company (l, r). **119** From *Powers of Ten* by Eames and Morrison. © 1982 by Scientific American Library. Reprinted with permission of W. H. Freeman and Company (t, c, b). **120** Allan Landau (l, r). **121** Susan Andrews. **122** From *Powers of Ten* by Eames and Morrison. © 1982 by Scientific American Library. Reprinted with permission of W. H. Freeman and Company (tl). **122-23** Aric Attas. **126–27** Aric Attas. **128** From *Powers of Ten* by Eames and Morrison. © 1982 by Scientific American Library. Reprinted with permission of W. H. Freeman and Company (tl). **128–29** Sharon Hoogstraten. **130** Sharon Hoogstraten. **131** Allan

Landau. **132–33** Sharon Hoogstraten. **134–135** Susan Andrews. **136–37** Sharon Hoogstraten. **138–39** Sharon Hoogstraten. **140** Allan Landau (l, c, r). **142–43** Aric Attas. **144–45** Sharon Hoogstraten. **145** Frances M. Roberts (tl). **146–47** Sharon Hoogstraten. **148** From *Powers of Ten* by Eames and Morrison. © 1982 by Scientific American Library. Reprinted with permission of W. H. Freeman and Company (tl); © Grant Heilman Photography, Inc. (br). **149** Allan Landau (l, c, r). **151** Sharon Hoogstraten. **152** Susan Andrews. **153** Sharon Hoogstraten; © Grant Heilman Photography, Inc. (r). **156** © Buck Miller Photography (tl). **157** Allan Landau (l, c, r, br). **158–59** Sharon Hoogstraten. **160** © Willard Clay, Tony Stone Worldwide. **162** © Art Wolfe, Allstock; Susan Andrews (t, tc, bc, b). **163** Aric Attas. **164–65** Sharon Hoogstraten. **166** Sharon Hoogstraten. **167** © Johnny Johnson, Allstock. **168–69** Sharon Hoogstraten. **170–71** Sharon Hoogstraten. **174** Allan Landau (l, r). **174–75** Sharon Hoogstraten. **175** Allan Landau (l, r). **176** Allan Landau. **178–79** Sharon Hoogstraten. **179** © Tony Stone Worldwide (l). **180–81** Sharon Hoogstraten. **182** Sharon Hoogstraten (t). **182–83** Allan Landau. **184** Copyright British Museum (tl). **184–85** Sharon Hoogstraten. **186–87** Allan Landau. **188–89** Sharon Hoogstraten. **190–91** Sharon Hoogstraten. **192–93** Sharon Hoogstraten. **194** Aric Attas. **195** Sharon Hoogstraten. **196–97** Sharon Hoogstraten. **198** © Erich Lessing, Art Resource (tr); Aric Attas (bl). **199** Allan Landau. **200** Aric Attas (l, c, r). **200–201** Aric Attas. **202** Ed Nagel (tl). **202–3** Aric Attas. **204** Allan Landau. **206** © Grant Heilman Photography (br). **206–7** Sharon Hoogstraten. **207** © Grant Heilman Photography (tl). **208** © Dallas and John Heaton, Westlight. **208–9** Sharon Hoogstraten. **210** © Hugh Sitton, Tony Stone Worldwide. **212** Aric Attas; Aric Attas (l, r). **213** Aric Attas (tl, tr); Allan Landau (b). **214–15** Ed Nagel. **216** Allan Landau (l). **216–17** Sharon Hoogstraten. **221** Sharon Hoogstraten. **222** Ed Nagel. **223** Aric Attas. **224–25** Ed Nagel. **226–27** Sharon Hoogstraten. **228–29** Ed Nagel. **229** © NASA (tr); © Lawrence Migdale, Tony Stone Worldwide (br). **230** © Dave Jacobs, Tony Stone Worldwide. **230–31** Sharon Hoogstraten. **231** © Tony Stone Worldwide (tr). **232** Allan Landau. **233** Aric Attas; Allan Landau (cr). **234–35** Sharon Hoogstraten. **238–39** Ed Nagel. **239** Allan Landau (l, r). **240** Aric Attas. **241** Sharon Hoogstraten. **242** Allan Landau (t, b). **242–43** Sharon Hoogstraten. **244–45** Sharon Hoogstraten. **246–47** Sharon Hoogstraten. **248–49** Sharon Hoogstraten. **250** Allan Landau. **253** Sharon Hoogstraten. **254** Sharon Hoogstraten; © Pete Saloutos, Tony Stone Worldwide (l). **257** Waterman, Chicago Historical Society (l). **258** Art Wise (l). **258–59** Sharon Hoogstraten. **259** Art Wise (l, r). **260** Sharon Hoogstraten. **261** Art Wise. **262** Art Wise. **263** Sharon Hoogstraten. **264–65** Sharon Hoogstraten. **267** Sharon Hoogstraten. **268** Sharon Hoogstraten. **269** Art Wise. **270** Art Wise (l, r). **270–71** Sharon Hoogstraten. **272** Art Wise (tl, bl). **272–73** Sharon Hoogstraten. **273** Art Wise (t, c). **274** UPI/BETTMANN. **275** Sharon Hoogstraten. **276** Sharon Hoogstraten; Sharon Hoogstraten (l, r). **277** Sharon Hoogstraten. **278** Art Wise. **279** Sharon Hoogstraten. **280** Art Wise. **281** Sharon Hoogstraten. **286–87** Sharon Hoogstraten. **288** Sharon Hoogstraten; Art Wise (t, c, b). **289** Sharon Hoogstraten; © 1993 , *USA Today*. Reprinted with permission; © 1993 Los Angeles Times Syndicate. Reprinted by permission; © 1993 World Journal. Reprinted with permission. **290** Allan Landau (t). **290–1** Sharon Hoogstraten (b); Copyright © 1993 USA TODAY. Reprinted with permission. **292** UPI/BETTMANN (bl). **292–3** Sharon Hoogstraten. **294–5** Allan Landau. **296–97** Allan Landau. **298** Sharon Hoogstraten. **299** Sharon Hoogstraten. **300–301** Sharon Hoogstraten. **302–3** Sharon Hoogstraten. **304–5** Sharon Hoogstraten. **306–7** Sharon Hoogstraten. **308** Allan Landau. **309** Sharon Hoogstraten. **310** Allan Landau. **311** Sharon Hoogstraten. **312–13** UPI/Andrews and McNeel. **314–15** Aric Attas. **317** Sharon Hoogstraten (tl, tr, b); Yale Babylonian Collection (br). **318** Sharon Hoogstraten (tl, tr); Allan Landau (b). **319** Sharon Hoogstraten (tl, tr). **322–23** Sharon Hoogstraten. **323** Sharon Hoogstraten (l). **324–25** Sharon Hoogstraten. **326–27** Allan Landau. **328** Sharon Hoogstraten. **329** Sharon Hoogstraten. **330–31** Sharon Hoogstraten. **334–35** Sharon Hoogstraten. **335** Sharon Hoogstraten (tr). **336** Sharon Hoogstraten. **337** © Cliff Hollenbeck, Tony Stone Worldwide. **338–39** Sharon Hoogstraten. **339** Allan Landau (b). **341** © Robin Smith, Tony Stone Worldwide (t). **342** Allan Landau. **344–45** Sharon Hoogstraten. **346** Sharon Hoogstraten. **347** Allan Landau. **348** Sharon Hoogstraten. **350** Sharon Hoogstraten. **352** UPI/BETTMANN. **352–53** © Robert Lautman. **353** © 1993 National Gallery of Art, Washington. **355** © Kisho Kurokawa. **356** Allan Landau. **357** Sharon Hoogstraten. **358** Allan Landau; © Tony Craddock, Tony Stone Worldwide (l). **359** Sharon Hoogstraten. **360–61** Sharon Hoogstraten. **364** Sharon Hoogstraten; Aric Attas (t); Sharon Hoogstraten (b). **365** Allan Landau. **366** Allan Landau; © Steve Elmore, Tony Stone Worldwide (l). **367** Allan Landau. **368** © William S. Hensel, Tony Stone Worldwide (tl); © Vince Streano, Tony Stone Worldwide (bl). **368–69** Allan Landau. **369** © Vince Streano, Tony Stone Worldwide (tr). **370–71** © Craig Aurness, Westlight. **373** © Dallas and John Heaton, Westlight. **374** Allan Landau (r); Book Press (bl). **374–75** Aric Attas. **375** Allan Landau (t, c, b). **376** Allan Landau (tr); Aric Attas. **377** Allan Landau. **378** © R. Ian Lloyd, Westlight. **379** © Image Finders, Westlight. **382–83** Sharon Hoogstraten. **384** Allan Landau (l, r). **384–85** Sharon Hoogstraten. **385** Allan Landau (tl, tr, bl, br). **387** Sharon Hoogstraten. **388** Aric Attas. **389** Sharon Hoogstraten. **390–91** Allan Landau. **392–93** Aric Attas. **394–95** Allan Landau. **398** Allan Landau (br). **398–99** Aric Attas. **400** Aric Attas. **401** Sharon Hoogstraten. **402–3** Sharon Hoogstraten (t); Allan Landau (b). **404–5** Sharon Hoogstraten. **405** Allan Landau (c). **406–7** Sharon Hoogstraten. **408–9** Sharon Hoogstraten. **410-11** Sharon Hoogstraten. **412** Allan Landau. **413** Sharon Hoogstraten; Sharon Hoogstraten (l, c, r). **414** Allan Landau. **415** Sharon Hoogstraten. **416** Sharon Hoogstraten. **417** Sharon Hoogstraten. **418** Sharon Hoogstraten. **419** Aric Attas. **420–21** Aric Attas. **422** Allan Landau. **423** Sharon Hoogstraten; © Tom Ulrich, Tony Stone Worldwide (tr); Allan Landau (l, c, r); © Geraldine Prentice, Tony Stone Worldwide (b). **426–27** Aric Attas. **428** Sharon Hoogstraten. **431** Sharon Hoogstraten. **432–33** Allan Landau. **434–35** Aric Attas. **435** Allan Landau (l). **436–37** Sharon Hoogstraten. **438** Allan Landau. **439** Aric Attas. **440–41** Aric Attas. **442** Allan Landau (b). **442–43** Aric Attas (t). **446–47** Aric Attas. **448** Aric Attas. **449** Aric Attas (tl, tr); Allan Landau (b). **450** Sharon Hoogstraten. **451** Sharon Hoogstraten. **452** Sharon Hoogstraten. **454** Allan Landau. **460** Allan Landau. **463** Allan Landau. **467** Aric Attas. **468–69** Sharon Hoogstraten. **469** Allan Landau (b). **470–71** Aric Attas.